International Norm Disputes

International Norm Disputes

The Link between Contestation and Norm Robustness

Lisbeth Zimmermann
Nicole Deitelhoff
Max Lesch
Antonio Arcudi
and
Anton Peez

OXFORD
UNIVERSITY PRESS

OXFORD
UNIVERSITY PRESS

Great Clarendon Street, Oxford, OX2 6DP,
United Kingdom

Oxford University Press is a department of the University of Oxford.
It furthers the University's objective of excellence in research, scholarship,
and education by publishing worldwide. Oxford is a registered trade mark of
Oxford University Press in the UK and in certain other countries

Published in the United States of America by Oxford University Press
198 Madison Avenue, New York, NY 10016, United States of America

British Library Cataloguing in Publication Data
Data available

Library of Congress Control Number: 2023930580

ISBN 978–0–19–887323–5

DOI: 10.1093/oso/9780198873235.001.0001

Printed and bound in the UK by
Clays Ltd, Elcograf S.p.A.

Acknowledgments

This book is the product of a decade-long research project on the effects of contestation on norm robustness in six comparative case studies. It started with the argument that challenges to the *validity* of international norms are more likely to weaken them whereas disputes about *application* strengthen them if they do not become permanent. We started working on this topic in 2011, when International Relations (IR) debates on contestation and crisis still mostly focused on individual norms such as the torture prohibition. The main project period in which we collected and analyzed our data lasted from 2015 to 2018, funded by the German Research Foundation (project number: 265442168). Finalizing the analyses and discussing drafts and a joint framework took some more years—during which the IR discourse turned to an overall debate of the "crisis" of a (liberal) international order. We are very happy to present the summary of our findings in this book with Oxford University Press (OUP)—and think that it makes for a very timely contribution to the ongoing IR debate on the dynamics of, and challenges to, international norms and institutions.

Although the outcome of this project is a monograph and based on our joint work on the overall framework and the final chapters, we divided the empirical work: data collection and analysis on the torture prohibition was done by Max Lesch, Antonio Arcudi covered the responsibility to protect and the duty to prosecute, the commercial whaling moratorium and privateering were examined by Lisbeth Zimmermann, and Anton Peez and Nicole Deitelhoff studied the transatlantic slave trade.

We are deeply thankful to our peers and colleagues who provided advice and comments along the way. We had fantastic discussions at the Frankfurt IR research colloquium at Goethe University ("RiesiKo") and the research council at Peace Research Institute Frankfurt (PRIF) as well as in research seminars at the Universities of St. Gallen, Leuven, and Konstanz. We also benefited immensely from comments at panels at the IR section of the German Political Science Association and the Drei-Länder-Tagung of the German, Swiss, and Austrian Political Scientists as well as at the general conference of the European Consortium of Political Research and several meetings of the International Studies Association.

Many of our arguments were deeply shaped by the discussions at a workshop series we organized along the theme of the book with fantastic colleagues—finding an outlet as a special issue in the Journal of Global Security Studies (2019). These were, among others, Tanja Börzel, Adam Bower, Jutte Brunnée, Raymond Duvall, Christopher Daase, Sidra Hamidi, Hyeran Jo, Phil Orchard, Sarah Percy, Richard Price, Thomas Risse, Wayne Sandholtz, Kathryn Sikkink, Beth Simmons, Stephen Toope, Jennifer Welsh, and Antje Wiener. We would also like to thank Deborah Avant, Tanja Börzel, Klaus Dingwerth, Nele Kortendiek, Diana Panke, Sarah Percy, Elvira Rosert, and Carmen Wunderlich for their helpful comments on article versions as well as Adam Bower, Matthias Dembinski, and Caroline Fehl for reading and commenting on draft chapters of this book.

Very importantly, Layan Abhari, Björn Dohl, Anna Ferl, Corinna Frey, Pauline Helms, Michael Pollok, Gözde Saziak, Ann-Kathrin Steger, Louisa Singer, and Tabea Zimmermann supported the project as student assistants at Goethe University, PRIF, and Zeppelin University Friedrichshafen.

We also would like to thank our two OUP readers for their very helpful and remarkably swift reports as well as Dominic Byatt at OUP for believing in this book right from the start. Finally, we thank Nancy du Plessis for turning our long, often awkward sentences and thoughts into (hopefully) an enjoyable read.

We have previously published some of these ideas and data in other outlets. We reused some of the ideas and updated versions of figures from "Nicole Deitelhoff and Lisbeth Zimmermann (2020). 'Things We Lost in the Fire: How Different Types of Contestation Affect the Robustness of International Norms.' *International Studies Review* 22 (1): pp. 51–76" and would like to thank OUP for permission to reuse it here. We also drew on our work on norm robustness which was published as "Nicole Deitelhoff and Lisbeth Zimmermann. 2019. 'Norms under Challenge: Unpacking the Dynamics of Norm Robustness.' *Journal of Global Security Studies* 4 (1): pp. 2–17". Earlier figures based on data for this project were also published in "Nicole Deitelhoff. 2020. 'What's in a Name? Contestation and Backlash against International Norms and Institutions.' *British Journal of Politics and International Relations* 22 (4): pp. 715–727" and "Antonio Arcudi. 2019. 'The Absence of Norm Modification and the Intensification of Norm Contestation: Africa and the Responsibility to Prosecute.' *Global Responsibility to Protect* 11(2): pp. 172–197".

Contents

List of figures

List of tables

List of abbreviations

ACHR	American Convention on Human Rights
ASP	Assembly of States Parties
ASW	Aboriginal subsistence whaling
AU	African Union
BRICS	Brazil, Russia, India, China, and South Africa
CAR	Central African Republic
CAT	Convention against Torture and Other Cruel, Inhuman or Degrading Treatment or Punishment
CICC	Coalition for the International Criminal Court
CIRI	Cingranelli and Richards Human Rights Data Project
CITES	Convention on International Trade in Endangered Species of Wild Fauna and Flora
CmAT	Committee against Torture
CRC	Convention on the Rights of the Child
CWC	Chemical Weapons Convention
DINA	Directorate for National Intelligence, Chile
DRC	Democratic Republic of the Congo
ECHR	European Convention on Human Rights and Fundamental Freedoms
ECommHR	European Commission on Human Rights
ECtHR	European Court of Human Rights
EU	European Union
GCR2P	Global Centre for the Responsibility to Protect
GSS	General Security Services, Israel
HLP	High-Level Panel on Threats, Challenges and Change, United Nations
HRC	Human Rights Committee
ICC	International Criminal Court
ICCPR	International Covenant on Civil and Political Rights
ICISS	International Commission on Intervention and State Sovereignty
ICJ	International Court of Justice
ICRW	International Convention for the Regulation of Whaling
ICTSD	International Centre for Trade and Sustainable Development
IIFFMCG	Independent International Fact-Finding Mission on the Conflict in Georgia
ILC	International Law Commission
IMT	International Military Tribunal
IO	International organization
IR	International Relations
IWC	International Whaling Commission
IWMC	Integrating Wildlife, Markets and Conservation

LIO	Liberal international order
LMG	Like-Minded Group
MP	Member of Parliament
NAM	Non-Aligned Movement
NAMMCO	North Atlantic Marine Mammal Commission
NATO	North Atlantic Treaty Organization
NGO	Non-governmental organization
NHRI	National Human Rights Institution
OAS	Organization of American States
ODM	Orange Democratic Movement, Kenya
OHCHR	Office of the High Commissioner for Human Rights
OPCAT	Optional Protocol to the Convention against Torture
OPCW	Organization for the Prohibition of Chemical Weapons
PRIF	Peace Research Institute Frankfurt
PSC	African Union Peace and Security Council
R2P	Responsibility to protect
RMP	Revised Management Procedure
RMS	Revised Management Scheme
SADC	Southern African Development Community
SOHR	Syrian Observatory for Human Rights
TRIPS	Trade-Related Aspects of Intellectual Property Rights
UCDP	Uppsala Conflict Data Program
UDHR	Universal Declaration of Human Rights
UK	United Kingdom
UN	United Nations
UNCLOS	United Nations Convention on the Law of the Sea
UNGA	United Nations General Assembly
UNHRC	United Nations Human Rights Council
UNSC	United Nations Security Council
UPR	Universal Periodic Review
US	United States of America
WSOD	World Summit Outcome Document

1

Introduction

Contestation and the dynamics of norm robustness

1.1 Introduction

"Crisis" is probably *the* buzzword of our age. It is used to describe liberal democratic governance, migration, arms control, the United Nations (UN) peace and security architecture, and the European Union (EU). Similar alarmism has also been suggested with respect to the liberal international order (LIO) (Sørensen 2011; Ikenberry 2018; Eilstrup-Sangiovanni and Hofmann 2020), which is generally described as a loose set of rules, norms, and institutions based on multilateralism, free trade, and individual rights (Acharya 2017; Eilstrup-Sangiovanni and Hofmann 2020). It is difficult to judge the plausibility of such diagnoses: The concept LIO seems too vague and the developments within it are just unfolding. However, we focus on one aspect of the LIO to provide insights into the plausibility of an "overall" crisis: the contestation of international norms. We explore the effects of contestation on their robustness and when and why international norms are weakened.

Contestation has inspired lively debate in International Relations (IR) and international law regarding the concept, how it might affect specific norms, and how to measure its consequences (Wiener 2014, 2018; Niemann and Schillinger 2017; Deitelhoff and Zimmermann 2019). In this book, we address these issues and focus on the consequences of contestation. Numerous studies warn that contestation causes the destabilization, or even erosion, of norms (see, for instance, Rosert and Schirmbeck 2007; McKeown 2009: 11; Heller et al. 2012: 283; Panke and Petersohn 2012, 2016). Still other studies argue that contestation actually strengthens norms by providing room for norm legitimation processes (Wiener 2004, 2008, 2010; Hurd 2013; Clark et al. 2018). We aim to contribute to this debate by presenting data on empirical cases of the contestation of international norms and their robustness. We define "contestation" as every verbal criticism of a norm's application and/or validity (Wiener 2014). We differentiate between *applicatory* and

International Norm Disputes. Lisbeth Zimmermann et al., Oxford University Press. © Lisbeth Zimmermann, Nicole Deitelhoff, Max Lesch, Antonio Arcudi, and Anton Peez (2023). DOI: 10.1093/oso/9780198873235.003.0001

validity contestations and assume that they affect norm robustness differently. Drawing on the discourse theory of law and normativity of Günther (1993) and Habermas (1996), we assume that as long as applicatory contestation does not become permanent (i.e. no temporary compromise or consensus of specific applicatory issues emerges), it does not negatively affect norm robustness. Validity contestation is more likely to weaken a norm. We evaluate our assertions by observing how contested norms become more or less robust through time, focusing on the discourse (concordance and negative reactions to norm violations) as well as the practice (compliance and implementation) regarding norms.

Our empirical analysis comprises six comparative case studies. Four are contemporary norms that have been repeatedly—or still are—heavily contested. These include the torture prohibition, which has been contested over the past five decades; the responsibility to protect (R2P), which has been contested since it was adopted in the 2005 World Summit Outcome Document (WSOD); the commercial whaling moratorium, contested since it was announced in the 1980s; and the international duty to prosecute, which was set out in the Rome Statute that established the International Criminal Court (ICC). Because all these norms may have been weakened but none has been completely eroded, we have added two historical case studies of norms that decayed and were replaced. One deals with the permissive norm of privateering, which was widely practiced from the beginning of the early modern period until it was banned in 1856. The other is the permissive norm of the transatlantic slave trade that flourished in the seventeenth and eighteenth centuries.

Our analysis demonstrates that the different types of contestations differently affect norm robustness. While all norms are contested, most contestation concerns their application, for example, a norm's precise meaning or when and where it applies and the action(s) its addressees must undertake. Such contestations do not usually weaken a norm—unless they become permanent. Negative effects can only be observed in cases of widespread validity contestation. Increases in the validity contestations of a norm (which happens rarely) lead to its weakening.

Our findings also shed light on when such a dynamic is likely to develop. Contrary to widespread assumptions (e.g. Panke and Petersohn 2012), our contemporary case studies show that the relative strength or power of contesters has little effect, whereas, in the two historical cases, the contester's power was a key factor. Law and legalization (Abbott and Snidal 2000; Kahler 2000) have also been much discussed with respect to contestation.

Some scholars argue that legal norms, which are often embedded in legal institutions and discourse, can better weather challenges regarding their application, prevent radicalization into validity contestation, and define the range of legitimate arguments and strategies (Bower 2015, 2019). However, the legal character of norms does not explain the contestation types and robustness trends we observed. We conclude that international institutionalization is key: Embeddedness in norm clusters shapes contestation dynamics (Lantis and Wunderlich 2018). When such a norm cluster fades, however, norms are weakened. Also, when norm challengers perceive that contestation is *unfairly* dealt with by international institutions, contestation becomes more radical. International institutions which have channels and procedures for managing objections and that are perceived as “fair” can help mitigate contestation and extract its productive potential for norms.

Contestation is widespread: Most international norms have been challenged and *all* of them have been contested. But contestation does not necessarily weaken international norms. Our findings show that once applicatory contestation is permanent and fundamental validity contestation is common, “harder law” or stronger enforcement cannot stop an international norm’s decline. Institutional settings that combine and embed norms and offer genuine recognition and fair processes seem better able to tame challenges. Some argue that the current challenges to the multilateral order are of a hitherto unknown scope and depth (Eilstrup-Sangiovanni and Hofmann 2020). According to Drezner (2020), McNamara and Newmann (2020), and Bettiza (2020), the COVID-19 pandemic could increase such challenges. However, these recent assessments ignore fundamental insights of international norms research. Our model is an excellent tool for analyzing and judging both the scope and depth of current contestations as well as understanding weakening and strengthening trends.

In Section 1.2, we situate our study in IR and international law norm research and conceptualize social norms. Section 1.3 shows that existing research on norm change and decay does not explain the ambiguous effects of contestation and presents a typology of applicatory and validity contestations based on the discourse theory of law and normativity in the tradition of Habermas and Günther. We first explain how these types of contestations relate to norm robustness. In Section 1.4, we present our concept and operationalization of norm robustness. Section 1.5 highlights our methods and data and introduces our cases; we discuss explanatory schemes for our findings in Section 1.6 and present the book’s main points in Section 1.7.

1.2 Conceptualizing social norms in international relations

Social norms are generically described as intersubjective standards of appropriate behavior for actors (Nadelmann 1990; Katzenstein 1996: 5; Finnemore and Sikkink 1998). Norms reflect the "temporally, socially, and substantively generalized behavioral expectations" of a given social group (Habermas 1996: 107). They both constitute and regulate interpersonal relationships. Norm claims also reflect normatively desirable behavior. As Finnemore and Sikkink (1998: 891) argue, "[I]t is precisely the prescriptive (or evaluative) quality of 'oughtness' that sets norms apart from other kinds of rules" (see also Chayes and Handler Chayes 1995). Social norms are intersubjective: They cannot be reduced to individual preferences but rather reflect normative obligations based on a given group's shared assessment of appropriate behavior. As deontological entities, norms primarily derive their validity from the addressees' shared intersubjective acceptance of their obligatory claims and only secondarily from their enforcement. We consider that many norms, like the international prohibition on the use of force and the prohibition of murder, are valid, although they are not fully complied with. Normative *obligation* ensures that a norm is not necessarily directly affected by being violated. Norms often only become visible when they are violated and provoke justifications because an intersubjective obligation appears to have been neglected (Finnemore and Sikkink 1998: 892).

There are various types of norms. *Proscriptive* norms, such as the prohibition of chemical weapons, require people to refrain from certain behaviors. *Prescriptive* norms ask addressees to engage in specific behaviors, such as granting all states the same trade terms as their most favored trading partner. *Permissive* norms may allow, or even encourage, addressees to engage in a specific behavior (Kratochwil 1989; Deitelhoff 2006)—as in the historical example of privateering. These different types of norms take varying forms. Social norms can become *legal* norms, enshrined in treaties and conventions, or be part of customary law like the torture prohibition. Or they can be mere *moral-political* norms, embodied in resolutions or codes of conduct, like R2P. Norms may also be *ethical*, prescribing a lifestyle for a specific community (Kratochwil 1989): Think of gender norms and the long-term ban on women fighting in the military (Percy 2019). Despite these many differences, all norms impose obligations on their addressees, who feel compelled to comply with them—to varying degrees and for various reasons (Sandholtz and Stiles 2009: 9–10).

1.3 Research on norms in international relations: The role of contestation

In the late 1980s, social constructivism (Kratochwil and Ruggie 1986; Wendt 1987; Nadelmann 1990) inspired systematic IR research on norms and their effects.[1] Early research understood international norms as having life cycles with limited contestation: A norm emerges, becomes diffused in the international system, and is finally internalized by actors (Finnemore and Sikkink 1998). The first phases of norm emergence were depicted as an inharmonious process in which norm entrepreneurs compete to win support for certain norms (Nadelmann 1990; Finnemore and Sikkink 1998; Price 1998). Models showed that this element of conflict vanished once the norm reached a "tipping point" (Finnemore and Sikkink 1998: 897), that is, after a critical mass of norm supporters (usually states) had embraced the nascent norm. Once a norm was established, its meaning and legitimacy were assumed to be stable (Wiener 2007). Risse, Ropp, and Sikkink (1999) studied disputes over norms during the diffusion phase when states individually reject well-established norms; Checkel (1999) examined controversies that arise when states are socialized into international or regional norm systems. According to norm diffusion models, successful socialization removes a norm from public debate: Its unquestioned presence—habitualization and internalization—was taken as a sign of its validity (Finnemore and Sikkink 1998: 895–96; Risse and Sikkink 1999: 17).

The early focus on *stable* norms can be attributed to the IR debate about whether ideational factors could independently affect state behavior. Social constructivists were eager to demonstrate that "norms mattered" (Finnemore and Sikkink 2001: 396). A norm that was repeatedly contested was thought to be weak—meaning that ideational factors could not have an influence.

However, the focus of research has shifted since then, with norms like the torture prohibition that were long perceived as deeply internalized and unquestionable portrayed as eroding (McKeown 2009) or already dead, like the anti-mercenary norms (Panke and Petersohn 2012, 2016). Even relatively recent norms, such as R2P, have been viewed as fading (Waal 2007; Rieff 2011; Hehir 2019). Lately, many have begun to argue that not only individual norms but also whole pillars of a multilateral order are challenged (Dunne 2007; Duncombe and Dunne 2018; Ikenberry 2018; Eilstrup-Sangiovanni and Hofmann 2020; Lake et al. 2021).

[1] This section draws on Deitelhoff and Zimmerman (2020).

As a result, research began on whether international norms that have been internalized can erode. Early research focused on norm decay or regression in reaction to contestation at the national level (Rosert and Schirmbeck 2007; McKeown 2009; Heller et al. 2012; Sikkink 2013; Kutz 2014) and at the international level (Deibert and Crete-Nishihata 2012; Keating 2014; Panke and Petersohn 2016; Clark et al. 2018; Gutterman and Lohaus 2018). However, many of these studies conceptualize norms in a rather linear way. They argue that a norm's contestation does not necessarily cause its full decay, although it definitely weakens it. As McKeown argues (2009: 11, emphasis added): "[E]ven if defenders are quite successful in rolling back some of the revisionists' gains, the norms will always lose some salience *just in virtue of being publicly challenged*" (see also Heller et al. 2012: 283; Panke and Petersohn 2012: 721). Each step from the norm's unquestioned internalization is equated with its potential weakening.

The stability bias of this field of norm research equates validity with the absence of contestation—and thus limits our understanding. Research on norm localization (Acharya 2004), norm change (Sandholtz and Stiles 2009; Krook and True 2012), and norm contestation (Wiener 2008, 2018; Deitelhoff and Zimmermann 2020) has sought hard to escape this focus by consistently emphasizing that norms remain dynamic and contested even after they emerge. From this perspective, contestation can even strengthen norms (Badescu and Weiss 2010; Brunnée and Toope 2010) by being a precondition for legitimation (Wiener 2007, 2010). However, few empirical analyse have been conducted on the limits of contestation.

Localization research investigates the reinterpretation and resistance of norms in different regional and national contexts (Acharya 2004; Zwingel 2016; Zimmermann 2017a, b; Zimmermann et al. 2017). But it does not analyze how localization globally influences norm robustness. In contrast, research on norm change studies the dynamics of norms and their interpretation at the international level (Badescu and Weiss 2010; Krook and True 2012; Müller and Wunderlich 2013). Contestation and interpretation processes are shown to strengthen or weaken norms (Sandholtz and Stiles 2009: 6–7; Krook and True 2012: 109), but *when* that happens is not explained. These scholars suggest that various factors, such as the discursive power of contesting actors, links to shared meta-norms, and precedents, can affect a norm's form and content (Sandholtz and Stiles 2009). So can norm entrepreneurship, conflicts between regimes, exogenous events, and technological developments (Müller and Wunderlich 2013). Yet, how these factors relate to norm robustness remains unexplained.

Disputes about how to interpret norms is another integral part of contestation research (Wiener 2004, 2008; van Kersbergen and Verbeek 2007). Wiener (2014, 2018) developed a "bifocal approach" to norms that applies both analytic and normative perspectives and explores how they are interrelated. She considers that contestation has a positive connotation because it can lead to shared understandings of the meaning of norms and can legitimize them (Wiener 2007: 48, 2010: 203). The proper framework for such deliberation can make contestation a strengthening, rather than destabilizing, force (Wiener 2007: 56, 2008: 204–208, 2010: 203). Wiener (2014: 59) also emphasizes that there can be *too much* contestation. Clark et al. (2018: 321) similarly assume that something akin to a "tipping point" exists—where contestation begins to seriously undermine a regime.

To sum up, this branch of research regards contestation as a standard practice that shapes the interpretation of norms. However, the research says little about the limits of contestation: How much can a norm be contested before its addressees stop considering it a shared normative expectation? When does controversy begin to weaken a norm? We evoke the discourse theory of law and normativity (Günther 1993; Habermas 1996) to differentiate between two ideal contestation types—applicatory and validity—so as to understand when and if contestation negatively affects norm robustness.[2]

1.3.1 Applicatory contestation

Applicatory contestation refers to disputes about how, when, and where a norm pertains. It questions the situation for applying a particular norm, as in "Does this include everything that makes the relevant norm applicable, or should a different norm prevail?," as well as the actions that addressees should or should not perform: "What should I do with respect to the norm in this situation?"

This kind of contestation affects norms in different ways. Ideally, applicatory contestation clarifies the various types of situations for individual norms and the types of actions required (Günther 1993: 40; Peterson 2015: 225–26).[3] Think of threshold regulations in international criminal law that try to clarify

[2] We introduced this distinction in Deitelhoff and Zimmermann (2020).
[3] For tensions that can cause disputes over norm application, see also O'Mahoney (2014: 841–42).

when a certain offense constitutes a "grave war crime" that is judiciable before the ICC. All norms have equivocal meanings and must apply to a whole class of social situations whose characteristics cannot be predetermined at the time they are established (Chayes and Handler Chayes 1993: 188–89). Furthermore, understandings and normative evaluations of certain practices change over time and norms must adapt if they are to remain useful. For example, norms for personal data protection emerged before the age of social media and need reviewing in light of the technological and societal changes. Sometimes, reevaluation leads to new discussions and compromises about how to interpret a norm.

Applicatory discourses take place regarding all norms and are hardly ever "solved." A case in point is the commercial whaling ban that exempts "aboriginal subsistence whaling" (ASW). Some actors understand subsistence whaling as pertaining only to clearly defined indigenous communities who use whales in strictly "uncommercial" ways; others understand it as also encompassing traditional coastal communities or accept that modern indigenous communities might want to buy whale meat in the local supermarket. Applicatory discourses aimed at working agreements can, and should, be reopened in the future. The interpretation of the "best interest of the child" in the Convention on the Rights of the Child (CRC 1989: Art. 3(1)) was also controversial, with heated discussions over the implications of the phrase and how the principle should be practically applied (Quennerstedt 2009). This applicatory discourse led the Committee on the Rights of the Child to finally publish General Comment 14, which explains its meaning. Of course, not every normative setting has a similar institutional body and General Comment 14 might not be the final word on this subject. Nevertheless, such pronouncements become important anchors in future applicatory discourses (see Reiners 2022; Lesch and Reiners 2023).

Applicatory contestation often broadens or restricts a norm's scope and temporarily stabilizes its behavioral implications. We emphasize temporality because applicatory debates can pop up at any time—a good example being Germany's compromise solution on abortion in the 1990s, which makes the procedure illegal but also exempts it from punishment in certain situations, and which has regularly remerged in public debates (Kamenitsa 2001). Technological inventions and normative societal changes can also narrow or broaden the scope of a norm (Günther 1993: 57; Peterson 2015: 221, 227). Such change does not necessarily weaken a norm: A new interpretation that creates broader acceptance of, and compliance with, a norm serves to strengthen it. However, constant applicatory contestation—when the meaning is repeatedly challenged over a long period of time—saps a norm. When norm addressees differ widely on how to interpret a norm, the claims become so blurry that addressees may begin to ignore the norm, resulting in non-compliance due to uncertainty about its meaning. Or they might get so frustrated that they begin to contest the norm's *validity*.

1.3.2 Validity contestation

Validity contestation questions the righteousness of the core claims of a norm (Günther 1993: 6–7; Peterson 2015: 218). For example, with regard to the torture prohibition, a state could argue, "We, State X, want the torture prohibition to be abolished because it violates the higher principle of national security." This is not just about where and when a norm pertains (applicatory contestation): State X *always* wants to prioritize national security. In the conflict over Japanese scientific whaling, Japan's Prime Minister Shinzo Abe argued that "[he] want[s] to aim for the resumption of commercial whaling by conducting whaling research" (Clapham 2015: 240). The debate was not just about whether Japanese scientific whaling is a legal exemption from commercial whaling (applicatory contestation): Abe aimed to *overthrow* the moratorium.

Validity is often discussed with respect to norm emergence discourse: when actors debate whether and what kind of normative claims they will intersubjectively accept in order to regulate their social relations (Finnemore and Sikkink 1998; Deitelhoff 2006). Such discourses can reoccur at any time if norm addressees perceive that effects are countering initial projections: International norms might create injustices, violate other equal or higher norms, or interfere with state interests.

It is rare for states to openly reject international norms—much less legal, non-derogable norms like the torture prohibition. But we often observe quite indirect forms of validity contestation (see also Schmidt and Sikkink 2019). For example, with respect to the ICC, a state may not declare that it wants to get rid of the duty to prosecute and instead describe the court as a tool of Western imperialism that creates injustice and dependency. Contestation of the torture prohibition is often similarly disguised. The United States (US) might argue, "We *do* support the torture ban but do not think it applies to *foreign* fighters." However, the torture ban is a non-derogable norm: It applies to all human beings in all circumstances (Nowak et al. 2019: 6). What, at first glance, appears to be applicatory contestation is actually an attack on the norm's core (normative) claims and challenges its *validity*.

Validity contestation threatens a norm's robustness by disturbing the intersubjective agreement about what actors ought or ought not to do. The more a norm's validity is contested, the more its robustness is likely to be weakened. But not every individual validity contestation depletes a norm: That only happens when a tipping point is reached. Finnemore and Sikkink (1998: 901) use that concept to show when a nascent norm is likely to become established. The tipping point is reached when around one-third of state actors including states that are critical to its implementation have adopted the new norm. After that, a "cascade" builds (Sikkink 2013) and states adopt new norms with or without domestic support for normative change. Other mechanisms also come into play such as praising and shaming by international organizations and transnational actors. States adopt new norms because they want to look like good members of the international community or because they think that a certain behavior is appropriate (Finnemore and Sikkink 1998: 902–903). We should remember that such norm creation processes are also linked to the weakening or "death" of norms. Finnemore and Sikkink's seminal article cites the "permission" to own slaves or use landmines in war. In their empirical applications of the norm life cycle, norm emergence always involves a legal norm replacing permissive norms which were not explicitly legal.

Clark et al. (2018) argue that reaching a tipping point creates a legitimacy crisis: A critical mass of different types of contestation shifts the burden of justification. In rare cases of contestation, norm challengers lose legitimacy as a result of their contestation and non-compliance. Past the tipping point, the legitimacy burden is reversed and additional contestation further erodes norm legitimacy. We conceptualize the tipping point as affecting contestation differently from Clark et al. (2018) and Finnemore and Sikkink (1998). We hold that when a critical mass of actors contest a norm's validity, a tipping point is reached, and other states may no longer know what the norm implies or if it is still upheld by the community of states. When intersubjective validity is in doubt, norm compliance is likely to decrease more rapidly.

Sandholtz (2019) argues that once an area has been regulated, we hardly ever see a process of "deregulation" or "norm death." Instead, one norm is replaced by other types, for example, a *pro*scriptive by a *pre*scriptive norm (Percy and Sandholtz 2022). With respect to the whaling moratorium, pro-whaling states are not seeking the complete deregulation of whaling: They want to replace the prohibition on commercial whaling with the permission to engage in sustainable commercial whaling. In certain cases, such a replacement can be very quick; more often, this might include a longer process of uncertainty, competition between different norms, and reinterpretation—as we can observe in the case of the replacement of the norms allowing for privateering with a ban.

Several IR scholars use similar distinctions of contestation types to indicate a norm's robustness or legitimacy (Price 2006: 262; Hurd 2013: 172; Keating 2014; Bellamy 2015: 167–68; Barnes 2016: 103). They argue that contesting implementation or enforcement processes indicates norm legitimacy or robustness. Norm researchers have also explored differences of contestation without studying how they are linked to norm robustness. Welsh (2013) and Ralph and Gallagher (2015) distinguish procedural contestation—the appropriate institutional context for making decisions—from more substantive contestations of a norm's content or outcomes (see also Adler-Nissen and Pouliot 2014: 895). Clark et al. (2018: 332) distinguish among challenges that are rejectionist, revisionist, and denialist but also argue that "the crisis is driven by this confluence of rejection, revision and denial in ways that question the very purpose of the regime." The simultaneous occurrence of these three types of challenges creates a legitimacy crisis for a norm. Stimmer and Wisken (2019) distinguish discursive from behavioral contestation: the former encompasses open, direct types, while the latter is indirect, more hidden, and linked to non-compliance and limited implementation. In our understanding, this approach conflates contestation with robustness—the very link we analyze in this volume. In her latest book, Wiener (2018) discusses *reactive* contestation, which encompasses non-compliance or breaches of norms, and *proactive* contestation that engages with the normative structure and aims to change it. Yet, the distinction seems to be more about specific procedural aspects (engagement with normative structures versus non-engagement) than about how these challengers substantially contest the norm.

1.3.3 Distinguishing applicatory from validity contestation

Theoretically, the distinction between these two ideal types is clear cut; empirically, their difference is muddy. Not only do actors often use both types, but also interpretive work is needed to establish if a certain argument attacks a norm's core claims or its application. Researchers must determine the former in order to distinguish applicatory from validity contestation—which is at odds with a more radical constructivist approach (Niemann and Schillinger 2017). Core normative claims are not defined objectively. For pragmatic reasons, we adopt the addressees' core normative claims at the widely acknowledged moment of "norm-setting." For example, with respect to R2P, we would not consult the first advisory report of 2001 by the International Commission on Intervention and State Sovereignty (ICISS) but refer to Articles 38 and 39 of the 2005 Millennium Summit resolution, the version adopted by UN member states (see Chapter 3).

Distinguishing applicatory from validity contestation often requires careful reading. Returning to the ICC: Contestation arguments describing the court as "flawed" might portray it as embodying Western imperialism or needing severe reform because it contradicts international law. While the former is a clear-cut example of validity contestation, the latter could be an instance of applicatory contestation that requests that the statute be aligned with the existing international legal framework (see Chapter 5). Below, we discuss in detail how we categorize applicatory and validity contestation for each case study (see the Appendix for coding schemes). While the coding schemes are, of course, adapted to each case study, the overall categories and coding rules are similar for all cases.

Validity contestation, in all of the cases, was attributed if statements prioritize a norm permanently over another norm or if a statement openly rejected a norm or described it as deeply unjust, for example, because of traces of colonialism. We classified statements as validity contestation if they introduced categorical exemptions which do not exist in the formerly agreed upon version of the norm, for example, enemy combatants in the case of the torture prohibition.

We classified statements as applicatory contestation if they pointed to hypocrisy or partial treatment (e.g. of the US in the context of the duty to prosecute), if they criticized the norm application (e.g. how certain concepts are defined, such as severity in the case of the torture prohibition), or if they criticized the performance of an institution centrally linked to the implementation of the norm (such as of the Committee against Torture).

1.4 Norm robustness: Understanding the dynamics of international norms

After conceptualizing our view of contestation and the way the various contestation types relate to norm robustness, we have to generate a conceptual understanding of norm robustness that is analytically distinct from contestation and applicable to various kinds of norms.[4] IR researchers differ widely

[4] This section draws on Deitelhoff and Zimmermann (2019).

about how to conceptualize and analyze norm robustness, which is often also referred to as norm "strength" or "legitimacy." This results in clashing descriptions of different norms (see also Ben-Josef Hirsch and Dixon 2021: 523). While some studies limit "robustness" to discourse and focus on the "acceptance" of norms, others only pay attention to practice and define robustness as the level of compliance that a norm can generate. In this book, we follow a third approach that combines discourse and practice to draw a more comprehensive picture of norm robustness.

1.4.1 Focus on either compliance or discourse

One strand of research links norm robustness to compliance: A norm's robustness is only measured by its facticity. Glennon (2004: 940) presents the most rigorous model, arguing that a "valid rule of international law [...] is a rule that few states often violate." If a norm is excessively violated "by a sufficient number of states," the violation is no longer a violation: Instead, the *freedom* principle rules—"another rule that permits unrestricted freedom of action."

Panke and Petersohn (2012) write that a violated norm is "challenged." The authors study norm erosion with respect to submarine warfare, the anti-mercenary norm, and sovereignty—arguing that all have degenerated. Although their conceptualization accepts a discursive dimension of norm robustness in which norms have only completely eroded if violations are no longer framed as non-compliance (Panke and Petersohn 2012: 723), they do not include this dimension in their empirical analysis. They consider state practice to be the most important indicator of norm robustness. It is difficult to apply such an approach to cases of significant non-compliance with norms whose validity is uncontested like the prohibition of murder.

Other works study norm robustness at the discursive level, focusing on contestation. In such a model, the level of contestation per se indicates norm robustness. Norm strength (legitimacy) resides in the degree of acceptance of a norm's claims by its addressees. The greatest robustness is equated with a norm's "taken-for-granted" quality (its complete internalization and habitualization by norm addressees).[5] However, in this approach, opening any discourse about the norm (even if it is supportive) enables erosion processes. Complete erosion is brought about by norm challengers that start a "domino

[5] Authors often start with norms which have been described as "taboo" in norm research (on taboos, see Tannenwald 1999; Bentley 2022).

effect of unthinkables" (Rosert and Schirmbeck 2007: 281, our translation), or "norm revisionists" that challenge a norm's resonance and start a "reverse cascade" (McKeown 2009: 6). One focus of this robustness research has been the domestic contestation of norms, including the torture ban and the nuclear non-proliferation treaty. However, contestation is common to international norms. Why does contestation not result in more cases of norm decay?

Hurd suggests that state practices of compliance do not explain norm robustness (he writes "legitimacy"). He considers that norm compliance is always contested and, given the general lack of international juridical institutions to mediate such conflicts, compliance claims will remain contested (Hurd 2013: 167): One actor's compliance is another's *non*-compliance. Hurd holds that research on compliance and discursive claims about compliance do not explain norm legitimacy. He argues that norms are legitimate if they are widely ratified and widely used rhetorically, and if "[t]here is little dissent from the idea that rules are binding on the states that have accepted them" (Hurd 2013: 172). Norms are important "because of how they invoke legal resources in the service of political ends" (Hurd 2013: 180).

Taking this approach, researchers define norm robustness in terms of support for the norm (the opposite of contestation) as measured by the number of treaty ratifications, the amount of verbal government support, or the absence of contestation (see also Ben-Josef Hirsch and Dixon 2021). Some also equate norm contestation with norm weakening. This approach does not account for relatively uncontested norms that no longer attract any significant compliance with their claims—possibly including the anti-mercenary norm.

Confusion also exists regarding discourse, practice, and norm content. Some descriptions automatically link normative change with a norm's strengthening or weakening. Panke and Petersohn (2016: 4) write, "[a] norm may be weakened if its applicatory scope is restricted through practice. In this process, actors still refer to the norm, but previously inappropriate behavior is now considered to be in accordance with the norm."[6] This description refers to proscriptive norms like the commercial whaling moratorium. Limiting the scope by including coastal whaling in the exemptions would be equated with weakening, whereas widening the scope to include small cetaceans not covered by the norm would imply strengthening. We argue that this indicates a normative bias: Only when widening the scope is assumed to be an improvement can that be equated with strengthening.

[6] Some authors similarly equate strength with precision: Legro (1997) and Finnemore and Sikkink (1998).

1.4.2 Bridging the gap between discourse and practice

Another group of scholars adopts a joint approach to studying norm robustness that disentangles norm content from robustness. They propose studying both practice and discourse and consider that a norm's robustness is constituted by its validity *and* facticity: Norm robustness is high when norm addressees broadly accept a norm's claims (*validity*) that generally guide their actions (*facticity*). This bi-dimensional perspective on robustness appeared in Kratochwil and Ruggie's (1986: 767) seminal article in which they argue that norm compliance alone does not explain norm robustness: "[W]hether or not violations also invalidate or refute a law (norm) will depend upon a host of other factors, not the least of which is how the community assesses the violation and responds to it."[7]

Price (2004, 2006) has elaborated a conceptual approach to norm robustness that is linked to international law debates about customary law. Most scholars support the claim that customary law can be identified by analyzing state practices and *opinio juris* (that a particular action was carried out because it is a legal obligation).[8] Price has used the focus on state practice and *opinio juris* to elaborate social science research on norm robustness. He gathers a whole range of possible indicators to assess norm robustness, specifically regarding the ban on anti-personnel landmines. His main question is: "How do we know (robust) international norms when we see them?" (Price 2006: 254). Price suggests assessing the discursive dimension according to: (1) general support, such as treaty status, general government statements, and government statements that specifically deal with the applicatory scope or central validity claims; (2) reactions to norm violations by a state that rejects the norm, shows no reaction, provides a special justification, denies violation, or supports criticism; and (3) third-party reactions that are passive, condemnatory, sanctioning, or instrumentalize accusations. This is combined with studying (non)-compliance practices: How often is a norm violated? Is non-compliance routine, widespread, normal, or uncontroversial? Or is it politicized, exceptional, aberrant, or abhorrent? Who decides what constitutes a violation? Are there production and export regulations, like for landmines? This list of possible indicators, some of which are norm-specific, can help us analyze a norm's robustness. But comparatively studying the whole range of indicators over long periods of time needs complex data sets.

[7] Similarly, Legro (1997: 33–34); Hurd (1999: 390–91; Sandholtz and Stiles (2009: 14).

[8] For debates, see Treves (2006).

Several other problems emerge during practical application (Deitelhoff and Zimmermann 2019; Ben-Josef Hirsch and Dixon 2021: 523). First, norms can be permissive, proscriptive, or prescriptive. While much research focuses on non-compliance rates at the practical level, this is not a fitting indicator for permissive norms. For example, the amount of privateering activity at any time could be centrally linked to other, primarily economic, factors or to wars—and thus reveal little about norm robustness. Second, non-compliance rates need interpretation. While the commercial whaling moratorium might be described as a solid norm if it is violated by just one fishing vessel catching a minke whale, the use of a nuclear weapon is very different: A norm breach's relative significance is always due to its specific policy field. Third, it is quite difficult to interpret strong differences in discourse and behavior. The torture prohibition, for example, is regularly violated but enjoys broad acceptance.

We examine four dimensions of robustness, two of which are more practical—compliance and implementation—and two more discursive—concordance and negative reactions to norm violations:

Compliance: In principle, norm addressees' behavior that is consistent with norms (Young 1979: 3) indicates that they feel bound by them. That said, we are very aware that behavior in agreement with a norm is not directly linked to its legitimacy (Martin 2013). We are also aware that interpretations change with respect to what constitutes "compliance." Nonetheless, we study if compliance is high, widespread, rare, or hardly existent—and if the trends are changing.

Implementation: Widespread inclusion in policy papers, protocols, and standards of regional and international organizations along with the founding of domestic, regional, and international institutions and the adoption of domestic legislation on norms also indicate that addressees feel bound by a norm (Betts and Orchard 2014: 2; Ben-Josef Hirsch and Dixon 2021: 526). We seek to learn whether implementation is high at more than one level (domestic, regional, or international), moderate, rare, or hardly existent. This indicator does easily not reveal a norm's weakening, however, because after an institution like the office of a human rights ombudsperson has been created, it is not easy to close.

Concordance with the norm:[9] This can be acceptance of a norm's legitimacy by a state and the general public or a more general belief in the legitimacy of the institution tasked with monitoring/

[9] Following Legro (1997: 35), "Concordance means how widely accepted the rules are in diplomatic discussions and treaties (that is, the degree of intersubjective agreement)." This also includes broader acceptance, including by non-governmental organizations (NGOs) and private citizens (Ben-Josef Hirsch and Dixon 2021).

implementing norms. The absolute and relative number of ratifications by addressees and the level and quality of opt-out clauses[10] can be helpful indicators for the subset of legal norms.

Negative reactions to norm violations: The reactions of other norm addressees to norm violations (including discursive sanctioning)[11] indicate whether norm violations are frequently criticized or tolerated.

This allows us to create ordinal scales of each dimension. A norm's trend is assessed by the shifts in the majority of indicator values (weakening/strengthening/constant). This conceptualization aims to analyze norm robustness through time and across cases. We do not assume that complete robustness has an ideal "endpoint," nor do we expect that norms will completely disappear. Instead, we expect to observe norms being strengthened or weakened—or replaced by other norms (Percy and Sandholtz 2022). We do not describe norms as either perfectly robust or irrelevant but rather try to indicate weakening or strengthening trends and explain the changes.

In such an approach, change in a norm's scope does not indicate that it is weakening or strengthening. For example, if the scope of a proscriptive norm, such as the prohibition of murder, is widened by permitting assisted suicide, this only implies that it is changing, not that it is weakening. The norm would only have become less robust if narrowing was accompanied by lower concordance, less negative reactions to norm violations, lower compliance, or reduced implementation.[12] Nevertheless, norm change and norm robustness are related. A norm can be fundamentally changed and reinterpreted—and at a certain point, the changes show that it has been replaced. A good example is the debate about waterboarding. We view questions about whether waterboarding is torture or cruel and degrading treatment as matters of *application*. However, others might argue that narrowing the scope of the ban on torture to exclude waterboarding or to allow torture in a ticking-bomb scenario fundamentally changes the norm. How far can a norm be "translated"—and its content changed—and remain the same? This is particularly important with respect to R2P which we discuss in Chapter 3.

The definition of core normative claims is based on scholarly or public interpretations and can vary over time. We pragmatically deal with this problem by reconstructing the core normative claims made at the time the norms were created. We study treaties, conventions, their negotiations, and so forth

[10] High ratification rates may be accompanied by large numbers of opt-out clauses or reservations, which makes it important to study the intermediate stages.

[11] We do not assume that the ability to materially sanction norm violations (e.g. by embargos) makes a specific norm more robust than when only discursive criticism is possible.

[12] See Percy (2014) for the anti-mercenary norm as an example for change instead of decay.

to figure out a norm's main normative claims and separate them from claims that imply derivative duties or applicatory conditions. When core claims are changed, we speak of norm *decay*—without claiming to solve the conundrum of norm change and norm replacement.

1.5 Case studies

For this study, we selected cases that are considered "under challenge" and historical cases that were completely replaced—albeit the cases showed different dominating contestation types over time. To study potential explanatory factors for contestation types and robustness trends, in a second step, our aim was to select cases that vary regarding robustness. Overall, we chose four current and two historical cases.[13] This allows studying the full spectrum of the dependent variable and enables us to better detect potential causes. While this is a small-N project, our cases allow for within-case variance as well (regarding shifting contestation types and variance in robustness over time), increasing our causal leverage (Blatter and Haverland 2012; Chapter 2).

The international prohibition of torture is a fundamental human rights norm deeply anchored in international treaty law (Rodley and Pollard 2009: 46–47). According to the International Covenant on Civil and Political Rights (ICCPR, Arts 7, 4) and the UN Convention against Torture (CAT, Arts 1, 2, 16), torture and cruel, inhuman, or degrading treatment or punishment are universally prohibited in war- and peacetime. This prohibition is not derogable: It applies to everyone, at all times, everywhere (Nowak and McArthur 2008: 157–58). We focus on the periods before and after CAT entered into force in 1987, studying norm challenges and robustness in the 1970s, 1990s, and early 2000s.

After much controversial debate, R2P was adopted at the UN World Summit and included in the WSOD. This makes every state responsible for protecting its population from genocide, ethnic cleansing, war crimes, and crimes against humanity. Following the WSOD formulation, we define R2P as the duty of every state to protect its population from these core crimes. The international community must help states to fulfill this duty. If a state manifestly fails to protect its population against these crimes and if peaceful means are inadequate, the international community is obligated to take collective action through the UN Security Council, including measures listed in

[13] Supplementary material and data for the four current case studies is available at the Harvard Dataverse. https://doi.org/10.7910/DVN/6VHFZK.

Chapter VII of the UN Charter. Chapter 3 in this volume studies the norm's development, especially the period between 2005 and 2016.

The commercial whaling moratorium can be described as a "soft" law. In 1982, the International Whaling Commission (IWC) decided to reduce all catch limits to zero.[14] When it came into force in 1986, it was planned to be temporary and termed a "moratorium." But because it has been in place ever since, it can now generally be referred to as the whaling "ban" (for background information, see Peterson 1992; Bailey 2008). It forbids commercial whaling of any kind but includes exemptions: "aboriginal subsistence whaling" based on IWC quotas, along with lethal whaling for scientific reasons.[15] The chapter focuses on the period between 1986 and 2016.

The duty to prosecute is based on the Rome Statute of 1998, which established the ICC. This norm covers the universal obligation to investigate and prosecute the most serious atrocities: genocide, war crimes, and crimes against humanity (aggression was added later). This duty is primarily national but passes to the ICC, which has been operating since 2002, if national jurisdictions are incapable or unwilling to prosecute (the complementarity principle) (Deitelhoff 2006: 181, 2009: 37–38). Under this norm, individuals, including heads of state, are no longer protected by the principles of sovereignty and immunity. We analyze the trends in norm robustness from 1998, when the Rome Statute was adopted, until 2016.

A widespread practice since the Middle Ages, privateering was a means of using government-issued "letters of marque" to seize private property at sea (Sicking 2018: 457). It is a *permissive* norm that allows, but does not dictate, certain behavior. Originally a means of gaining compensation, privateering later became part of maritime warfare (Kempe 2010: 45; Starkey 2011: 129). It was a legal enterprise under the domestic laws of many states that considered piracy—conducted by individuals whose actions were *not* state-sanctioned—unlawful. Privateering was regulated both domestically and by intra-state customs. While the distinction between piracy and privateering was often blurry, the latter remained legal until it was finally banned in 1856 by the Paris Declaration Respecting Maritime Law.

The slave trade was similarly linked to permissive norms. Any description of a normative field that lasted for centuries and stretched across countries risks oversimplification, but we can safely say that European slave trading was based on participating countries' two normative assumptions: (1) their perceived duty to spread Christianity and "industrious labor" and (2) the belief

[14] The basic international convention, the International Convention for the Regulation of Whaling was not changed.

[15] See IWC Schedule, para. 13.

that Europeans were morally superior to Africans (Dahomay 2003: 5). For these reasons, the slave trade was widely believed to be a *morally desirable* undertaking (see, e.g. Clay 2016: 269). The transatlantic slave-trading norm was underpinned by states' rights to capture, transport, and sell Africans (Drescher 2009: 4–5). This chapter focuses on the norm's surprising robustness in Great Britain and Portugal. It remained quite stable from the sixteenth to the nineteenth centuries—and then ended swiftly.

Detailed data collection and analytic strategies are presented for each case study. For the two historical cases, we generally examined patterns of contestation and robustness trends in archival material, newspaper discourses, and secondary literature. The contemporary cases are supplemented by interviews, protocols of speeches and debates, newspaper content, and participatory observation—as well as data sets, for example, on compliance with the torture prohibition. Contestation types were assessed using qualitative content analysis, which was also used for several robustness indicators, such as concordance with the torture ban and R2P.

1.6 Argument: How contestation types and robustness are linked

The case studies show that contestation types and robustness can be linked. For the torture prohibition and R2P, most contestation was applicatory, while robustness either remained stable or increased. For the torture prohibition, compliance with the norm was more or less stable and implementation increased. We observed no lasting decline in either concordance or negative reactions to norm violations by norm addressees, and the international community generally did not accept attempts by the US and Israel to challenge the validity of the torture prohibition. In contrast, we observed that the norms regarding the duty to prosecute and the commercial whaling moratorium weakened. The validity of both norms was increasingly contested, and applicatory contestation of the commercial whaling moratorium became permanent. That said, neither norm was completely eroded or replaced. In the case of the commercial whaling ban, whaling activities increased while other IWC member states' negative reactions to them decreased.

The two historical cases were different. Both privateering and the slave trade were surprisingly stable for centuries. States vigorously contested privateering's application, which resulted in several processes of adaptation and more regulation. Yet, its legitimacy was hardly questioned until the mid-nineteenth century, when validity contestation finally arose, particularly in

Great Britain—and the applicatory contestation of privateering became permanent. Inspired by Great Britain's early-nineteenth-century transnational abolitionist movement, privateering was banned in 1856 and slowly replaced.

What explains these patterns of contestation? Why do norm challengers sometimes radicalize their contestations? When do they only critique the application? Research on norm erosion and weakening addresses several factors, most importantly the power of norm challengers and the legal characteristics of a norm. We demonstrate that institutional characteristics, such as the embeddedness of norms in norm clusters and perceptions of procedural fairness, play more determinant roles.

1.6.1 Role of law and norm clusters

Norm dynamics research describes a norm's legal character as key to preventing it from weakening. IR scholars traditionally equate legal character with robustness. Abbott et al. (2000) wrote that a law is "*harder*" when its obligation is higher, more precise, and linked to more delegation.[16] International treaties—which codify—are better protected from radical challenges and non-compliance and more binding than communiqués or resolutions (see Kahler 2000: 679). It is assumed that a norm's *precision*—that spells out when, how, and the conditions under which it is to be applied—prevents norm contestation (and weakening). *Delegation*, the practice of using courts and centralized enforcement, serves to strengthen norms. When there are no institutions that can rule on contested issues, norms are at greater risk of decaying. Adjudication bodies—in the best case, courts—can help settle disputes over a norm's application and decide its meanings (see, e.g. Romano et al. 2014; Lesch 2023). Enforcement mechanisms prevent contestation and non-compliance.

However, whether a norm's legalization makes it more robust is open to question. For example, with respect to the prohibition on women engaging in combat, Percy (2019) argues that the absence of any relevant international law long helped to keep the norm robust. Eventually, a growing body of legislation created access points for contestation and accelerated the prohibition's decay. Some scholars argue that precision does not preclude contestation and that very "tight" behavioral rules can stimulate it, while less precision makes it possible to link a plentitude of interests and interpretations to

[16] Of course, this take on legalization did have critics in Finnemore and Toope (2001), Deitelhoff (2009), and Firscher-Lescano and Liste (2005). Moreover, international law scholars do not accept that a legal norm can be *more or less* binding: For them, it is either binding or not.

a norm (Widmaier and Glanville 2015). Greater scope lowers sovereignty costs and increases behavioral latitude. Panke and Petersohn (2016) maintain that precise norms do not lend themselves to adaptation: While *im*precise norms can be adapted and reinterpreted when challenged, *precise* norms allow no leeway—which leads challengers to eliminate them. The same holds for delegation: Although centralized decisions and sanctioning might help to consolidate norm meanings and enforce norms, they can also create high costs and backlash. As Price (2019) shows in the context of the Chemical Weapons Convention (CWC), highly institutionalized norms are costly to uphold because states are expected to materially sanction non-compliance. When states are either unwilling or unable to uphold a high bar, a norm may become weakened because other norm addressees interpret inaction as less norm legitimacy. Moreover, sanctioning mechanisms can raise issues of fairness in targeted states, leading to radicalization and the shift from applicatory toward validity contestation.

The debate over "hard" versus "soft" law differs from research on legal argumentation; that is, a specific form of legal discourse could tame contesting actors by limiting the range of legitimate arguments (Müller 2004; Fischer-Lescano and Liste 2005; Deitelhoff 2009; Bower 2019; Brunnée and Toope 2019). According to Bower (2019), legal argumentation curtails applicatory contestation and protects the ICC from effective challenges. However, our case data shows that the ICC is being weakened (see Chapter 5).

Norms are also embedded in broader normative fields or clusters: Norms that are connected and linked to a dense field of higher principles, like human rights, are harder to isolate and attack because the whole cluster has legitimacy and is interrelated (Lantis and Wunderlich 2018; Deitelhoff and Zimmermann 2019). It is not clear how embeddedness works: Contestation aimed at the underlying *principle* rather than at an individual norm could be particularly devastating because that would erode the whole cluster. Moreover, cluster membership is a discursively constructed category. Targeted killing was long embedded in the clusters of sovereignty and liberal norms and only became disconnected from the latter in recent decades because of shifts in the discursive process (Großklaus 2017). Linkages and cluster membership do not merely "exist": They can also be grafted (Fehl 2019; Gholiagha et al. 2020).

As we explain in detail in the following chapters, the role of law is not what we had assumed. In the two cases that exhibit radicalized contestation, the ICC represents hard law and the whaling moratorium soft. At the same time, the (soft-law) R2P principle, which we had expected to be particularly vulnerable to validity contestation, and the (hard-law) torture prohibition have both survived extensive contestation quite well. Moreover, as both the torture prohibition and the ICC cases show, legal arguments do not preclude validity contestation. Challengers seem to adapt their argumentation to the legal, normative, or scientific context—and to specific audiences (see Zimmermann 2021).

Embeddedness in normative clusters played a central role in our historical case studies. Privateering was part of a more general norm set that organized warfare and states' economic relationships; its robustness dynamics were linked to the rise of capitalism and the consolidation of statehood in Europe. Embeddedness also influenced the torture prohibition. Its tight embeddedness in a broader cluster of human rights norms made it very hard to attack. Not only is it included in regional and international human rights treaties, but it is also codified in international humanitarian and criminal law. In many of the treaties, the prohibition's special position makes it non-derogable and applicable to both international and non-international conflicts. In the other contemporary cases, embeddedness in complex norm clusters fueled contestation but cannot explain shifts in contestation patterns.

1.6.2 Role of powerful actors

Much norm research identifies the power of norm challengers as largely shaping norm dynamics and erosion processes. Although studies focus on the power to coerce or indirectly shape agendas and institutions, other forms of power are also relevant (see Barnett and Duvall 2005).

This discussion concerns *hard* power, which is usually understood as the distribution of material power or wealth. Norm challengers who have much more material power than supporters can change or erode a norm (Panke and Petersohn 2016). Hard power stimulates various dynamics: Powerful challengers can bribe or sanction norm supporters, who might not want to risk encouraging the former to adopt critical positions or specific behaviors; that is, norm supporters may refrain from publicly condemning non-compliance or contestation in the hopes of avoiding difficulties in other policy areas. One example of this is the way European states did not openly condemn US torture practices in the first years after allegations were publicized (Keating 2014). Furthermore, powerful norm challengers like the US are not easily impressed by sanctions or shaming and can more easily weather condemnations of their non-compliance than less powerful states since they generally need not rely on cooperation. That said, many researchers argue that softer forms of power can also matter. Some challengers are powerful because they have communicative resources to promote their preferred interpretations of norms or are viewed as enjoying a certain moral authority (Sandholtz and Stiles 2009: 16–17). They can thus persuade other norm addressees to radicalize their contestation.

Nonetheless, it is not entirely clear whether hard and soft power can directly shape norm dynamics. Sometimes, middle powers manage to establish new norm interpretations that conflict with the interests of powerful states—as in the Rome Statute that created the ICC and the landmine ban (Price 1998; Deitelhoff 2009). Norm changes can also sometimes be brought about by weaker coalitions. For example, Trade-Related Aspects of Intellectual Property Rights (TRIPS) was reinterpreted in light of public health crises, and generics were sold despite the organized opposition of many Western states (Deere 2009). How important, then, is the agential "power" of specific norm challengers? Our case studies focus on policy fields and essential resources (information, communication, moral authority, wealth, and military might) to assess the role of power. This may involve veto power, quotas, or other procedures in decision-making bodies that are linked to the norm or control over the flow of resources to institutions involved in its implementation.

Our contemporary case studies present no clear picture with respect to the power factor. Norms were not weakened by hard power, nor did soft power materialize as a central factor. With respect to the duty to prosecute, the main African norm challengers had much less hard *and* soft power than the supporters, and although the main pro-whaling states—Norway, Iceland, and Japan—have more soft power than African states, they feared US sanctions and consumer boycotts coordinated by coalitions of NGOs (see Chapters 4 and 5). In contrast, with respect to the torture prohibition, which remained robust despite the hard and soft power of the US, Israel, and the United Kingdom, few states imitated their contestations or practices (see Chapter 2).

In the historical case studies, the power of norm challengers had much more direct effects. Imperial Great Britain experienced an internal change of policy with respect to its slave trade that led it to internationally push for similar policy change using a new form of transnational campaigning. A similar constellation is observable with respect to privateering: Great Britain was the major power pushing for privateering to be banned, which it accomplished by reinterpreting the rights of neutral states in warfare (see Chapters 6 and 7).

1.6.3 Role of institutions: Procedural characteristics

Many scholars see the role of international institutions as linked to delegation: the use of courts and centralized enforcement. They equate institutionalization with legalization (Abbott et al. 2000). Our broader conceptualization considers that the institutional structures and organizational schemes in which international norms are negotiated and challenged are significant as well as their characteristics. We are concerned about their types, decision-making rules, and "negotiation cultures."

Although many studies of norm emergence and diffusion emphasize the importance of institutional settings, studies dealing with norm erosion surprisingly do not. The IR debate about "arguing" (exchanging points of view with the aim of reaching consensus) and bargaining (Risse 2000; Müller 2004; Deitelhoff and Müller 2005; Panke 2010) has been influential. Identifying the institutional preconditions that facilitate arguing helps us to understand how institutionalization can prevent contestation from radicalizing. The more institutions are conducive to arguing, the more likely they are to hinder radicalization. Theories on argumentation and deliberation (Bohman 1996; Habermas 1996) view institutional settings as helping to channel and manage disputes and prevent them from degenerating into hostile confrontation. They serve to tame disputes so actors can agree on new norms and their interpretations (Deitelhoff 2009: 44, 61). Institutional settings that are perceived as "fair" can provide these functions through generating equal and effective access to actors, having non-hierarchical negotiating modes (Dryzek 1992: 412; Risse 2000, 15; Sikkink 2002), and providing space for shared learning (Deitelhoff 2009; Risse and Kleine 2010: 715). According to Wiener (2008: 204–208), international institutions help to establish shared understandings, thereby preventing greater conflict, and also provide dispute settlement procedures. By sharing evaluation criteria and processes for managing objections, institutional fora similarly facilitate the emergence of common concepts and procedural norms for channeling developing conflicts (Deitelhoff 2009; Panke 2010). Dembinski and Peters (2019) examine procedural justice and encourage the study of just how "fair" international institutions are perceived to be when international norms are implemented (see also Dembinski 2016). But this field of research does not link this to broader processes of norm strengthening or decline.

Recently, with respect to radicalized contestation, researchers on backlash to international institutions and courts (Madsen et al. 2018; Alter and Zürn

2020) have discussed how institutional characteristics create resilience to radical contestation (Soley and Steininger 2018) and that perceptions of lost status and unfair treatment in shaming campaigns stimulate more radical backlash (Freedman 2020; Snyder 2020). When certain procedural characteristics are absent from international negotiations over norms, contesting actors might perceive them as unfair and radicalize their positions.

With respect to norm weakening, fair institutions help to enshrine and channel contestation by offering actors equal recognition: Temporarily fixing meaning in institutions[17] can lead to applicatory contestation instead of complete resistance. Such institutions take contestation seriously. They are perceived as opening effective institutional channels for change and encouraging, rather than subduing, critique. In our case studies, this included the formalized sanctioning of norm violations without exploiting power asymmetries.

Our case studies reveal the crucial role of fair institutions. A central outcome of our contemporary cases studies is that contestation expands and increases also at the validity level when contesting states do not find (or at least perceive it as such) access to contestation in the relevant institutions. The two cases of norm weakening, the international duty to prosecute and the commercial whaling ban, were driven by institutional features. Some pro-whalers felt they were not taken seriously and were being cheated by anti-whaling groups who exploited the decision-making structures. Rather than bolstering support for the norm, the threat of sanctions by anti-whaling states and a coalition of anti-whaling NGOs exacerbated feelings of unfairness that resulted in confrontational interactions and radicalization. With respect to the international duty to prosecute, the ICC represents the norm's institutionalization, although it is not the only institution or even the decisive one. Contestation became radicalized when the UN Security Council refused to consider the African Union's appeal to have the ICC stop investigating the situation in Darfur once an arrest warrant for Omar al-Bashir had been issued.

In contrast, with respect to the torture prohibition and R2P, norm challenges were often made through UN institutions or within the European human rights framework—settings which, in contrast to the IWC and the ICC's Assembly of States, allowed for a more open debate about norm content. The US sent a delegation to Geneva to engage in "constructive dialogue" with the Committee against Torture, and states critical of R2P are

[17] For more on fixing meaning in international organizations, see Barnett and Finnemore (1999: 710–15). See also Finnemore and Sikkink (1998: 900) and Sandholtz (2007: 8).

still debating the norm at the UN General Assembly; that is, these institutional settings have been able to help prevent radicalization. Without their moderating effects, states who felt excluded from the R2P debate might have radicalized their contestation, while the US and Israel, feeling that their perspectives were not taken seriously, might have stopped engaging with human rights treaty bodies. Both norms also show that contestation does not necessarily intensify over time. The responsibility to protect "lives" with constant applicatory contestation. The severe challenges to the torture prohibition ceased over time.

1.7 Outline of the book

We address the burgeoning diagnoses regarding the crisis of LIO by zooming in on the dynamics of six international norms. First, we present links between contestation patterns and norm robustness trends and explain our findings. This comparative study allows us to demonstrate that it is premature to talk about a crisis of LIO, much less its demise. We show that the amount of contestation is not in itself a strong indicator for a crisis of norms or a crisis of the liberal international order.

To develop our argument, Chapters 2–5 on the four contemporary case studies—the torture prohibition, R2P, the commercial whaling moratorium, and the international duty to prosecute—share a common structure. We begin by assessing the main characteristics of each norm and introducing our data. Then, we examine how the two types of contestation developed over time. After that, we look at the compliance, implementation, concordance, and negative reactions to norm violations and study the plausibility of four factors: law and norm clusters, power, and procedural fairness perceptions. In Chapters 6 and 7, we trace the close links between contestation and norm robustness in privateering and the transatlantic slave trade and identify factors that drive contestation.

Our comparisons show that norms can weather high amounts of contestation. This is particularly evident with respect to the anti-torture norm (Chapter 2) and R2P (Chapter 3). A norm only risks becoming weakened when applicatory contestation is accompanied by validity contestation and/or if it becomes permanent, as shown by the whaling moratorium and the ICC (Chapters 4 and 5). Yet, even in this subset, the norms remain in place, while validity contestation regarding the ICC is generally confined to the African continent. Only in our historical case studies—privateering and the transatlantic slave trade—were the norms completely replaced (Chapters

6 and 7). This demonstrates that contestation cannot easily erode a norm. This probably holds for international institutions and even more so for the current international order built on these institutions and norms. The empirical chapters present insight into the factors that spur or tame contestation, thereby impacting robustness. As the historical case studies indicate, power mostly plays a role in situations of consolidated hegemonies with little international institutionalization, such as the British Empire (Chapters 6 and 7). The contemporary cases show that embeddedness in norm clusters and the fair institutionalization of norms are more decisive in preventing applicatory contestation from becoming permanent or so radicalized that the validity of norms is contested.

Our book presents six case studies that offer original insights into the link between applicatory and validity contestations and norm robustness. However, we expect to find similar dynamics in other policy fields. We conclude by contextualizing our findings, outlining possible avenues for further research, and offering recommendations for preventing crises of norms, institutions, and orders. Contestation must be *encouraged*, and fora and procedures must be put in place to manage conflicts regarding norms and institutions. Neither contestation nor change are always negative: Sometimes they are needed to make an order run smoothly. Our empirical approach to the study of norm dynamics does not consider the overarching normative question of *which* norms and values should be upheld. But it is an essential first step to better understanding the forces that drive contestation and trends in norm robustness.

Reference list

Abbott, Kenneth W., and Duncan Snidal. 2000. "Hard and Soft Law in International Governance." *International Organization* 54 (3): pp. 421–56. doi: 10.1162/002081800551280.

Abbott, Kenneth W., Robert O. Keohane, Andrew Moravcsik, Anne-Marie Slaughter, and Duncan Snidal. 2000. "The Concept of Legalization." *International Organization* 54 (3): pp. 401–19. doi: 10.1162/002081800551271.

Acharya, Amitav. 2004. "How Ideas Spread: Whose Norms Matter? Norm Localization and Institutional Change in Asian Regionalism." *International Organization* 58 (2): pp. 239–75. doi: 10.1017/S002081830458202.

Acharya, Amitav. 2017. "After Liberal Hegemony: The Advent of a Multiplex World Order." *Ethics & International Affairs* 31 (3): pp. 271–85. doi: 10.1017/S089267941700020X.

Adler-Nissen, Rebecca, and Vincent Pouliot. 2014. "Power in Practice: Negotiating the International Intervention in Libya." *European Journal of International Relations* 20 (4): pp. 889–911. doi: 10.1177/1354066113512702.

Alter, Karen J., and Michael Zürn. 2020. "Conceptualising Backlash Politics: Introduction to a Special Issue on Backlash Politics in Comparison." *British Journal of Politics and International Relations* 22 (4): pp. 563–84. doi: 10.1177/1369148120947958.

Badescu, Cristina G., and Thomas G. Weiss. 2010. "Misrepresenting R2P and Advancing Norms: An Alternative Spiral?" *International Studies Perspectives* 11 (4): pp. 354–74. doi: 10.1111/j.1528-3585.2010.00412.x.

Bailey, Jennifer L. 2008. "Arrested Development: The Fight to End Commercial Whaling as a Case of Failed Norm Change." *European Journal of International Relations* 14 (2): pp. 289–318. doi: 10.1177/1354066108089244.

Barnes, Jamal. 2016. "The 'War on Terror' and the Battle for the Definition of Torture." *International Relations* 30 (1): pp. 102–24. doi: 10.1177/0047117815587775.

Barnett, Michael, and Raymond Duvall. 2005. "Power in International Politics." *International Organization* 59 (1): pp. 39–75. doi: 10.1017/S0020818305050010.

Barnett, Michael N., and Martha J. Finnemore. 1999. "The Politics, Power, and Pathologies of International Organizations." *International Organization* 53 (4): pp. 699–732. doi: 10.1162/002081899551048.

Bellamy, Alex J. 2015. "The Responsibility to Protect Turns Ten." *Ethics & International Affairs* 29 (2): pp. 161–85. doi: 10.1017/S0892679415000052.

Ben-Josef Hirsch, Michal, and Jennifer M. Dixon. 2021. "Conceptualizing and Assessing Norm Strength in International Relations." *European Journal of International Relations* 27 (2): pp. 521–47. doi: 10.1177/1354066120949628.

Bentley, Michelle. 2022. "A New Model of 'Taboo': Disgust, Stigmatization, and Fetishization." *International Studies Review* 24 (3): pp. 1–25. doi: 10.1093/isr/viac028.

Bettiza, Gregorio. 2020. "Pandemipolitics and the (Potential) Unmaking of the Liberal World Order." Accessed September 23, 2022. http://www.gregoriobettiza.com/publication_3276.html.

Betts, Alexander, and Phil Orchard, eds. 2014. *Implementation and World Politics: How International Norms Change Practice*. Oxford: Oxford University Press.

Betts, Alexander, and Phil Orchard. 2014. "Introduction: The Normative Institutionalization-Implementation Gap." In Betts and Orchard 2014, pp. 1–26.

Blatter, Joachim, and Markus Haverland. 2012. *Designing Case Studies: Explanatory Approaches in Small-N Research*. London: Palgrave Macmillan.

Bohman, James. 1996. *Public Deliberation: Pluralism, Complexity, and Democracy*. Cambridge, MA: MIT Press.

Bower, Adam. 2015. "Arguing with Law: Strategic Legal Argumentation, US Diplomacy, and Debates over the International Criminal Court." *Review of International Studies* 41 (2): pp. 337–60. doi: 10.1017/S0260210514000217.

Bower, Adam. 2019. "Contesting the International Criminal Court: Bashir, Kenyatta, and the Status of the Nonimpunity Norm in World Politics." *Journal of Global Security Studies* 4 (1): pp. 88–104. doi: 10.1093/jogss/ogy037.

Brunnée, Jutta, and Stephen J. Toope. 2010. *Legitimacy and Legality in International Law: An Interactional Account.* Cambridge: Cambridge University Press.

Brunnée, Jutta, and Stephen J. Toope. 2019. "Norm Robustness and Contestation in International Law: Self-Defense against Nonstate Actors." *Journal of Global Security Studies* 4 (1): pp. 73–87. doi: 10.1093/jogss/ogy039.

Chayes, Abram, and Antonia Handler Chayes. 1993. "On Compliance." *International Organization* 47 (2): pp. 175. doi: 10.1017/S0020818300027910.

Chayes, Abram, and Antonia Handler Chayes. 1995. *The New Sovereignty: Compliance with International Regulatory Agreements.* Cambridge, MA: Harvard University Press.

Checkel, Jeffrey T. 1999. "Norms, Institutions, and National Identity in Contemporary Europe." *International Studies Quarterly* 43 (1): pp. 83–114. doi: 10.1111/0020-8833.00112.

Clapham, Phillip J. 2015. "Japan's Whaling Following the International Court of Justice Ruling: Brave New World—or Business as Usual?" *Marine Policy* 51 (Suppl. C): pp. 238–41. doi: 10.1016/j.marpol.2014.08.011.

Clark, Ian, Sebastian Kaempf, Christian Reus-Smit, and Emily Tannock. 2018. "Crisis in the Laws of War? Beyond Compliance and Effectiveness." *European Journal of International Relations* 24 (2): pp. 319–43. doi: 10.1177/1354066117714528.

Clay, Lauren R. 2016. "'Cruel Necessity': Capitalism, the Discourse of Sympathy, and the Problem of the Slave Trade in the Age of Human Rights." *Slavery & Abolition* 37 (2): pp. 256–83. doi: 10.1080/0144039X.2015.1120103.

CRC (Convention on the Rights of the Child). 1989. "Convention on the Rights of the Child." United Nations Treaty Series, no. 27531, vol. 1577 at 3 (November 20, 1987).

Dahomay, Jacky. 2003. "Slavery and Law: Legitimations of an Insurrection." In *The Abolitions of Slavery: From Léger Félicité Sonthonax to Victor Schoelcher, 1793, 1794, 1848*, ed. Marcel Dorigny. New York: Berghahn Books, pp. 3–16.

Deere, Carolyn. 2009. *The Implementation Game: The TRIPS Agreement and the Global Politics of Intellectual Property Reform in Developing Countries.* Oxford: Oxford University Press.

Deibert, Ronald J., and Masashi Crete-Nishihata. 2012. "Global Governance and the Spread of Cyberspace Controls." *Global Governance* 18 (3): pp. 339–61. doi: 10.5555/1075-2846-18.3.339.

Deitelhoff, Nicole. 2006. *Überzeugung in der Politik: Grundzüge einer Diskurstheorie internationalen Regierens*. Frankfurt am Main: Suhrkamp.

Deitelhoff, Nicole. 2009. "The Discursive Process of Legalization: Charting Islands of Persuasion in the ICC Case." *International Organization* 63 (1): pp. 33–65. doi: 10.1017/S002081830909002X.

Deitelhoff, Nicole, and Harald Müller. 2005. "Theoretical Paradise—Empirically Lost? Arguing with Habermas." *Review of International Studies* 31 (1): pp. 167–79. doi: 10.1017/S0260210505006364.

Deitelhoff, Nicole, and Lisbeth Zimmermann. 2019. "Norms under Challenge: Unpacking the Dynamics of Norm Robustness." *Journal of Global Security Studies* 4 (1): pp. 2–17. doi: 10.1093/jogss/ogy041.

Deitelhoff, Nicole, and Lisbeth Zimmermann. 2020. "Things We Lost in the Fire: How Different Types of Contestation Affect the Robustness of International Norms." *International Studies Review* 22 (1): pp. 51–76. doi: 10.1093/isr/viy080.

Dembinski, Matthias. 2016. "Procedural Justice and Global Order: Explaining African Reaction to the Application of Global Protection Norms." *European Journal of International Relations* 23 (4): pp. 809–32. doi: 10.1177/1354066116 681059.

Dembinski, Matthias, and Dirk Peters. 2019. "The Power of Justice: How Procedural Justice Concerns Affect the Legitimacy of International Institutions." *Global Governance* 25 (1): pp. 149–70. doi: 10.1163/19426720-02501010.

Drescher, Seymour. 2009. *Abolition: A History of Slavery and Antislavery*. Cambridge: Cambridge University Press.

Drezner, Daniel W. 2020. "The Song Remains the Same: International Relations after COVID-19." *International Organization* 74 (S1): E18–E35. doi: 10.1017/S0020818320000351.

Dryzek, John S. 1992. "How Far Is It from Virginia and Rochester to Frankfurt? Public Choice as Critical Theory." *British Journal of Political Science* 22 (4): pp. 397–417. doi: 10.1017/S0007123400006463.

Duncombe, Constance, and Tim Dunne. 2018. "After Liberal World Order." *International Affairs* 94 (1): pp. 25–42. doi: 10.1093/ia/iix234.

Dunne, Tim. 2007. "'The Rules of the Game Are Changing': Fundamental Human Rights in Crisis after 9/11." *International Politics* 44 (2–3): pp. 269–86. doi: 10.1057/palgrave.ip.8800188.

Eilstrup-Sangiovanni, Mette, and Stephanie C. Hofmann. 2020. "Of the Contemporary Global Order, Crisis, and Change." *Journal of European Public Policy* 27 (7): pp. 1077–89. doi: 10.1080/13501763.2019.1678665.

Fehl, Caroline. 2019. "Bombs, Trials, and Rights: Norm Complexity and the Evolution of Liberal Intervention Practices." *Human Rights Quarterly* 41 (4): pp. 893–915. doi: 10.1353/hrq.2019.0066.

Finnemore, Martha J., and Kathryn Sikkink. 1998. "International Norm Dynamics and Political Change." *International Organization* 52 (4): pp. 887–917. doi: 10.1162/002081898550789.

Finnemore, Martha J., and Kathryn Sikkink. 2001. "Taking Stock: The Constructivist Research Program in International Relations and Comparative Politics." *Annual Review of Political Science* 4 (1): pp. 391–416. doi: 10.1146/annurev.polisci.4.1.391.

Finnemore, Martha J., and Stephen J. Toope. 2001. "Alternatives to 'Legalization': Richer Views of Law and Politics." *International Organization* 55 (3): pp. 743–58. doi: 10.1162/00208180152507614.

Fischer-Lescano, Andreas, and Philip Liste. 2005. "Völkerrechtspolitik: Zur Trennung und Verknüpfung von Politik und Recht in der Weltgesellschaft." *Zeitschrift für Internationale Beziehungen* 12 (2): pp. 209–49. doi: 10.5771/0946-7165-2005-2-209.

Freedman, Joshua. 2020. "Back of the Queue: Brexit, Status Loss, and the Politics of Backlash." *British Journal of Politics and International Relations* 22 (4): pp. 631–43. doi: 10.1177/1369148120949824.

Gholiagha, Sassan, Anna Holzscheiter, and Andrea Liese. 2020. "Activating Norm Collisions: Interface Conflicts in International Drug Control." *Global Constitutionalism* 9 (2): pp. 290–317. doi: 10.1017/S2045381719000388.

Glennon, Michael J. 2004. "How International Rules Die." *Georgetown Law Journal* 93 (3): pp. 939–91.

Großklaus, Mathias. 2017. "Friction, Not Erosion: Assassination Norms at the Fault Line Between Sovereignty and Liberal Values." *Contemporary Security Policy* 38 (2): pp. 260–80. doi: 10.1080/13523260.2017.1335135.

Günther, Klaus. 1993. *The Sense of Appropriateness: Application Discourses in Morality and Law*. Albany, NY: SUNY.

Gutterman, Ellen, and Mathis Lohaus. 2018. "What Is the 'Anti-Corruption' Norm in Global Politics? Norm Robustness and Contestation in the Transnational Governance of Corruption." In *Corruption and Norms: Why Informal Rules Matter*, ed. Ina Kubbe and Annika Engelbert. Cham: Springer, pp. 241–68.

Habermas, Jürgen. 1996. *Between Facts and Norms: Contributions to a Discourse Theory of Law and Democracy*. Cambridge, MA: MIT Press.

Hehir, Aidan. 2019. *Hollow Norms and the Responsibility to Protect*. Cham: Palgrave Macmillan.

Heller, Regina, Martin Kahl, and Daniela Pisoiu. 2012. "The 'Dark' Side of Normative Argumentation: The Case of Counterterrorism Policy." *Global Constitutionalism* 1 (2): pp. 278–312. doi: 10.1017/S2045381711000049.

Hurd, Ian. 1999. "Legitimacy and Authority in International Politics." *International Organization* 53 (2): pp. 379–408. doi: 10.1162/002081899550913.

Hurd, Ian. 2013. "Torture and the Politics of Legitimation in International Law." In *Legitimacy of International Human Rights Regimes*, ed. Andreas Føllesdal, Johan K. Schaffer, and Geir Ulfstein. Cambridge: Cambridge University Press, pp. 165–89.

Ikenberry, G. John. 2018. "The End of Liberal International Order?" *International Affairs* 94 (1): pp. 7–23. doi: 10.1093/ia/iix241.

Kahler, Miles. 2000. "Conclusion: The Causes and Consequences of Legalization." *International Organization* 54 (3): pp. 661–83. doi: 10.1162/002081800551244.

Kamenitsa, Lynn. 2001. "Abortion Debates in Germany." In *Abortion Politics, Women's Movements, and the Democratic State: A Comparative Study of State Feminism*, ed. Dorothy E. McBride. Oxford: Oxford University Press, pp. 111–34.

Katzenstein, Peter J. 1996. "Introduction: Alternative Perspectives on National Security." In *The Culture of National Security: Norms and Identity in World Politics*, ed. Peter J. Katzenstein. New York: Columbia University Press, pp. 1–32.

Keating, Vincent C. 2014. "Contesting the International Illegitimacy of Torture: The Bush Administration's Failure to Legitimate Its Preferences within International Society." *British Journal of Politics & International Relations* 16 (1): pp. 1–27. doi: 10.1111/1467-856X.12024.

Kempe, Michael. 2010. *Fluch der Weltmeere: Piraterie, Völkerrecht und internationale Beziehungen 1500–1900*. Wiesbaden: Campus Verlag.

Kratochwil, Friedrich. 1989. *Rules, Norms and Decisions: On the Conditions of Practical and Legal Reasoning in International Relations and Domestic Affairs*. Cambridge: Cambridge University Press.

Kratochwil, Friedrich, and John Gerard Ruggie. 1986. "International Organization: A State of the Art on an Art of the State." *International Organization* 40 (4): pp. 753–75. doi: 10.1017/S0020818300027363.

Krook, Mona Lena, and Jacqui True. 2012. "Rethinking the Life Cycles of International Norms: The United Nations and the Global Promotion of Gender Equality." *European Journal of International Relations* 18 (1): pp. 103–27. doi: 10.1177/1354066110380963.

Kutz, Christopher. 2014. "How Norms Die: Torture and Assassination in American Security Policy." *Ethics & International Affairs* 28 (4): pp. 425–49. doi: 10.1017/S0892679414000598.

Lake, David A., Lisa L. Martin, and Thomas Risse. 2021. "Challenges to the Liberal Order: Reflections on International Organization." *International Organization*, pp. 1–33. doi: 10.1017/S0020818320000636.

Lantis, Jeffrey S., and Carmen Wunderlich. 2018. "Resiliency Dynamics of Norm Clusters: Norm Contestation and International Cooperation." *Review of International Studies* 44 (3): pp. 570–93. doi: 10.1017/S0260210517000626.

Legro, Jeffrey W. 1997. "Which Norms Matter? Revisiting the 'Failure' of Internationalism." *International Organization* 51 (1): pp. 31–63. doi: 10.1162/002081897550294.

Lesch, Max. 2023. "From Norm Violations to Norm Development: Deviance, International Institutions, and the Torture Prohibition." *International Studies Quarterly*, forthcoming.

Lesch, Max, and Nina Reiners. 2023. "Informal Human Rights Law-making: How Treaty Bodies Use General Comments to Develop International Law." *Global Constitutionalism*, online first: pp. 1–24. doi: 10.1017/S2045381723000023.

Madsen, Mikael Rask, Pola Cebulak, and Micha Wiebusch. 2018. "Backlash against International Courts: Explaining the Forms and Patterns of Resistance to International Courts." *International Journal of Law in Context* 14 (02): pp. 197–220. doi: 10.1017/S1744552318000034.

Martin, Lisa L. 2013. "Against Compliance." In *Interdisciplinary Perspectives on International Law and International Relations: The State of the Art*, ed. Jeffrey L. Dunoff and Mark A. Pollack. Cambridge: Cambridge University Press, pp. 591–610.

McKeown, Ryder. 2009. "Norm Regress: US Revisionism and the Slow Death of the Torture Norm." *International Relations* 23 (1): pp. 5–25. doi: 10.1177/0047117808100607.

McNamara, Kathleen R., and Abraham L. Newman. 2020. "The Big Reveal: COVID-19 and Globalization's Great Transformations." *International Organization* 74 (S1): E59–E77. doi: 10.1017/S0020818320000387.

Müller, Harald. 2004. "Arguing, Bargaining and All That: Communicative Action, Rationalist Theory and the Logic of Appropriateness in International Relations." *European Journal of International Relations* 10 (3): pp. 395–435. doi: 10.1177/1354066104045542.

Müller, Harald, and Carmen Wunderlich, eds. 2013. *Norm Dynamics in Multilateral Arms Control: Interests, Conflicts, and Justice*. Athens: University of Georgia Press.

Nadelmann, Ethan A. 1990. "Global Prohibition Regimes: The Evolution of Norms in International Society." *International Organization* 44 (4): pp. 479–526. doi: 10.1017/S0020818300035384.

Niemann, Holger, and Henrik Schillinger. 2017. "Contestation 'All the Way Down'? The Grammar of Contestation in Norm Research." *Review of International Studies* 43 (1): pp. 29–49. doi: 10.1017/S0260210516000188.

Nowak, Manfred, and Elizabeth McArthur. 2008. *The United Nations Convention against Torture: A Commentary*. Oxford: Oxford University Press.

Nowak, Manfred, Moritz Birk, and Giuliana Monina. 2019. *The United Nations Convention against Torture and Its Optional Protocol: A Commentary*. 2nd edn. Oxford: Oxford University Press.

O'Mahoney, Joseph. 2014. "Rule Tensions and the Dynamics of Institutional Change: From 'To the Victor Go the Spoils' to the Stimson Doctrine." *European Journal of International Relations* 20 (3): pp. 834–57. doi: 10.1177/1354066113483781.

Panke, Diana. 2010. "Why Discourse Matters Only Sometimes: Effective Arguing beyond the Nation-State." *Review of International Studies* 36 (1): pp. 145–68. doi: 10.1017/s0260210509990544.

Panke, Diana, and Ulrich Petersohn. 2012. "Why International Norms Disappear Sometimes." *European Journal of International Relations* 18 (4): pp. 719–42. doi: 10.1177/1354066111407690.

Panke, Diana, and Ulrich Petersohn. 2016. "Norm Challenges and Norm Death: The Inexplicable?" *Cooperation and Conflict* 51 (1): pp. 3–19. doi: 10.1177/0010836715597948.

Percy, Sarah. 2014. "The Unimplemented Norm." In Betts and Orchard 2014, pp. 68–84.

Percy, Sarah. 2019. "What Makes a Norm Robust: The Norm against Female Combat." *Journal of Global Security Studies* 4 (1): pp. 123–38. doi: 10.1093/jogss/ogy044.

Percy, Sarah V., and Wayne Sandholtz. 2022. "Why Norms Rarely Die." *European Journal of International Relations* 28 (4): 934–54. doi: 10.1177/13540661221126018.

Peterson, M. J. 1992. "Whalers, Cetologists, Environmentalists, and the International Management of Whaling." *International Organization* 46 (1): pp. 147–86. doi: 10.2307/2706954.

Peterson, Victor. 2015. "Creativity in Application Discourses." *Constellations* 22 (2): pp. 218–32. doi: 10.1111/1467-8675.12111.

Price, Richard. 1998. "Reversing the Gun Sights: Transnational Civil Society Targets Land Mines." *International Organization* 52 (3): pp. 613–44. doi: 10.1162/002081898550671.

Price, Richard. 2004. "Emerging Customary Norms and Anti-Personnel Landmines." In *The Politics of International Law*, ed. Christian Reus-Smit. Cambridge: Cambridge University Press, pp. 106–30.

Price, Richard. 2006. "Detecting Ideas and Their Effects." In *The Oxford Handbook of Contextual Political Analysis*, ed. Robert E. Goodin and Charles Tilly. Oxford: Oxford University Press, pp. 252–65.

Price, Richard. 2019. "Syria and the Chemical Weapons Taboo." *Journal of Global Security Studies* 4 (1): pp. 37–52. doi: 10.1093/jogss/ogy040.

Quennerstedt, Ann. 2009. "Balancing the Rights of the Child and the Rights of Parents in the Convention on the Rights of the Child." *Journal of Human Rights* 8 (2): pp. 162–76. doi: 10.1080/14754830902897270.

Ralph, Jason G., and Adrian Gallagher. 2015. "Legitimacy Faultlines in International Society: The Responsibility to Protect and Prosecute after Libya." *Review of International Studies* 41 (3): pp. 553–73. doi: 10.1017/S0260210514000242.

Reiners, Nina. 2022. *Transnational Lawmaking Coalitions for Human Rights*. Cambridge: Cambridge University Press.

Rieff, David. 2011. "R2P, R.I.P." New York Times, November 7. Accessed January 6, 2023. http://www.nytimes.com/2011/11/08/opinion/r2p-rip.html?_r=0.

Risse, Thomas. 2000. "'Let's Argue!' Communicative Action in World Politics." *International Organization* 54 (1): pp. 1–39. doi: 10.1162/002081800551109.

Risse, Thomas, and Mareike Kleine. 2010. "Deliberation in Negotiations." *Journal of European Public Policy* 17 (5): pp. 708–26. doi: 10.1080/135017610037 48716.

Risse, Thomas, and Kathryn Sikkink. 1999. "The Socialization of International Human Rights Norms into Domestic Practices: Introduction." In *The Power of Human Rights: International Norms and Domestic Change*, ed. Thomas Risse, Stephen C. Ropp, and Kathryn Sikkink. Cambridge: Cambridge University Press, pp. 1–38.

Risse, Thomas, Stephen C. Ropp, and Kathryn Sikkink, eds. 1999. *The Power of Human Rights: International Norms and Domestic Change*. Cambridge: Cambridge University Press.

Rodley, Nigel S., and Matt Pollard. 2009. *The Treatment of Prisoners under International Law*. Oxford: Oxford University Press.

Romano, Cesare, Karen J. Alter, and Yuval Shany, eds. 2014. *The Oxford Handbook of International Adjudication*. Oxford: Oxford University Press.

Rosert, Elvira, and Sonja Schirmbeck. 2007. "Zur Erosion internationaler Normen: Folterverbot und Nukleares Tabu in der Diskussion." *Zeitschrift für Internationale Beziehungen* 14 (2): pp. 253–87.

Sandholtz, Wayne. 2007. *Prohibiting Plunder: How Norms Change*. Oxford: Oxford University Press.

Sandholtz, Wayne. 2019. "Norm Contestation, Robustness, and Replacement." *Journal of Global Security Studies* 4 (1): pp. 139–46. doi: 10.1093/jogss/ogy042.

Sandholtz, Wayne, and Kendall W. Stiles. 2009. *International Norms and Cycles of Change*. Oxford: Oxford University Press.

Schmidt, Averell, and Kathryn Sikkink. 2019. "Breaking the Ban? The Heterogeneous Impact of US Contestation of the Torture Norm." *Journal of Global Security Studies* 4 (1): pp. 105–22. doi: 10.1093/jogss/ogy036.

Sicking, Louis. 2018. "The Pirate and the Admiral: Europeanisation and Globalisation of Maritime Conflict Management." *Journal of the History of International Law* 20 (4): pp. 429–70. doi: 10.1163/15718050-12340098.

Sikkink, Kathryn. 2002. "Restructuring World Politics: The Limits and Asymmetries of Soft Power." In *Restructuring World Politics: Transnational Social Movements, Networks and Norms*, ed. Sanjeev Khagram, James V. Riker, and Kathryn Sikkink. Minneapolis: University of Minnesota Press, pp. 301–18.

Sikkink, Kathryn. 2013. "The United States and Torture: Does the Spiral Model Work." In *The Persistent Power of Human Rights: From Commitment to Compliance*, ed. Thomas Risse, Stephen C. Ropp, and Kathryn Sikkink. Cambridge: Cambridge University Press, pp. 145–63.

Snyder, Jack. 2020. "Backlash against Naming and Shaming: The Politics of Status and Emotion." *British Journal of Politics and International Relations* 22 (4): pp. 644–53. doi: 10.1177/1369148120948361.

Soley, Ximena, and Silvia Steininger. 2018. "Parting Ways or Lashing Back? Withdrawals, Backlash and the Inter-American Court of Human Rights." *International Journal of Law in Context* 14 (2): pp. 237–57. doi: 10.1017/S1744552318000058.

Sørensen, Georg. 2011. *A Liberal World Order in Crisis: Choosing between Imposition and Restraint*. Ithaca, NY: Cornell University Press.

Starkey, David J. 2011. "Voluntaries and Sea Robbers: A Review of the Academic Literature on Privateering, Corsairing, Buccaneering and Piracy." *Mariner's Mirror* 97 (1): pp. 127–47. doi: 10.1080/00253359.2011.10709036.

Stimmer, Anette, and Lea Wisken. 2019. "The Dynamics of Dissent: When Actions Are Louder Than Words." *International Affairs* 95 (3): pp. 515–33. doi: 10.1093/ia/iiz019.

Tannenwald, Nina. 1999. "The Nuclear Taboo: The United States and the Normative Basis of Nuclear Non-Use." *International Organization* 53 (3): pp. 433–68. doi: 10.1162/002081899550959.

Treves, Tullio. 2006. "Customary International Law." In *Max Planck Encyclopedia of Public International Law*, ed. Anne Peters and Rüdiger Wolfrum. Oxford: Oxford University Press. Last updated November 2006. Accessed January 6, 2023. https://opil.ouplaw.com/view/10.1093/law:epil/9780199231690/law-9780199231690-e1393.

van Kersbergen, Kees, and Bertjan Verbeek. 2007. "The Politics of International Norms: Subsidiarity and the Imperfect Competence Regime of the European Union." *European Journal of International Relations* 13 (2): pp. 217–38. doi: 10.1177/1354066107076955.

Waal, Alex de. 2007. "Darfur and the Failure of the Responsibility to Protect." *International Affairs* 83 (6): pp. 1039–54. doi: 10.1111/j.1468-2346.2007.00672.x.

Welsh, Jennifer M. 2013. "Norm Contestation and the Responsibility to Protect." *Global Responsibility to Protect* 5 (4): pp. 365–96. doi: 10.1163/1875984X-00504002.

Wendt, Alexander E. 1987. "The Agent-Structure Problem in International Relations Theory." *International Organization* 41 (3): pp. 335–70. doi: 10.1017/S002081830002751X.

Widmaier, Wesley W., and Luke Glanville. 2015. "The Benefits of Norm Ambiguity: Constructing the Responsibility to Protect across Rwanda, Iraq and Libya." *Contemporary Politics* 21 (4): pp. 367–83. doi: 10.1080/13569775.2015.1014178.

Wiener, Antje. 2004. "Contested Compliance: Interventions on the Normative Structure of World Politics." *European Journal of International Relations* 10 (2): pp. 189–234. doi: 10.1177/1354066104042934.

Wiener, Antje. 2007. "The Dual Quality of Norms and Governance beyond the State: Sociological and Normative Approaches to 'Interaction.'" *Critical Review of International Social and Political Philosophy* 10 (1): pp. 47–69. doi: 10.1080/13698230601122412.

Wiener, Antje. 2008. *The Invisible Constitution of Politics: Contested Norms and International Encounters*. Cambridge: Cambridge University Press.

Wiener, Antje. 2010. "Normative Baggage in International Encounters: Contestation All the Way." In *On Rules, Politics and Knowledge: Friedrich Kratochwil, International Relations, and Domestic Affairs*, ed. Oliver Kessler, Rodney B. Hall, Cecilia Lynch, and Nicholas G. Onuf. Basingstoke: Palgrave Macmillan, pp. 202–12.

Wiener, Antje. 2014. *A Theory of Contestation*. Heidelberg: Springer.

Wiener, Antje. 2018. *Contestation and Constitution of Norms in Global International Relations*. Cambridge: Cambridge University Press.

Young, Oran R. 1979. *Compliance & Public Authority: A Theory with International Applications*. Baltimore, MD: Taylor and Francis.

Zimmermann, Lisbeth. 2017a. *Global Norms with a Local Face? Rule-of-Law Promotion and Norm Translation*. Cambridge: Cambridge University Press.

Zimmermann, Lisbeth. 2017b. "More for Less: The Interactive Translation of Global Norms in Postconflict Guatemala." *International Studies Quarterly* 61 (4): pp. 774–85. doi: 10.1093/isq/sqx044.

Zimmermann, Lisbeth. 2021. "Law and Science in Environmental Governance: The Effects of Legal and Scientific Argumentation in the International Whaling Commission." In *Talking International Law: Legal Argumentation outside the Courtroom*, ed. Ian Johnstone and Steven R. Ratner. Oxford: Oxford University Press, pp. 263–81.

Zimmermann, Lisbeth, Nicole Deitelhoff, and Max Lesch. 2017. "Unlocking the Agency of the Governed: Contestation and Norm Dynamics." *Third World Thematics: A TWQ Journal* 2 (5): pp. 691–708. doi: 10.1080/23802014.2017.1396912.

Zwingel, Susanne. 2016. *Translating International Women's Rights: The CEDAW Convention in Context*. London: Palgrave Macmillan.

2
International torture prohibition
A contested norm endures

2.1 Introduction

Following the 2004 scandal in Abu Ghraib prison in Iraq, scholars of International Relations (IR) became concerned about challenges to the international norm prohibiting torture. In the notorious "Torture Memos," lawyers for the United States (US) government challenged the international law on torture (Dratel and Greenberg 2005). Some IR scholars suggest that contestation and/or violations of the norm against torture have weakened it in the US and perhaps worldwide (Foot 2006: 140; Rosert and Schirmbeck 2007: 262; McKeown 2009: 19–20; Brunnée and Toope 2010: 270; Sikkink 2013: 162; Kutz 2014: 437–38). These studies either conflate contestation with robustness or narrowly interpret robustness through compliance rates. Other researchers decouple norm robustness from compliance, arguing that the torture prohibition is robust because it continues to shape state discourse (Hurd 2013: 185; Barnes 2017: 7). However, most of the studies only analyze the early 2000s in the US (but see Liese 2009; Barnes 2017); they do not include global trends over time. This chapter fills this research gap by studying the norm dynamics of the international torture prohibition over four decades, using our four-dimensional approach to robustness.

Contestation of the anti-torture norm is not new: Chile and the United Kingdom (UK) in the 1970s, Israel in the 1990s, and the US in the early 2000s all challenged its validity and application. On one hand, they invoked the ticking bomb scenario to challenge the norm's non-derogability, and, on the other, they disputed allegations of using torture in interrogations. We observe fewer validity contestations than applicatory contestations in most of the countries studied and low levels of both types of contestation in international discourse. These challenges to the prohibition of torture have been widely rejected. The rare contagious effects—for instance, when other states emulated US contestation (Schmidt and Sikkink 2019: 111)—did not

International Norm Disputes. Lisbeth Zimmermann et al., Oxford University Press. © Lisbeth Zimmermann, Nicole Deitelhoff, Max Lesch, Antonio Arcudi, and Anton Peez (2023). DOI: 10.1093/oso/9780198873235.003.0002

create a global tipping point. This leads us to argue that contestation has not weakened the international prohibition of torture.

We develop our argument by first sketching out how the torture prohibition developed and defining its normative core. We then introduce empirical material to assess contestation and norm robustness—before and after the adoption of the United Nations (UN) Convention against Torture (CAT) in 1984 (Section 2.2). Section 2.3 analyzes contestation trends in international discourse over time, and Section 2.4 traces the dynamics of the norm's robustness. Finally, we discuss the explanatory factors, particularly perceptions of procedural fairness.

2.2 International torture prohibition: History and data

2.2.1 Norm evolution

The prohibition of torture is deeply anchored in international and regional human rights treaties, international criminal law, and the law of armed conflict (Rodley and Pollard 2009: 46–47). The Universal Declaration of Human Rights (UDHR) of 1948 laid the groundwork for developing the torture prohibition: "No one shall be subjected to torture or to cruel, inhuman or degrading treatment or punishment" (UDHR 1948: Art. 5). In 1950, the Council of Europe codified the prohibition of torture in the European Convention on Human Rights (ECHR 1950: Art. 3). Then, in 1966, the International Covenant on Civil and Political Rights (ICCPR) that prohibits torture was globally adopted by the United Nations General Assembly (UNGA) (ICCPR 1966: Art. 7). In 1969, the American Convention on Human Rights (ACHR) codified the prohibition of torture in the Americas (ACHR 1969: Art. 5(2)).

None of these international legal instruments defined torture, but the ECHR, ICCPR, and ACHR specified the norm's applicatory scope by codifying the prohibition of torture as a *non-derogable* right: They have emergency clauses that allow a state party to derogate from the conventions in times of war or public emergency—but not from the prohibition of torture (ECHR 1950: Art. 15(1); ICCPR 1966: Art. 4(1); ACHR 1969: Art. 27). The first international law treaty to define torture was the Convention against Torture and Other Cruel, Inhuman or Degrading Treatment or Punishment adopted in 1984 (CAT 1984). Its first article states that torture:

> means any act by which severe pain or suffering, whether physical or mental, is intentionally inflicted on a person for such purposes as obtaining from him or a third person information or a confession, punishing him for an act he or a third

> person has committed or is suspected of having committed, or intimidating or coercing him or a third person, or for any reason based on discrimination of any kind, when such pain or suffering is inflicted by or at the instigation of or with the consent or acquiescence of a public official or other person acting in an official capacity.
>
> **(CAT 1984: Art. 1(1))**[1]

This definition of torture has four dimensions—involvement of a public official, infliction of severe pain or suffering, intention, and specific purpose—but does not clearly distinguish between "torture" and "cruel, inhuman treatment" (Nowak and McArthur 2008: 28, 118, 539–40). CAT universalizes the duty to prevent torture (Art. 2(1)) and cruel, inhuman or degrading treatment or punishment (Art. 16). It underlines the non-derogability and absoluteness of the torture prohibition by stating that no "exceptional circumstance whatsoever [. . .] may be invoked as a justification of torture" (CAT 1984: Art. 2(2)). Whether or not the prohibition of ill-treatment was also non-derogable was left to interpretive discretion, which contesting states would try to exploit. This loophole was only closed by the second General Comment made by the Committee against Torture (CmAT) in 2008 (Lesch 2023; Lesch and Reiners 2023: 14–15).

The torture prohibition's normative development was accompanied by its delegation to (quasi-) legal authorities, both regional and global. The European Commission on Human Rights (ECommHR) and the European Court of Human Rights (ECtHR) were set up to monitor compliance with the ECHR (Bates 2010: 119),[2] and the Inter-American human rights system generally mirrors ECHR institutions (Goldman 2009: 866). Within the UN, the ICCPR and CAT established committees to monitor compliance with the respective treaties: the Human Rights Committee (HRC) in 1977 and CmAT in 1989. The 2002 Optional Protocol to the Convention against Torture (OPCAT) established an international system to inspect places of detention with the aim of guaranteeing the prohibition of torture. This separate treaty entered into effect in 2006 (Murray et al. 2011: 68–69). The prohibition of torture has also been integrated into international criminal law, most importantly the International Criminal Court's Rome Statute definitions of crimes against humanity and war crimes (Schabas 2010: 166–67, 215–16).

[1] This definition built on the wording of the Declaration on the Protection of All Persons from Being Subjected to Torture and Other Cruel, Inhuman or Degrading Treatment or Punishment adopted by UNGA in 1975, which drew on the definition of torture developed by the European Commission on Human Rights in the "Greek Case" (Rodley 2002).

[2] When the ECHR system was reformed in 1998, the commission was dismantled (Bates 2010: 461).

2.2.2 Normative core claims

"No one shall be subjected to torture or to cruel, inhuman or degrading treatment or punishment." The UDHR wording is unequivocal. Yet, there is more to the prohibition of torture: It is one of the few individual human rights from which no derogation is allowed and which is absolute: "[I]t is [. . .] ensured without any restriction whatsoever" (Nowak 2005: 157–58). We identify the torture prohibition's core normative claims thus: *Torture and cruel, inhuman or degrading treatment or punishment are universally prohibited in war- and peacetime. This prohibition is not derogable under any circumstances. The prohibition of torture is applicable to everyone, all the time, everywhere.* We define challenges to these core claims as *validity contestation*. The most radical form of contestation is outright rejection; contesting the torture prohibition's universality, absoluteness, or non-derogability are other ways to challenge its validity. One example of validity contestation argues for exceptions during wars. When states challenge the appropriateness of norms in specific situations, we speak of *applicatory contestation*, for example, by denying that a state is violating the prohibition or maintaining that certain practices do not amount to torture.[3] Even with the codified CAT definition, debate continues about whether certain practices constitute "torture."

2.2.3 Data collection and analysis

We focus on broad trends of contestation in international institutions as well as on the specific discourse of four different states charged with torture. To do this, we examine the longitudinal and cross-sectional dimensions of contestation and norm robustness. Taking CAT's 1987 entry into force as a watershed, we studied a period *before* that—the 1970s—and one *after*—the 1990s and early 2000s. Before CAT, the UK faced allegations of torture during its 1971 counter-insurgency campaign in Northern Ireland, and allegations of torture arose in Chile after Pinochet's coup d'état in 1973. After CAT, Israel (mainly in the 1990s) and the US (in the early 2000s) were accused of using torture in their counter-terrorism campaigns. Our study ends in 2010, two years after the Bush presidency, so we can observe the effects of contestation on norm robustness after his tenure.

We began analyzing contestation by broadly assessing UNGA debates between 1990 and 2010,[4] where contestation was very rare (Section 2.3).

[3] For a detailed coding scheme, see the Appendix, Table A.1.
[4] Digitalized summary records were only available from 1986.

We analyzed the cases of Chile, the UK, Israel, and the US in more detail because they were the main contesting actors discussed in literature on the prohibition of torture (for a comprehensive overview, see Barnes 2017). They were also useful as case studies because of the variety of contestation periods, and regional and institutional settings. Despite their differences, these four states share an important similarity: All were alleged to practice torture when the state believed it was existentially threatened (see Liese 2009: 21).[5]

UNGA's Third Committee is the principal organ for human rights issues. In 1984, it was the venue for final debates over CAT (Burgers and Danelius 1988: 102–107). Other UN bodies also deal with torture but only in UNGA does each state have a voice. That makes Third Committee debates a good entry point for analyzing international human rights discourse. We conducted a full text search on torture in all Third Committee minutes to assess global trends of contestation from 1990 to 2010. We coded all the statements that mention torture (852 in total).[6] In addition, we compiled individual data sets for Chile, the UK, Israel, and the US. A combination of statements by states in international organizations and by states in national newspaper articles[7] allowed us to depict not only diplomatic communications but also the broader political discourse. For Chile, we relied on the very broad UNGA debate and analyzed all the minutes listed in UN yearbooks under "The Human Rights Situation in Chile"—reaping 515 state statements between 1974 and 1980.[8] We based our newspaper research for the UK, Israel, and the US on a full text search for "torture" in newspaper archives and coded all the articles with references to torture by state representatives. For the UK, we coded the 54 relevant statements in 589 articles in the *Times* and the *Guardian* between 1970 and 1978; for Israel, we coded the 81 relevant statements in 671 *Jerusalem Post* articles between 1990 and 2001;[9] and for the US, we coded the 66 relevant statements in a random sample of 1,100 articles from a total of 6,126 articles in the *New York Times* and the *Washington Post* between 2001 and 2008. We complemented the data sets for the UK, Israel, and the US using statements made at

[5] Supplementary material and data is available at the Harvard Dataverse: https://doi.org/10.7910/DVN/6VHFZK.

[6] Per year, the number of statements is distributed as follows: 1990: 52, 1991: 37, 1992: 41, 1993: 47, 1994: 42, 1995: 40, 1996: 26, 1997: 32, 1998: 40, 1999: 34, 2000: 32, 2001: 31, 2002: 58, 2003: 28, 2004: 39, 2005: 47, 2006: 39, 2007: 52, 2008: 41, 2009: 41, 2010: 53.

[7] Accessed June 5, 2018. https://www.nexis.com and the Guardian archive: accessed June 5, 2018. https://theguardian.newspapers.com.

[8] No computer-based full text search was possible for Chile because the minutes have not been digitalized. They have been collected and scanned at the UN Depository Library in Heidelberg.

[9] The *Jerusalem Post* was the only newspaper with an online archive of English articles that covers the entire study period. Ideally, this should have been balanced with articles from *Haaretz*, for example.

the human rights treaty bodies and at UNGA's Third Committee (UK total: 54, Israel total: 95, USA total: 90).[10]

Empirical material for analyzing the *discursive dimensions* of norm robustness was also gathered from statements mentioning torture to the Third Committee. We coded each statement with respect to affirmations of the prohibition of torture and negative reactions to norm violations. We also analyzed the UN Universal Periodic Review (UPR)[11] and secondary literature. To assess states' concordance with the norm, we combined a content analysis of affirmative statements in the Third Committee with an assessment of the rates of states ratifying the ICCPR, CAT, and OPCAT as well as results from public opinion polls. We used existing data sets to study the *practice dimension* of the torture prohibition's strength. Compliance with the prohibition of torture is hard to measure because torture usually takes place clandestinely, which means that quantitative data on torture must rely on proxies: the annual reports of Amnesty International and the US State Department's Country Reports on Human Rights Practices (Hathaway 2002: 1969–70; Simmons 2009: 266–67; Cingranelli and Richards 2010: 406; Conrad et al. 2013: 201–202).[12] The Cingranelli and Richards Human Rights Data Project (CIRI) provides the most comprehensive data set on torture between 1981 and 2010 (Cingranelli and Richards 2010). CIRI distinguishes three levels: "torture did not occur/nonreported," "torture occurred occasionally" (1–49 instances), and "torture was practiced frequently" (50 and more instances).[13] It is important to note that the data set is biased by an "information effect": As the awareness of torture grows, national and international monitoring generate more and better information on the issue, creating "a false perception that a phenomenon has increased in prevalence" (Clark and Sikkink 2013: 567–68). Furthermore, the data set cannot control for the changing definitions of torture used in allegations. Human rights reports include more cases of torture in 1999 than in 1989 because they employ a broader concept of torture (Clark and Sikkink 2013). The data must be carefully interpreted, keeping in mind that human rights reports note more norm violations as information improves and the concept of torture broadens over time (Fariss 2014). Despite these caveats, CIRI offers the most

[10] Per year, the number of statements is distributed as follows: Israel: 1990: 4, 1991: 6, 1992: 6, 1993: 7, 1994: 9, 1995: 11, 1996: 2, 1997: 5, 1998: 9, 1999: 20, 2000: 4, 2001: 12. US: 2002: 10, 2003: 12, 2004: 16, 2005: 14, 2006: 17, 2007: 14, 2008: 7.

[11] The UPR is the peer review about how all UN member states are implementing their human rights commitments and obligations. Every four-and-a-half years, each state receives "recommendations" from other states—suggestions for improving its human rights practices that it can "note" or "accept."

[12] The Political Terror Scale is based on the same material. However, it cannot be disaggregated to only show scales of torture (Wood and Gibney 2010: 375–76).

[13] The CIRI data set only measures allegations of torture—not actual behavior (Conrad et al. 2013: 202).

comprehensive means for assessing compliance with the prohibition of torture—both globally and long term. To study the torture prohibition's implementation, we used data regarding its incorporation into national constitutional and criminal law worldwide (Goderis and Versteeg 2014; Versteeg 2015; Berlin 2021). We also used the National Human Rights Institution's (NHRI) Data Collection Project, which includes NHRIs in 153 countries (with populations over a million) between 1991 and 2012 (Welch et al. 2021).

2.3 Contestation trends

Contestation of the torture prohibition is not new. Before and after CAT, states made applicatory contestations of the norm and, to a lesser degree, also challenged its validity. States regularly argue that the exceptional circumstances of fighting terrorism justify the use of torture. Comparing the pre- and post-CAT phases shows that US contentions do not constitute an outlier case—as the literature has often assumed by focusing only on the early 2000s. However, neither before nor after CAT's adoption did contestation—especially with respect to its validity—become dominant in the broader international discourse.

In the 1970s, Chile (Sections 2.3.1) and the UK (Section 2.3.2) challenged allegations of torture. The debate about human rights in Chile mainly evolved in the UN after observers, international media, and non-governmental organizations (NGOs) had raised concerns, including that of torture by General Augusto Pinochet's military junta following the 1973 coup (Ensalaco 2000). During and after that, the notorious Directorate for National Intelligence (DINA) used a combination of electrical and water torture, beatings, stress positions, and other practices (Rejali 2007: 205–206). Allegations of torture in Northern Ireland became the object of the ECHR case, *Ireland v. United Kingdom*. The Republic of Ireland took the United Kingdom to court over the "five techniques": hooding, wall-standing, white noise, and food and sleep deprivation that UK security forces introduced when the conflict escalated in 1971 (Rejali 2007: 363).

After CAT was adopted, the torture prohibition was little contested in Third Committee debates at UNGA, where states almost never challenge its validity (Figure 2.1). They do, however, challenge allegations of torture as untrue or inaccurate and contest the torture prohibition's unfair application, accusing the UN of turning a blind eye to alleged cases of torture in other, often Western, states. Whereas the 1995 peak was due to growing contestation of torture

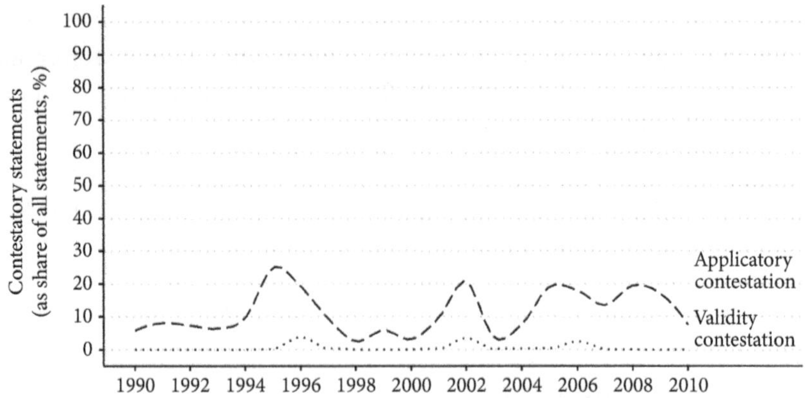

Figure 2.1 Contestation of the international torture prohibition, 1990–2010
Source: Based on 852 statements on "torture" in the UNGA Third Committee.

allegations, the 2002 high reflects the contentious negotiations over OPCAT. Overall, only a few statements on torture contest the norm—and thus do not seriously challenge the torture prohibition's validity.

The picture changes, however, when we take a closer look at Israel and the United States, both of whom challenged the torture prohibition in counter-terrorism campaigns. Israel was accused of using torture in interrogations during the first *intifada* (1988–93) (Section 2.3.3). After the Abu Ghraib prison scandal (2004) revealed the use of torture by US soldiers, concerns mounted about their interrogation techniques (Section 2.3.4). Both Israel and the US contested the torture prohibition by challenging the allegations of torture.

2.3.1 Chilean human rights debated at the United Nations

In the early 1970s, the UN had not yet begun to investigate domestic human rights situations: It only addressed human rights violations as part of threats to international peace and security (Kamminga 1992: 94; Hawkins 2002: 62). Then, in 1974, the UN Human Rights Commission established the Ad Hoc Working Group on the Human Rights Situation in Chile, one of the first UN fact-finding missions tasked with making on-the-spot visits (Lesch 2022: 48). The reports, first by the Ad Hoc Working Group and later by the UN Special Rapporteur, constituted the starting point for debates and resolutions at the

UN (for a comprehensive overview, see Vargas Viancos 1990). The political divisions of the Cold War shaped the debates in which Chile was usually supported by several Latin American states (Eckel 2014: 630). Beginning in 1973, the UNGA Plenary and Third Committee debated Chile's human rights situation for more than a decade.

Throughout the 1970s, Chile challenged allegations of its human rights violations along three major lines: the competence of the Ad Hoc Working Group and UN procedures; findings of reports and resolutions on its human rights situation, particularly regarding torture; and whether the UN was treating Chile fairly, given the general ignorance about human rights violations in *other* countries. Contestation—especially with respect to validity—began to lessen after 1977 (Figure 2.2), when there was a careful reconciliation between Chile and the UN (Eckel 2014: 672–77).

In 1976, a Portuguese UNGA delegate expressed Chile's longstanding critique of the UN's role and the Ad Hoc Working Group's competence:

> [T]he United Nations was competent to analyse the situation in Chile, but the Third Committee was not a court of law. Everyone tended to forget that fact, including Chile itself, for in document A/C.3/31/6, it stated: "In requesting information to identify the individual cases, we are exercising a minimum right accorded in a court of law to any person charged with an offence or subject to an investigation, namely, that specific questions be addressed to him before the results of the trial or investigation are announced."
>
> **(Portugal in UNGA 1976)**

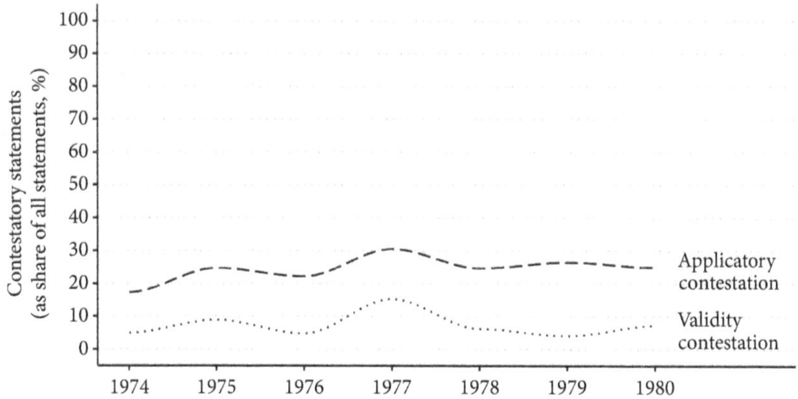

Figure 2.2 Contestation of the international torture prohibition, 1974–80

Source: Based on 515 statements on Chile's human rights situation in the UNGA Plenary and Third Committee.

Chile challenged the working group's procedures and demanded the right of defense, which is usual in domestic legal systems. More broadly, Chile questioned the need for UN action—referring to the regional activities of the Inter-American Commission on Human Rights, an organ of the Organization of American States (OAS). Chile contested the competence of the Ad Hoc Working Group and denied it entry until 1978.

Chile also challenged the working group's finding of "institutionalized torture," which Chile criticized as exaggerated and based on limited, if not false, information: "That gratuitous slander has no other basis but the politically biased depositions obtained from Chileans who live abroad and are the declared enemies of their Government" (Chile in UNGA 1975c: para. 124). Disputing allegations of torture is a paradigmatic case of applicatory contestation: What was the evidence for the allegations? Was the torture norm correctly applied to a specific situation? Chile mainly denied the allegations and the evidence presented by the group but did not systematically rebut them (Eckel 2014: 633). Many states—not just Chile and its allies—criticized the UN for lacking fairness and balance in its approach to human rights. The Ad Hoc Working Group was framed as a new, politicized instrument that unfairly focused on Chile and overlooked human rights violations in many other countries. The Chilean delegation charged, "The word 'universal,' when it comes to this subject, has become a synonym for falsehood and hypocrisy" (Chile in UNGA 1977: para. 39).

Chile sometimes used this applicatory argument in more radical contestations, vehemently criticizing UNGA resolutions for illegally interfering in its sovereignty because they violated "the principle of non-intervention in the internal affairs of a State enshrined in the Charter of the United Nations" (Chile in UNGA 1980: para. 205). Although the Ad Hoc Working Group was indeed a novel instrument, Chile had ratified the ICCPR and signed the UDHR. Chile's rejection of the application of international human rights norms on the grounds of national sovereignty constituted a categorical exception to the torture prohibition's validity as a *universal* human rights norm (see also Bossuyt 1978: 464–67). Chile accompanied its fundamental rejection of the applicability of human rights norms by referring to post-regime-change civil unrest as moments that did not always allow for defending human rights and preventing torture (Chile in UNGA 1974: paras. 95–96, 1975a, para. 35).

In sum, Chile mainly used its statements, along with those from its Latin American allies, to respond to challenges about the *way* the torture prohibition was applied as well as the working group's related reports and resolutions.

2.3.2 *Ireland v. United Kingdom*: Torture allegations in ECHR institutions

After launching an operation to detain and interrogate terrorism suspects in Northern Ireland on August 9, 1971, the UK challenged the application and validity of the torture prohibition. Late that month, it created the Compton Committee, which published its findings about "allegations of physical brutality" and their legality in November 1971 (Brownlie 1972: 501; O'Boyle 1977: 676–77). On December 16, 1971, after having failed to place the Northern Ireland conflict on the UN agenda (Bonner 2014: 49),[14] despite UK pressure to refrain, the Republic of Ireland turned to the ECHR institutions (Bonner 2014: 55–56) and presented an inter-state complaint to the ECommHR (Schabas and O'Sullivan 2007: 10–11). The case was admitted. In 1976, the ECommHR published its report; the ECtHR's judgment came in 1978.[15] During those two years, contestation declined (Figure 2.3).

We identify two major lines of contestation: First, the UK disagreed that the five techniques constitute torture under international law. Second, the UK contested the torture prohibition's non-derogability with reference to the special circumstances of fighting terrorism in Northern Ireland, a *validity*

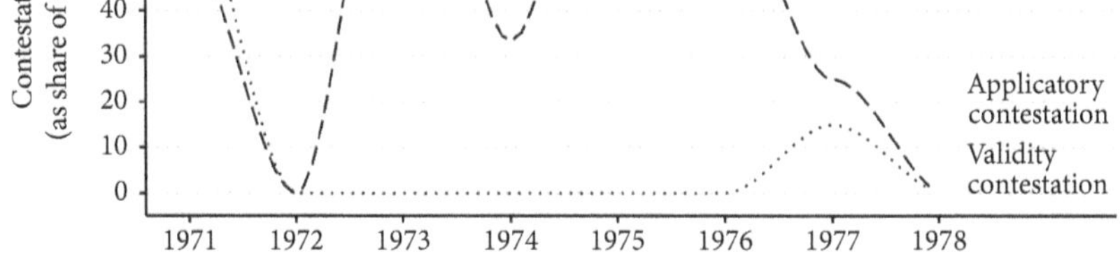

Figure 2.3 British contestation of the international torture prohibition, 1971–78
Source: Based on 54 statements on torture in the *Times*, *Guardian*, and at the HRC.

[14] In 1978, however, the UN HRC reviewed the UK's periodic report to the ICCPR, including the issue of torture and ill-treatment during internment in Northern Ireland (HRC 1978a, b, c).

[15] For the development of the meaning of torture and ill-treatment in the ECHR context, see Mavronicola (2021) and Yildiz (2020).

contestation that was only salient in 1971. In the following years and during the ECHR proceedings, *applicatory* contestation mainly questioned whether the five techniques constitute torture.

In December 1971, after the Compton Report's release, Reginald Maudling, the British Home Secretary responsible for Northern Ireland, stated to the House of Commons that the Compton Committee "found no evidence of physical brutality by the British Army or the Royal Ulster Constabulary, still less of torture or brain-washing." He added that in the course of the arrest of 342 men on August 9, "a small number of them suffered what the committee describe as a measure of ill-treatment or hardship" (UK in *Times* 1971a). In both the Compton Committee and the broader political discourse, British officials discussed "brutality"—not torture. The report concluded that each of the five techniques constituted "physical ill treatment" (Compton Committee 1971: paras 92–96) but did not assess the techniques' psychological and "cumulative effects" (Brownlie 1972: 502; O'Boyle 1977: 676). The Compton Report refuted the torture allegations by Ireland and Amnesty International. Yet, neither the report nor the broader UK discourse explicitly discussed the allegation in Northern Ireland with respect to their international obligations (Foley 2021: 115).

British officials resorted to arguing about the "special circumstances" in Northern Ireland, with statements like Maudling's targeting the validity of the torture prohibition, namely, its non-derogability under the ECHR and the ICCPR:

> Mr Maudling told MPs that the methods used in Northern Ireland had yielded information of great value that would not otherwise have been available. [. . .] Without that they could not have defended civilians against the campaign of terror. [. . .] Torture, he emphasized, was not acceptable, but on the other hand one could not go along to those people and ask them politely to help in one's investigations. Somewhere a line had to be drawn.
>
> **(UK in *Times* 1971b)**

They justified the UK's interrogation methods by their success in gathering intelligence when civilian lives were at stake. This statement and similar positions did not argue for allowing torture in light of terrorist threats but blurred the distinction between the methods that could be used to "defend innocent people against such terrorism" and challenged the torture prohibition's non-derogability—thus contesting its validity.

In 1972, the UK used both lines of argument in its initial submissions to the ECommHR in Strasbourg, denying that the five techniques constitute torture (UK in ECommHR 1976: 261) and terming terrorism a "special circumstance for interrogations" (UK in ECommHR 1976: 264–65). In early 1972, the Parker Committee had revisited the torture allegations. Lord Gerald Gardiner, a former lord chancellor, rejected the majority's justification for using the five techniques under exceptional circumstances and deemed the interrogation procedures illegal (Parker Committee 1972: 14). The UK concurred with Lord Gardiner and declared the five techniques were being terminated (O'Boyle 1977: 679). This is one reason why there was almost no validity contestation after 1972.

Finally, the ECommHR's 1976 report concluded—based on the definition of torture developed in the Greek Case[16]—that use of the five techniques *does* constitute torture and is a breach of ECHR Article 3 (ECommHR 1976: 399–422). The case was referred to the ECtHR for a final decision. There, the head of the British delegation reiterated the position made before the ECommHR "that the 'five techniques' will not in any circumstances be reintroduced as an aid to interrogation" (UK in ECtHR 1978: 36). The UK explicitly did *not* contest the ECommHR finding (UK in *Guardian* 1977). But the ECtHR came to a different conclusion: The five techniques involve inhuman and degrading treatment—and thus breach the ECHR—*but are not torture* (ECtHR 1978: 59).

In sum, contestation of UK interrogation methods in Northern Ireland shifted from the validity to the applicatory level—especially after proceedings began at ECHR institutions, whose verdict the UK eventually accepted.[17]

2.3.3 Israel: "Moderate physical pressure" or torture?

At the heart of the debate about torture in Israel was the Landau Commission report of 1987. Amid growing criticism of its General Security Services (GSS), the Israeli government had tasked the commission to clarify the legality of "violent interrogations methods" used in counter-terrorism (Meydani 2015: 87). The Landau Commission argued that "moderate physical pressure" was legally allowed during interrogations under exceptional circumstances (Landau Commission 1987: 80). The NGO *B'Tselem*—The Israeli Information Center for Human Rights in the Occupied Territories—said

[16] In April 1967, Greek colonels seized power and ousted the democratic government. Soon after the coup d'état, reports of torture began to circulate. As a consequence, in September 1967, Denmark, Norway, Sweden, and the Netherlands lodged inter-state complaints against Greece, including torture allegations, under the ECHR. As one of the first torture cases, it led the ECommHR to articulate a first definition of torture (Becket 1970).

[17] For a discussion of the long-term effects of the disputes about the five techniques and British torture during the "war on terror" in the early 2000s, see Blakeley and Raphael (2017); Foley (2021).

these interrogation practices "fit accepted definitions of torture," including verbal threats to life and family, sleep and food deprivation, a combination of stress positions used for days at a time, hooding, and beatings (Cohen and Golan 1991: 8, 54–74).

In the 1990s, international disputes about Israel and the prohibition of torture took place at the UN in CmAT and in the HRC. Torture and human rights violations have also been debated in Israeli public discourse, politics, and courts (see Meydani 2015: ch. 5). Contestation peaked in 1997 and 1998, when Israel appeared twice before CmAT to discuss a special report (CmAT 1997a)[18] as well as its second periodic CAT report (CmAT 1998a). In 1998, Israel presented its first ICCPR periodic review to the HRC. In 2001, applicatory contestation again increased when Israel appeared before CmAT for its third periodic review (Figure 2.4). Israel challenged allegations of torture by contesting or denying that it used torture in interrogations as well as by citing the special circumstances of the fight against terrorism to justify employing "moderate physical pressure" and also by challenging CmAT's competence to interpret CAT.

To begin with, the Israeli delegation tried to exploit the norm's ambiguity. This debate was mainly about whether "moderate physical pressure" amounted to torture under international law. In 2001, Israel's delegation to CmAT presented the following statement that echoed its argumentation

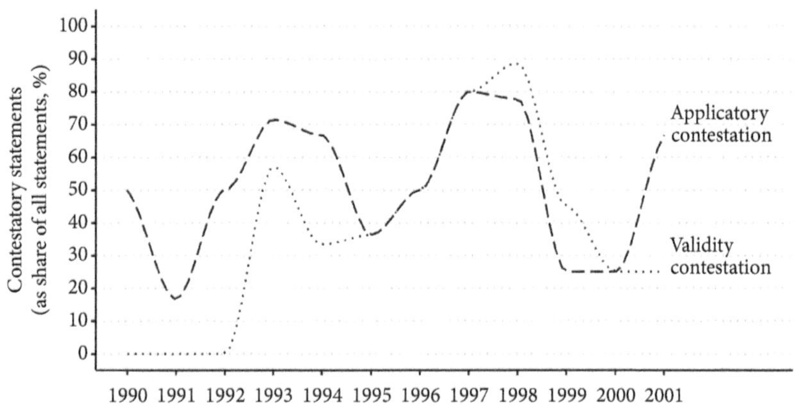

Figure 2.4 Israeli contestation of the international torture prohibition, 1990–2001

Source: Based on 95 statements in the *Jerusalem Post*, the UNGA's Third Committee, the HRC, and CmAT.

[18] CmAT had requested the report in 1996 to clarify whether Israel was respecting the torture prohibition's non-derogability (see UNGA 1997: paras. 24–25).

throughout the 1990s (see Grosso 2000: 327–28), claiming its interrogation practices:

> did not constitute torture as defined in article 1 of the Convention or cruel, inhuman or degrading treatment or punishment within the meaning of article 16. [. . .] Nevertheless, his Government maintained that a careful reading of the Convention suggested that pain and suffering did not in themselves necessarily constitute torture. Interrogation procedures had to be examined taking account of the severity of the pain or suffering inflicted on a person. Each act or measure of alleged misconduct must be examined on its own merits and in the light of specific circumstances.
>
> **(Israel in CmAT 2001: para. 10)**

This argument rejects the view of NGOs like *B'Tselem* and of CmAT that Israeli security forces' interrogation practices constitute torture. The Israeli delegation proposed an interpretation of torture that focuses only on the *severity* of the methods in question, disregarding the fact that ill-treatment with a *purpose* (e.g. to extract confessions) is a central aspect of the torture prohibition (Israel in CmAT 1997b: paras 12, 48). It invoked the Landau Commission that had applied the ECtHR's decision in *Ireland v. United Kingdom* (Landau Commission 1987: 71–76; see also Grosso 2000: 328). That decision—distinguishing torture and ill-treatment on the basis of pain and suffering inflicted—had become a useful precedent for states seeking to justify torture.

Israel further argued that its criminal law only permitted moderate physical pressure under existential threats: the "necessity" defense. In 1999, Israel's High Court of Justice had ruled that moderate physical pressure is illegal and urged legislators to establish clear guidelines for interrogation. An article in the *Jerusalem Post* quoted Ehud Barak, at the time both Prime Minister and Defense Minister:

> "There should be a mechanism to enable the use of physical pressure in certain interrogations." [. . .] Barak reportedly reiterated the government's "commitment to combat terrorism using every means at its disposal, with determination and persistence." [. . .] [H]e believes "there must be an authority that can, in time of need, take rapid action to approve necessary interrogations in 'ticking bomb' situations which present an immediate danger."
>
> **(Israel in *Jerusalem Post* 1999)**

In a clear example of validity contestation, Barak used the ticking bomb scenario to underscore the need to take exceptional measures in exceptional circumstances of "an immediate danger." This raised suspicions that the High Court ruling—despite declaring moderate physical pressure illegal—provided loopholes to legally use such interrogation techniques (Laursen 2000: 424–25). The Israeli government further claimed that CAT and the ICCPR are not applicable in the Occupied Territories—adding more exceptions to the torture prohibition (Israel in CmAT 1994: para. 22; Israel in HRC 1998: paras 21, 22). After 1999, however, this line of validity contestation ebbed.

Israeli delegations to CmAT also attacked the committee's competence: The UN "could not empower international judges to implement the articles of the Convention in Israel; it was up to the country's judges to decide whether there had been cruel, inhuman or degrading treatment in a particular case" (Israel in CmAT 1997b: para. 50). These and similar arguments were mostly tied to the torture definition and the concept of "moderate physical pressure." They were *applicatory* contestations. Israel's claim that CmAT as "a specialized expert forum whose competence was recognized in a specific field [. . .] should avoid taking generalized positions" (Israel in CmAT 1998b: para. 2) leaves little leeway for international institutions to apply international norms. When the application and interpretation of the torture prohibition are framed as a purely *national* matter, contestation veers toward the validity of the *international* norm.

In sum, Israel long contested both the application and the validity of the prohibition on torture, but validity contestation faded around 2001.

2.3.4 United States: "Enhanced interrogation" and torture

In the US, the debate about torture gained momentum when Department of Justice memoranda were leaked in June 2004 (Birdsall 2016: 184). Intended to provide the George W. Bush administration with a legal opinion on interrogation techniques, the memos detailed attempts to anchor its "enhanced interrogations" in international law (for a detailed analysis, see Sanders 2018: ch. 3). They limited the CAT torture definition by focusing on the severity of the pain inflicted, restricted the Geneva Conventions' applicability by removing "illegal enemy combatants" from their protection, and argued that presidential war powers release a US president from international law (Hurd 2013: 177–79; Sikkink 2013: 150–51). US enhanced interrogations use techniques similar to those employed by Chile, the UK, and Israel, including stress positions, white noise, and food and sleep deprivation as well as waterboarding (simulated drowning).

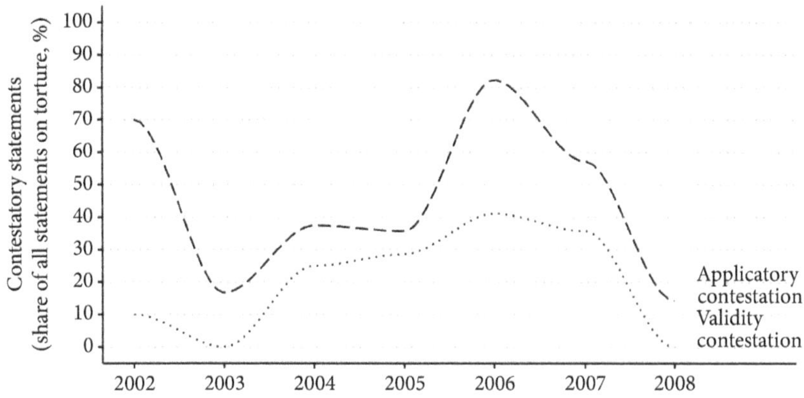

Figure 2.5 US contestation of the international torture prohibition, 2002–08
Source: Based on 90 statements in the UNGA Third Committee, the HRC, and CmAT as well as the *New York Times* and the *Washington Post*.

The high level of contestations in 2002 was mostly due to US criticisms of the new OPCAT, adopted that December (OPCAT 2006). Contestations peaked in 2006, when the US defended itself against international allegations of torture during discussion of its periodic human rights reports at CmAT and the HRC. In 2008, as George W. Bush's tenure was nearing its end, contestation declined (Figure 2.5). In 2007, the US position shifted in legal memoranda revoking earlier interpretations (Birdsall 2016: 188–90). The US generally echoed Israel, arguing that allegations of torture were untrue or that the practices in question did not amount to torture. Then, it introduced several arguments that aimed to narrow the scope of the norm. Finally, the US claimed to hold interpretive sovereignty over CmAT.

The US began by rejecting "that torture and ill-treatment were widespread or systemic; the allegations made related to a minute percentage of the overall number of detainees. Moreover, not all the allegations were true" (US in CmAT 2006a: para. 26). The *Washington Post* quoted George W. Bush: "This country doesn't torture, we're not going to torture" (US in *Washington Post* 2006). In a more legalistic approach, the US questioned whether specific practices employed by its intelligence officers and military constituted torture. In 2006, the head of the US delegation to CmAT formulated his disagreement, rejecting that:

> the interpretation of both memorandums was more restrictive than previous United Nations standards, including the Declaration on the Protection of All Persons from Being Subjected to Torture and Other Cruel, Inhuman or Degrading Treatment or Punishment [. . .]. The interpretation of the term "severe" in the

> December 2004 memorandum reflected the understanding that torture constituted a more aggravated form of abuse than that covered by cruel, inhuman or degrading treatment or punishment. The distinction was not only expressed in the text of the Convention, and apparent from the negotiating history, the United States ratification record and other international law sources; it was also consistent with, and not more restrictive than, the 1975 Declaration on Torture, which distinguished torture from other lesser forms of abuse in part on the basis of the severity of the underlying acts.
>
> **(US in CmAT 2006a: para. 21)**

US delegates exploited specific elements of the definition of torture: whether US practices were "severe," the unclear line between torture and inhumane treatment, and the history of drafting CAT. Both the ECtHR and the UN Declaration on Torture had distinguished torture as an *aggravated* form of ill-treatment. The US argument levered the key elements of the torture definition.[19] In isolation, such arguments tend to concern application. However, when combined with the arguments outlined below, they can also contest validity (for a similar argument, see Schmidt and Sikkink 2019: 106).

The legal memos challenged the crux of the torture prohibition. US officials also invoked exceptional circumstances—often ticking bomb scenarios—to justify enhanced interrogation. For instance, referring to US counter-terrorism measures and allegations of torture, George W. Bush stated, "[T]he techniques that we use have been fully disclosed to appropriate members of the United States Congress. The American people expect their government to take action to protect them from further attack" (US in *Washington Post* 2007). In addition, the US delegation to CmAT argued that the Geneva Conventions, not CAT, applied. US detainee operations in Guantanamo, Afghanistan, and Iraq "were governed by the law of armed conflict—the *lex specialis* applicable." They argued that when negotiating CAT, states "had focused on rights afforded under domestic legislation and not on provisions governing armed conflict" (US in CmAT 2006a: para. 14; original emphasis). The argument was linked to the concept of "unlawful combatants" which the US defended before CmAT (US in CmAT 2006a: para 56). The US viewed unlawful combatants as neither prisoners of war nor civilians: As such, they could be detained until the end of hostilities, the end of the "war on terror" (Venzke 2009: 169–70). Moreover, the US challenged CAT's applicability in territories under its de facto control, such as Guantanamo Bay or detention

[19] When ratifying CAT in 1994, the US lodged an "Understanding" that constituted "notable limitations on the scope of the definition" (Nowak and McArthur 2008: 50).

centers in Iraq, Afghanistan, and elsewhere, which were not de jure US territory. The head of the US delegation to CmAT claimed that the obligation to prevent ill-treatment "did not apply to activities undertaken outside that territory, and his Government rejected the concept that 'de facto control' equated to territory under its jurisdiction" (US in CmAT 2006a: para. 60; see also US in HRC 2006: para. 5). Although these arguments carved out exceptions from the torture prohibition, thereby contesting its validity, most of the statements contested application.

Finally, the US delegation also challenged CmAT's competences. It rejected a committee member's statement that "in the event of a difference of opinion between the Committee against Torture and the state party as to the interpretation of the Convention, the opinion of the Committee should prevail over that of the state party" because the US "had not recognized the [Committee] as an absolute authority in the matter of interpretation" (CmAT 2006b: para. 3). The US had similarly challenged international institutions during the debates over OPCAT when the US criticized the sub-committee for infringing on its sovereignty (US in UNGA 2002a: paras 86–88, 2002b: paras 7, 8). We view these arguments as contesting *application* because they specifically challenge the competence of international institutions. They do not challenge their validity.

US contestation has been observed with great concern: McKeown (2009: 19–20) cautions that US contestation would weaken the torture prohibition internationally. Indeed, US arguments did generate interest in a few other states. As a long-standing observer of CmAT noted, the US position in the early 2000s "has made it more difficult to raise the discussion about torture in countries because [. . .] they have [. . .] lost respect for the absolute nature of the prohibition."[20] Some states, like Sudan, used US arguments and practices to "justify their own misdeeds" (Schmidt and Sikkink 2019: 110). That said, our data on contestation trends in UNGA shows that US validity contestation did *not* affect the broader international discourse (see Figure 2.1). While this might be due to UNGA diplomatic practices, public statements by states outside the UN (Keating 2014: 15) and statements in diplomatic cables (Schmidt and Sikkink 2019: 109) show similar results regarding international discourse: US argumentation could not even rally its European allies, whose initial discursive support declined over the years and finally transformed into coordinated pushback. There was no cascade of contestation (see also Keating 2014: 16; Schmidt and Sikkink 2019: 110; Stimmer 2019: 277). Indeed,

[20] Interview with Asger Kjærum (International Rehabilitation Council for Torture Victims) during the 57th session of CmAT in May 2016.

after Barack Obama took office, the US re-aligned its policies with the international torture prohibition. So did Chile, the UK, and Israel (see also Barnes 2017: 141, 172). In fact, all four states eventually stopped challenging the torture prohibition, especially its validity.

2.4 Norm robustness trends

Contestation of the international torture prohibition has never reached a tipping point. That leads us to assume that the torture prohibition remained robust both before and after the adoption of CAT. We hold that applicatory contestation can even strengthen a norm. In contrast to diagnoses of norm erosion (Section 2.1), our findings on norm robustness show that with respect to practice and discourse, contestation has not weakened the torture prohibition.

2.4.1 Practice: Stable compliance and growing implementation

We used quantitative human rights data on compliance and implementation of the prohibition in national constitutions and human rights institutions to study the practical dimension of the torture norm.

The CIRI data set shows that between 1990 and 2010, most states were alleged to practice torture at least occasionally (see Figure 2.6); historical and comparative studies indicate that torture has never been absent from

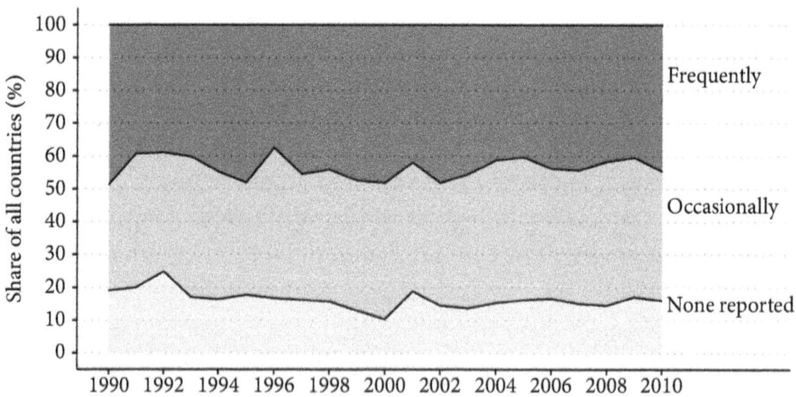

Figure 2.6 Countries alleged to have practiced torture, 1990–2010
Source: Based on the CIRI data set (Cingranelli and Richards 2010).

state practice (Rejali 2007; Klose 2013; Austin 2017; Barnes 2017). After CAT entered into force, on average, less than 20 percent of states were *not* alleged to torture. In around 40 percent of states, torture is allegedly only practiced occasionally—between one and forty-nine times each year. In the remaining 40 percent, torture is allegedly practiced frequently, or more than 49 times per year. Based on CIRI, norm compliance slightly decreased in the 1990s; compliance was stable between 2002 and 2010.

As discussed in Section 2.2.3, the data is biased toward showing increasing allegations of torture over time because of the changing "standard of accountability." As Fariss (2014: 309) argues, reported instances of torture only appear to be stable or rising when compared to earlier numbers because "monitoring agencies look harder for torture, look in more places for torture, and classify more acts as torture." From this perspective, compliance with the prohibition of torture has actually increased worldwide (Fariss 2014: 311–12). However, Schmidt and Sikkink (2019: 114) show that the forty states actively participating in the US rendition program between 2001 and 2009 were less compliant during those years. That said, the broader global non-compliance trends do not appear to be linked to US policies or torture programs:

> A huge part of the torture that happens in the world has nothing to do with this [the US interrogation program and contestation; author's note] but is basically just system error in individual countries. This can both be in the form of failed implementation of safeguards to prevent torture. But very often we experience that unrealistic crime solving targets imposed on the police result in them arresting random poor and marginalized person and torturing them to confess to crimes so that they can be solved and the target met.[21]

Overall compliance patterns remained similar or slightly improved.

Implementation of the torture prohibition increased before and after CAT as human rights treaties impacted national laws and institutions. In 2006, of 188 countries, 84 percent had included the prohibition of torture in their constitutional rights: 47 percent more than in 1946 (Goderis and Versteeg 2014: 6). Versteeg (2015: 108) concludes, "[T]he entry into force of ECHR and CAT has inspired constitution-makers around the globe, even in the absence of treaty ratification" (see also Sandholtz 2017). However, one of the most contentious questions in CmAT's "constructive dialogues" is whether states have adopted the CAT definition of torture in their criminal law codes.

[21] Interview with Asger Kjærum (International Rehabilitation Council for Torture Victims) during the 57th session of CmAT in May 2016.

Many states use narrower definitions. Nonetheless, research on implementation of the torture definition and prohibition shows that CAT signatories are increasingly defining torture in their laws (Berlin 2021: 8–9)—and if they do so, they are less likely to torture (Berlin 2021: 11). Moreover, since 1990, the number of national human rights institutions has continued to grow (Welch et al. 2021: 1014), stimulating compliance and decreasing instances of torture, especially in states that have ratified CAT (Welch 2017: 106–107). NHRI monitoring, annual reporting, and punishing of norm violations reduce the frequency of torture and increase the chances of eliminating it (Welch et al. 2021: 1019–20). Creamer and Simmons (2015: 597) show that NHRIs improve the overall interactions of states parties with CmAT through better and more timely reporting, which, in turn, can positively impact compliance rates (Creamer and Simmons 2019: 1057).

With respect to the practice dimension, compliance with the torture prohibition appears to be stable (or perhaps slightly increasing), while implementation seems to be increasing. Research reveals a positive correlation between implementation of the torture prohibition and compliance.

2.4.2 Discourse: Growing concordance and stable negative reactions

With respect to discourse, we studied concordance with the torture prohibition using ratification rates and affirmations in diplomatic discourse and public opinion polls as well as negative reactions to norm violations in UNGA.

The ICCPR and CAT are two of the most widely ratified human rights treaties, with ratifications rising constantly since CAT entered into force in 1987 (OHCHR 2022). We observe that human rights treaties have continued to be ratified since 1970—both before and after CAT entered into force. OPCAT was adopted in 2002 and entered into force in 2006; in 2010, it had 58 members (OPCAT 2006). Ratification rates of CAT (in 2010, 147 states parties) and the ICCPR (in 2010, 167 states parties) indicate continued concordance with the norm (Figure 2.7). Increased ratification—despite contestations—indicates that the torture prohibition continues to have normative appeal (see also Liese 2009: 35).[22]

We looked more carefully at CAT ratifications and which specific norms and institutional mechanisms of the treaty (opt-in clauses) states accept.

[22] As of December 2021, ICCPR had 173, CAT 171, and OPCAT 91 states parties. CAT and ICCPR are thus headed toward universal ratification.

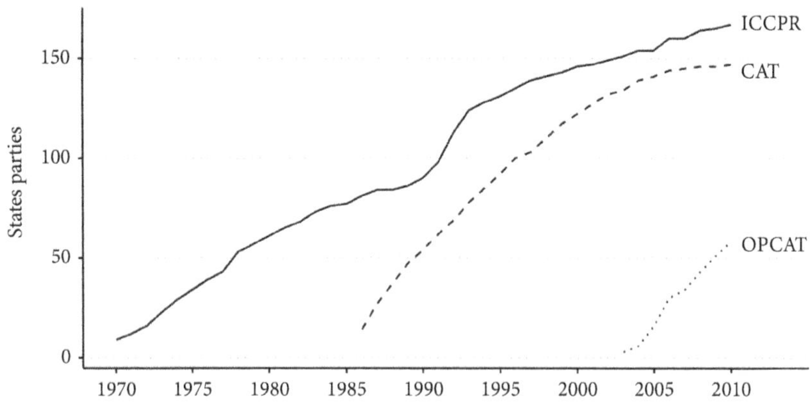

Figure 2.7 Ratification status of the ICCPR, CAT, and OPCAT, 1970–2010
Source: Based on the OHCHR (2022) database on human rights treaty ratifications.

Besides CmAT's state reporting system, three types of action trigger committee inquiries: CmAT's own "confidential" inquiries (Art. 20), state-to-state complaints (Art. 21), and communications by individuals claiming to have been violated by a party to the convention (Art. 22). By 2010, 138 states (94 percent of all states parties) had accepted the inquiry system and 64 signatories (44 percent of the total) had accepted individual complaints (OHCHR 2022). However, recent ratifying states parties have been increasingly reluctant to accept individual communications to CmAT, which could undermine that critical enforcement mechanism. Several states, including the US in 1994, have issued reservations or observations about the applicability and scope of the definition of torture (Nowak and McArthur 2008: 50), although their reservations have not gone unchallenged: A group of European states filed objections against them and similar "far-reaching reservations" that CmAT had regularly criticized (Nowak and McArthur 2008: 50–51). Schmidt and Sikkink (2019: 109) observe that since 2000, criticism of opt-outs and reservations has grown, indicating higher concordance with the prohibition of torture.

We observe a similar trend of affirmations of the torture prohibition in the UNGA Third Committee between 1990 and 2010 (Figure 2.8). This pattern closely resembles debates about the human rights situation in Chile before CAT came into force.[23] Most states—both critics of Chile and Chile and its allies who contested the prohibition of torture—affirmed the prohibition and human rights in general. Before CAT, many states rejected Chilean challenges

[23] Based on the analysis of UN meeting records.

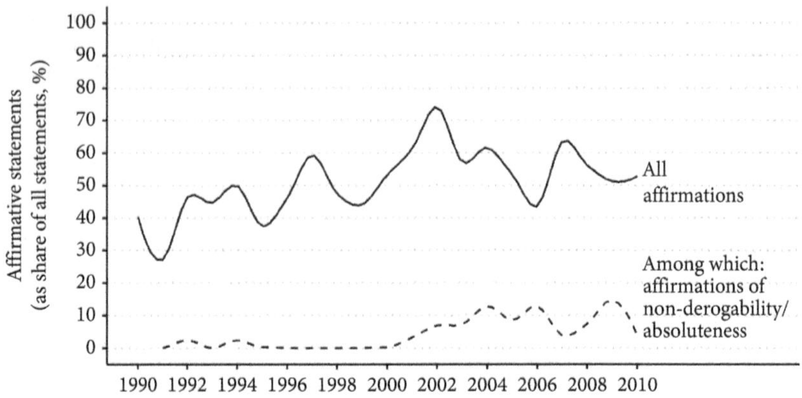

Figure 2.8 Affirmations of the international torture prohibition, 1990–2010
Source: Based on 852 statements on "torture" in UNGA's Third Committee.

to the UN's competence by affirming norms and demanding that institutions be developed to deal with human rights violations. Following CAT's entry into force, states continued to affirm the torture prohibition in the Third Committee. Then, after 2001, states began to explicitly affirm the torture ban's absoluteness or non-derogability in UNGA. With reference to fighting terrorism, they noted that there are no exceptions to the prohibition of torture: They not only affirmed the norm but also refuted post-2001 arguments to limit it. Currently, at the UN, "[T]here's no doubt that torture is prohibited. So, all states come to the table with that perspective."[24] Disputes about the US enhanced interrogation program have reinforced international commitment to the norm against torture (see also Brunnée and Toope 2010: 250; Birdsall 2016: 193).

Opinion polls on whether the general public supports upholding the prohibition of torture do not reveal clear global trends. A 2006 BBC survey of 25 countries found that most citizens disapproved of using torture—although 43 percent of Israelis favored it, along with 36 percent of US respondents (Brunnée and Toope 2010: 244). Gronke et al. (2010: 437) argue that in the US, the majority never supported torture under President George W. Bush (see also Barnes 2017: 167). That said, a meta-analysis of public opinion polls on the torture prohibition found that support for torture increased in the US between 2004 and 2012—although, upon taking office in 2008, the Obama administration quickly ended enhanced interrogations (Miller et al. 2014: 21–22). It is difficult to compare attitudinal changes over the long term. The

[24] Interview with Matthew Sands (at the time, Association for the Prevention of Torture) during the 57th session of CmAT in May 2016.

few opinion polls made in the US in the 1940s, 1980s, and early 1990s show US citizens strongly opposed torture by *other* countries (Miller et al. 2014: 18–21). However, these surveys did not ask about torture when a terrorist attack was imminent, and the wording appears to suggest that people might condone "torture" while strongly opposing waterboarding or electroshocks (Miller et al. 2014: 27). Nylen and Carpenter (2019: 155–56) have shown that more recent survey questions in the US were designed to convey a particular understanding of the torture prohibition that harmonized with the Bush administration's interpretation. It is possible that a majority of US nationals accepted torture at the time—a finding that comes with caveats—while opinion polls in other countries suggest that other nationals did not.

Internationally, we observe a fairly constant trend of *negative reactions to norm violations* matching the constant level of (non-)compliance before and after CAT. Throughout the 1970s (before CAT), across the East–West divide and despite politicization of the debate in UNGA, member states criticized violations of the prohibition of torture, particularly in Chile. Outside the UN, states and non-state actors also reacted negatively to norm violations. For their part, NGOs raised awareness of the human rights situation in Chile and lobbied the UN and other international organizations to respond to Pinochet's junta. In the Northern Ireland case, too, "Condemnation of the interrogation methods came from all over the world [. . .]. Anti-internment rallies were held not only in Britain but in many American cities" (Kennedy-Pipe and Mumford 2007: 123). NGOs pressured Ireland to take legal action against the UK over the Northern Ireland conflict. Ireland's 1971 inter-state complaint to the ECommHR was a strong reaction to British violations of the torture prohibition and considered an unlikely step for a fellow European State to take—"unless the circumstances were most dramatic" (Bates 2010: 85). Despite the ECtHR's ambivalent judgment, the ECHR institutions eventually found the UK in violation of the prohibition of torture and ill-treatment (Art. 3 ECHR).

We observe that between 1990 and 2010, states regularly condemned norm violations in their statements on torture to the UNGA's Third Committee (Figure 2.9). After the 1990s, when Israel was heavily criticized for violating the torture norm during the first *intifada*, negative reactions ebbed. The initial decline in condemnations after 2000 reflects relatively high compliance levels (Section 2.4.1). Negative reactions peaked in 2006, with states increasingly condemning US violations of the torture prohibition. The fact that the US was criticized for its interrogation practices indicates that even powerful states cannot escape the torture prohibition's normative pressure. At the UN, states have consistently named and criticized torture as violation of international

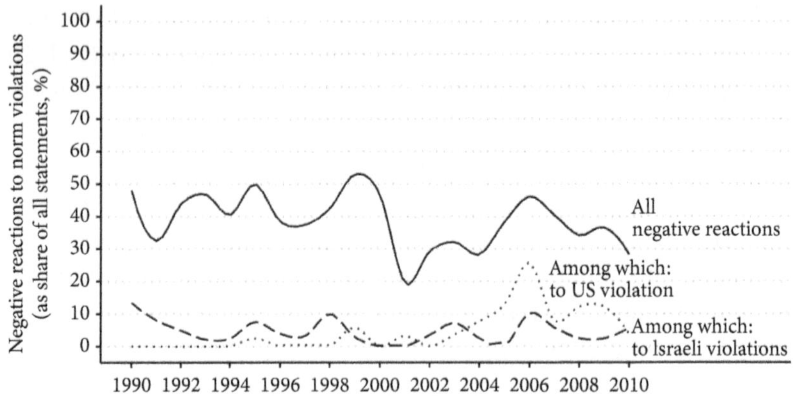

Figure 2.9 Negative reactions to violations of the international torture prohibition, 1990–2010

Source: Based on 852 statements on "torture" in UNGA's Third Committee.

human rights law. Between 2005 and today, states have consistently condemned torture and other forms of cruel, inhuman, and degrading treatment during the Human Rights Council Universal Periodic Review. Torture is one of the top five issues discussed in all review sessions.[25] Negative reactions to violations of the torture prohibition have also figured in diplomatic interactions between 2004 and 2008 (Schmidt and Sikkink 2019: 109–12) and the broader state-level international discourse (Keating 2014: 15).

In sum, the torture prohibition remained robust throughout the 1970s, 1990s, and early 2000s. As for the impact of US actions, we concur with the mixed conclusions of Schmidt and Sikkink (2019: 118) that states participating in the US rendition program respected the torture ban less. Despite that, the stable and even positive trends in our four dimensions of norm robustness suggest that the torture prohibition could well be gaining strength. Constant non-compliance stimulates constant negative reactions to norm violations. Both the implementation of and concordance with the torture prohibition are increasing slightly. We observe no global decrease in the norm's robustness between 1970 and 2010.

2.5 Explanatory factors

Contestations of the torture prohibition mainly target its application but rarely its validity. As expected, the torture prohibition remains robust—and

[25] See "Database of Recommendations" by *UPR Info*: accessed January 7, 2023. https://upr-info-database.uwazi.io/.

may even be strengthening. How did international law and norm clusters, the relative power of norm challengers, and institutionalization contribute to this outcome? How was the torture prohibition able to weather validity contestation?

The prohibition of torture is a legal norm enshrined in many instruments of international treaty law (Section 2.2.1). A *jus cogens* norm, its very high degree of obligation binds all states. CAT made the prohibition of torture a very precise norm, both in terms of the meaning of torture as defined in Article 1 and the legal obligations of states parties to prevent torture and ill-treatment (Lutz and Sikkink 2000: 635–36). Does this enhanced precision block contestation as theories about legalization assume? Contestation of the torture prohibition, and especially of its validity, is rare. However, *when* states challenge the norm, they often use CAT terms. This is well illustrated by the shift from understanding torture as *brutality*—used before CAT—toward the focus on *severity* to distinguish torture from ill-treatment based on CAT's definition. When Israel and the US engaged with CmAT, they did not use the denial strategy pursued by most delegations but rather appeared to admit certain practices and used legalistic argumentations to reconcile them with international law.[26]

We do not contend that contesting the torture prohibition in legal language indicates its robustness, as some have argued (Hurd 2013: 185; Birdsall 2016: 192). International law does not block challenges to the torture prohibition: Instead, it provides pathways for contestation. Nor does contestation using the language of the law indicate a "weak law," as Percy (2007: 390) has argued with respect to the prohibition of mercenaries. Rather, it shows that legal and social norms are always indeterminate. Although CAT codified the torture prohibition, there is some leeway in its definition and the question of how torture differs from ill-treatment.

The legal framework to prohibit torture created international organs that can play decisive roles in disputes over the norm. In response to anti-terrorism challenges, CmAT (2008) adopted General Comment No. 2 to CAT that affirms the non-derogability of the torture prohibition and, by rejecting Israeli and US arguments, reinforces the norm (Lesch 2023; Lesch and Reiners 2023: 16–17). Not only is the prohibition of torture highly legalized, but it is also deeply embedded in a dense norm cluster of international human rights law, humanitarian law, and criminal law. This cluster includes a plethora of international treaties enshrining the prohibition of torture, with every state committed to at least one of them (Rodley and Pollard 2009: 46–47). In fact, the prohibition of torture is at the center of this norm cluster

[26] Interview with an NGO representative during the 57th session of CmAT.

(see also Percy and Sandholtz 2022: 938). Our case study of the torture prohibition shows that norm clusters can "insulate individual norm cores from validity challenges" (Lantis and Wunderlich 2018: 577). Contestation of the torture prohibition's validity, in contrast, could well challenge the validity of the entire human rights cluster (Sandholtz 2019: 146).

Norm clusters and legalization reinforce each other (Lantis and Wunderlich 2018: 579). Legalizing the torture prohibition has created an abundance of institutional means to address norm violations nationally, regionally, and globally. This is evident not only in ECHR institutions, UN special procedures, and human rights treaty bodies but also in national legal proceedings against torture. For example, in the early 2000s, often facilitated by transnational litigation networks (Wiener 2018: 159), national courts began to scrutinize European cooperation with the US rendition program (Schmidt and Sikkink 2019: 116–17). In 2020, the International Criminal Court finally opened an investigation of war crimes and crimes against humanity in the Afghanistan situation but subsequently decided to remove allegations against US forces from the case (see Chapter 5). This has raised deep concerns about international jurisdiction (Zvobgo 2021). Yet, the density and institutionalization of the human rights, humanitarian, and criminal law norm cluster, along with the centrality of the torture prohibition, safeguard the tenets of its normative core claims.

The relative power of contesting states did not play a decisive role. The torture prohibition has been challenged by very powerful actors: Before CAT, the UK was a regional power in Europe and relatively powerful vis-à-vis Ireland; Chile's regional position was similar. The US may have been *the* most powerful state in the early 2000s, and Israel is a regional power, backed by the US. All *unsuccessfully* challenged the torture prohibition. The power of challengers—especially that of the US—should have made it easier to win support for contesting the torture prohibition (for this argument, see McKeown 2009: 19; Schmidt and Sikkink 2019: 117). But the US got no help from its close allies. In the 1970s, Chile was able to garner some regional support but never managed to turn debates around at the UN. Similarly, the UK was not able to halt Ireland from launching its inter-state complaint with the ECHR institutions. Nor did the UK manage to determine CAT's definition of torture—despite having US support (Lesch 2023). The "powerful" norm challengers were unable to compel broader coalitions. This is one reason why the norm remained stable throughout the period we have studied. Despite US contestation, the norm prohibiting torture and its institutions proved resilient.

The institutionalization of the torture prohibition shaped contestation dynamics. Before CAT, perceptions of institutional unfairness were salient when Chile was scrutinized by the UN Ad Hoc Working Group—a novel mechanism specifically created to examine human rights in the country. Singling out Chile was termed "unfair," a case of the UN refusing to acknowledge torture elsewhere (Section 2.3.1). Moreover, the procedure was challenged for not taking "the accused country's defence into account" (Chile in UNGA 1975b: para. 59). Chile demanded to have its position recognized in the proceedings of the Ad Hoc Working Group and UNGA. Chile's critique of the UN triggered more universal debates that resulted in procedures for addressing norm violations and formalizing contestations to prevent the General Assembly from being politicized. One outcome of the debates was CAT and the establishment of CmAT to monitor all member states' compliance with the torture prohibition. Similarly, the UK did not question the ECHR's fairness and embraced its role as a formal respondent government. The UK delegation was generally satisfied with the handling of the case, which is partly why it recognized the authority of the ECommHR and ECtHR and accepted their decisions (Lesch 2023).

After the adoption of CAT, states rarely accused international institutions of unfairness; when they did, the focus was on specific procedural aspects. Both CAT and the ICCPR have expert committees to monitor compliance and implementation, with each treaty party required to regularly submit reports to the UN human rights treaty bodies. One reason to create the treaty bodies was to avoid having the UN accused of selectivity with respect to human rights: singling out some states while ignoring the practices of other (often Western) states. The UN organs examine compliance by all states parties and evaluate the reports in "constructive dialogues" between the expert committee and the state delegations. Although some CAT signatories continue to be late or not report at all, Creamer and Simmons (2015: 601–603) show that they engage more with CmAT after submitting their first report, a sign that the constructive dialogues are generally perceived as fair. Indeed, both Israel and the US used them to present their interpretations of the torture prohibition, and in 1997, Israel swiftly responded to the committee's request for additional details regarding its compliance.

This is not to suggest that there is no room for contestation in these institutions. That often happens at CmAT, where allegations of torture are usually controversially discussed. When the UN human rights treaty bodies rejected Israeli and US interpretations, both states challenged the procedural approach and the legal nature of their "concluding observations." Israel claimed that their "previous report clearly demonstrated the need to study each interrogation procedure on its merits and not to make hasty generalizations" (Israel in CmAT 1998b: para. 2; see also Israel in CmAT 2001: para. 10). Yet, neither Israel, the US, nor other states parties to the human rights treaties questioned the treaty bodies' general competence. As an NGO representative in Geneva pointed out with respect to CmAT, "States recognize the expertise of the Committee. They come before them with some trepidation because they know their performance will be reviewed but I don't think they leave feeling that they have been under attack."[27] The treaty bodies are perceived as less politicized than the Human Rights Council because they conduct few biased reviews (Carraro 2017: 956). Evidence is growing that the constructive dialogues "may indeed disseminate new perspectives, advice, and potentially produce pressure for change in practice" (Creamer and Simmons 2019: 1062). In a similar vein, the end of contestation, along with domestic policy changes in Israel and the US, indicates that both countries at least implicitly accept institutional findings that result from open dialogue (see Grosso 2000: 333; Stimmer 2019: 277). States' perception that the committee's procedures are fair helps prevent the radicalization and spread of contestation.

2.6 Conclusion

The torture prohibition was not contested for the first time in the early 2000s during the US "war on terror." Although IR literature has recently focused on that period, we show that in our cases, as early as the 1970s, states alleged to torture have challenged the prohibition—but have not weakened it. The norm's stability is mostly due to the predominance of *applicatory* contestations. States have rarely challenged the torture prohibition's fundamental *validity*. On those rare occasions, most states rejected the more radical contestation, which did not become part of international discourse. Contestation has not weakened the torture prohibition because institutional access and the norm's deep embeddedness help keep contestation at the applicatory level and hamper the validity contestations that could weaken it. International institutions that are viewed as fair help contain contestation of the torture prohibition by clarifying and stabilizing its meaning.

[27] Interview with Matthew Sands (at the time, Association for the Prevention of Torture) during the 57th session of CmAT in May 2016.

Reference list

ACHR (American Convention on Human Rights). 1969. "American Convention on Human Rights." OAS Treaty Series, no. 36 (November 21).

Austin, Jonathan Luke. 2017. "We Have Never Been Civilized: Torture and the Materiality of World Political Binaries." *European Journal of International Relations* 23 (1): pp. 49–73. doi: 10.1177/1354066115616466.

Barnes, Jamal. 2017. *A Genealogy of the Torture Taboo*. London: Routledge.

Bates, Ed. 2010. *The Evolution of the European Convention on Human Rights: From Its Inception to the Creation of a Permanent Court of Human Rights*. Oxford: Oxford University Press.

Becket, James. 1970. "The Greek Case before the European Human Rights Commission." *Human Rights* 1 (1): pp. 91–117.

Berlin, Mark S. 2021. "Does Criminalizing Torture Deter Police Torture?" *American Journal of Political Science*, online first: pp. 1–24. doi: 10.1111/ajps.12684.

Birdsall, Andrea. 2016. "But We Don't Call It 'Torture'! Norm Contestation during the US 'War on Terror.'" *International Politics* 53 (2): pp. 176–97. doi: 10.1057/ip.2015.42.

Blakeley, Ruth, and Sam Raphael. 2017. "British Torture in the 'War on Terror.'" *European Journal of International Relations* 23 (2): pp. 243–66. doi: 10.1177/1354066116653455.

Bonner, David. 2014. "Of Outrage and Misunderstanding: Ireland v United Kingdom—Governmental Perspectives on an Inter-State Application under the European Convention on Human Rights." *Legal Studies* 34 (1): pp. 47–75. doi: 10.1111/lest.12005.

Bossuyt, Marc J. 1978. "The United Nations and Civil and Political Rights in Chile." *International and Comparative Law Quarterly* 27 (2): pp. 462–71. doi: 10.1093/iclqaj/27.2.462.

Brownlie, Ian. 1972. "Interrogation in Depth: The Compton and Parker Reports." *Modern Law Review* 35 (5): pp. 501–507. doi: 10.2307/1094477.

Brunnée, Jutta, and Stephen J. Toope. 2010. *Legitimacy and Legality in International Law: An Interactional Account*. Cambridge: Cambridge University Press.

Burgers, J. Herman, and Hans Danelius. 1988. *The United Nations Convention against Torture: A Handbook on the Convention against Torture and Other Cruel and Inhuman or Degrading Treatment*. Dordrecht: Martinus Nijhoff Publishers.

Carraro, Valentina. 2017. "The United Nations Treaty Bodies and Universal Periodic Review: Advancing Human Rights by Preventing Politicization?" *Human Rights Quarterly* 39 (4): pp. 943–70. doi: 10.1353/hrq.2017.0055.

CAT (Convention against Torture). 1984. "United Nations Convention against Torture, Cruel, Inhumane, and Other Degrading Treatment and Punishment." United Nations Treaty Series, no. 24841, vol. 1465 at 85 (December 10).

Cingranelli, David L., and David L. Richards. 2010. "The Cingranelli and Richards (CIRI) Human Rights Data Project." *Human Rights Quarterly* 32 (2): pp. 401–24. doi: 10.1353/hrq.0.0141.

Clark, Ann Marie, and Kathryn Sikkink. 2013. "Information Effects and Human Rights Data: Is the Good News about Increased Human Rights Information Bad News for Human Rights Measures?" *Human Rights Quarterly* 35 (3): pp. 539–68. doi: 10.1353/hrq.2013.0046.

CmAT (Committee against Torture). 1994. "Summary Record: 12th Session, 184th Meeting." UN Doc. CAT/C/SR.184 (April 25).

CmAT. 1997a. "Second Periodic Reports of States Parties Due in 1996, Addendum: Israel." UN Doc. CAT/C/33/Add.2/Rev.1 (February 18).

CmAT. 1997b. "Summary Record: 18th Session, 296th Meeting." UN Doc. CAT/C/SR.296 (May 7).

CmAT. 1998a. "Second Periodic Reports of States Parties Due in 1996, Addendum: Israel." UN Doc. CAT/C/33/Add.3 (March 6).

CmAT. 1998b. "Summary Record: 20th Session, 336th Meeting." UN Doc. CAT/C/SR.336 (May 15).

CmAT. 2001. "Summary Record: 27th Session, 496th Meeting." UN Doc. CAT/C/SR.496 (November 20).

CmAT. 2006a. "Summary Record: 36th Session, 703rd Meeting." UN Doc. CAT/C/SR.703 (May 5).

CmAT. 2006b. "Summary Record: 36th Session, 706th Meeting." UN Doc. CAT/C/SR.706 (May 8).

CmAT. 2008. "General Comment No. 2: Implementation of Article 2 by States Parties." UN Doc. CAT/C/GC/2 (January 24).

Cohen, Stanley, and Daphna Golan. 1991. *The Interrogation of Palestinians during the Intifada: Ill-Treatment, 'Moderate Physical Pressure' or Torture?* Jerusalem: B'Tselem—The Israeli Information Center for Human Rights.

Compton Committee. 1971. "Report of the Enquiry into Allegations against the Security Forces of Physical Brutality in Northern Ireland Arising Out of Events on the 9th August, 1971." London: Her Majesty's Stationery Office.

Conrad, Courtenay R., Jillienne Haglund, and Will H. Moore. 2013. "Disaggregating Torture Allegations: Introducing the Ill-Treatment and Torture (ITT) Country–Year Data." *International Studies Perspectives* 14 (2): pp. 199–220. doi: 10.1111/j.1528-3585.2012.00471.x.

Creamer, Cosette D., and Beth A. Simmons. 2015. "Ratification, Reporting, and Rights: Quality of Participation in the Convention against Torture." *Human Rights Quarterly* 37 (3): pp. 579–608. doi: 10.1353/hrq.2015.0041.

Creamer, Cosette D., and Beth A. Simmons. 2019. "Do Self-Reporting Regimes Matter? Evidence from the Convention against Torture." *International Studies Quarterly* 63 (4): pp. 1051–64. doi: 10.1093/isq/sqz043.

Dratel, Joshua L., and Karen J. Greenberg, eds. 2005. *The Torture Papers: The Road to Abu Ghraib*. Cambridge: Cambridge University Press.

ECHR (European Convention on Human Rights and Fundamental Freedoms). 1950. "European Convention on Human Rights." European Treaty Series, no. 5 (November 4).

Eckel, Jan. 2014. *Die Ambivalenz des Guten: Menschenrechte in der internationalen Politik seit den 1940ern*. Göttingen: Vandenhoeck & Ruprecht.

ECommHR (European Commission on Human Rights). 1976. "Ireland v. The United Kingdom: Report of the Commission." European Commission on Human Rights, no. 5310/71 (January 25).

ECtHR (European Court of Human Rights). 1978. "Ireland v. United Kingdom: Judgment on the Merits." European Court of Human Rights, no. 5310/71 (January 18).

Ensalaco, Mark. 2000. *Chile under Pinochet: Recovering the Truth*. Philadelphia, PA: University of Pennsylvania Press.

Fariss, Christopher J. 2014. "Respect for Human Rights Has Improved over Time: Modeling the Changing Standard of Accountability." *American Political Science Review* 108 (2): pp. 297–318. doi: 10.1017/S0003055414000070.

Foley, Frank. 2021. "The (De)Legitimation of Torture: Rhetoric, Shaming and Narrative Contestation in Two British Cases." *European Journal of International Relations* 27 (1): pp. 102–26. doi: 10.1177/1354066120950011.

Foot, Rosemary. 2006. "Torture: The Struggle over a Peremptory Norm in a Counter-Terrorist Era." *International Relations* 20 (2): pp. 131–51. doi: 10.1177/0047117806063844.

Goderis, Benedikt, and Mila Versteeg. 2014. "The Diffusion of Constitutional Rights." *International Review of Law and Economics* 39 (3): pp. 1–19. doi: 10.1016/j.irle.2014.04.004.

Goldman, Robert K. 2009. "History and Action: The Inter-American Human Rights System and the Role of the Inter-American Commission on Human Rights." *Human Rights Quarterly* 31 (4): pp. 856–87. doi: 10.1353/hrq.0.0108.

Gronke, Paul, Darius Rejali, Dustin Drenguis, James Hicks, Peter Miller, and Bryan Nakayama. 2010. "U.S. Public Opinion on Torture, 2001–2009." *PS: Political Science & Politics* 43 (3): pp. 437–44. doi: 10.1017/S1049096510000697.

Grosso, Catherine M. 2000. "International Law in the Domestic Arena: The Case of Torture in Israel." *Iowa Law Review* 86 (1): pp. 305–37.

Guardian. 1977. "Strasbourg to Rule on Torture." The Guardian, February 16.

Hathaway, Oona A. 2002. "Do Human Rights Treaties Make a Difference?" *Yale Law Journal* 111 (8): pp. 1934–2042.

Hawkins, Darren G. 2002. *International Human Rights and Authoritarian Rule in Chile*. Lincoln, NE: University of Nebraska Press.

HRC (Human Rights Committee). 1978a. "Summary Record: 3rd Session, 67th Meeting." UN Doc. CCPR/C/SR.67 (January 30).

HRC. 1978b. "Summary Record: 3rd Session, 69th Meeting." UN Doc. CCPR/C/SR.69 (January 31).

HRC. 1978c. "Summary Record: 3rd Session, 70th Meeting." UN Doc. CCPR/C/SR.70 (February 1).

HRC. 1998. "Summary Record: 63rd Session, 1675th Meeting." UN Doc. CCPR/C/SR.1675 (July 15).

HRC. 2006. "Summary Record: 87th Session, 2379th Meeting." UN Doc. CCPR/C/SR.2379 (July 17).

Hurd, Ian. 2013. "Torture and the Politics of Legitimation in International Law." In *Legitimacy of International Human Rights Regimes*, ed. Andreas Føllesdal, Johan K. Schaffer, and Geir Ulfstein. Cambridge: Cambridge University Press, pp. 165–89.

ICCPR (International Covenant on Civil and Political Rights). 1966. "International Covenant on Civil and Political Rights." United Nations Treaty Series, no. 14668, vol. 999 at 171 (December 16).

Jerusalem Post. 1999. "Barak Hints of Ways to Bypass Anti-Torture Ruling." Jerusalem Post, September 9.

Kamminga, Menno T. 1992. *Inter-State Accountability for Violations of Human Rights*. Philadelphia, PA: University of Pennsylvania Press.

Keating, Vincent C. 2014. "Contesting the International Illegitimacy of Torture: The Bush Administration's Failure to Legitimate Its Preferences within International Society." *British Journal of Politics & International Relations* 16 (1): pp. 1–27. doi: 10.1111/1467-856X.12024.

Kennedy-Pipe, Caroline, and Andrew Mumford. 2007. "Torture, Rights, Rules and Wars: Ireland and Iraq." *International Relations* 21 (1): pp. 119–26. doi: 10.1177/0047117807073777.

Klose, Fabian. 2013. *Human Rights in the Shadow of Colonial Violence: The Wars of Independence in Kenya and Algeria*. Philadelphia, PA: University of Pennsylvania Press.

Kutz, Christopher. 2014. "How Norms Die: Torture and Assassination in American Security Policy." *Ethics & International Affairs* 28 (4): pp. 425–49. doi: 10.1017/S0892679414000598.

Landau Commission. 1987. "Commission of Inquiry into the Methods of Interrogation of the General Security Service Regarding Hostile Terrorist Activity: Report, Part One." English translation provided by the Government Press Office. Jerusalem: State of Israel.

Lantis, Jeffrey S., and Carmen Wunderlich. 2018. "Resiliency Dynamics of Norm Clusters: Norm Contestation and International Cooperation." *Review of International Studies* 44 (3): pp. 570–93. doi: 10.1017/S0260210517000626.

Laursen, Andreas. 2000. "Israel's Supreme Court and International Human Rights Law: The Judgement on 'Moderate Physical Pressure.'" *Nordic Journal of International Law* 69 (4): pp. 413–47. doi: 10.1163/15718100020296396.

Lesch, Max. 2023. "From Norm Violations to Norm Development: Deviance, International Institutions, and the Torture Prohibition." *International Studies Quarterly*, forthcoming.

Lesch, Max. 2022. "Devianz als Vermittlung zwischen Fakt und Norm: Epistemische Praktiken und fact-finding internationaler Organisationen." *Zeitschrift diskurs* (8): pp. 42–56.

Lesch, Max, and Nina Reiners. 2023. "Informal Human Rights Law-making: How Treaty Bodies Use General Comments to Develop International Law." *Global Constitutionalism*, online first: pp. 1–24. doi: 10.1017/S2045381723000023.

Liese, Andrea. 2009. "Exceptional Necessity: How Liberal Democracies Contest the Prohibition of Torture and Ill-Treatment When Countering Terrorism." *Journal of International Law and International Relations* 5 (1): pp. 17–47.

Lutz, Ellen L., and Kathryn Sikkink. 2000. "International Human Rights Law and Practice in Latin America." *International Organization* 54 (3): pp. 633–59. doi: 10.1162/002081800551235.

Mavronicola, Natasa. 2021. *Torture, Inhumanity and Degradation under Article 3 of the ECHR: Absolute Rights and Absolute Wrongs*. Oxford: Hart.

McKeown, Ryder. 2009. "Norm Regress: US Revisionism and the Slow Death of the Torture Norm." *International Relations* 23 (1): pp. 5–25. doi: 10.1177/0047117808100607.

Meydani, Assaf. 2015. *The Anatomy of Human Rights in Israel: Constitutional Rhetoric and State Practice*. Cambridge: Cambridge University Press.

Miller, Peter, Paul Gronke, and Darius Rejali. 2014. "Torture and Public Opinion: The Partisan Dimension." In *Examining Torture: Empirical Studies of State Repression*, ed. Tracy Lightcap and James P. Pfiffner. New York: Palgrave Macmillan, pp. 11–41.

Murray, Rachel, Elina Steinerte, Malcolm D. Evans, and Antenor Hallo de Wolf. 2011. *The Optional Protocol to the UN Convention against Torture*. Oxford: Oxford University Press.

Nowak, Manfred. 2005. *U.N. Covenant on Civil and Political Rights: CCPR Commentary*. 2nd edn. Kehl: N.P. Engel.

Nowak, Manfred, and Elizabeth McArthur. 2008. *The United Nations Convention against Torture: A Commentary*. Oxford: Oxford University Press.

Nylen, Alexandria, and Charli Carpenter. 2019. "Questions of Life and Death: (De)Constructing Human Rights Norms through US Public Opinion Surveys." *European Journal of International Security* 4 (2): pp. 142–62. doi: 10.1017/eis.2019.3.

O'Boyle, Michael. 1977. "Torture and Emergency Powers under the European Convention on Human Rights: Ireland v. The United Kingdom." *American Journal of International Law* 71 (4): pp. 674–706. doi: 10.2307/2199581.

OHCHR (Office of the High Commissioner for Human Rights). 2022. "Status of Ratification." Accessed September 21, 2022. https://indicators.ohchr.org.

OPCAT (Optional Protocol to the Convention against Torture). 2006. "Optional Protocol to the Convention against Torture and Other Cruel, Inhuman or Degrading Treatment or Punishment." United Nations Treaty Series, no. 24841, vol. 2375 at 237 (December 18).

Parker Committee. 1972. "Report of the Committee of Privy Counsellors Appointed to Consider Authorised Procedures for the Interrogation of Persons Suspected of Terrorism." London: Her Majesty's Stationery Office.

Percy, Sarah. 2007. "Mercenaries: Strong Norm, Weak Law." *International Organization* 61 (2): pp. 367–97. doi: 10.1017/S0020818307070130.

Percy, Sarah V., and Wayne Sandholtz. 2022. "Why Norms Rarely Die." *European Journal of International Relations* 28 (4): 934–54. doi: 10.1177/13540661221126018.

Rejali, Darius. 2007. *Torture and Democracy*. Princeton, NJ: Princeton University Press.

Rodley, Nigel S. 2002. "The Definition(s) of Torture in International Law." *Current Legal Problems* 55 (1): pp. 467–93. doi: 10.1093/clp/55.1.467.

Rodley, Nigel S., and Matt Pollard. 2009. *The Treatment of Prisoners under International Law*. Oxford: Oxford University Press.

Rosert, Elvira, and Sonja Schirmbeck. 2007. "Zur Erosion internationaler Normen: Folterverbot und nukleares Tabu in der Diskussion." *Zeitschrift für Internationale Beziehungen* 14 (2): pp. 253–87.

Sanders, Rebecca. 2018. *Plausible Legality: Legal Culture and Political Imperative in the Global War on Terror*. Oxford: Oxford University Press.

Sandholtz, Wayne. 2017. "Domestic Law and Human Rights Treaty Commitments: The Convention against Torture." *Journal of Human Rights* 16 (1): pp. 25–43. doi: 10.1080/14754835.2015.1103164.

Sandholtz, Wayne. 2019. "Norm Contestation, Robustness, and Replacement." *Journal of Global Security Studies* 4 (1): pp. 139–46. doi: 10.1093/jogss/ogy042.

Schabas, William A. 2010. *The International Criminal Court: A Commentary on the Rome Statute*. Oxford: Oxford University Press.

Schabas, William A., and Oliver O'Sullivan. 2007. "Of Politics and Poor Weather: How Ireland Decided to Sue the United Kingdom under the European Convention on Human Rights." *Irish Yearbook of International Law* 2: pp. 3–29.

Schmidt, Averell, and Kathryn Sikkink. 2019. "Breaking the Ban? The Heterogeneous Impact of US Contestation of the Torture Norm." *Journal of Global Security Studies* 4 (1): pp. 105–22. doi: 10.1093/jogss/ogy036.

Sikkink, Kathryn. 2013. "The United States and Torture: Does the Spiral Model Work." In *The Persistent Power of Human Rights: From Commitment to Compliance*, ed. Thomas Risse, Stephen C. Ropp, and Kathryn Sikkink. Cambridge: Cambridge University Press, pp. 145–63.

Simmons, Beth A. 2009. *Mobilizing for Human Rights: International Law in Domestic Politics*. Cambridge: Cambridge University Press.

Stimmer, Anette. 2019. "Beyond Internalization: Alternate Endings of the Norm Life Cycle." *International Studies Quarterly* 63 (2): pp. 270–80. doi: 10.1093/isq/sqz001.

Times. 1971a. "Privy Councillors to Hold Inquiry on Interrogation Methods." The Times, November 17.

Times. 1971b. "Brutality Charges 'Demolished.'" The Times, November 18.

UDHR (Universal Declaration of Human Rights). 1948. "UNGA Resolution 217 (III) A: Universal Declaration of Human Rights." UN Doc. A/810 at 71 (December 10).

UNGA (United Nations General Assembly). 1974. "UN GAOR: 29th Session, 2278th Plenary Meeting." UN Doc. A/PV.2278 (November 6).

UNGA. 1975a. "UN GAOR: 30th Session, 2152nd Third Committee Meeting." UN Doc. A/C.3/SR.2152 (November 7).

UNGA. 1975b. "UN GAOR: 30th Session, 2155th Third Committee Meeting." UN Doc. A/C.3/SR.2155 (November 11).

UNGA. 1975c. "UN GAOR: 30th Session, 2433rd Plenary Meeting." UN Doc. A/PV.2433 (December 9).

UNGA. 1976. "UN GAOR: 31st Session, 46th Third Committee Meeting." UN Doc. A/C.3/31/SR.46 (November 11).

UNGA. 1977. "UN GAOR: 32nd Session, 105th Plenary Meeting." UN Doc. A/32/PV.105 (December 16).

UNGA. 1980. "UN GAOR: 35th Session, 96th Plenary Meeting." UN Doc. A/35/PV.96 (December 15).

UNGA. 1997. "Report of the Committee against Torture." UN Doc. A/52/44, Supp. no. 44.

UNGA. 2002a. "UN GAOR: 57th Session, 31st Third Committee Meeting." UN Doc. A/C.3/57/SR.31 (October 31).

UNGA. 2002b. "UN GAOR: 57th Session, 36th Third Committee Meeting." UN Doc. A/C.3/57/SR.36 (November 5).

Vargas Viancos, María C. 1990. "El Caso Chileno en la Asamblea General y la Comisión de Derechos Humans de la Organización de las Naciones Unidas." *Revista Chilena de Derechos Humanos* 12: pp. 31–59.

Venzke, Ingo. 2009. "Legal Contestation about 'Enemy Combatants': On the Exercise of Power in Legal Interpretation." *Journal of International Law and International Relations* 5 (1): pp. 155–84.

Versteeg, Mila. 2015. "Law Versus Norms: The Impact of Human-Rights Treaties on National Bills of Rights." *Journal of Institutional and Theoretical Economics* 171 (1): pp. 87–111. doi: 10.1628/093245615X14204441572731.

Washington Post. 2006. "Most Ridiculous Moment?" Washington Post, October 26.

Washington Post. 2007. "Bush's Feeble Torture Dodge." Washington Post, October 9.

Welch, Ryan M. 2017. "National Human Rights Institutions: Domestic Implementation of International Human Rights Law." *Journal of Human Rights* 16 (1): pp. 96–116. doi: 10.1080/14754835.2015.1103166.

Welch, Ryan M., Jacqueline H. R. DeMeritt, and Courtenay R. Conrad. 2021. "Conceptualizing and Measuring Institutional Variation in National Human Rights Institutions (NHRIs)." *Journal of Conflict Resolution* 65 (5): pp. 1010–33. doi: 10.1177/0022002720982349.

Wiener, Antje. 2018. *Contestation and Constitution of Norms in Global International Relations*. Cambridge: Cambridge University Press.

Wood, Reed M., and Mark Gibney. 2010. "The Political Terror Scale (PTS): A Re-Introduction and a Comparison to CIRI." *Human Rights Quarterly* 32 (2): pp. 367–400. doi: 10.1353/hrq.0.0152.

Yildiz, Ezgi. 2020. "A Court with Many Faces: Judicial Characters and Modes of Norm Development in the European Court of Human Rights." *European Journal of International Law* 31 (1): pp. 73–99. doi: 10.1093/ejil/chaa014.

Zvobgo, Kelebogile. 2021. "The ICC's Flawed Afghan Investigation: Why the Court Shouldn't Let America Off the Hook." Foreign Affairs, November 3. Accessed January 7, 2023. https://www.foreignaffairs.com/articles/afghanistan/2021-11-03/iccs-flawed-afghan-investigation.

3

Responsibility to protect

A robust but changing norm?

3.1 Introduction

Every state is responsible for protecting its population against genocide, ethnic cleansing, war crimes, and crimes against humanity. Should a state be unable or unwilling to do so, the responsibility to act lies with the international community. This is the essence of the "responsibility to protect" (R2P), a political norm adopted at the United Nations (UN) 2005 World Summit. Although its unanimous endorsement was seen as a breakthrough in reconciling cross-border protection of human rights and state sovereignty (Evans 2006: 714, 2008, 284), R2P is contested. Skeptics question whether the norm has any effect. Alex de Waal (2007) describes international reactions to the crisis in Darfur (Sudan) as the "Failure of the Responsibility to Protect." The 2011 intervention in Libya authorized by the UN Security Council (UNSC) and led by the North Atlantic Treaty Organization (NATO) was subsequently heavily contested (Brockmeier et al. 2016). Controversies over how to deal with the crisis in Syria also point to R2P's controversial nature (Welsh 2019: 55–56). Some authors conclude that R2P has lost acceptance (see Dembinski and Mumford 2012) or even collapsed (Rieff 2011; Nuruzzaman 2013; Hehir 2019). Others argue that the norm remains robust or has even been strengthened (Gifkins 2016; Scherzinger 2023). These competing findings are mainly due to different ways of measuring norms, especially those with positive obligations like R2P (Welsh 2019: 57). Those who foretell the norm's demise mainly focus on R2P practice (Reinold 2010: 69–74; Hehir 2019), whereas those who describe it as robust rely on discursive indicators (e.g. Gifkins 2016; Scherzinger 2023). In this chapter we empirically analyze the norm's contestation and robustness between the 2005 World Summit and 2016 using our four-dimensional approach to norm robustness.

We argue that despite some rough years, R2P remains robust because challenges have mainly concerned its *application*. Although widespread,

International Norm Disputes. Lisbeth Zimmermann et al., Oxford University Press. © Lisbeth Zimmermann, Nicole Deitelhoff, Max Lesch, Antonio Arcudi, and Anton Peez (2023). DOI: 10.1093/oso/9780198873235.003.0003

contestation about the norm does not challenge its fundaments, unlike the challenges to the International Criminal Court (ICC) and the moratorium on commercial whaling (see Chapters 4 and 5). This is because the UN's institutional setting for discussing and interpreting R2P is generally perceived as fair and because of the specific embeddedness of the norm in a complex norm cluster of human rights and sovereignty. We do observe, however, that some of R2P's core claims have begun to change, with states and civil society organizations favoring non-violent measures that could ultimately do away with R2P's military dimension. This might be reflected in the latest data on robustness.

We begin by outlining how the norm's core claims developed and defining them. We then introduce empirical material to assess its contestation and robustness in two phases—before and after the NATO-led coalition intervened in Libya in 2011 (Section 3.2). Section 3.3 analyses R2P contestation in international discourse and Section 3.4 examines its robustness. We end by discussing explanatory factors (Section 3.5), particularly perceptions of procedural fairness and embeddedness in strong norm clusters and whether continual reinterpretation of R2P could hollow it out.

3.2 Responsibility to protect: History and data

3.2.1 Norm evolution

The approval of R2P at the UN 2005 World Summit was seen as a milestone: R2P was viewed as a way of bridging longstanding tensions between the cross-border protection of human rights and the principles of sovereignty and non-interference (Bellamy and Drummond 2011: 180; Williams and Bellamy 2012: 283). The debate about the need to protect people in other countries from atrocities was not new: R2P builds on established legal, political, and moral principles (Staunton and Glanville 2022: 4–6). Yet, R2P's "universal endorsement and scope" as laid out in the 2005 World Summit Outcome Document (WSOD) (Staunton and Glanville 2022: 8) significantly developed international norms regarding sovereignty and protection. It was actually an attempt to calm the heated debates about humanitarian intervention.

The humanitarian crises of the 1990s, especially in Rwanda and Srebrenica, focused attention on the potentially harmful tension between sovereignty and protection from atrocities. In his "We the Peoples" report in 2000, UN Secretary-General Kofi Annan appealed to the international community:

> If humanitarian intervention is, indeed, an unacceptable assault on sovereignty, how should we respond to a Rwanda, to a Srebrenica—to gross and systematic violations of human rights that offend every precept of our common humanity?
>
> **(Annan 2000: 48)**

Annan pushed the UN member states to reinterpret state sovereignty as the responsibility to protect the population from atrocities (Deng et al. 1996; Annan 1999; Lu 2006; see also Bellamy 2011: 10).

A Canadian initiative led to the creation of the International Commission on Intervention and State Sovereignty (ICISS), headed by Gareth Evans, in 1999 (Thakur 2005: 182). It was tasked to study the inherent tension between cross-border protection of human rights and state sovereignty (Bellamy 2009b: 35). The commission's report emphasized that states are primarily responsible for protecting their citizens from grave human rights violations. If states are incapable or unwilling to accept that responsibility, it is incumbent on the international community to do so (Bellamy 2011: 16). Military intervention should only be a last resort to end massive human rights violations such as genocide (ICISS 2001: 33). However, the ICISS report did not clarify whether the responsibility to protect was a *legal* or a *moral* principle and only vaguely formulated what would trigger international action: "large scale loss of life, whether real or apprehended" (ICISS 2001: XII). Finally, it left open the crucial question of *who* was responsible for initiating international action (Welsh 2013: 370). The report was well aware of power politics in the UNSC—the only institution that could authorize a military intervention—and called on its five permanent members to waive their veto rights in R2P-relevant situations (ICISS 2001: XIII). It also stipulated that the UN General Assembly (UNGA) should be enabled to authorize the use of force in accordance with the "Uniting for Peace" resolution (UNGA 1950) if the UNSC cannot, or does not, act (Bellamy 2011: 18; Tiewa 2012: 155).

The terror attacks of September 2001 overshadowed the R2P debate (Molier 2006; Rotmann et al. 2014). The 2003 intervention in Iraq, which was not authorized by the UNSC, was another setback for the norm's development (Murthy and Kurtz 2016: 41). However, norm entrepreneurs continued to promote R2P (Staunton and Glanville 2022: 11–12). One important step was when Kofi Annan created the UN High-Level Panel on Threats, Challenges and Change (HLP) to discuss threats to international peace and security. Its report, "A More Secure World: Our Shared Responsibility," listed 101 recommendations and proposed rules regarding the use of force (Weiss 2006: 746). Crucially, it referred to the "emerging norm that there is a collective international responsibility to protect" (High Level Panel on Threats, Challenges and Change 2004: 66). The UN 2005 World Summit then provided the opportunity to establish the still highly controversial R2P as an international norm (Murthy and Kurtz 2016: 42).

Criticism of R2P mounted during the run-up to the 2005 World Summit. States in the Global South with longstanding concerns about their sovereignty worried that R2P could undermine the UN Charter by justifying unilateral interventions (Williams and Bellamy 2005: 37; Serrano 2011). Russia emphasized that the UN Charter risked being weakened if unilateral interventions in the name of R2P were tolerated (Bellamy 2009a: 112). The Non-Aligned Movement (NAM) argued that the UNSC was already well equipped to deal with humanitarian emergencies (Bellamy 2006: 152), while states that had initially supported R2P were concerned about who would authorize interventions to halt R2P crimes, the criteria for using force to halt serious human rights violations, and potential abuse in terms of territorial disputes and regime change (Bellamy 2009b: 83–84).

In 2005, despite all the controversies, the WSOD adopted R2P (UNGA 2005), indicating broad and express commitment to its core normative claims (Staunton and Glanville 2022: 8). Yet, the WSOD did not go as far as the ICISS, and some commented that it was "R2P-light" (Bellamy 2008: 616; Luck 2012b: 40–41; Weiss 2016: 117). The WSOD states that R2P applies to the four core crimes (genocide, war crimes, ethnic cleansing, and crimes against humanity), whereas the ICISS had defined its scope as situations of "large scale loss of life" (ICISS 2001: XII). The WSOD names the UNSC as the only organ that can authorize military interventions: It neither infringes on the five permanent members' veto rights nor allows UNGA to authorize intervention when the UNSC is blocked. The WSOD is an UNGA resolution without any formal legal character: R2P is a political norm (see Stahn 2007; Welsh and Banda 2010; Byers 2015; Daase 2015). Yet, based on the "new configuration" of existing (legal) provisions, "R2P has become a leading norm of human protection" (Staunton and Glanville 2022: 3). As we will see, its broad and often abstract formulations leave a lot of leeway for interpretation (Section 3.5). Primarily, R2P guides the debate about how to react to atrocities (Welsh 2019; Staunton and Glanville 2022).

3.2.2 Normative core claims

The WSOD enshrined R2P in paragraphs 138 and 139, defining three responsibilities that constitute its core normative claims: (1) Each state must protect its population against genocide, war crimes, ethnic cleansing, and crimes against humanity; (2) the international community is responsible for helping states fulfill their duty; (3) if a state manifestly fails to protect its population against these crimes and peaceful means prove inadequate, the international community must consider collective action through the UNSC, including by taking possible measures under Chapter VII of the UN Charter (UNGA 2005). Under R2P, national sovereignty and, thus, the norm of non-interference are conditional upon whether states fulfill their responsibility to protect. This is the essence of Annan's notion of "sovereignty as responsibility" (Annan 1999). The division in "three pillars of R2P" (Ban 2009) indicates that R2P should not be treated as a single norm, because it formulates both negative *and* positive responsibilities of individual states and the international community, and instead be viewed as a set of distinct but coherent norms (Welsh 2014: 125, 2019; Deitelhoff 2019). At its core, R2P is about not only military interventions to protect populations from atrocities but also prevention and assistance. This link was instrumental in R2P's acceptance because it shifted the debate from the deep concerns about "humanitarian intervention" to the notion of protection (Staunton and Glanville 2022: 12–13).

R2P's Pillar 1 enshrines a positive duty for individual states to protect their populations and a negative duty to refrain from harming them. Pillars 2 (responsibility to assist) and 3 (responsibility to respond) are positive obligations for the "wider international community," particularly the UNSC, to protect people from atrocities. Challenges to these core claims constitute *validity contestations*, the most glaring of which is total rejection of one of the pillars. Contestations that invoke colliding (incompatible) norms, such as absolute non-intervention or traditional notions of sovereignty, also contest the validity of R2P. We speak of *applicatory contestation* when, in specific situations, states challenge the appropriateness of applying norms or taking certain measures to comply with the norm. Examples include skepticism about the use of force because of its potential negative effects, questioning whether mass atrocities occurred, and claiming that R2P is being used for political ends.[1] It is difficult to distinguish the three pillars because actors

[1] For a detailed coding scheme, see the Appendix, Table A.2.

often just refer to R2P. Furthermore, its complex nature implies that contesting one pillar, such as international responsibility, could mean affirming another, like national responsibility (see also Welsh 2019: 56).

3.2.3 Data collection and analysis

We begin our analysis in 2005, when the UN member states adopted R2P at the World Summit, and take the intervention in Libya in 2011 as a turning point because it was the first time the UNSC authorized a military intervention based on R2P. We thus divide our analysis into two parts, from 2005 to 2010 and from 2011 to 2016. We also discuss the latest developments as far as data is available.

We examine international contestation trends, focusing on the debates about R2P within the UN, as well as statements by state representatives and diplomats in domestic newspapers, to better understand patterns of contestation.[2] For the qualitative content analysis, we compiled 840 statements from states, regional organizations, and state groups.[3] Almost half of the statements (391 documents) were retrieved from UNGA's Informal Interactive Dialogue on the Responsibility to Protect (hereafter "Informal Dialogue"). Because it is the main forum for discussing R2P's development within the UN, we coded all the documents available. We also coded a randomly selected sample of meeting records of the UNSC (225 documents) and UNGA and its committees (164) selected through a full-text search in the UN documents archive. Because these debates address R2P in concrete situations, we were able to examine specific political processes. Finally, we coded statements from a randomly selected sample of newspaper articles (60 documents) in a full-text search of R2P in the "All English and German Language News" Nexis database.[4]

We based our analysis of the *discursive dimension* of norm robustness on data compiled for analyzing contestation trends, coding each statement regarding affirmations of R2P and negative reactions to violations. To complement the results of our content analysis to assess concordance with R2P, we measured changes in the number of states participating in the Informal Dialogue. Since its launch in 2010, this has become the most important platform

[2] Supplementary material and data is available at the Harvard Dataverse: https://doi.org/10.7910/DVN/6VHFZK.

[3] Number of documents per year: 2005: 29, 2006: 33, 2007: 19, 2008: 34, 2009: 79, 2010: 49, 2011: 84, 2012: 81, 2013: 101, 2014: 82, 2015: 166, 2016: 85, 2017: 69.

[4] Most articles came from *Africa News* (20) and *BBC Monitoring* (7).

for R2P debates. R2P is not a formal treaty, so there are no ratification numbers (an indicator used in other case studies). Instead, we used the number of participating states as a proxy for how they perceive the norm's importance. For the *practical dimension* of robustness, it is difficult to track compliance rates and implementation efforts because R2P is an abstract norm that includes some positive obligations. Here, we use the UNSC resolutions referencing R2P as a proxy for compliance with its positive obligations because the UNSC is the most important international body concerned with global peace and security and the only UN organ that can authorize R2P military interventions. We discuss these findings in light of relevant potential R2P cases based on data sets on violence against civilians (Pettersson et al. 2021) and secondary literature (Bellamy 2015; Hofmann 2019). To observe trends in military R2P responses, we use recent data on humanitarian military interventions (Gromes and Dembinski 2019).

These steps allow us to assess whether, and how, the UNSC has applied R2P in situations that involved protecting populations from atrocities and the measures adopted by the international community (including without UN mandate). Acknowledging that different potential R2P situations warrant different responses (Gallagher 2015; Ralph 2018), the data is not solely focused on military coercion. We do not assess R2P's effectiveness with regard to successful protection. Following Welsh (2019: 57), we analyze compliance in terms of whether or not the UNSC and other actors address (potential) atrocities with respect to R2P's core principle, the positive obligation to protect.

For R2P *implementation*, we look at international and national practice. For the former, we track several implementation initiatives at the UN; for the latter, we mainly study the development of the "R2P Focal Point Initiative," which aims to institutionalize national responses to atrocities and create international networks to implement them (Serrano 2015).

3.3 Contestation trends

Between 2005 and 2016, international disputes over R2P mostly addressed its application (see Figure 3.1). R2P was already very controversial before its inclusion in the WSOD in 2005 and it continues to be contested. In the literature, the Libya intervention of 2011 is viewed as pivotal (Scherzinger 2023: 84), although states had already challenged R2P regarding the conflict in Darfur and post-election violence in Kenya.

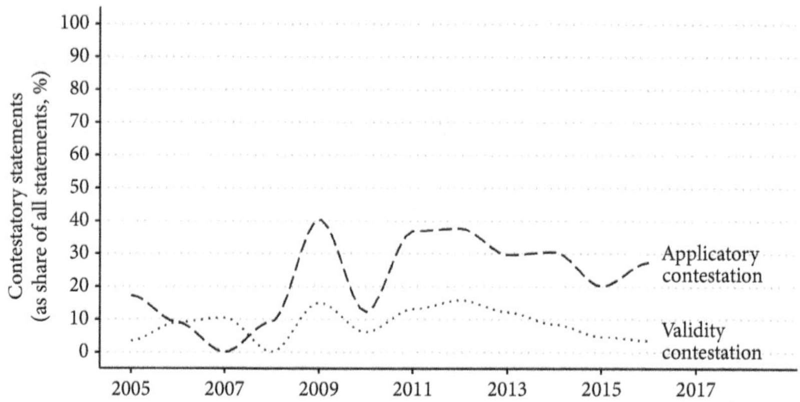

Figure 3.1 Contestation of the responsibility to protect, 2005–16

Source: Based on 840 statements on the responsibility to protect in UN documents, the Informal Interactive Dialogue on Responsibility to Protect, and in newspapers. Updated and adapted with permission from Deitelhoff and Zimmermann 2020. "Things We Lost in the Fire: How Different Types of Contestation Affect the Robustness of International Norms." *International Studies Review* 22 (1): pp. 51–76. doi: 10.1093/isr/viy080.

Contestation peaked in 2009, when the first official post-2005 debate on R2P took place in UNGA. It mainly concerned how R2P should be applied. Starting in 2011, challenges centered around the Libya intervention and if—and how—the international community should react to the conflict in Syria. Contestation grew about applying R2P but not challenges to its validity.

3.3.1 From the UN World Summit to first R2P applications, 2005–2010

After R2P was included in the WSOD, the UNSC debated about whether the council should adopt a resolution reaffirming its responsibility. Especially, the United Kingdom (UK), France, and Denmark wanted a resolution. But China, Russia, Algeria, and Brazil were cautious, arguing that UNGA had only agreed to deliberate R2P and that it was too early to discuss it at the UNSC (Bellamy 2010: 145). Russia argued:

> We believe that it is clearly premature to advance that concept [R2P] in Security Council documents. We all remember well the complex compromise that was required to reflect that issue in the 2005 Summit Outcome document. In that connection—and the outcome documents states this—we need to have a detailed discussion in the General Assembly of the issue of the responsibility to protect before we can discuss its implementation.
>
> **(Russia in UNSC 2005: 19)**

Eventually, the UK and France could reach a compromise with China and Russia—strictly based on the language of the WSOD (Gifkins 2016: 155). Security Council Resolution 1674 (UNSC 2006) confirmed the 2005 version of R2P.

The norm was first applied in 2005, with Darfur described as the first test of the international community's commitment to R2P (Matthews 2008: 144). Official Sudanese actions resembled a "textbook illustration of a government unwilling to live up its responsibility to protect its citizens" (Badescu and Bergholm 2009: 294), and in 2005, the UNSC referred the situation in Sudan to the ICC (Chapter 5). That was followed by UNSC Resolution 1706 adopted in late August 2006, which invoked R2P—after six months of negotiations—when deciding to deploy a UN mission to Darfur (UNSC 2006). Yet, because Sudan did not consent to this resolution, it was never implemented. This could only be achieved by the compromise for a hybrid African Union (AU)-UN mission in UNSC resolution 1769—now without reference to R2P (Gifkins 2016: 156–57).

Another central issue during the first phase of R2P is illustrated by France's effort to apply the norm after Cyclone Nargis caused more than 138,000 deaths and displaced 800,000 persons in Myanmar in May 2008 (Haacke 2009: 157). Despite the catastrophic natural disaster, Burmese authorities obstructed international humanitarian efforts (Badescu and Weiss 2010: 362). The proposal by French Foreign Minister Bernard Kouchner that R2P should be applied to facilitate aid deliveries (Bellamy 2008: 633) was rejected by China, Indonesia, and Viet Nam, among others (Security Council Report 2008: 3). Cautious states rejected the use of R2P in Myanmar—and so did R2P supporters (Steinberg 2009: 437). Although some commentators supported the French call (Badescu and Weiss 2010: 362), it received little support.

R2P made headlines again in August 2008 when Russia referred to R2P, attempting to justify its military operation in Georgia (Evans 2009). In that case, a Russian citizen of South Ossetian origin, Eduard Kokoiti, had been elected president of South Ossetia. Russia distributed Russian passports in South Ossetia, and Russian security personal increased its presence in South Ossetian territory, which led the Georgian government to believe that Russia was pursuing "a process of de facto absorption of South Ossetia [. . .] into Russia" (Allison 2008: 1147). The tension erupted into an armed conflict on Georgian soil involving Georgian troops, South Ossetian separatists, and Russian forces (IIFFMCG 2009). Russia justified its intervention, citing R2P (BBC 2008) and claiming it had acted to stop a "genocide of the Ossetian population by Georgian forces" (IIFFMCG 2009: 21). However, much of the international community rejected the R2P justification because the genocide claim did not hold and because Russia had intervened with disproportionate military force and without UNSC authorization (Evans 2009: 27).

These cases were viewed as failures or unjustified attempts to invoke R2P. But international response to the conflict regarding Kenya's election results in December 2007 was viewed as its successful application (Crossley 2016: 149). Kenyan president Mwai Kibaki's electoral victory was unexpected because the opposition Orange Democratic Movement (ODM) had achieved a comfortable majority in the latest parliamentary elections (Sharma 2012: 28). After the ODM refused to accept the allegedly fraudulent election, violence broke out in various parts of Kenya, claiming more than 1,000 lives, with 300,000 injured and 600,000 displaced (Höhn 2014: 567; Sharma 2015: 283). The severity of the crisis quickly stimulated international rhetoric—and also led to contested investigations by the ICC (see Chapter 5). On December 31, 2007, UN Secretary-General Ban Ki-moon called for restraint on the part of Kenya's security forces (UN 2007; see also Junk 2016). Viewing the Kenyan crisis from an R2P perspective (Luck 2012a: 98), a few days later, Moon invoked the norm, reminding "the Government, as well as the political and religious leaders of Kenya, of their moral responsibility to protect the lives of innocent people" (UN 2008). After one initiative to resolve the conflict failed, Kofi Annan chaired the AU Panel of Eminent Personalities, which pushed the hostile parties to agree that Kibaki would be president and Odinga prime minister (Crossley 2013: 204–206; Junk 2016: 56).

These cases reflect the general challenges to R2P during the first phase, which mainly concerned application. In particular, China, Pakistan, and Sudan addressed R2P triggers, fears about its politicization and misuse, feelings of unequal treatment, and the exact measures to be implemented. During the second official UNGA debate about R2P, Indonesia referred to Cyclone Nargis:

> [T]here have been efforts by some to misuse the concept of R2P by applying it to situations that are clearly outside its scope. For instance, some have tried to link R2P to humanitarian access in the wake of natural disasters. That is patently unhelpful.
>
> **(Indonesia in UNGA 2009b, 7)**

The issue of triggers is often intertwined with the second line of applicatory arguments: States complained that R2P is applied or abused for political reasons and highlighted the risk of politicizing the norm. For instance, Georgia referred to South Ossetia, arguing:

> The potential to misuse this principle could lead to its perversion and subversion. We would therefore like to join our voice to those that have highlighted the perils associated with the insidious or even cynical misapplication of the principle.
>
> (UNGA 2009d: 7)

The dangers of abuse and politicization were accompanied by demands for safeguards and guidelines (e.g. Israel in UNGA 2009b: 15). Some states invoked the need for equal treatment in similar situations (Pakistan in UNGA 2009b) and for impartiality (China in UNSC 2005).

During the first phase, the measures to be applied in R2P were also contested, with Costa Rica expressing skepticism about the use of force and other enforcement procedures: "Likewise, any decision to take measures of force must be based on careful assessments, always keeping human beings at the centre of their concerns" (Costa Rica 2010). Challenges to R2P's *validity*—from a much smaller group of states that included Bolivia, Venezuela, and Cuba—employed two main arguments: sovereignty and the categorical exclusion of specific measures. Although sovereignty-based arguments can be regarded as applicatory contestation because sovereignty is a conflicting norm, we classify them as *validity* contestations because R2P includes an understanding of conditional sovereignty (Section 3.2.2). Nicaragua argued that:

> The concept cannot be placed above the sovereignty of States or the United Nations Charter. Relevant organs, such as the Human Rights Council and the Peacebuilding Commission, already exist, and we believe that they must be strengthened in that regard.
>
> (UNGA 2009c: 13)

Another subject of validity contestation is the absolute exclusion of specific measures linked to R2P: Their rejection is not restricted to specific circumstances. That had been one of the main issues at the 2005 World Summit. Qatar rejected the use of military force across the board because it "believe[s] that the military option is not conductive to the resolution of any crisis, regardless of its source" (Qatar in UNSC 2007). During the first phase, there were few blanket rejections of R2P or allegations of neocolonialism and imperialism except for Ecuador (in UNGA 2009b: 9), while Sudan stated that R2P "can be misused by some powerful countries to achieve imperial hegemony over less powerful ones" (Sudan in UNGA 2009d: 11).

In sum, debates during the first years after R2P's adoption by the WSOD mainly concerned its potential application to specific situations and contestation about triggers and applicatory scope. States rarely fundamentally challenged the norm's core claims.

3.3.2 R2P during and after the Libya intervention, 2011–2016

The intervention in Libya triggered debate about forcible regime change and changed the issues regarding contestation. The Libyan crisis was induced by the "Arab Spring" that erupted there in mid-February 2011. Muammar Gaddafi had ruled Libya for more than 40 years, and young Libyans in particular sought to replicate the uprisings in Tunisia and Egypt. The government reacted violently (Ulfstein and Christiansen 2013: 159–60). On February 21, 2011, Secretary-General Ban Ki-moon called on Gaddafi to end the violence and respect fundamental human rights (UN News Centre 2011). The UNSC, the European Union, NATO, the AU, and the Arab League also condemned it, with the latter suspending Libya's membership (Security Council Report 2011b; UN 2011c).

As the demonstrations grew and government forces reacted even more violently, protesters requested assistance from the international community. The UNSC responded by unanimously adopting Resolution 1970, which called upon Libyan authorities to end its lethal violence, and imposed sanctions, including an arms embargo, travel bans, and asset freezes. It also referred the situation to the ICC (UNSC 2011a). Resolution 1970 was ineffective, however, and attacks on revolutionaries and civilians continued. The UN Human Rights Council suspended Libya on March 1, 2011 (UN 2011a) and shortly thereafter, the Gulf Cooperation Council and the Arab League called for a no-fly zone over Libya (League of Arab States 2011: para. 1; Security Council Report 2011a). After Gaddafi announced that government forces would "chase the traitors from Benghazi. Destroy their fortifications. Show them no mercy" (*Telegraph* 2011), the UNSC adopted Resolution 1973 authorizing UN member states "to take all necessary measures [. . .] to protect civilians and civilian populated areas [. . .] while excluding a foreign occupation force" and "to enforce compliance with the ban on flights" (UNSC 2011b: 3). The resolution was strongly supported by France, the United States (US), and the UK. South Africa, Colombia, Nigeria, Gabon, Bosnia and Herzegovina, Portugal, and Lebanon also voted in favor; China, Germany, India, and Russia abstained. Contestation flared up soon after the NATO-led coalition began its operations.

Also in early 2011, largely peaceful demonstrators in Syria began protesting poverty, political oppression, corruption, and restrictions on freedom of speech. But the demonstrations quickly escalated into a fully fledged civil war with numerous internal and external conflict parties (for a detailed account of the conflict, see Phillips 2016). Various actors have documented numerous violations of human rights and humanitarian law, including the use of chemical weapons. In 2022, estimated casualties of the war in Syria vary between conservative estimates of 350,000 (OHCHR 2021) to over 600,000 deaths (SOHR 2022). According to most recent estimates, this includes 300,000 *civilian* deaths alone (UNHRC 2022).

The Security Council has responded cautiously. Only in August 2011, almost five months after the conflict began, did the UNSC condemn the use of force against civilians (UN 2011d). In October 2011, the UNSC discussed a draft resolution which included sanctions that Russia and China rejected (UN 2011b). Since then, Russia and China have blocked a series of draft resolutions that threaten to sanction Syria or refer it to the ICC (Welsh 2019: 57; Staunton and Glanville 2022: 9). Despite that, the international community has not been idle: Allegations of chemical weapons use have triggered responses ranging from fact-finding missions by the Organization for the Prohibition of Chemical Weapons (OPCW) and the UN and destroying Syria's weapons under the auspices of the OPCW to unilateral military strikes carried out by the US, the UK, and France in retaliation to the renewed use of chemical weapons (Price 2019). A UNSC resolution in February 2014 referred to Syria's primary responsibility to protect its citizens, called on the Assad regime to grant humanitarian access, and threatened further actions. But Syria did not change course (UNSC 2014a, b, c).

Some states contested the application of R2P to Libya and Syria, but, surprisingly, after the Libya intervention there was less contestation than during the first phase (see Figure 3.1), when challenges had mainly addressed whether, and how, to apply R2P. Validity contestation dwindled and, by 2016, almost disappeared. After 2011, Russia, China, and, of course, Syria, expressed the most criticism regarding R2P's application and validity.

Applicatory contestation continued to address similar issues, but, in contrast to the period before 2011, most debate concerned measures, largely in discussions regarding regime change. Ecuador argued that the "possible regime change of a sovereign state, is outside of the concept of Responsibility to Protect and completely lacks legal standing" (Ecuador 2013). Other states also opposed external forces bringing about regime change as part of R2P:

> [The] intervention in Libya did not put an end to violence and had the unintended effect of exacerbating tensions on the ground and causing more harm than good to the very same civilians it was supposed to protect. It soon became clear that the interventions' goal was not the protection of civilians but regime change.
>
> **(Venezuela 2016)**

Military reaction was said to be the wrong response to the conflict in Syria:

> Military intervention to resolve political conflicts, as we have seen in other parts of the world—most recently in the Libyan situation—has unintended consequences not only for the country in question but for the wider region. That is something the Middle East can ill afford.
>
> **(South Africa in UNSC 2012: 30)**

Other states opined that force should only be used as a last resort (e.g. Pakistan 2012). The general reluctance to use force or coercive measures is often justified by their negative implications (Argentina in UNSC 2015). Raising concerns about politicizing R2P, Russia (in UNSC 2015) warned of "cynical political calculation" in the Syrian conflict, while Cuba complained, "[T]he Security Council can in no way ensure a non-abusive and non-selective action when implementing the Responsibility to Protect" (Cuba 2011).

Only from 2010 to 2012 did *validity contestation* increase—mainly from China, Russia, India, Nicaragua, Syria, and Venezuela—and then decline (see Figure 3.1). Once again, sovereignty was the top issue—along with the categorical exclusion of measures and allegations of neocolonialism and imperialism. The latter, however, were evoked less frequently than before 2011. Validity contestation did not catch on and cascade and remained limited to a small group of states.

Arguments about sovereignty mainly concerned Libya and Syria. In UNGA, Venezuela argued that the "free Libyan people must define their own destiny [. . .]. Sovereign peoples are the only protagonists of history, no foreign force is authorized to intervene in the internal affairs of the Libyan nation" (Venezuela in UNGA 2009a). Some states still rejected all use of force. Cuba stated that it:

> opposes, and will categorically oppose, any use of force that is not included in the provisions of the Charter, for which there can be no justification. The current unjust

> and deeply unequal global order cannot be succeeded by a more primitive one, based on the reinterpretation of the Charter and the International Law.
>
> **(Cuba 2011)**

Although these states were dissatisfied by the way the situation in Libya was handled, even after the intervention, challenges to R2P did not diffuse further and actually fewer and fewer states questioned its validity. As for Syria, proponents of R2P did not call for military force and generally focused on Pillars 1 and 2 and the non-violent measures in Pillar 3. This approach may have kept further contestation at bay but weakened a key feature of the norm, as we discuss in Sections 3.4 and 3.5.

3.4 Norm robustness trends

After 2011, contestation regarding the responsibility to protect remained mainly applicatory. We found—unlike several authors who assumed that R2P was becoming less robust—that contestation did not weaken the norm in practice or discourse: R2P increasingly shaped UNSC practice, while states criticized the fact that atrocities did not call forth responses. National, regional, and international implementation increased, and concordance was constant. However, we detect decreasing willingness to respond to state-inflicted atrocities by invoking R2P.

3.4.1 Practice: Stable compliance and growing implementation

With respect to the practical dimension of robustness, we now look at R2P's role in UNSC resolutions and debates along with military responses to atrocities inside and outside the UN as a way of assessing compliance. We also analyze R2P implementation by tracing its international, regional, and national institutionalization.

R2P resolutions by the UNSC and military responses by the UN and other actors must be seen in light of the "universe of cases" of potential R2P applications. Bellamy (2013b: 337–39, 2015, 164, 167) and Hofmann (2019: 316–17) used the Uppsala Conflict Data Program (UCDP) on one-sided violence[5]

[5] The UCDP defines one-sided violence as the "use of armed force by the government of a state or by a formally organised group against civilians which results in at least 25 deaths in a year" (Eck and Hultman 2007: 235).

to identify conflicts featuring civilian atrocities as potential cases for applying R2P. It is difficult to fully account for "R2P test cases" because the data excludes cases of successful prevention. Nonetheless, it is shown that after 2005, when R2P was written into the WSOD, fatalities from one-sided violence remained constant until at least 2010 (Pettersson and Eck 2018: 539). From 2011 until 2014, the case number grew, then declined, which can also be attributed to the overall decline of fatalities in the Syrian conflict (Pettersson et al. 2021: 814–16). With one-sided violence continuing unabated after 2005, we should observe a stable number of R2P responses.

Because the UNSC is the main body empowered to authorize R2P measures internationally, we examined the number of resolutions referring to R2P to assess whether the UNSC is fulfilling the "duty of conduct on the part of members of the international community: to identify when atrocity crimes are being committed or are imminent, and to deliberate [. . .] how different actors [. . .] should respond" (Welsh 2019: 57). This may include military measures, but they are not essential for a "successful" application of R2P (Welsh 2013: 368, 2019: 57). Figure 3.2 shows that, especially since 2012, more and more thematic and country-specific resolutions refer to the norm (GCR2P 2022; see also Staunton and Glanville 2022: 8–9).[6] Most of the resolutions refer to Pillar 1 and state responsibility; a few mandate international assistance under Pillar 2. Only Resolution 1973 on Libya explicitly authorized military action under R2P's Pillar 3 (Hofmann 2019: 318–19),

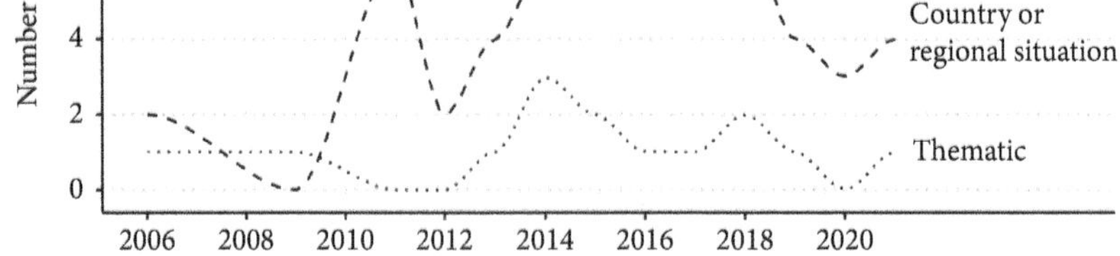

Figure 3.2 UNSC resolutions referring to the responsibility to protect, 2006–21
Source: Global Center for the Responsibility to Protect (GCR2P 2022).

[6] Between 2005 and 2021, most situation-specific resolutions referred to the Central African Republic (14), South Sudan (12), the Democratic Republic Congo (11), and Syria (7). Thematic resolutions referenced R2P with regard to international peace and security (5) and civilian protection (5).

while several resolutions "reaffirm[ed] the entirety of the WSOD's provisions on R2P" (Staunton and Glanville 2022: 8). There is a clear tendency to address conflicts in terms of "responsibility" and "protection" after 2005 and the WSOD's adoption of R2P. As Bellamy (2015: 163) notes, in most relevant cases of the 1990s and early 2000s, "the protection of people from genocide and mass atrocities was a peripheral concern." This did not change immediately after 2005: Only a few potential cases were discussed in terms of a responsibility to protect, let alone linked to the norm in UNSC resolutions (Hofmann 2019: 250). In 2007 and 2008, references to R2P were deleted from draft resolutions on Sudan and Somalia (Hofmann 2019: 249).

The picture changes after 2010. Beginning—but not ending, as some had supposed—with UNSC Resolutions 1970 and 1973 on Libya, the UNSC invoked the responsibility to protect in several country-specific and regional resolutions (see also Bellamy 2015; Hofmann 2019; Welsh 2019). Referring to R2P became less controversial and was usually—except for the Libyan case—unanimously adopted (Bellamy 2015: 166). Bellamy (2015: 166–67) and Hofmann (2019: 315–16) argue that the UNSC has increasingly applied R2P in relevant conflict situations, meaning that the UNSC is at least partially living up to what Welsh (2019: 57) has termed the international community's "duty of conduct" when faced with (potential) atrocities. This does not mean that the UNSC is responding to all relevant R2P cases in a manner that satisfies all actors (Ralph 2018: 194–95). Indeed, states often criticize inaction under R2P (Section 3.4.2). Moreover, UNSC resolutions do not always improve the situation on the ground, as seen in Syria (Hofmann 2019: 317).

Figure 3.2 shows that after 2017, the number of UNSC resolutions referring to R2P—especially in specific situations—began to decline. Observers note UN actors' reluctance to use R2P language in an attempt to avoid controversies (Welsh 2019: 55), particularly in resolutions authorizing the use of force (Scherzinger 2022: 14). The Syria case is a good example of this: Although the UNSC adopted resolutions on Syria that mention R2P, the council and the international community rarely addressed the situation in terms of an *international* responsibility to protect, apart from cases involving chemical weapons (Welsh 2019: 64; Deitelhoff and Zimmermann 2020: 62). If R2P no longer influences actions of the UN and its member states, it risks being weakened—especially if states do no longer protest inaction. Inertia regarding Syria, and especially the absence of any military response by the UN, is often taken as evidence that the R2P norm is not respected (although it is not clear whether a military response could have improved the situation on the ground). Yet, R2P continues to shape UNSC practice beyond Libya and Syria.

Figure 3.3 Ongoing humanitarian military interventions, 1990–2016
Source: Practices and Outcomes of Humanitarian Military Interventions Data Set (Gromes and Dembinski 2019).

How is this reflected in military responses to atrocities? Gromes and Dembinski (2019: 1033) define a "humanitarian military intervention" as "a cross-border use or threat of force by a state, a coalition of states, or an international organization for the purpose of protecting citizens of the target country from an acute violent emergency." This conceptualization captures how, both inside and outside the UN framework, responses to atrocities in the sense of the norm's Pillar 3 evolved over time. Data shows that military action with a humanitarian aim was not entirely unheard of before 1990 but that the vast majority (35 out of 41 cases) occurred after (Gromes and Dembinski 2019: 1041). Since the WSOD of 2005 adopted R2P, military responses to protect have continued—with and without UNSC mandates, as shown in Figure 3.3. Examples include the Libya intervention in 2011, robust UN peacekeeping missions in Darfur (since 2007) and Côte d'Ivoire (2011), and the AU mission in Somalia (since 2007) (Gromes and Dembinski 2019: 1039). This trend does not directly indicate "compliance" with R2P. Yet, it points to the at least stable, if not slightly increasing, tendency to protect populations from atrocities using military force and states' general willingness to do so—one of the core claims of R2P.

R2P's *implementation* in terms of international, regional, and national institutionalization is progressing. This is reflected at the international level through the UN Office on Genocide Prevention and the Responsibility to Protect established in 2008 (see Hofmann 2015: 29–30), mainly due to Secretary-General Ban Ki-moon's efforts. The office is not supposed to generate information on emerging crises but rather "collect, collate, analyze, and disseminate information" (Welsh 2014: 143). In 2007, Ban Ki-moon appointed Francis Deng, who was instrumental in developing R2P, as his Special Advisor for the Prevention of Genocide and Edward Luck as his Special Adviser on the Responsibility to Protect (Ban 2007). Initially, the UNGA Fifth Committee, which deals with budget issues, was reluctant to fund the new office. Despite having a small staff, its work is important for developing R2P, especially its annual reports used in the Informal Interactive Dialogue on the Responsibility to Protect (Hofmann 2015: 29–30). In 2014, the office published a framework for detecting the risk of mass atrocities early on (UN 2014).

A sign of R2P's national implementation is the "R2P Focal Point Initiative" and the steadily growing number of R2P Focal Points: "a senior official within a government who facilitates mechanisms for atrocity prevention" (GCR2P 2016). These persons are intended to improve the capacity to prevent and respond to the threat or commission of atrocities and "integrate atrocity prevention within national policy" (Welsh 2014: 140). Focal points show that especially the second pillar of R2P "has become even more action-guiding" (Welsh 2019: 62). The R2P Focal Point Network was initiated in 2010 by Costa Rica, Denmark, Ghana, and the Global Centre for the Responsibility to Protect. Since then, the number of Focal Points has increased to more than 60 (GCR2P 2020). Meeting at least once a year, the Focal Point Network provides a platform for developing strategies and capacities to respond to atrocities at the regional and state levels, thereby implementing R2P from the bottom up (Serrano 2015: 90–91).

Ever more national, regional, and global mechanisms exist to prevent atrocities, such as the Atrocities Prevention Board (now the "Atrocity Early Warning Task Force") in the US (Welsh 2019: 62), the Latin American Network for Genocide and Mass Atrocity Prevention, and the Global Action against Mass Atrocity Crimes (Hofmann 2019: 358–60). All these initiatives, which include ever more state and non-state actors, are important for realizing R2P's normative aspiration, particularly its non-military dimension.

With respect to R2P's practical dimension, we conclude that *compliance* with R2P has been stable since 2005, even after the controversial Libya intervention in 2011, which some had seen as R2P's death knell. Yet, we must follow the incremental departure from R2P in UNSC practice and state reactions inside and outside the council. That said, R2P is increasingly being implemented nationally, regionally, and internationally.

3.4.2 Discourse: Stable concordance and negative reactions

We examine discourse about the responsibility to protect by looking at participation in the UNGA Informal Interactive Dialogue and R2P affirmations to assess norm concordance as well as negative reactions to norm violations in international debates.

The Informal Dialogue on the Responsibility to Protect, which began in 2010, has become the most important forum for discussing R2P and its development. The number of participating states and regional organizations rose steadily from 44 in 2010 to 85 in 2017. That indicates the perceived importance of, and concordance with, the norm. Following the UN 2005 World Summit, UNGA held just one official debate on R2P: In 2009, it opted to continue to study R2P within the framework of the annual Informal Dialogue. However, in September 2017, UNGA voted by 113 to 21 to place "The Responsibility to Protect and the prevention of genocide, war crimes, ethnic cleansing and crimes against humanity" on its formal agenda (GCR2P 2017) as several states and the Secretary-General were demanding (Ghana 2016; Brazil 2017; Canada 2017; Guterres 2017: 17). This broad international agreement is further evidence of widespread concordance with the norm (Welsh 2019: 62).

For a more comprehensive picture, we analyzed affirmations of R2P in our data (Figure 3.4). Except for the significant variation between 2007 and 2009 during the general debate on R2P in UNGA, most statements affirmed the international community's responsibility to protect. Surprisingly, fewer statements affirm the responsibility of the individual state. We find no clear decline in affirmations after the contentious application of R2P in Libya. Affirmations of the international community's responsibility only slightly slackened after 2009 (see also Scherzinger 2023: 91–93). This trend appears to continue beyond 2016, with generally positive statements regarding R2P in the UNSC (Scherzinger 2023: 88), indicating overall concordance with the norm.

International responses to R2P are often characterized as insufficient. Do states respond negatively to "norm violations"? Before 2011, it is difficult to identify a clear trend (see Figure 3.5). Especially since 2014, however, there has been a steep increase in statements on R2P that condemn both atrocities and international inaction in response to them. This can be attributed to the debates about the conflict in Syria. The UK, for example, criticized "[T]he collective response by the international community to the situation in Syria has been thwarted by a lack of consensus in the United Nations Security Council" and called on the UNSC "to shoulder their responsibility in

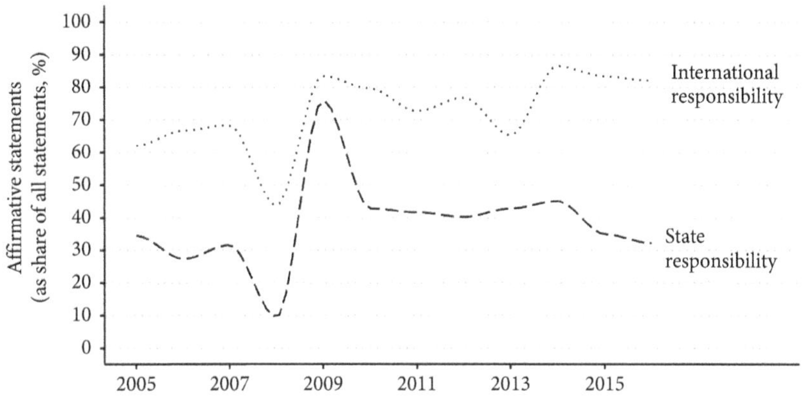

Figure 3.4 Affirmations of the responsibility to protect, 2005–16

Source: Based on 840 statements on the responsibility to protect in UN documents, the Informal Interactive Dialogue on Responsibility to Protect, and in newspapers.

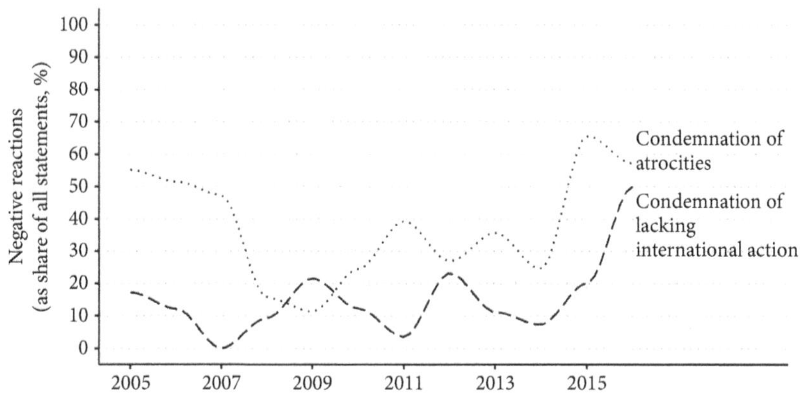

Figure 3.5 Negative reactions to violations of the responsibility to protect, 2005–16

Source: Based on 840 statements on the responsibility to protect in UN documents, the Informal Interactive Dialogue on Responsibility to Protect, and in newspapers.

taking the decisive action required to compel the Assad regime to cease the violence and engage in a political process" (UK Government 2012). These and similar statements indicate that even with spotty compliance, R2P helps states evaluate how the international community should protect at-risk civilians. It is worth noting that this kind of responses did not decline—and, in fact, even increased—after 2011 and the controversial Libya intervention. The consolidation of this tendency around 2016 leads us to conclude that negative reactions to norm violations did not decline during the period studied.

Based on these four dimensions of norm robustness (compliance, implementation, concordance, and negative reactions), we conclude that, at least between 2005 and 2016, the responsibility to protect remained robust. Even after the controversial Libya intervention, UNSC resolutions increasingly referred to R2P, which is a sign of growing compliance. This is also reflected in the military responses, which remain, however, the exception. Driven mainly by norm advocates, especially the UN Secretary-General but also by the Focal Points Network, R2P is increasingly being implemented regionally, nationally, and internationally. Besides positive trends in practice, norm concordance (mainly in norm affirmations and participation in the Interactive Dialogue) and negative reactions to norm violations (principally, the international community's inaction) remain stable. R2P is shaping how the UN and other actors respond to potential atrocities. However, recent developments indicate that the core claims of the norm have begun to change, which is also accompanied by a reduced willingness to use R2P in practice. Both trends could lead to a weakening of R2P's robustness.

3.5 Explanatory factors

We have seen that contestations of the responsibility to protect mainly target its application and rarely its validity, and the norm has generally remained stable. How have international law and norm clusters, the relative power of norm challengers, and R2P's institutionalization contributed to this? Neither legalization nor the relative power of norm challengers accounts for its robustness. Contestation remained largely applicatory due to the widespread perception that challenges were fairly addressed by institutional mechanisms and by its embeddedness in a complex norm cluster of human rights and sovereignty. That said, we observe a shift in R2P's core claims that is facilitated by its imprecision and embeddedness in a norm cluster.

R2P is not a legal norm. It also does not precisely lay out positive obligations. It does, however, delegate decisions to the UNSC regarding application and possible intervention (Section 3.2.1). Does R2P's non-legal character facilitate contestation because it lacks precision and delegation? Even without them, as we have shown, R2P's validity was rarely contested. States do not question *whether* there is a responsibility to protect but struggle about *how* to do that. The lack of precision seems to be a virtue, not a vice, because complexity and ambiguity create wiggle room for compromise (Staunton and Ralph 2020: 663; Staunton and Glanville 2022: 13–14). Unlike other norms, such as the duty to prosecute in Chapter 5, R2P's imprecision could create opportunities to discuss the norm. Despite not being legalized, contestation about R2P did not shift to validity and the norm did not become less robust.

R2P's embeddedness in a broader norm cluster has played a more decisive role in stabilizing the norm. R2P is anchored in several longstanding normative and legal principles—about sovereignty and non-interference, on one hand, and human rights protection and the notion that sovereigns are responsible to their subjects, on the other (Staunton and Glanville 2022: 4–6). This can create contestation when states use traditional understandings to oppose R2P. At the same time, however, R2P's embeddedness can shield it from validity contestation because a fundamental challenge to its underlying claim to protect civilians from atrocities impinges on the broader human rights cluster and international criminal law's commitment to prosecute such crimes (see Fehl 2019: 908–10). This embeddedness makes it difficult to replace R2P's core normative claims. As Staunton and Glanville (2022: 14) conclude: "[T]he notions that sovereign states and the international community have a responsibility to protect have lineages that go back far beyond 2001 and they are unlikely to disappear anytime soon." This lowest common denominator—whose application remains contested—has rarely been attacked in the debates we analyze.

However, R2P's ability to accommodate contestation (due to its imprecision) and mitigate it with the embedding norm cluster might have some drawbacks. With the Libya intervention and during debates about Syria, even states and civil society actors who supported R2P shifted the focus from military toward non-violent means, placing stronger emphasis on the norm's Pillars 1 and 2 (Hofmann and Suthanthiraraj 2019). This was driven by concerns about regime change in the course of R2P—like what happened in Libya. Has the shift from military intervention hollowed out R2P's normative core claims (Welsh 2019: 60–61)? Even after 2011, "[P]revention responsibilities have proven to be one of the few things that the international community has consistently agreed on" (Staunton and Glanville 2022: 13). In both the ICISS report and the WSOD, military intervention was seen as the last resort for stopping the most massive atrocities such as the Rwandan genocide. For the time being, there is broad consensus that the international community must assist states and react to atrocities. So far, R2P's core claims remain intact, but it is unclear how, and to what extent, R2P will be adapted—and perhaps weakened—in the coming years.

The relative power of contesting states was not a decisive factor. R2P has been challenged by many countries of the Global South at the "receiving end" of potential R2P interventions. Although militarily and economically less powerful than their Northern counterparts, they can also wield power—especially by joining forces in international fora such as the UN and acting through alliances like the NAM. Some of R2P's most constant critics, including Russia and China, are among the most powerful in the international system. Yet, the effect of their contestations is not clear. They were unable to rally enough states behind their cause to shift the discourse against R2P, which is one reason why the norm has remained robust. The US and other major Western states could not convince Russia and China to permit R2P missions in Syria. Following the Libya intervention, when Western states successfully secured support for R2P (Adler-Nissen and Pouliot 2014), the Syrian case can be seen as a backlash against alleged misuse of R2P and power politics before Libya (Ralph and Gifkins 2016). The latter clearly impact R2P effectiveness in specific cases such as the civil war in Syria. As we have argued, this does not imply the norm's general weakening because it remained at least stable in all four dimensions of robustness. Overall, the power of norm challengers did not directly affect R2P contestations and strength.

Having an institutional mechanism that is perceived as fair to deal with challenges to the norm helped restrict contestations to the level of application. The main debates about R2P's role in the UN take place in the Informal Interactive Dialogue on the Responsibility to Protect and the UNSC. The interactive dialogue is a space for debating fundamental issues about R2P, where every state has equal access and voice. The Informal Dialogue is based on the Secretary-General's annual "Report on R2P." Various UN agencies and civil society actors are also attempting to mainstream R2P by introducing the norm to very different and broad topics and in different agencies (see Bellamy 2013a; Ralph 2014; Hofmann and Suthanthiraraj 2019).

Addressing R2P in a fair institutional framework seems to help resolve disputes about its application and has helped prevent contestation becoming radicalized (see also Dembinski 2016). The Interactive Dialogue provides an important corrective to UNSC power politics, deadlock, and inertia. It permits interpretation and reinterpretation based on state concerns reflected in efforts to institutionalize and reform the norm: The refocus on prevention is reflected in Brazil's concept of "Responsibility while Protecting" (see Tourinho et al. 2016) and the UN's "Human Rights up Front" action plan, a reform process that aims to strengthen human rights throughout the UN system (see Hofmann 2019: 356–57). No major frustration regarding challenges was expressed in the Interactive Dialogue, which we think contributes to the fact that few states have contested R2P's validity.

The perception of procedural fairness and acknowledgment that criticism is justified with respect to R2P stands in stark contrast to our findings in the whaling moratorium (see Chapter 4) and the duty to prosecute (see Chapter 5) case studies, in which the International Whaling Commission and the ICC have spurred frustration about what are often perceived as hierarchical and inaccessible institutions that do prevent genuine dialogue. States' recognition that their claims are taken up in R2P debates at the UN has helped prevent the radicalization and spread of contestation. However, this accommodative approach, along with the norm's ambiguity, as discussed, has created room for norm change that could alter R2P's core normative claims and affect its robustness.

3.6 Conclusion

The responsibility to protect has been contested since Kofi Annan coined the notion of "sovereignty as responsibility" in 1999. Disputes continued after R2P was adopted in the 2005 WSOD. Yet, it has remained robust and has become an ever more frequent point of reference in UNSC practice; military missions to protect have not declined. States regularly affirm the norm and criticize insufficient international responses to atrocities. This is mainly due to the predominance of applicatory contestation—both before and after the intervention in Libya. We have found that R2P has remained robust despite challenges because of the norm's ambiguity and embeddedness in a complex cluster of human rights norms and sovereignty that accommodates contestation. This was facilitated by the UN Interactive Dialogue, While some scholars maintain that R2P's reinterpretation toward non-military means has already altered its core claims and made it toothless, we argue that the norm's critical claim to protect from mass atrocities is so far being upheld. However, R2P could be reinterpreted—and change our findings on norm robustness.

Reference list

Adler-Nissen, Rebecca, and Vincent Pouliot. 2014. "Power in Practice: Negotiating the International Intervention in Libya." *European Journal of International Relations* 20 (4): pp. 889–911. doi: 10.1177/1354066113512702.

Allison, Roy. 2008. "Russia Resurgent? Moscow's Campaign to 'Coerce Georgia to Peace'." *International Affairs* 84 (6): pp. 1145–71. doi: 10.1111/j.1468-2346.2008.00762.x.

Annan, Kofi. 1999. "Two Concepts of Sovereignty." The Economist, September 18.

Annan, Kofi. 2000. *We the Peoples: The Role of the United Nations in the 21st Century.* New York: United Nations.

Badescu, Cristina G., and Linnea Bergholm. 2009. "The Responsibility to Protect and the Conflict in Darfur: The Big Let-Down." *Security Dialogue* 40 (3): pp. 287–309. doi: 10.1177/0967010609336198.

Badescu, Cristina G., and Thomas G. Weiss. 2010. "Misrepresenting R2P and Advancing Norms: An Alternative Spiral?" *International Studies Perspectives* 11 (4): pp. 354–74. doi: 10.1111/j.1528-3585.2010.00412.x.

Ban, Ki-moon. 2007. "Letter Dated 31 August 2007 from the Secretary-General Addressed to the President of the Security Council." UN Doc. S/2007/721 (August 31, 2007).

Ban, Ki-moon. 2009. "Implementing the Responsibility to Protect: Report of the Secretary-General." UN Doc. A/63/677 (January 12).

BBC. 2008. "Interview by Minister of Foreign Affairs of the Russian Federation Sergey Lavrov." BBC. August 9. Accessed January 7, 2023. http://www.mid.ru/brp_4.nsf/0/F87A3FB7A7F669EBC32574A100262597.

Bellamy, Alex J. 2006. "Whither the Responsibility to Protect? Humanitarian Intervention and the 2005 World Summit." *Ethics & International Affairs* 20 (2): pp. 143–69. doi: 10.1111/j.1747-7093.2006.00012.

Bellamy, Alex J. 2008. "The Responsibility to Protect and the Problem of Military Intervention." *International Affairs* 84 (4): pp. 615–39. doi: 10.1111/j.1468-2346.2008.00729.x.

Bellamy, Alex J. 2009a. "Realizing the Responsibility to Protect." *International Studies Perspectives* 10 (2): pp. 111–28. doi: 10.1111/j.1528-3585.2009.00365.x.

Bellamy, Alex J. 2009b. *Responsibility to Protect: The Global Effort to End Mass Atrocities.* Malden: Polity Press.

Bellamy, Alex J. 2010. "Responsibility to Protect: Five Years On." *Ethics & International Affairs* 24 (2): pp. 143–69. doi: 10.1111/j.1747-7093.2010.00254.x.

Bellamy, Alex J. 2011. *Global Politics and the Responsibility to Protect: From Words to Deeds.* New York: Routledge.

Bellamy, Alex J. 2013a. "Mainstreaming the Responsibility to Protect in the United Nations System: Dilemmas, Challenges and Opportunities." *Global Responsibility to Protect* 5 (2): pp. 154–91. doi: 10.1163/1875984X-00502003.

Bellamy, Alex J. 2013b. "The Responsibility to Protect: Added Value or Hot Air?" *Cooperation and Conflict* 48 (3): pp. 333–57. doi: 10.1177/0010836713482448.

Bellamy, Alex J. 2015. "The Responsibility to Protect Turns Ten." *Ethics & International Affairs* 29 (2): pp. 161–85. doi: 10.1017/S0892679415000052.

Bellamy, Alex J., and Catherine Drummond. 2011. "The Responsibility to Protect in Southeast Asia: Between Non-Interference and Sovereignty as Responsibility." *Pacific Review* 24 (2): pp. 179–200. doi: 10.1080/09512748.2011.560958.

Brazil. 2017. "Statement Delivered by the Government of Brazil during the September 2017 United Nations General Assembly Informal Interactive Dialogue on the Responsibility to Protect." September 6. Accessed January 7, 2023. https://www.globalr2p.org/resources/statement-by-brazil-at-the-2017-un-general-assembly-informal-interactive-dialogue-on-the-responsibility-to-protect.

Brockmeier, Sarah, Oliver Stuenkel, and Marcos Tourinho. 2016. "The Impact of the Libya Intervention Debates on Norms of Protection." *Global Society* 30 (1): pp. 113–33. doi: 10.1080/13600826.2015.1094029.

Byers, Michael. 2015. "International Law and the Responsibility to Protect." In *Theorising the Responsibility to Protect*, ed. Ramesh Thakur. Cambridge: Cambridge University Press, pp. 101–24.

Canada. 2017. "Statement by Canada at the 2017 UN General Assembly Informal Interactive Dialogue on the Responsibility to Protect." September 6. Accessed January 7, 2023. https://www.globalr2p.org/resources/statement-by-canada-at-the-2017-un-general-assembly-informal-interactive-dialogue-on-the-responsibility-to-protect.

Costa Rica. 2010. "Statement Delivered by the Government of Costa Rica during the August 2010 United Nations General Assembly Informal Interactive Dialogue on the Responsibility to Protect." September 5. Accessed January 7, 2023. https://www.globalr2p.org/resources/statement-by-costa-rica-at-the-2012-un-general-assembly-informal-interactive-dialogue-on-the-responsibility-to-protect.

Crossley, Noële. 2013. "A Model Case of R2P Prevention? Mediation in the Aftermath of Kenya's 2007 Presidential Elections." *Global Responsibility to Protect* 5 (2): pp. 192–214. doi: 10.1163/1875984X-00502004.

Crossley, Noële. 2016. *Evaluating the Responsibility to Protect: Mass Atrocity Prevention as a Consolidating Norm in International Society*. Abingdon: Routledge.

Cuba. 2011. "Statement by Cuba at the July 2011 UN General Assembly Informal Interactive Dialogue on the Responsibility to Protect." July 12. Accessed January 7, 2023. https://www.globalr2p.org/resources/statement-by-cuba-at-the-2011-un-general-assembly-informal-interactive-dialogue-on-the-responsibility-to-protect.

Daase, Christopher. 2015. "Legalizing Legitimacy: A Critique of the Responsibility to Protect as an Emerging Norm." *Telos* 2015 (170): pp. 67–87. doi: 10.3817/0315170067.

Deitelhoff, Nicole. 2019. "Is the R2P Failing? The Controversy about Norm Justification and Norm Application of the Responsibility to Protect." *Global Responsibility to Protect* 11 (2): pp. 149–71. doi: 10.1163/1875984X-01102003.

Deitelhoff, Nicole, and Lisbeth Zimmermann. 2020. "Things We Lost in the Fire: How Different Types of Contestation Affect the Robustness of International Norms." *International Studies Review* 22 (1): pp. 51–76. doi: 10.1093/isr/viy080.

Dembinski, Matthias. 2016. "Procedural Justice and Global Order: Explaining African Reaction to the Application of Global Protection Norms." *European Journal of International Relations* 23 (4): pp. 809–32. doi: 10.1177/1354066116681059.

Dembinski, Matthias, and Densua Mumford. 2012. "Die Schutzverantwortung nach Libyen: Ohne Einbeziehung der Regionalen Sicherheitsorganisationen wird diese wichtige Norm scheitern." HSFK Standpunkte 4/2012. Hessische Stiftung Friedens- und Konfliktforschung.

Deng, Francis M., Sadikiel Kimaro, Terrence Lyons, Donald Rothchild, and Ira W. Zartman. 1996. *Sovereignty as Responsibility: Conflict Management in Africa.* Washington, DC: Brookings Institution.

Eck, Kristine, and Lisa Hultman. 2007. "One-Sided Violence against Civilians in War." *Journal of Peace Research* 44 (2): pp. 233–46. doi: 10.1177/0022343307075124.

Ecuador. 2013. "Statement by Ecuador at the 2013 UN General Assembly Informal Interactive Dialogue on the Responsibility to Protect." September 11. Accessed January 7, 2023. https://www.globalr2p.org/resources/statement-by-ecuador-at-the-2013-un-general-assembly-informal-interactive-dialogue-on-the-responsibility-to-protect.

Evans, Gareth. 2006. "From Humanitarian Intervention to R2P." *Wisconsin International Law Journal* 24 (3): pp. 703–22.

Evans, Gareth. 2008. "The Responsibility to Protect: An Idea Whose Time Has Come . . . And Gone?" *International Relations* 22 (3): pp. 283–98. doi: 10.1177/0047117808094173.

Evans, Gareth. 2009. "Russia, Georgia and the Responsibility to Protect." *Amsterdam Law Forum* 1 (2): pp. 25–28.

Fehl, Caroline. 2019. "Bombs, Trials, and Rights: Norm Complexity and the Evolution of Liberal Intervention Practices." *Human Rights Quarterly* 41 (4): pp. 893–915. doi: 10.1353/hrq.2019.0066.

Gallagher, Adrian. 2015. "The Responsibility to Protect Ten Years on from the World Summit: A Call to Manage Expectations." *Global Responsibility to Protect* 7 (3–4): pp. 254–74. doi: 10.1163/1875984X-00704003.

GCR2P (Global Centre for the Responsibility to Protect). 2016. "Global Network of R2P Focal Points." Accessed January 20, 2019. https://www.globalr2p.org/the-global-network-of-r2p-focal-points.

GCR2P. 2017. "Statement on the Inclusion of the Responsibility to Protect on the Formal Agenda of the 72nd Session of the UN General Assembly." Global Centre for the Responsibility to Protect, Statement. September 15. Accessed January

7, 2023. https://www.globalr2p.org/publications/statement-on-the-inclusion-of-the-responsibility-to-protect-on-the-formal-agenda-of-the-72nd-session-of-the-un-general-assembly.

GCR2P. 2020. "Members of the Global Network of R2P Focal Points." Global Centre for the Responsibility to Protect, Signatory List. November 8. Accessed January 7, 2023. https://www.globalr2p.org/resources/members-of-the-global-network-of-r2p-focal-points.

GCR2P. 2022. "R2P References in United Nations Security Council Resolutions and Presidential Statements." Global Centre for the Responsibility to Protect, List of Resolutions. June 2. Accessed January 7, 2023. https://www.globalr2p.org/wp-content/uploads/2022/04/UNSC-R2P-Resolutions-2-June-2022.pdf.

Ghana. 2016. "Statement by Ghana at the 2016 UN General Assembly Informal Interactive Dialogue on the Responsibility to Protect." September 6. Accessed January 7, 2023. https://www.globalr2p.org/resources/statement-by-ghana-at-the-2016-un-general-assembly-informal-interactive-dialogue-on-the-responsibility-to-protect.

Gifkins, Jess. 2016. "R2P in the UN Security Council: Darfur, Libya and Beyond." *Cooperation and Conflict* 51 (2): pp. 148–65. doi: 10.1177/0010836715613365.

Gromes, Thorsten, and Matthias Dembinski. 2019. "Practices and Outcomes of Humanitarian Military Interventions: A New Data Set." *International Interactions* 45 (6): pp. 1032–48. doi: 10.1080/03050629.2019.1638374.

Guterres, António. 2017. "Implementing the Responsibility to Protect: Accountability for Prevention." UN Doc. S/2017/556 (August 10).

Haacke, Jürgen. 2009. "Myanmar, the Responsibility to Protect, and the Need for Practical Assistance." *Global Responsibility to Protect* 1 (2): pp. 156–84. doi: 10.1163/187598409X424289.

Hehir, Aidan. 2019. *Hollow Norms and the Responsibility to Protect*. Cham: Palgrave Macmillan.

High Level Panel on Threats, Challenges and Change. 2004. *A More Secure World: Our Shared Responsibility*. New York: United Nations.

Hofmann, Gregor P. 2015. "Ten Years R2P: What Doesn't Kill a Norm Only Makes It Stronger? Contestation, Application and Institutionalization of International Atrocity Prevention and Response." PRIF Report no. 133. Peace Research Institute Frankfurt.

Hofmann, Gregor P. 2019. *Gerechtigkeitskonflikte und Normentwicklung: Die internationale Umstrittenheit der Responsibility to Protect*. Wiesbaden: Springer.

Hofmann, Gregor P., and Kavitha Suthanthiraraj. 2019. "Norm Contestation and Norm Adaptation: R2P's Reframing over Time." *Global Responsibility to Protect* 11 (2): pp. 226–53. doi: 10.1163/1875984X-01102006.

Höhn, Sabine. 2014. "New Start or False Start? The ICC and Electoral Violence in Kenya." *Development and Change* 45 (3): pp. 565–88. doi: 10.1111/dech.12087.

ICISS (International Commission on Intervention and State Sovereignty). 2001. "The Responsibility to Protect: Report of the International Commission on Intervention and State Sovereignty." Ottawa: International Development Research Centre.

IIFFMCG (Independent International Fact-Finding Mission on the Conflict in Georgia). 2009. "Independent International Fact-Finding Mission on the Conflict in Georgia: Report, Volume I." September. Accessed September 12, 2022. https://www.mpil.de/files/pdf4/IIFFMCG_Volume_I2.pdf.

Junk, Julian. 2016. "Bringing the Non-coercive Dimensions of R2P to the Fore: The Case of Kenya." *Global Society* 30 (1): pp. 54–66. doi: 10.1080/13600826.2015.1092422.

League of Arab States. 2011. "Letter Dated 14 March 2011 from the Permanent Observer of the League of Arab States to the United Nations Addressed to the President of the Security Council." UN Doc. S /2011/137 (March 14).

Lu, Catherine. 2006. *Just and Unjust Interventions in World Politics: Public and Private*. Basingstoke: Palgrave Macmillan.

Luck, Edward C. 2012a. "From Promise to Practice: Implementing the Responsibility to Protect." In *The Responsibility to Protect: The Promise of Stopping Mass Atrocities in Our Time*, ed. Jared Genser and Irwin Cotler. Oxford: Oxford University Press, pp. 85–106.

Luck, Edward C. 2012b. "The Responsibility to Protect: The Journey." In *Responsibility to Protect: From Principle to Practice*, edited by Julia Hoffmann and André Nollkaemper, pp. 39–46. Amsterdam: Amsterdam University Press.

Matthews, Max W. 2008. "Tracking the Emergence of a New International Norm: The Responsibility to Protect and the Crisis in Darfur." *Boston College International & Comparative Law Review* 31 (1): pp. 137–52.

Molier, Gelijn. 2006. "Humanitarian Intervention and the Responsibility to Protect after 9/11." *Netherlands International Law Review* 53 (1): pp. 37–62. doi: 10.1017/S0165070X06000374.

Murthy, C.S.R., and Gerrit Kurtz. 2016. "International Responsibility as Solidarity: The Impact of the World Summit Negotiations on the R2P Trajectory." *Global Society* 30 (1): pp. 38–53. doi: 10.1080/13600826.2015.1094451.

Nuruzzaman, Mohammed. 2013. "The 'Responsibility to Protect' Doctrine: Revived in Libya, Buried in Syria." *Insight Turkey* 15 (2): pp. 57–66.

OHCHR (Office of the High Commissioner for Human Rights). 2021. "Oral Update on the Extent of Conflict-Related Deaths in the Syrian Arab Republic: Background Note on the Statistical Analysis." Office of the High Commissioner of Human Rights. September 24. Accessed January 7, 2023. https://www.ohchr.org/sites/default/files/Documents/Countries/SY/BackgroundTechnicalNote_Syria.pdf.

Pakistan. 2012. "Statement Delivered by the Government of Pakistan during the September 2012 United Nations General Assembly Informal Interactive Dialogue on the Responsibility to Protect." September 5. Accessed January 7, 2023. https://www.globalr2p.org/resources/statement-by-pakistan-at-the-2012-un-general-assembly-informal-interactive-dialogue-on-the-responsibility-to-protect.

Pettersson, Therése, and Kristine Eck. 2018. "Organized Violence, 1989–2017." *Journal of Peace Research* 55 (4): pp. 535–47. doi: 10.1177/0022343318784101.

Pettersson, Therése, Shawn Davies, Amber Deniz, Garoun Engström, Nanar Hawach, Stina Högbladh, and Margareta Sollenberg Magnus Öberg. 2021. "Organized Violence 1989–2020, with a Special Emphasis on Syria." *Journal of Peace Research* 58 (4): pp. 809–25. doi: 10.1177/00223433211026126.

Phillips, Christopher. 2016. *The Battle for Syria: International Rivalry in the New Middle East*. New Haven, CT: Yale University Press.

Price, Richard. 2019. "Syria and the Chemical Weapons Taboo." *Journal of Global Security Studies* 4 (1): pp. 37–52. doi: 10.1093/jogss/ogy040.

Ralph, Jason G. 2014. "Mainstreaming the Responsibility to Protect in UK Strategy." UNA–UK Briefing Report no. 2. United Nations Association—UK.

Ralph, Jason G. 2018. "What Should Be Done? Pragmatic Constructivist Ethics and the Responsibility to Protect." *International Organization* 72 (1): pp. 173–203. doi: 10.1017/S0020818317000455.

Ralph, Jason G., and Jess Gifkins. 2016. "The Purpose of United Nations Security Council Practice: Contesting Competence Claims in the Normative Context Created by the Responsibility to Protect." *European Journal of International Relations* 23 (3): pp. 630–53. doi: 10.1177/1354066116669652.

Reinold, Theresa. 2010. "The Responsibility to Protect—Much Ado About Nothing?" *Review of International Studies* 36 (S1): pp. 55–78. doi: 10.1017/S0260210510000446.

Rieff, David. 2011. "R2P, R.I.P." New York Times, November 7. Accessed January 7, 2023. http://www.nytimes.com/2011/11/08/opinion/r2p-rip.html?_r=0.

Rotmann, Philipp, Gerrit Kurtz, and Sarah Brockmeier. 2014. "Major Powers and the Contested Evolution of a Responsibility to Protect." *Conflict, Security & Development* 14 (4): pp. 355–77. doi: 10.1080/14678802.2014.930592.

Scherzinger, Johannes. 2022. "'Acting under Chapter 7': Rhetorical Entrapment, Rhetorical Hollowing, and the Authorization of Force in the UN Security Council, 1995–2017." *International Relations*, online first: 1–22. doi: 10.1177/00471178221082870.

Scherzinger, Johannes. 2023. "Unbowed, Unbent, Unbroken? Examining the Validity of the Responsibility to Protect." *Cooperation and Conflict* 58 (1): pp. 81–101. doi: 10.1177/00108367221093155.

Security Council Report. 2008. "Update Report No. 4: Myanmar." Security Council Report, Update Report, May 14. Accessed January 7, 2023. https://www.securitycouncilreport.org/update-report/lookup_c_glkwlemtisg_b_4130257.php.

Security Council Report. 2011a. "Update Report No. 1: Libya." Security Council Report, Update Report. March 14. Accessed January 7, 2023. https://www.securitycouncilreport.org/update-report/lookup_c_glkwlemtisg_b_6621881.php.

Security Council Report. 2011b. "Update Report No. 3: Libya." Security Council Report, Updated Report. February 25. Accessed January 7, 2023. https://www.securitycouncilreport.org/update-report/lookup_c_glkwlemtisg_b_6586331.php.

Serrano, Mónica. 2011. "The Responsibility to Protect and Its Critics: Explaining the Consensus." *Global Responsibility to Protect* 4 (3): pp. 425–37. doi: 10.1163/187598411X602017.

Serrano, Mónica. 2015. "National Focal Points for R2P: Institutionalizing the Responsibility to Protect." In *The Responsibility to Prevent. Overcoming the Challenges of Atrocity Prevention*, ed. Serena K. Sharma and Jennifer M. Welsh. Oxford: Oxford University Press, pp. 83–101.

Sharma, Serena K. 2012. "The 2007–08 Post-Election Crisis in Kenya: A Success Story for the Responsibility to Protect?" In *Responsibility to Protect: From Principle to Practice*, edited by Julia Hoffmann and André Nollkaemper, pp. 27–38. Amsterdam: Amsterdam University Press.

Sharma, Serena K. 2015. "The 2007–8 Post-Election Crisis in Kenya: A Case of Escalation Prevention." In *The Responsibility to Prevent: Overcoming the Challenges of Atrocity Prevention*, edited by Serena K. Sharma and Jennifer M. Welsh, pp. 280–303. Oxford: Oxford University Press.

SOHR (Syrian Observatory for Human Rights). 2022. "Syrian Revolution 11 Years On: SOHR Documents by Names Nearly 161,000 Civilian Deaths, Including 40,500 Children and Women." Syrian Observatory for Human Rights. March 15. Accessed January 7, 2023. https://www.syriahr.com/en/243125.

Stahn, Carsten. 2007. "Responsibility to Protect: Political Rhetoric or Emerging Legal Norm?" *American Journal of International Law* 101 (1): pp. 99–120. doi: 10.1017/S0002930000029559.

Staunton, Eglantine, and Luke Glanville. 2022. "Selling the Responsibility to Protect: The False Novelty But Real Impact of a Norm." *International Studies Review* 24 (3): pp. 1–18. doi: 10.1093/isr/viac014.

Staunton, Eglantine, and Jason G. Ralph. 2020. "The Responsibility to Protect Norm Cluster and the Challenge of Atrocity Prevention: An Analysis of the European Union's Strategy in Myanmar." *European Journal of International Relations* 26 (3): 660–86. doi: 10.1177/1354066119883001.

Steinberg, Donald. 2009. "Responsibility to Protect: Coming of Age?" *Global Responsibility to Protect* 1 (4): pp. 432–41.

Telegraph. 2011. "Libya: Celebrations in Benghazi as UN Backs No-Fly Zone." The Telegraph, March 18. Accessed January 7, 2023. https://www.telegraph.co.uk/news/worldnews/africaandindianocean/libya/8389639/Libya-celebrations-in-Benghazi-as-UN-backs-no-fly-zone.html.

Thakur, Ramesh, ed. 2016. *Theorising the Responsibility to Protect*. Cambridge: Cambridge University Press.

Tiewa, Liu. 2012. "China and Responsibility to Protect: Maintenance and Change of Its Policy for Intervention." *Pacific Review* 25 (1): pp. 153–73. doi: 10.1080/09512748.2011.632978.

Tourinho, Marcos, Oliver Stuenkel, and Sarah Brockmeier. 2016. "'Responsibility While Protecting': Reforming R2P Implementation." *Global Society* 30 (1): pp. 134–50. doi: 10.1080/13600826.2015.1094452.

UK Government. 2012. "Statement by the United Kingdom at the 2012 UN General Assembly Informal Interactive Dialogue on the Responsibility to Protect." September 5. Accessed January 7, 2023. https://www.globalr2p.org/resources/statement-by-the-united-kingdom-at-the-2012-un-general-assembly-informal-interactive-dialogue-on-the-responsibility-to-protect.

Ulfstein, Geir, and Hege Føsund Christiansen. 2013. "The Legality of the NATO Bombing in Libya." *International & Comparative Law Quarterly* 62 (1): pp. 159–71. doi: 10.1017/S0020589312000565.

UN (United Nations). 2007. "Secretary-General Concerned by Kenya Violence Following Election Results: Appeals for Calm, Patience, Respect for Law." UN Press Release SG/SM/11354-AFR/1639 (December 31).

UN. 2008. "Secretary-General Troubled by Escalating Kenyan Tensions, Violence." UN Press Release SG/SM/11356-AFR/1641 (January 2).

UN. 2011a. "General Assembly Suspends Libya from Human Rights Council." UN Press Release GA/11050 (March 1).

UN. 2011b. "Security Council Fails to Adopt Draft Resolution Condemning Syria's Crackdown on Anti-Government Protestors, Owing to Veto by Russian Federation, China, Security Council Meeting Coverage." UN Press Release SC/10403 (October 4).

UN. 2011c. "Security Council Press Statement on Libya." UN Press Release SC/10180-AFR/2120 (February 22).

UN. 2011d. "Security Council, in Statement, Condemns Syrian Authorities for 'Widespread Violations of Human Rights, Use of Force against Civilians.'" UN Press Release SC/10352 (August 3).

UN. 2014. *Framework of Analysis for Atrocity Crimes: A Tool for Prevention*. New York: United Nations.

UNGA (United Nations General Assembly). 1950. "UNGA Resolution 377 (V): Uniting for Peace." UN Doc. A/1775 at 10 (November 3).

UNGA. 2005. "2005 World Summit Outcome." UN Doc. A/60/L.1 (September 20, 2005).

UNGA. 2009a. "UN GAOR: 63rd Session, 76th Plenary Meeting." UN Doc. A/63/PV.76 (March 2).

UNGA. 2009b. "UN GAOR: 63rd Session, 98th Plenary Meeting." UN Doc. A/63/PV.98 (July 24).

UNGA. 2009c. "UN GAOR: 63rd Session, 100th Plenary Meeting." UN Doc. A/63/PV.100 (July 28).

UNGA. 2009d. "UN GAOR: 63rd Session, 101st Plenary Meeting." UN Doc. A/63/PV.101 (July 28).

UNHRC (United Nations Human Rights Council). 2022. "Report of the United Nations High Commissioner for Human Rights: Civilian Deaths in the Syrian Arab Republic." UN Doc. A/HRC/50/68 (June 28).

UN News Centre. 2011. "Ban Strongly Condemns Qadhafi's Actions against Protesters, Calls for Punishment." UN News Centre. February 23. Accessed January 7, 2023. https://news.un.org/en/story/2011/02/367342-ban-strongly-condemns-qadhafis-actions-against-protesters-calls-punishment.

UNSC (United Nations Security Council). 2005. "UN SCOR: 60th Session, 5319th Meeting." UN Doc. S/PV.5319 (December 9).

UNSC. 2006. "UNSC Resolution 1706." UN Doc. S/RES/1706 (August 31, 2006).

UNSC. 2007. "UN SCOR: 62nd Session, 5655th Meeting." UN Doc. S/PV.5655 (April 4).

UNSC. 2011a. "UNSC Resolution 1970." UN Doc. S/RES/1970 (February 26).

UNSC. 2011b. "UNSC Resolution 1973." UN Doc. S/RES/1973 (March 17).

UNSC. 2012. "UN SCOR: 67th Session, 6710th Meeting." UN Doc. S/PV.6710 (January 31).

UNSC. 2014a. "UNSC Resolution 2139." UN Doc. S/RES/2139 (February 22).

UNSC. 2014b. "UNSC Resolution 2165." UN Doc. S/RES/2165 (July 14).

UNSC. 2014c. "UNSC Resolution 2191." UN Doc. S/RES/2191 (December 17).

UNSC. 2015. "UN SCOR: 70th Session, 7419th Meeting." UN Doc. S/PV.7419 (March 27).

Venezuela. 2016. "Statement Delivered by the Government of Venezuela during the September 2016 United Nations General Assembly Informal Interactive Dialogue on the Responsibility." September 6. Accessed January 7, 2023. https://www.globalr2p.org/resources/statement-by-venezuela-at-the-2016-un-general-assembly-informal-interactive-dialogue-on-the-responsibility-to-protect.

Waal, Alex de. 2007. "Darfur and the Failure of the Responsibility to Protect." *International Affairs* 83 (6): pp. 1039–54. doi: 10.1111/j.1468-2346.2007.00672.x.

Weiss, Thomas G. 2006. "R2P After 9/11 and the World Summit." *Wisconsin International Law Journal* 24 (3): 741–60.

Weiss, Thomas G. 2016. *Humanitarian Intervention: Ideas in Action*. 3rd edn. Cambridge: Polity.

Welsh, Jennifer M. 2013. "Norm Contestation and the Responsibility to Protect." *Global Responsibility to Protect* 5 (4): pp. 365–96. doi: 10.1163/1875984X-00504002.

Welsh, Jennifer M. 2014. "Implementing the 'Responsibility to Protect.'" In *Implementation and World Politics: How International Norms Change Practice*, ed. Alexander Betts and Phil Orchard. Oxford: Oxford University Press, pp. 125–43.

Welsh, Jennifer M. 2019. "Norm Robustness and the Responsibility to Protect." *Journal of Global Security Studies* 4 (1): pp. 53–72. doi: 10.1093/jogss/ogy045.

Welsh, Jennifer M., and Maria Banda. 2010. "International Law and the Responsibility to Protect: Clarifying or Expanding States' Responsibilities?" *Global Responsibility to Protect* 2 (3): pp. 213–31. doi: 10.1163/187598410X500363.

Williams, Paul D., and Alex J. Bellamy. 2005. "The Responsibility to Protect and the Crisis in Darfur." *Security Dialogue* 36 (1): pp. 27–47. doi: 10.1177/0967010605051922.

4

Contesting the international moratorium on commercial whaling

A norm weakens at the international level

4.1 Introduction

The anti-whaling movement saw its heyday in the 1970s and 1980s, when conservation groups around the world rallied to "*Save the whales!*" Whaling activities still cause outrage and attract enormous media attention. In 2014, German newspapers reported that customs officials confiscated whale-meat snacks for sale at a Norwegian stall in a trade fair in Berlin, with the case referred to city prosecutors (Oltermann 2014). Whaling by indigenous peoples regularly garners coverage and creates conflict in cases like that of the Makah tribe in the Pacific Northwest of the United States (US), who, for decades, have fought for the right to hunt gray whales off their coast (Ager 2019). A 2017–18 Japanese whale hunt justified by special research permits also sparked indignation, with the *Sydney Morning Herald* running an article titled "Japan Slaughtered 122 Pregnant Whales to Prove They Were Fertile" (Hasham 2018). But instead of changing their behavior, pro-whaling states contested the ban more. Has the norm regarding the ban on commercial whaling remained stable or been weakened over time? This chapter analyzes the effects of contestation around a moratorium temporarily prohibiting commercial whaling in the 1980s that has remained in place and is now regarded by many as a commercial whaling "ban."

We show that in the International Whaling Commission (IWC), the primary negotiating forum for pro- and anti-whaling states, validity contestation of the ban has increased and applicatory contestation regarding several key issues has become permanent. In the 2000s, the commercial whaling ban lost considerable strength and barely recouped over the next decade. Neither the role of law nor the relative power of norm challengers affected trends in contestation and robustness. Instead, it was the IWC's institutional structure—which includes super-majority rules but no

International Norm Disputes. Lisbeth Zimmermann et al., Oxford University Press. © Lisbeth Zimmermann, Nicole Deitelhoff, Max Lesch, Antonio Arcudi, and Anton Peez (2023). DOI: 10.1093/oso/9780198873235.003.0004

adjudication process—that caused norm challengers to view channels of normative change as blocked. Anti-whaling states and non-governmental organizations (NGOs) also adopted informal sanctions, which "radicalized" contestations by norm challengers and weakened the norm. The perception that institutions were unfair shaped contestation types and robustness trends.

This chapter outlines the whaling norm and related contestation. Section 4.2 provides historical background and describes the evolution of the norm, its core claims, and the IWC structure, along with the sources and methods used for data collection and analysis. Section 4.3 defines and analyzes contestation and Section 4.4 robustness trends. Validity contestation became more prevalent and applicatory contestation permanent—and the norm was weakened. Section 4.5 discusses the explanatory factors, particularly perceptions of procedural fairness.

4.2 Commercial whaling moratorium: History and data

4.2.1 Norm evolution

Commercial whaling was a common practice that inspired no moral discussion until the second half of the twentieth century. European countries and the US had started hunting whales for monetary gain in industrial fashion in the seventeenth century. Then, in the 1930s, the first international conventions were signed to improve the inter-state management of whaling. The industrial-scale harvesting of whale oil and whale meat continued—so many stocks were quickly exhausted (see also Bailey 2008: 294).

The IWC was established under the International Convention for the Regulation of Whaling (ICRW) (ICRW 1946), which was signed by 14 states[1] in 1946 and took effect in 1948 (Norway joined in 1960). The ICRW's Preamble states that it aims to ensure "the proper conservation of whale stocks" and "the orderly development of the whaling industry." However, the convention only covers the management of great baleen and toothed whales and member states also disagree about whether the IWC's mandate applies to small cetaceans such as smaller whale species and dolphins.

[1] Argentina, Australia, Brazil, Canada, Chile, Denmark, France, the Netherlands, New Zealand, Peru, the USSR, the United Kingdom (UK), the US, and South Africa.

For decades, whaling industry interests in the IWC prevailed over science with respect to sustainable catch limits. The industrial exploitation of whales caused its demise: IWC catch quotas were too high and lacked monitoring and enforcement mechanisms, as well as sound scientific models to reliably study whale populations and their development (Peterson 2019). Many whale species became critically endangered. With whale stocks depleted, the profitability of most large-scale Antarctic whaling declined (Bailey 2008: 295). The declining profitability was hastened by technological developments in the first half of the twentieth century that eliminated the need for whale blubber, the main object of Western industrial whaling.[2]

Then, in the 1970s, a transnational movement of environmental and animal rights groups, among them British and US animal welfare organizations, rapidly changed the West's perception of whales, which came to be seen as a species deserving special protection. The first groups included the Universities Federation for Animal Welfare and the World Federation for the Protection of Animals; Friends of the Earth, the World Wildlife Fund, and Greenpeace later joined the protest. They sought to make wildlife preservation the IWC's guiding norm. Internationally successful campaigns focused on the scientific uncertainty around whale stocks and the dangerous influence of commercial interests within the IWC; the intelligence, longevity, and humanity of whales; and the cruelty of whale-hunting practices.[3] These activities led to a change in US policy: from supporting whaling to supporting a whaling ban. Other whaling nations, such as the UK, Australia, and New Zealand, followed suit. With whaling no longer of any economic interest to many businesses and governments, it was easy to support the issue.

Successful domestic lobbying in the US and the UK, coupled with recruiting non-whaling states for the IWC, brought about a general shift of majorities in the organization, which had been a "whalers' club" for whaling states.[4] In addition, the outcome document of the 1972 United Nations Conference on the Human Environment in Stockholm called for a 10-year moratorium on commercial whaling. After intense debates in the IWC and the admission of new non-whaling member states, in 1982, a moratorium on commercial whaling gained the necessary three-quarters majority (Friedheim 2001: 6; Bailey 2008: 198; Sakaguchi 2013: 199).

[2] Whale oil made from blubber was used for products such as lamp oil, candle wax, and cosmetics.

[3] For details of the anti-whaling discourse, see Epstein (2008); for the Euro-American anti-whalers' framing of whales as super-whales or "charismatic megafauna," see Friedheim (2001: 3).

[4] When a state ratifies the ICRW, it automatically becomes a member of the IWC. However, in October 2002, IWC members voted on whether Iceland, which had left in 1992, should be allowed to join a second time because Iceland sought to make its membership conditional.

4.2.2 Normative core claims

The norm against commercial whaling has specific features. With the moratorium, IWC member states did not change the underlying convention (the ICRW), but rather whaling catch limits. The norm is not "hard" but "soft" law (Abbott and Snidal 2000). The IWC set all catch limits to zero for up to five years.[5] The moratorium was justified as a measure to create time to discuss and implement sustainable catch limits and introduce more efficient monitoring of whaling activities. It entered into force for the 1985–86 whaling season.[6]

The moratorium rules out all types of commercial whaling but permits limited whaling by indigenous communities, termed "aboriginal subsistence whaling" (ASW) based on IWC quotas. It also allows lethal whaling for scientific purposes under domestically issued permits ("special permit" whaling or scientific whaling). ASW was created as a new category to ensure whaling activities by indigenous groups (see discussions at IWC 1982).[7] Special permit whaling is contained in the convention (see ICRW 1946: Art. VIII).

The norm includes a temporal dimension: The compromise version justified the ban as a measure that would be scientifically reviewed after a certain period of time.[8] Following its passage, anti-whaling states repeatedly stated that it was intended to be temporary (see, e.g. UK in IWC 1989: 55). In the 1990s, anti-whalers stopped referring to a review—but pro-whaling states did not. Anti-whaling states increasingly stressed their support for an unlimited moratorium.[9] According to Western media, the debate concerned a "general commercial whaling ban" (Howe Verhovek 1998; see also Spiegel 1992; Struck 2002; *Guardian* 2003; McCurry 2005). Scholars write that the moratorium "profoundly changed the IWC as a regime" (Lieberman et al. 2012: 519) and that the commercial whaling ban is the "principal *norm*" in the field (Sigvaldsson 1996: 314; emphasis in original; see also Friedheim 2001: 3).

In line with this volume's main theoretical framework, *applicatory* contestation describes contestation regarding exemptions from the norm: ASW, scientific permits, and attempts to include a new exemption for coastal whaling or "small-type whaling." *Validity* contestation prioritizes other norms concerning the commercial whaling ban (sovereignty, indigenous rights, and

[5] See paragraph 10(e) of the IWC Schedule of 1982.

[6] A blanket moratorium failed to gain a three-quarters majority. See the debates in IWC (1982: 21).

[7] The ASW category is not in the convention itself but is in the IWC Schedule. The US introduced ASW in order to ensure hunts for Alaskan Inuit and an ASW regime was approved in 1982 (IWC 1982: 28–29). To gain support for the new category, the US helped ensure similar exemptions for Greenland and for Soviet catches. In 1987, ASW was added for Saint Vincent and the Grenadines (IWC 1987a).

[8] See IWC Schedule amendment para. 10(e) (IWC 1982: 40).

[9] See, e.g. Germany, IWC (2000: 185); the US, IWC (1997b: 34); and Italy and the UK, IWC (1998: 58, 166–67).

cultural identity) or more generally rejects the ban because of its negative effects or inherent flaws (imperialism, colonialism, and so forth). The IWC's anti-whaling majority considers that the norm has no time limit and regards debate about whether sustainable whaling is again possible (e.g. by arguing that the moratorium has become superfluous) as validity contestation.[10]

4.2.3 International Whaling Commission (IWC)

The IWC had 15 members in 1975, 24 in 1980, and 36 in 1990. Its current membership is 88 (see Figure 4.1). Growth is mostly due to the ongoing polarization about commercial whaling that has overshadowed all IWC work; Japan's official withdrawal in 2019 could affect membership dynamics in coming years.

States are divided into the "pro-whaling" camp (most importantly Iceland, Japan before it withdrew from the IWC in 2019, Norway, several Caribbean and African states, and South Korea)[11] and the "anti-whaling" camp (especially European Union (EU) member states, the UK, the US, New Zealand, Australia, and Latin American states).[12] Denmark's role is complicated because it has to balance support for indigenous whaling in Greenland

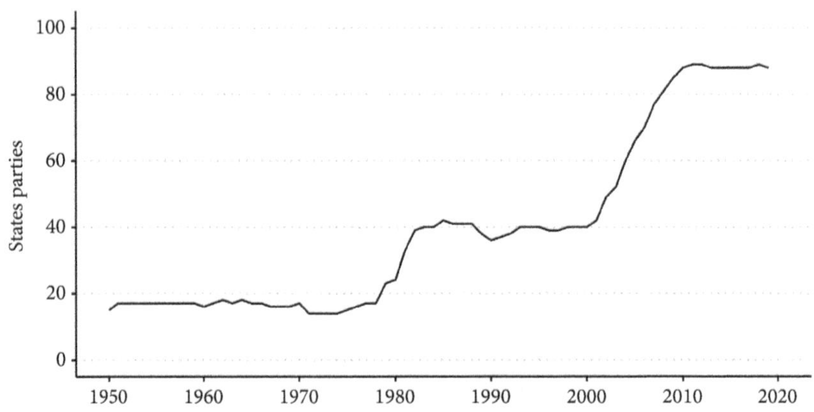

Figure 4.1 International Whaling Commission membership, 1950–2019
Source: Based on IWC reports and the IWC website.

[10] For a detailed coding scheme, see the Appendix, Table A.3.

[11] In-depth research has only been conducted on Japanese whaling policies. See Friedheim (1996); Wong (2001); Miyaoka (2004); Catalinac and Chan (2005); Hirata (2005); Flowers (2008); Strausz (2018). On Icelandic whaling, see Ivarsson (1994) and Brydon (2006); for Norwegian whaling, see Andresen (2004) and Bailey (2009).

[12] Since 2008, the EU has voted as a bloc (sometimes without Denmark). Most Latin American states have also voted as a bloc (the "Buenos Aires Group").

and for the Faroe Islands pilot whale hunt[13] (it externally represents both territories) with its EU membership. The same goes for the US and Russia, which need to ensure ongoing support for their ASW quotas. In the 1990s and 2000s, IWC members also included an active group of states that were open to compromise (South Africa, Oman, and Switzerland).

The anti- and pro-whaling camps generally try to persuade other countries to join the IWC and support their side. In the 1970s and 1980s, anti-whaling NGOs helped to swell the anti-whalers by financing new memberships (Catalinac and Chan 2005: 139; Andresen 2019: 116). Many European states were asked to join the IWC (and its anti-whalers) as part of joining the EU (see US Embassy Helsinki 2007). The US also tried hard to attract more members to the anti-whaling side.[14] In the opposite camp, Japan persuaded many African and Caribbean states to join in the 1990s and 2000s, thereby ensuring that the anti-whaling states no longer held a three-quarters majority.[15] On both sides, NGO networks used lobbying and praise and shame to keep states in their respective camps.[16]

The IWC is a rather small international organization. The IWC plenary, a meeting of the contracting states, is its forum for passing non-binding, majority vote resolutions and changing the ICRW Schedule (binding, three-quarters majority, objections allowed). In 2012, the IWC switched from holding annual meetings to meeting every other year. Several committees and working groups, like the scientific and conservation committees, report to the plenary.

4.2.4 Data collection and analysis

With regard to the ban on commercial whaling, we focused on IWC member states' contestation from 1986, when the moratorium entered into force, to 2016. To trace robustness trends regarding practice, we focused on

[13] Pilot whales are small cetaceans not officially covered by the IWC.

[14] For Turkey, see US Embassy Ankara (2006); for Israel, see US Embassy Tel Aviv (2006).

[15] Many researchers hold that Japan also linked foreign aid to fishing policies. See Gillespie (2005), Miller and Dolšak (2007); Darby (2008); Strand and Tuman (2012). Linking foreign aid to IWC voting has also been discussed in the anti-whaling camp. See New Zealand's comments about Pacific states in WikiLeaks Cable (US Embassy Wellington 2006).

[16] These groups have changed slightly over time. At first, the protectionist camp included Greenpeace and the World Wildlife Fund; more specialized NGOs such as the Whale and Dolphin Conversation, the International Fund for Animal Welfare, and the Environmental Investigation Agency joined later. In the other camp, we find several domestic Japanese groups linked to fishery and whaling as well as groups like the Integrating Wildlife, Markets and Conservation (IWMC)—World Conservation Trust that promotes the sustainable management and use of wildlife resources. In the late 1990s and early 2000s, there was a transnational alliance of indigenous and other state and non-state pro-whaling groups called the World Council of Whalers. Representatives of indigenous groups (the Alaska Eskimo Whaling Commission and, recently, the Chukotka Traditional Marine Mammal Hunting Association) have routinely attended the IWC to support indigenous whaling.

compliance levels as shown through member states' whaling activities. It does not help to focus on regional or national implementation because, worldwide, only a handful of states hunt whales. With respect to discourse, we analyzed negative reactions to norm violations in IWC resolutions. We also studied concordance. General IWC membership trends mean little with respect to concordance because they generally represent the confrontation of the commission's two blocs. Instead, we discuss attempts to shift fora and whaling states withdrawing from the IWC, both of which indicate the ban's institutional weakening and potential cascading norm rejection. We also studied opinion polls to learn about popular views of the commercial whaling ban.

Contestation types were analyzed by qualitatively coding the minutes of all IWC meetings between 1986 and 2016 (plenary sessions were documented in "Verbatim Records" until 2000; since then, summarized "Chair's Reports" have been used)[17] along with interviews and secondary literature.[18] This rather state-centric data is supplemented by NGO actors' views in interviews, IWC documentation, and secondary literature.

To analyze robustness trends with respect to compliance, we used IWC data, interviews, and secondary literature. We analyzed negative reactions by examining IWC resolutions criticizing commercial or scientific whaling. To retrace closed-door negotiations on the commercial whaling ban, as well as diplomatic condemnation of whaling activities, we used diplomatic cables published by WikiLeaks. Concordance was assessed using existing (albeit limited) survey data and secondary literature.

4.3 Contestation trends

4.3.1 Radicalized contestation in the 1990s and 2000s

Contestation of the commercial whaling ban includes permanent applicatory contestation and a rise in validity contestation.[19] In the 1980s, both applicatory and validity contestations were rare. Figure 4.2 shows that in the 1980s, less than 20 percent of member states contested the ban's applicability in one or more statements at IWC meetings, but nearly 50 percent did that in the 2000s. Validity contestation rose from less than 5 percent in the 1980s to

[17] The IWC's 1994 Verbatim Report is incomplete and has not been included in our analysis.

[18] Supplementary material and data is available at the Harvard Dataverse: https://doi.org/10.7910/DVN/6VHFZK.

[19] This section analyzes contestation trends over time. Supporters of the commercial whaling ban of course engage with the various lines of contestation and present elaborate and detailed rebuttals, but we do not examine them in detail here.

nearly 50 percent in 2006. In view of the sharp growth of IWC members in the 1990s, it is clear that many new states—aside from the EU members—were pro-whalers.

In reaction to this escalation, IWC member states agreed to negotiate and refrain from controversy, which caused a stark drop in both types of contestations between 2007 and 2010. Following the breakdown of negotiations in 2010, controversial issues gradually returned, although contestations have not reached the level of the early 2000s. Here, we discuss the general shift to greater contestation, along with the increased validity contestation that began in the 1990s and continued until 2006, and explain why contestation declined at the end of the decade. We observe three distinct phases: disputes over application from 1986 to 1991; the radicalization of contestation between 1992 and 2006; and the failure of efforts to reach a compromise after 2007.

Throughout the 1980s and early 1990s, disputes were mainly over application as pro-whaling states thought they were debating a limited moratorium. They assumed that, after a review in 1990, they would be able to resume some whaling. Although these states, especially Norway and Iceland, might have never agreed to a *ban* on commercial whaling, within the IWC they engaged in mostly applicatory debates (see Figure 4.2), seeking to learn more about whaling populations, scientific whaling, and improving sustainability, and humane killing methods.[20] On the rare occasion that they minimally

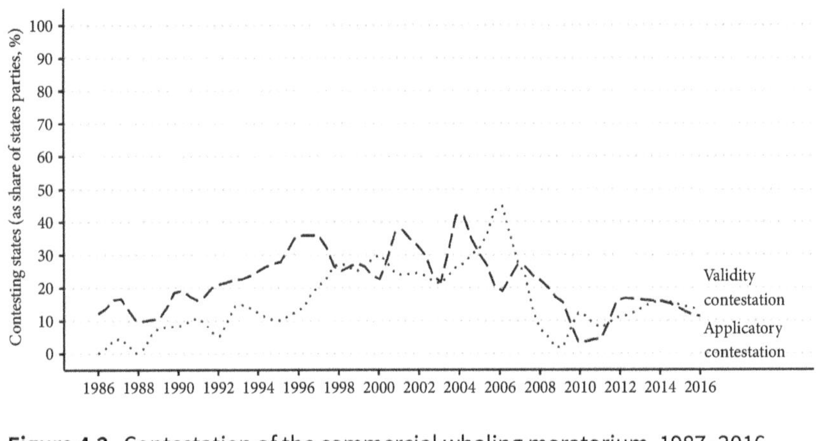

Figure 4.2 Contestation of the commercial whaling moratorium, 1987–2016

Source: Based on the verbatim records and chair's reports of IWC meetings.
Note: The figure shows the percentage of member states that uttered at least one contestation aiming to broaden the whaling exemptions (applicatory) or challenge the norm's validity. 1994 (missing) and 2013 and 2015 (switched to biennial meetings) interpolated.

[20] Summary of arguments based on analyzing IWC debates.

contested validity, they mainly critiqued the way the US coerced other states into accepting the ban: "The intrusion of political and economic considerations into scientific research through interference by the Commission and coercion by the United States will not contribute to, but will impede the IWC receiving the best scientific advice" (Iceland in IWC 1987b: 36).

Pro-whaling states threatened to leave the organization if no compromise was found (IWC 1986b, 1987b, 1989, 1991), however. In addition, the Nordic countries threatened to develop the North Atlantic Marine Mammal Commission (NAMMCO), which at the time only focused on small cetaceans and other marine mammals, into an alternative to the IWC (IWC 1990b: 58–60).

After 1992, it became clear that the anti-whaling states would not agree to changing the moratorium. A new model for calculating sustainable catch limits (the Revised Management Procedure, RMP) was approved by the IWC Scientific Committee in 1991 and approved by the commission in 1994 (see Lieberman et al. 2012: 525–27; Tallberg et al. 2013: 225).[21] Pro-whaling states thought that the RMP would open a path for limited commercial whaling. But debates over monitoring, enforcing, and managing the RMP dragged on into the new millennium.

Contestation intensified in the 1990s and increasingly challenged the validity of the moratorium. The pro-whaling states, led by Iceland, Norway, and Japan and supported by new members from Africa and the Caribbean, increasingly contested the moratorium's validity. They argued that limited sustainable whaling was now possible because some stocks were considered healthy (or at least, healthier), the practice was scientifically sound, and it was important to acknowledge cultural identity. As Japan stated in 1993: "In order to achieve successful sustainable utilization of marine living resources, mutual respect of food habits and cultures indigenous to each nation is essential. We must not abandon ourselves to emotional and political considerations, but base our consideration on scientific evidence" (IWC 1993b: 2).

The Caribbean and African states also contested the moratorium's validity, based on the right to sustainably use domestic resources for "food security" and "cultural identity" (Dominica in IWC 1997b: 104; Mali in IWC 2006a: 5) and accused the IWC of "cultural imperialism" and "racism." "We have to be careful, Mr. Chairman, that decisions that are made in this Commission is [sic] not seen as racist decision [sic] and cultural imperialism upon people

[21] For details on the background deals related to the resolution on the RMP's sustainable catch limits, see Kalland (2009: 123–24).

that should be given the right to exploit the resources that are available to them" (Antigua and Barbuda in IWC 1997b: 100).

In contrast, Norway and Iceland no longer spearheaded validity contestations (Iceland withdrew from the IWC in 1992 and rejoined in 2002). The Nordic countries supported the sustainable use of natural resources as laid out in other conventions on international resource management (Epstein 2008: 221–22). The pro-whaling states threatened to leave the IWC or at least look for other solutions. These included Japan (IWC 1992a, 1993a, 2004, 2005), Norway (IWC 1992a, 1995, 1996a), Denmark (IWC 1993a, 2004, 2005), and Saint Kitts and Nevis (IWC 2005).

Between 2000 and 2004, pro-whalers increasingly voiced their frustration about how the majority anti-whaling bloc kept discussing a monitoring scheme for commercial whaling without wanting to approve it.[22] Contestation intensified after two more failed attempts to negotiate compromises. The "Irish proposal" (1997) and the "Chair's proposal" (2004) aimed to limit commercial whaling by introducing strong safeguards. Pro-whaling states demonstrated their frustration by blocking the passage of ASW quotas for the US and Russia (2002), which was a major affront because the quotas had generally been passed by consensus.

At the 2006 IWC meeting in Saint Kitts and Nevis, contestation peaked when the pro-whaling states surprisingly passed the Saint Kitts and Nevis Declaration, their first successful *pro-whaling* IWC resolution since 1982. The declaration called for:

> [N]ormalising the functions of the IWC based on the terms of the ICRW and other relevant international law, respect for cultural diversity and traditions of coastal peoples and the fundamental principles of sustainable use of resources, and the need for science-based policy and rulemaking that are accepted as the world standard for the management of marine resources.
>
> **(IWC 2006b)**

However, by the next IWC meeting, anti-whaling sentiment was once again in the majority.

This intensification of validity contestation was accompanied by an increase in applicatory contestation (see Figure 4.2; for a thematic review see Section 4.3.2). Moreover, in the late 1990s and the early 2000s, pro-whalers regularly made highly emotional accusations of hypocrisy—as in Grenada's

[22] Personal interview with an international organization (IO) observer (a person delegated from another international organization to observe the IWC proceeding) at the 2016 IWC plenary in Portorož, Slovenia.

statement about how anti-whalers emphasized the need to humanely kill whales:

> If we talk about humane killing of whales, are we going to apply the same to sheep or deer or fox or kangaroos? Mr. Chairman, we are very much concerned because in countries where there is capital punishment, you know quite recently we heard someone was executed in an electric chair and it took a good three or four jolts of power before that person could be pronounced dead.
>
> **(IWC 1998: 19)**

After 2007, intensified contestation led to a more serious attempt to negotiate a solution in the "Future of the IWC" process that was established in 2007. This stipulated low whaling quotas for commercial whaling along with the end of objections and reservations regarding new items on the IWC Schedule (see Hurd 2012: 106). In 2007, IWC members agreed to a kind of temporary rapprochement that halted debate on contentious issues and required that decisions be made by consensus. In 2010, still lacking a solution, pro-whaling states increased their application and validity contestation—but not to the levels of the early 2000s.[23] Denmark (IWC 2008, 2010) and Japan (IWC 2007a, 2012) again threatened to leave the forum. In 2018, Japanese efforts to restart negotiations left anti-whaling states indifferent (see IWC 2018a). Attempts to compromise failed.

In this third phase, validity contestation mostly argued that since sustainable whaling had become possible, there was no longer a need to ban all commercial whaling. Iceland, Norway, and many other pro-whaling states emphasized that sustainable whaling is scientifically grounded: "From its [Icelandic] perspective, what was important was sustainability, and it considered there were only two categories of whaling, sustainable whaling and non-sustainable whaling" (IWC 2011a: 18). Pro-whaling states also leveled charges of colonialism and domestic interference against the anti-whaling bloc, which countered that these attacks were a "show" funded and staged by the Japanese.[24] However, Caribbean and African states resented not having their positions and interests taken seriously.[25]

[23] The pro-whaling camp had to contend with internal divisions. Some states resented the Japanese negotiating a package that would have prevented new states from whaling. Interview with Lars Walløe, head of the Norwegian delegation to the IWC Scientific Committee (1988–2016), during the 2016 IWC Scientific Committee meeting in Bled, Slovenia.

[24] Two interviews with members of the US delegation to the 2016 IWC Scientific Committee meeting in Bled and with an independent expert at the 2016 IWC Plenary meeting in Portorož, Slovenia.

[25] Interview with the head of a Caribbean delegation at the 2016 IWC Plenary meeting in Portorož, Slovenia.

A more general human rights discourse was also introduced to whaling debates, with pro-whaling states increasingly invoking human rights and indigenous rights:

> St. Kitts and Nevis saw the position of the EU to be an unjustifiable attempt to deny the human rights of a group of indigenous people. At a time of acute world food shortages, it viewed this as a small group of countries, purported to be world leaders, denying marginal people of the right to eat.
>
> **(IWC 2008: 21)**

This human rights discourse was also used by pro-whaling NGOs. Addressing the IWC plenary in 2012, Eugene Lapointe of the IWMC—World Conservation Trust described his belief that:

> [A]ccess to food was a basic right and it was demeaning that proud people had to beg to exercise their culture and traditions. He was unhappy that human rights were ignored to the advantage of animal rights. He was unhappy when wild animals were humanised and when humans were demonised for making use of animals.
>
> **(see IWC 2012: 60)**

To sum up: In the early years of the moratorium (1986–91), pro-whalers thought that they were debating a limited moratorium and that their arguments would eventually win over the preservationists. In the 1990s, the anti-whaling IWC majority showed no intention of lifting the moratorium, and between 1992 and 2006, the whaling states' contestation shifted toward more fundamental validity contestation. That peaked in the early 2000s. The subsequent "Future of the IWC" renegotiation process, which lasted from 2007 to 2010, failed and moderate contestation persisted.

4.3.2 Applicatory contestation becomes permanent

Several lines of applicatory contestation around exemptions to the commercial whaling moratorium have become permanent during the past three decades.[26] Particularly with regard to scientific and "small-type whaling" (a term which Japan introduced to describe small-scale traditional, coastal whaling), contestations have not led to any new temporal stabilizations and

[26] We only discuss the main themes of applicatory contestation. Almost all issues discussed at the IWC are, in one way or another, related to the main debate: a ban on whaling.

have created confusion about the norm. ASW is another contested issue. Debates can be particularly intense when new quotas are being decided. However, addressees' shared understandings have increased more with respect to the AWS norm than for all other issues.

The ICRW only permits lethal whaling with domestically issued permits "for purposes of scientific research" (ICRW 1946: Art. VIII). It contains no other provisions regarding scientific whaling. This issue is particularly prone to contestation because the IWC has no mandate to regulate domestic permits. In the 1980s, the IWC created broad criteria for scientific whaling (IWC 1986a) and in the 2010s, a specific review procedure for scientific whaling programs was developed and applied in the IWC Scientific Committee.

Before the whaling moratorium of 1982, IWC member states often conducted scientific whaling programs. After the moratorium on commercial whaling took effect in the 1985–86 season, Norway and Iceland continued scientific whaling until the early 1990s. Japan started using scientific permits for whaling in the 1980s and continued until 2019. Japan's withdrawal from the IWC may lead to the (perhaps temporary) end of this exemption. Often, more scientific-permit whaling was conducted by Japan than commercial whaling by Norway and Iceland (see Section 4.4.1). Japan remained the only whaler in the Antarctic after the moratorium took effect, arguing that the ICRW permits it to engage in scientific whaling in the whale sanctuary established there in 1994. The Japanese government rationalized that it was seeking to better understand biological and ecological parameters related to whales, investigate developments and alterations in the composition of whale species and their distribution, and analyze how environmental change affects marine ecosystems (IWC 2007b; Government of Japan 2015). Japan has gone to great effort to establish that its whaling is a sovereign right permitted by the ICRW. It has also stated that the findings of its whaling research are valuable to the IWC Scientific Committee. Most recently, Japan announced that in light of its withdrawal from the IWC, it would halt hunting in the Antarctic and only whale commercially in its exclusive economic zone (Holm 2019).

After the commercial whaling ban was passed, anti-whaling states became highly critical of scientific programs—especially Japan's. Many observers viewed them as a way of getting around the commercial whaling ban, while the Japanese government argued that scientific whaling would help keep the industry alive until commercial whaling was once again permitted (Clapham 2015: 240). Japan also authorized the domestic sale of whale meat caught during its scientific hunts, which, besides the number and type of whales hunted, was one of the major bones of contention regarding its scientific whaling. Anti-whaling states in the IWC argued that scientific research on whales needed to be more closely regulated. They also charged that the Japanese program did not heed IWC decisions, that it targeted endangered stocks and species, and that it was not necessary to obtain the data of interest through lethal methods.[27]

An international NGO coalition has consistently challenged Japanese scientific whaling, with Sea Shepherd and Greenpeace taking direct action to stop Japanese whaling in the Antarctic and by blocking and ramming whaling ships to protest Norwegian and Icelandic whaling (McCurry 2008; Riese 2017). In the early 1990s, Greenpeace halted direct actions, and in 2008, it stopped tracking Japanese whaling ships (McCurry 2008; Scarce 2016). Sea Shepherd continued these activities until the 2010s and was banned from IWC meetings in 1986. However, Japan has not managed to also get Greenpeace banned.

After the "Future of the IWC" process collapsed in 2010, Australia brought the case of Japanese scientific whaling to the International Court of Justice (ICJ).[28] There, Japan again argued that its scientific whaling program was legal. In its 2014 decision, the court did not rule against lethal scientific whaling or the domestic sale of whale meat caught in the process but decided that Japan's Antarctic whaling program did not meet the criteria for "scientific" research (ICJ 2014; see also Caddell 2014). Although Japan agreed to respect this decision and stop its Antarctic whaling program, this did not resolve the general dispute over scientific whaling.[29] In 2014, Japan started two new research programs, one in the Antarctic and one in the North Pacific, which were ended when Japan withdrew from the IWC and resumed commercial whaling.

In general, while some procedural developments observed over time pointed to some compromise regarding the interpretation of this applicatory issue (e.g. the "Annex P process" for reviewing scientific whaling programs),[30] patterns of argumentation had largely remained unchanged. This repetitiveness is reflected by a member of the US delegation to the IWC Scientific Committee:

> We used to have these excruciatingly long debates on scientific permits [. . .] and the Japanese would put in some proposal, we would write an extensive critique

[27] Summary of arguments based on analyzing IWC debates.

[28] For possible motivations, see Scott (2014). New Zealand joined the case in 2012 (ICJ 2012).

[29] Japan has also decided to exempt any future disputes on marine resources that involve it from ICJ competency.

[30] This led to a slight depoliticization of scientific permit discourses. Interview with a participant invited to the 2016 IWC Scientific Committee in Bled. Interview with IWC secretariat staff at the 2016 IWC Plenary meeting in Portorož, Slovenia. This shifted again, however, when the IWC established a Standing Working Group on Special Permit Programmes in the plenary in 2016.

> on how bad the science was, they'd write a long rebuttal, other people will come in and support on either side, et cetera. [. . .] But at the Agadir Meeting [in 2010], at the very beginning of the Special Permits session, I put up my hand and I said, "I propose we have absolutely no discussion about this, because it's pointless. And we just each write a paragraph for the Scientific Committee report, which will mostly refer back to what we've said in previous years." And the Japanese were quite happy to agree to that. So afterwards I sat down and wrote a paragraph for the report; and, following that, I then wrote the Japanese response. And I walked over to the Japanese delegation, and I handed it to them. I said, "Here's what I'm saying, here's what you're going to say in response." And I put all the citations in and everything, you know. And they said, "You wrote our response?" I said, "Well, it's your response. You can do whatever you want with it." And they used it. I mean, they modified it somewhat, but they used it. They jokingly asked me if I wanted to be a co-author and I said, "I think not. But you can write mine next year." So that kind of summarizes just how awfully predictable and stalemated the whole thing is.[31]

In sum, hardly any joint understanding of the scientific whaling exemption to the commercial whaling ban emerged over time. Applicatory contestation became permanent.

The IWC's interpretation of indigenous whaling (ASW) is another contentious issue. Although commercial whaling is banned, the IWC issues ASW quotas for specific communities, currently in Greenland (Denmark), the US, Russia, and Saint Vincent and the Grenadines. Whaling quotas are only given to indigenous communities that can demonstrate that they need whale meat to subsist. The IWC admits, however, that there are no relevant definitions of "aboriginal" and "subsistence."[32]

ASW is less fiercely contested than other issues. Although pro-whaling states generally support ASW quotas, at the 2002 IWC meeting, they strategically blocked them in order to force renegotiation of the moratorium. Anti-whaling states, including New Zealand and Australia, have been reluctant to voice criticism of indigenous subsistence needs but do criticize specific hunts. In recent years, India and Latin American states have become more outspoken and direct in their critique (see IWC 2018a: 16–17).

Based on the different hunts, the targets of contestation have gradually shifted. In the 1990s and early 2000s, the main target was Siberian Chukotka

[31] Interview with Philip Clapham, US delegation, at the 2016 IWC Scientific Committee meeting in Bled.

[32] See the IWC homepage: Aboriginal Subsistence Whaling. Accessed September 23, 2022. https://iwc.int/aboriginal.

whaling: How was the meat used and were the hunts sufficiently "authentic"? In 1997, the Makah's application for a license to hunt gray whales along the US Pacific Northwest was controversial.[33] Since the 2010s, criticism has focused on Saint Vincent and the Grenadines, as well as Greenland (IWC 2012, 2014). With respect to Saint Vincent and the Grenadines, questions were raised regarding IWC compliance, sustainability, and "authenticity," whereas criticism of Greenland focused on commercial elements in the hunt, sustainability, and justifications for bigger quotas. In contrast, pro-whaling and ASW states generally stress the sustainability of their hunts as well as the IWC Scientific Committee's support for their requested quotas, the hunting communities' nutritional needs, and cultural aspects of their whaling traditions. They reject narrow interpretations of "commerciality" and "authenticity" and stress that ASW complies with IWC rules. That said, pro-whaling states also attempt to link ASW with sustainable whaling, which ASW states try to avoid. Denmark has recently tried harder to connect the ASW debate to debates on indigenous rights at the UN (IWC 2016).

Applicatory contestation over the whaling ban increased as indigenous voices became louder. Before the 1990s, they had hardly been heard in the IWC. But more and more indigenous organizations have been observing and attending IWC meetings as members of state delegations—where they have been successfully organizing calls to recognize cultural autonomy (Bailey 2008: 302–303; Epstein 2008: 235–43).[34] Indigenous whale-hunting communities claim that they are not against the commercial whaling ban per se but rather the relevant whaling policies of the IWC and domestic institutions.[35]

The passage of ASW quotas is generally guaranteed through intensive background negotiations and by linking the ASW quota proposals of the US, Russia, and Saint Vincent and the Grenadines (see IWC 1997a: 27–29, 51).[36] In 2012, however, anti-whaling states blocked a new quota for Greenland (IWC 2012: 23).

Many debates repeat similar patterns of argumentation. That said, there have been some important developments in applicatory debates about ASW, specifically with regard to more humane and efficient hunting strategies. Moreover, the IWC Scientific Committee has developed quite a sound

[33] Industrial whaling had fully depleted gray whale stocks along the Makah tribe's coast; for 70 years, they were unable to hunt whales—although coastal whaling had been permitted in an 1855 treaty with the US. Supported by the US government, the Makah continue to fight to legally regain this right. Clashes with anti-whaling NGOs were most intense in the 1990s, when the Makah harvested one gray whale (Erikson 1999).

[34] Interview with an indigenous group representative at the 2016 IWC Plenary in Portorož, Slovenia. On the (contested) Maori calls for whaling, see *New Zealand Herald* (July 5, 2012).

[35] Interview with a representative of an indigenous group at the 2016 IWC Plenary in Portorož, Slovenia.

[36] Interview with a representative of an indigenous group at the 2016 IWC Plenary in Portorož, Slovenia.

strategy regarding sustainable quotas. States with ASW quotas also attempt to depoliticize and streamline the debate. Recently, ASW states have pushed for more concrete rules demonstrating "need," a new procedure to automatically renew quotas, and giving more attention to human rights and indigenous rights perspectives in IWC decision-making (IWC 2015). Partial success was evident at the 2018 meeting, where the necessary three-quarters majority favored the automatic renewal of quotas approved by the IWC Scientific Committee, that is, without needing any vote by the IWC plenary (IWC 2018a: 17).

The ASW debate is linked to another field of applicatory contestation regarding the commercial whaling ban: disputes about exempting "small-type whaling" or hunting close to the shore with smaller vessels. States with small-type whaling activities (such as Japan and Norway) considered the category of ASW artificial (Kalland 2009: 110) and the distinction unjust. It remains to be seen whether this topic will remain on the IWC agenda now that Japan has left the commission.

In the 1980s, pro-whaling states began to fight for exemptions from the whaling ban for small coastal communities. Japan requested a small-type whaling quota for four communities in 1987 and kept the issue on the IWC agenda.[37] However, these catch quotas have not been approved; this issue remained the IWC's most obvious "stuck" contestation.[38]

Japan pursued the issue, claiming that poor rural populations needed help. Then, Japan justified its request for small-type whaling quotas by citing the cultural and subsistence arguments of the aboriginal whaling exemption. The patterns of arguments on both sides had remained essentially the same since the 1990s: One side argued that the current situation harms local communities and that its plans for small-type whaling are scientifically sound and sustainable and have little to do with commerce. Supporters also usually argued that small-type whaling is like ASW. Opponents argued that commercial aspects remain, that ASW is different from small-type whaling, and that there was no universal monitoring scheme for whaling. Applicatory contestation—using repetitive statements at the biannual IWC meetings—became permanent, with no further attempts to achieve a common interpretation.[39]

[37] In 1993, the IWC recognized the special distress of Japanese whaling communities but has regularly rejected a Japanese action plan for "un-commercial" whaling.

[38] The four communities did not hunt great whales but rather small cetaceans that were not in the IWC's purview during this period. Since Japan withdrew from the IWC, this has changed—and now Japanese fishers also catch great whales, following government quotas for the number of whales of each species authorized.

[39] Based on analysis of these IWC meetings.

In sum, both applicatory and validity contestation rose significantly in the IWC until 2006. After norm challengers failed to push through compromise in 2010, contestation continued, but less vehemently. At least two of three issues of applicatory contestation had become largely repetitive. No compromise was reached on an interpretation of the exemptions.

4.4 Norm robustness trends

Paralleling contestation trends, robustness declined in the observed period. Although commercial whaling was restarted and expanded in the 1990s and 2000s, these whaling activities were less openly condemned by other states and the level of concordance has remained fairly constant.

4.4.1 Practice: Commercial whaling is restarted in several states

With regard to the practical dimension of the commercial whaling ban, we focus on non-compliance. That said, the kind of behavior that can be categorized as "non-compliant" is controversial. Although approval of the moratorium brought commercial whaling to a standstill in 1988, beginning in 1992, whaling figures rose significantly—but not to pre-moratorium levels (see Figure 4.3).

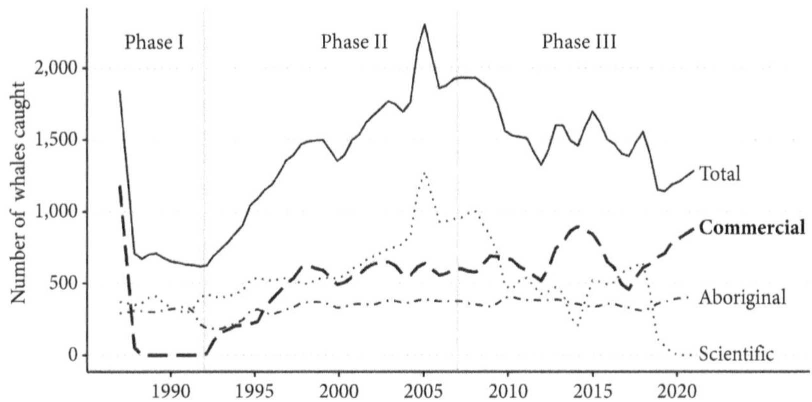

Figure 4.3 Whaling catches by type in three phases, 1987–2021

Source: Based on IWC data. Updated and adapted with permission from Deitelhoff and Zimmermann 2020. "Things We Lost in the Fire: How Different Types of Contestation Affect the Robustness of International Norms." *International Studies Review* 22 (1): pp. 51–76. doi: 10.1093/isr/viy080.

The first phase was marked by relatively swift "enforcement" of the commercial whaling ban: From 1988 to 1992, compliance was universal, apart from a special phase-out for Japan, which halted after the 1987–88 season. Only whaling permitted by ASW quotas and scientific licenses was practiced. After the moratorium came into force, many states stopped commercial whaling. Spain and Brazil began to oppose whaling, while Chile, Iceland, and South Korea ceased commercial whaling without much resistance but did not adopt strong anti-whaling positions. The ICRW rules allow countries to formally object to changes in the ICRW Schedule and, as a result, not be legally bound by them: Japan and Peru lodged objections to the moratorium that they later withdrew,[40] and Norway lodged an objection but stopped commercial whaling in 1986. Similarly, Russia lodged an objection but does not engage in commercial whaling.[41]

The ban's early "success" was facilitated by US support (Nadelmann 1990: 518; Sakaguchi 2013). In 1971, the US Congress passed the Pelly Amendment to the Fishermen's Protective Act, which authorizes the president to ban the import of seafood products from any country that is diminishing the effectiveness of international fishery conventions. The 1979 Packwood-Magnuson Amendment to the Magnuson Fishery Conservation and Management Act allowed fishing allocations in the US exclusive economic zone to be stopped for the same reasons. The US used these tools to pressure states to cease whaling activities and support the moratorium—a step that worked with Japan and which was also effective against Iceland, Brazil, Chile, Peru, and South Korea (Sakaguchi 2013: 200, see also Section 4.5).

Scientific whaling was widespread before the moratorium was passed, with the US, the Soviet Union, South Africa, Canada, and Japan issuing special permits (Kalland 2009: 22–23). After that, only Iceland, Japan, and Norway continued to issue scientific permits (Iceland in IWC 1985: 20; Japan in IWC 1987a: 14; Norway in IWC 1988: 12), and only Japan began a large-scale scientific program. Both South Korea (in IWC 1985: 20) and the USSR (in IWC 1990a: 12–13) contemplated issuing permits—but did not.

ASW was the least controversial category. In the first phase, Inuit in Alaska hunted bowhead whales, Greenlanders hunted fin and minke whales, Chukotka in Siberia hunted bowhead and gray whales, and Bequians of Saint Vincent and the Grenadines hunted humpback whales. In 1982, Canada was the only whaling country to react to the moratorium by immediately withdrawing from the IWC, although it neither defended whaling in

[40] Chile and Peru recently switched to being "anti-whaling." See Sakaguchi (2013: 201).

[41] For an overview of the marked reduction of whaling activities in the 1980s, see Zangl (1999: 218–25).

international fora nor whaled commercially (Epstein 2008: 220). The country authorizes small aboriginal whaling quotas for Canadian Inuit. Some other non-IWC member states also have small-scale whaling activities, such as the Philippines (which left the IWC in 1988 after a brief membership) and Indonesia.[42]

Whaling activities grew significantly between 1992 and 2006. After the Norwegian government concluded that the moratorium would not be altered in the near future, Norway replaced its scientific whaling with commercial whaling.[43] By objecting to the moratorium, Norway is not legally bound by it. Norway started to hunt minke whales in 1993 (157 that year) and caught around 600 in the 2000s.[44] Expecting that the moratorium would be continued, Iceland left the IWC in 1992. It then rejoined in 2002, promptly lodged an objection to the moratorium, and resumed scientific whaling that year.[45]

The Convention on International Trade in Endangered Species of Wild Fauna and Flora (CITES) from 1973, which includes all major pro-whaling states as members, heavily restricts or bans the international trade of whale products from any species.[46] Iceland, Japan, and Norway are not officially bound by the ban because of their objections (see Kalland 2009: 87–88). However, Iceland and Norway only started to trade in the 2000s after a Norwegian domestic law from 1986 that banned exports was abolished in 2001. After Iceland rejoined the IWC and became a member of CITES, Norway exported whale meat to Iceland and the Faroe Islands (see Altherr 2003; Animal Welfare Institute 2013; Hurd 2013; Altherr et al. 2016).

In the early 2000s, Japan significantly raised its scientific permit catch numbers—including species considered more endangered than minkes. In 2006, for example, Japan caught 605 minke whales in the Antarctic, the Pacific and its coastal waters, as well as 51 Bryde's whales, 101 sei whales, and 6 sperm whales in the Pacific, and 3 fin whales in the Antarctic. Officially bound by the ban, South Korea indicated its wish to start commercial or scientific whaling several times.[47] However, South Korea's very lax bycatch policy that allowed the marketing of unintentionally caught whale meat satisfied domestic demand (Tatar 2014; Bale 2016).

[42] Although the Philippines banned whaling in 1997, some illegal whaling may continue. For hunting by the Lamalera in Indonesia, see Emont (August 3, 2017).

[43] Interview with Lars Walløe, head of the Norwegian delegation to the IWC Scientific Committee (1988–2016), during the 2016 IWC Scientific Committee meeting in Bled.

[44] Norway uses a slightly modified version of the RMP, including higher risk, to calculate catch quotas.

[45] The legality of this step is contested. See the IWC homepage for Iceland. Accessed January 8, 2023. https://iwc.int/_iceland.

[46] CITES bases its prohibition on the IWC moratorium on commercial whaling.

[47] See IWC (1987b, 2000) for scientific whaling and IWC (1993a) for small-type whaling.

There was no significant rise in overall whaling activities after 2007 but commercial whaling has increased. The increased commercial catches by Iceland and Norway that peaked around 2014 and Greenland's ASW were offset by a reduction in Japanese scientific whaling. Iceland officially restarted commercial whaling in 2006 with low quotas for minke and fin whales.[48] Catches increased significantly until 2015 (155 fin whales and 29 minke whales that year), followed by significant ups and downs during the following years. Both Iceland and Norway started exporting whale meat to Japan in 2008 (Sakaguchi 2013: 204). Japan was both countries' most important whale-meat trading partner.

In the third phase, Japan reduced its scientific whaling and offered to end specific hunts like those for endangered humpbacks in the Atlantic as part of the "Future of the IWC" negotiations (US Embassy Tokyo 2007). After the ICJ ruling on Japanese scientific whaling in 2014 (see Section 4.3.2), Japan's new scientific whaling programs had slightly lower catch quotas—a trend that has continued, although Japan withdrew from the IWC in 2019 and restarted commercial whaling. In 2019, the Japanese fisheries agency issued a quota for its coastal waters that is significantly lower than those before (McCurry 2019). This decision has effects on the whale hunt in other states. In Iceland, the extension of quotas is currently under discussion as Japanese demand for imports is falling (Jonassen 2022).

In contrast, Denmark's demand for higher catch quotas for indigenous whaling in Greenland from 2010 to 2014 was strongly criticized by anti-whaling activists (IWC 2010, 2012, 2014)—particularly because it included the endangered bowhead and humpback whales. In 2012, South Korea announced a new scientific whaling program (IWC 2012: 42–43), but did not start it. South Korea continues to tolerate bycatch whaling.

Rising catches have not been paralleled by a widespread rise in the number of IWC whaling states. Nor do we observe any general cascade of non-compliance by pro-whaling states. In fact, there were never many of them: From around 12 IWC whaling states in the 1970s, their number sank from 9 in the 1980s to a low of 4 in 1991, before rising to 8 in the 2000s. Today, there are seven IWC whaling member states and three whaling states that do not belong to the IWC.[49]

[48] Iceland also uses the IWC RMP catch-limit algorithm, albeit a slightly modified version.

[49] Currently, three states officially engage in commercial whaling: IWC member states Norway and Iceland and the non-IWC-member state Japan. South Korea tolerates bycatch whaling. Canada and Indonesia, which do not belong to the IWC, continue to pursue (limited) indigenous whaling, as do IWC member states Denmark, Russia, St Kitts and Nevis, and the US. Some whaling might be ongoing in the Philippines.

4.4.2 Discourse: Fewer negative reactions and ongoing polarization

This section focuses on the discursive reaction to non-compliance with the whaling ban. It also studies the more general development of acceptance in whaling countries and forum-shifting attempts.

Open condemnation of whaling activities by IWC anti-whaling member states decreased between 1986 and 2016—as shown by the general decrease in condemnatory resolutions (see Figure 4.4). Between 1986 and 1991, when no commercial whaling took place, condemnations of Japan, Norway, and Iceland mostly addressed scientific permit whaling in annual resolutions. Between 1992 and 2006, anti-whaling states mainly critiqued Norway's commercial whaling (see debates in IWC 1993b, 1994, 1996b). In the 1990s, anti-whaling states also condemned the fact that one of the original IWC members, Canada, which had left the IWC in 1982 over the moratorium, authorized indigenous whaling but did not rejoin the IWC.[50] In the early 2000s, strong condemnation ebbed—including criticism of the fact that the whaling states had begun to export whale meat again (Andresen 2019: 120).[51]

From 2001 on, although now Iceland also engaged in commercial whaling activities, no majority resolutions condemned it. This was probably because

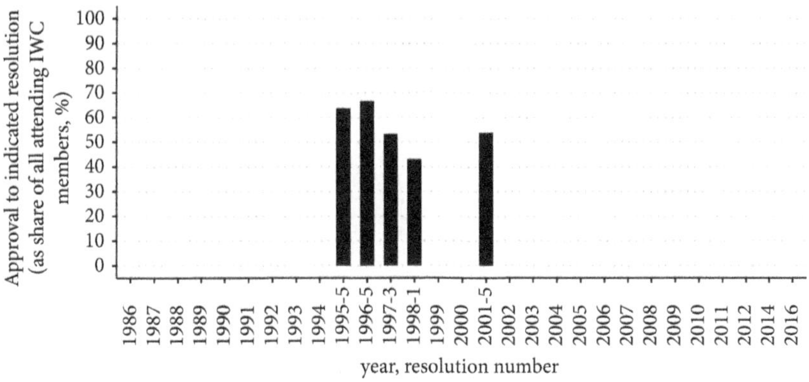

Figure 4.4 Support for resolutions condemning commercial whaling, 1986–2016

Source: Based on IWC reports. The percentage may be lower than 50 percent due to abstentions.

Note: 2013 and 2015 missing due to a switch to biennial meetings. No bar indicates that no resolution was voted on in the indicated year.

[50] See the debates in IWC (1992b); see also resolutions IWC 1993-18, 1996-9, and 1998-13.

[51] Resolutions on the trade of whale meat were only passed in 1995 and 1996 (IWC Res. 1995-5 and 1996-3).

open dispute was halted for the duration of the "Future of the IWC" process. Iceland's resumption of whaling was criticized by anti-whaling states diplomatically (see US Department of State 2009b; US Embassy Reykjavik 2009a, b) but there was hardly any public protest. Resolutions condemning scientific whaling have also become less frequent and support for them has diminished (see Figure 4.5).

In sum, negative reactions to whaling have lessened since the 1990s. Many anti-whaling NGOs have noticed the general decline in open condemnation and lobbied for stronger public criticism of whaling states.[52] For example, at the 2016 IWC meeting, NGOs were unable to persuade anti-whaling states to pass a resolution supporting the moratorium's thirtieth anniversary.[53] An observer of IWC meetings argues, "The whaling countries will continue whaling under opposition more from the conservation NGOs than [from] anti-whaling governments" (Iliff 2008b: 337)—though the 2018 IWC meeting included, if not a condemnation of whaling, at least an affirmation of the moratorium and non-lethal scientific research in a resolution (IWC 2018b). NGOs' fundamental opposition to certain types of whaling also seems to be vanishing. Contrary to their public statements, in bilateral talks with IWC commissioners before the Japanese withdrawal, at least one important NGO indicated behind closed doors that they could accept Japan's request

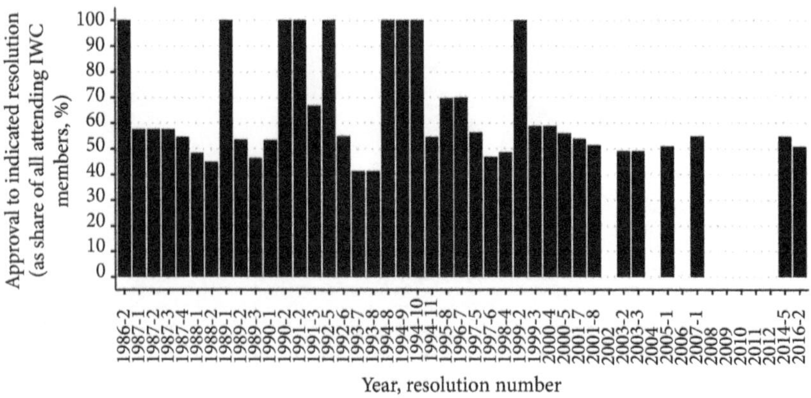

Figure 4.5 Support for resolutions condemning or criticizing scientific whaling, 1986–2016

Source: Based on IWC reports. The percentage may be lower than 50 percent due to abstentions.
Note: 2013 and 2015 missing due to a switch to biennial meetings. No bar indicates that no resolution was voted on in the indicated year.

[52] Conversations with NGO activists at the 2016 IWC plenary in Portorož, Slovenia.
[53] Interview with an NGO activist at the 2016 IWC plenary in Portorož, Slovenia.

for small-type whaling: "Let them eat their mercury-contaminated whale meat."[54]

NGOs and anti-whaling states have begun to think that with the barely profitable whaling industry dying out (in Norway and Japan it is aging),[55] restraint might achieve more than confrontation. Whale-meat consumption has continuously decreased in pro-whaling states, although the general public supports whaling in principle (Epstein 2008: 224–25; Sakaguchi 2013: 202).[56] Animal Protection Norway took the following approach: "The organization has found it effective to quietly monitor what appears to be a slowly dying industry, rather than protest and 'stir things up,' which might risk making things worse" (US Embassy Oslo 2009).

This suggests a more general decrease in discursive sanctioning by IWC members (Andresen 2019: 121). No longer fearing a dramatic weakening of the commercial whaling ban, most anti-whaling states seem to tacitly accept whaling activities and use the IWC as a forum to appease protectionist NGOs with some mildly critical rhetoric.

As for concordance, the rather polarized acceptance levels remain stable—as shown by opinion polls and forum-shifting efforts. No long-term comparative opinion polls have been made on whaling. Most of the polls were conducted by scientific institutes with pro- or anti-whaling agendas or by environmentalist NGOs—mostly in the US, Australia, and New Zealand, along with a few in Norway and Japan. This means that we can say very little about global trends. Sakaguchi (2013: 203) argues that in the 1990s, the domestic activities of anti-whaling states and NGOs increased support for whaling in Japan, Norway, and Iceland, where whaling had previously been quite a political issue. Starting in the 1990s, polls revealed stable public attitudes. In non-whaling countries, a large majority disapproved of whaling and whale-meat consumption but not in the whaling states of Japan and Norway (Freeman and Kellert 1992). In the 2000s, country-specific polls revealed similar results: strong disapproval of commercial whaling in Australia and New Zealand (for New Zealand, see Stoett 1997; for Australia, see Dorsey 2013) but support for commercial whaling in Japan (Bowett and Hay 2009; Meadows 2013; Smith 2015). Scientific whaling continued to enjoy high levels of support among the Japanese in the 2010s (Strausz 2018: 387). While whale-meat consumption seems to be declining and the whaling industry is small, support for whaling is significant in whaling states. The Japanese may

[54] Interview with an IWC commissioner, 2015.
[55] See NGO discourse and state reception in the WikiLeaks Cables (US Embassy Oslo 2009).
[56] It declined in both Norway and Japan and has never been high in Iceland.

not have strong opinions on whaling, but they decidedly reject "anti-whaling" campaigns and foreign criticism of domestic whaling (Ishii 2011).

We observed only two withdrawals from the IWC by outspoken pro-whalers after the moratorium. Iceland withdrew in 1992 but rejoined ten years later. Although Japan's 2018 withdrawal, which became effective in 2019, garnered much attention, Norway, Iceland, and South Korea do not appear to be interested in following suit.

Attempts to shift fora have been unsuccessful. According to the United Nations Convention on the Law of the Sea (UNCLOS) (UNCLOS 1982: Arts 64–65), whaling activities must be managed by an international organization. But there is only the IWC. Observers repeatedly discuss NAMMCO as a possible alternative forum for pro-whaling states. Created after Iceland temporarily left the IWC in 1992, NAMMCO members include Iceland, Norway, Greenland, and the Faroe Islands—because they were all unhappy with the IWC. Canada, Denmark, Japan, Namibia, and Russia have been observers (Knauss 1997: fn. 37). In the 1990s, some observers imagined that Japan and Norway could leave the IWC and use NAMMCO to coordinate their activities (Knauss 1997: fn. 83). In the 1990s, Japan threatened, in vain, to establish a similar institution in the Asia-Pacific (Kalland 2009: 202) and again threatened to found an alternative institution during the "Future of the IWC" process (2007–10). An alternative institution in the Asia-Pacific seems to be the variant preferred by current NAMMCO members following Japan's withdrawal from the IWC. In its opening statement to the NAMMCO meeting in 2019, the Faroe Islands (2019) government supported Japan's exit from the IWC but stopped short of inviting Japan to join NAMMCO. It suggested instead that Japan found a "sister organization"—but Japan has not yet made any effort to do that.

The rise in whaling activities, coupled with the overall decrease in open condemnation of them and polarized concordances, indicates that the commercial whaling ban has been weakened but not thoroughly eroded.

4.5 Explanatory factors

With respect to the commercial whaling ban, applicatory contestation became permanent on certain issues and validity contestation increased (Section 4.3). The robustness trends showed a pattern in line with our proposed theoretical argument that increased validity contestation and permanent applicatory contestation weaken norm robustness. In the case of the commercial whaling ban, we observe increasing whaling activity and diminishing negative reactions to norm violations (Section 4.4). This section analyzes the role of international law and the relative power of norm challengers as well as how the whaling ban's international institutionalization impacted shifts in contestation and patterns of robustness. We show that for the commercial whaling ban, perceptions of the procedural quality of the norm's international institutionalization explain differences in contestation and robustness. Within the IWC, pro-whaling states viewed anti-whaling states as using their majority to hierarchically install their normative vision and block any change. The anti-whaling camp also instituted unofficial "sanctions" of pro-whaling states, especially NGO consumer boycotts and direct action against whaling ships. These created feelings of unfairness among the challengers and helped to shift contestation toward questioning the validity of the commercial whaling ban and to also intensify the challenge.

Neither the role of law nor embeddedness in norm clusters explains shifts in contestation and robustness. The commercial whaling ban is a "soft" law: based on the IWC Schedule, not a convention or treaty. As we saw in Section 4.3, imprecise exemptions and the lack of delegation drive applicatory contestation but do not explain a shift to validity contestation. Nor does the expectation hold that a norm that is embedded in a tight normative cluster will not be weakened. The 1946 ICRW is based on a paradigm of conservation and resource management whose principles clash with the commercial whaling moratorium, which is based on preservation. Sustainable resource management has become the guiding principle in many other environmental regimes: the 1972 Stockholm Declaration (on the "human environment") as well as the Brundtland Report ("Our Common Future") from 1987 and the Rio Declaration from 1992, both of which concern sustainable development. States can justify pro-whaling positions by drawing on a legal document, the ICRW, as well as on the central paradigm of sustainable use (Zimmermann 2021). Although this constellation fueled contestation, it remained quite stable and did not shift contestation patterns during the period analyzed.

Scholars also suggest that the relative power of norm challengers explains trends in contestation patterns and robustness because powerful challengers can more strongly challenge a norm and more easily gain support from other states. In contrast, powerful norm supporters have more resources to enforce a ban. Challenger power does not seem to be a decisive factor with respect to whaling.

Japan, Norway, and Iceland—the major pro-whaling states in the IWC—are not great powers. They belong to a Western "community of states": well-developed countries with considerable economic strength that are known to be generally law-abiding and are commonly acclaimed for their domestic "green politics." This is especially true for Norway (Teigen 2018). The pro-whalers' power is definitely soft. All three countries also paid considerable membership fees to the IWC, where Japan worked hard to gain a decisive majority. The 2006 IWC Annual Meeting, where pro-whalers laid the foundation for the "Future of the IWC" renegotiations, testified to Japan's success. However, that process did not manage to change the norm.

At the same time, the principal advocates of the commercial whaling moratorium, the coalition of norm supporters that includes the US and anti-whaling NGOs, enjoyed considerable *enforcement* power. No pro-whaling state was immune to anti-whaling state sanctions. Japan, Norway, and Iceland all had to carefully balance their whaling interests with international public opinion and the threat of sanctions (Catalinac and Chan 2005; Sakaguchi 2013: 202–204; Strausz 2018). US pressure forced Japan to accept the moratorium.[57] Japan has to deal with its reputation as a "villain" with regard to whaling. Norway gave in to US pressure and consumer boycotts in the 1980s and first stopped commercial and then scientific whaling—before resuming commercial whaling in 1993, once again eliciting threats of US sanctions and consumer boycotts (Andresen 2019: 121). Similarly, Iceland first caved in to US threats with regard to its commercial whaling in the 1980s, then stopped scientific whaling in 1990 as a result of a consumer boycott of its seafood products (see Brydon 2006: 213–35).[58] Despite US threats, Iceland restarted scientific whaling and then, in the 2000s, commercial whaling (The White House 2014).

In recent decades, no very powerful states have joined the pro-whaling side, whose support had grown significantly in the 1990s—mostly from African countries and Caribbean and Pacific microstates. However, these states used the most radical validity contestation: the discourse of marginalization and colonialism. Validity contestation thus grew with the increasing support of "non-powerful" states. As we will see below, the anti-whaling coalition's weight fueled feelings of unfairness and frustration among pro-whalers.

That said, anti-whaling states never completely dominated the IWC. As the main "enforcer" of the commercial whaling moratorium, the US tried to not apply too much pressure because whaling is less important than other foreign policy issues. It also had to ensure a three-quarters majority for indigenous whaling quotas inside the IWC. Therefore, the US government tried not

[57] Some argue that US sanction power declined during the 1980s because the strong sanctioning instrument of foreign fishing rights in the US exclusive economic zone was scheduled to be eliminated in 1988 (see Catalinac and Chan 2005: 150; Strausz 2018: 385).

[58] For a list of threatened sanctions, see Kalland (2009: 140).

to antagonize Japan, Norway, and Iceland.[59] Meanwhile, domestic NGOs unsuccessfully sued to compel the US administration to enforce sanctions under US regulations. Some scholars argue that US action remained limited to threats, which gradually diminished (Couzens 2013: 45). In effect, the anti-whaling side created space for pro-whalers to challenge the ban.

Perceptions of the procedural quality of international institutions seem to have pushed pro-whaling states to more radical contestation and weakened the whaling ban. Pro-whalers criticized the IWC as a hierarchical organization that did not acknowledge their positions as well as the informal sanctions of norm violations.

In the view of pro-whalers, the highly polarized IWC came to be dominated by "protectionists." In reaction, Japan vainly tried to recruit more pro-whaling members in the late 1990s and 2000s. Observers maintain that after the failure of the "Future of the IWC" renegotiation process in 2010, the anti-whaling coalition "tightened its hand" on the IWC's agenda and policy-making process (Couzens 2013: 101–102).

No formal hierarchy exists: The IWC decides all matters with a simple majority. But binding decisions require a three-quarters majority (IWC 2011b: E, 3a). In the 1990s, the pro-whalers created a coalition big enough to block binding changes by the anti-whalers, who still held the majority and were regularly able to enforce their normative position by passing resolutions bolstering institutional protectionism, for example, with regard to scientific whaling. Although these were non-binding resolutions, pro-whaling states felt that their positions, particularly those regarding sustainability, went unheard and that the anti-whalers did not accept any normative visions in the IWC besides those promoting preservation.[60]

Pro-whalers also complained that the anti-whaling camp repeatedly held lengthy debates on how to reopen limited commercial whaling without ever actually approving the negotiated results or making any concessions: Channels for norm change were proposed time and again—then blocked. This is captured in reports of IWC meetings, for example, in discussions about the proposed Revised Management Scheme (RMS):

> So often they have come with all kinds of impediments. [. . .] Next year they will come up with something else. The [Revised Management Procedure] might never

[59] Interview with a US member at the 2016 IWC plenary in Portorož. See also negotiations about gaining support for ASW quotas in US Embassy Reykjavik (2007); US Embassy London (2007); US Embassy Tokyo (2006).

[60] For a discussion of the confrontation of principled discourse with scientific discourse, see Mitchell (1998). For a comparison with positions in CITES, see Peez and Zimmermann (2022).

> come into being, the RMS might never come into being, and there'll be continued delay in tactics all the time because the idea is not one whale must be killed.
>
> **(Dominica in IWC 1993b: 87).**

Similar frustration is echoed in a statement by Norway:

> The New Zealand Commissioner states again and again I am against commercial whaling anywhere, anytime, but is he willing to sit down and talk about compromises? What compromises? You need to lay out what is his form of compromise. I asked in Antigua, let somebody look up in the Dictionary what the word compromise means. Does it mean that somebody should give up everything and the others cash in? Is that a New Zealand dictionary for compromise? It is not mine. So I get a bit agitated when I hear those statements. We sit down in good faith with you to negotiate and discuss the items in order to allow you to understand the concerns of all parties and I thought we had very good discussions but when we come to the Plenary we need to make postures for the outside world. Here we go again, traditional IWC.
>
> **(IWC 1998: 166)**

With the IWC having no formalized adjudication and sanctioning mechanisms, applicatory contestation for scientific and small-type whaling has become permanent. But that lack has also led to anti-whaling states and NGOs using informal sanctions, which have fueled feelings of unfairness among pro-whalers. Large NGO campaigns condemned whaling activities in Norway, Iceland, Japan, Greenland, and the Caribbean and organized or threatened consumer boycotts, while Greenpeace and Sea Shepherd took direct action that included pursuing whaling ships and other protest activities (Bailey 2008: 310–12; Sakaguchi 2013).[61] In a case of unintended consequences, after Sea Shepard sabotaged a Norwegian whaling vessel in 1992, support *grew* for Norway to resume commercial whaling (*Independent* 1992). Something similar can be observed with respect to Iceland's withdrawal from the IWC in 1992. Pro-whaling sentiments were stirred when two US members of Sea Shepherd sank two whaling ships in Reykjavík in 1986 and by broader NGO campaigns. Prior to these events, Iceland's population was little interested in its rather small whaling industry (Brydon 2006: 231–33). But threats of sanctions against countries like Norway and Iceland that saw themselves as "green" outraged their citizens.[62] Along with accusations of

[61] Both Sea Shepherd and Japanese whaling ships allege that the other side committed acts of violence that included disabling, boarding, and ramming vessels (Couzens 2013: 112).

[62] For a similar argument regarding frustration and a detailed description of threatened sanctions, see Sakaguchi (2013: 196, 202–204).

hypocrisy (especially directed at the US because of its high meat consumption and failure to act on climate change), pro-whaling states shifted toward more radical contestations of the commercial whaling ban.[63]

Of course, not all former whaling states resisted. Some, like Spain and the Soviet Union, quietly gave in and abandoned their pro-whaling positions—either because whaling was unprofitable or they had been persuaded. For others, the right to hunt became a matter of principle, although whaling no longer had any significant economic benefit. As former Norwegian Minister of Foreign Affairs Johan Jørgen Holst put it, it was about "small countries [fighting] pressure from major powers" (cited in Sakaguchi 2013: 203). This explains why some NGOs have changed strategies and do not want to "stir up things" (see Section 4.4.2). Citing the sanctioned states' greater resistance and combativeness, they now fear that powerfully sanctioning whaling activities might "have made things worse."

Given this impasse, why do we not observe more decay regarding the commercial whaling ban? Its particular type of institutionalization explains both why renegotiations have failed and why most pro-whaling states remain members. The ICRW allows for broad exemptions. Most IWC members do not see any major benefit from changing the status quo (Victor 2001: 303–304; Iliff 2010: 365). Whaling continues to reap objections, but only Japan has sought to evade additional debate over scientific whaling by withdrawing from the IWC. At the same time, anti-whaling states need not accept public blame for supporting the reopening of limited commercial whaling or take any responsibility for it.[64]

Thus, negotiations have repeatedly failed: In 1997, the IWC chair presented the "Irish proposal," which would have permitted strictly regulated commercial whaling based on small quotas in exchange for ending scientific whaling.[65] A similar proposal was presented as the "Chair's proposal" in 2004 (Iliff 2008a, 2010: 360). After 2006, the then IWC Chair renewed joint negotiations (the "Hogarth initiative" on the "Future of the IWC"), and brought in international experts to reduce the polarization (Iliff 2010). However, no consensus could be found on the most controversial points (scientific

[63] Of course, this argument does not exclude political elites in whaling countries invoking such perceived unfairness to boost their legitimacy.

[64] Interview with a US commission member and with an IWC observer at the 2016 IWC plenary in Portorož. Maquieira (2019) holds a similar view. The strong opposition to whaling by domestic audiences and NGOs in many anti-whaling countries makes compromising on commercial whaling too costly for most anti-whaling governments in the IWC.

[65] It permitted limited coastal whaling by Norway, Japan, and Iceland.

whaling, sanctuaries, small-type whaling, and limited commercial whaling). The negotiations were unsuccessful.[66]

4.6 Conclusion

Both applicatory and validity contestation intensified significantly until 2006. Several themes of applicatory contestation have become permanent and no new shared meanings have become established. Through 2016, whaling activities rose moderately, negative reactions to whaling activities decreased, and public attitudes remained polarized. The norm banning commercial whaling was weakened but not completely eroded.

Legal status and precision remained stable over time and did not influence the observed changes in contestation regarding the whaling ban. Similarly, the constellation of the moratorium on commercial whaling and the ICRW's link to different meta-principles, preservation, and sustainable use fed the arguments of norm challengers but cannot explain the changes in contestation. In the IWC, the pro-whaling bloc of mostly smaller states that had to cope with the anti-whalers' threats of sanctions remained the minority, leading to frustration. The IWC's dialogue-stifling institutionalization, which permitted anti-whalers to pass majority anti-whaling resolutions and included no adjudication processes for many issues, caused contestation to intensify in the 1990s and 2000s—and the norm lost strength.

Reference list

Abbott, Kenneth W., and Duncan Snidal. 2000. "Hard and Soft Law in International Governance." *International Organization* 54 (3): pp. 421–56. doi: 10.1162/002081800551280.

Ager, Simon. 2019. "For the Whales: A Shepherd on Makah Tribe's Request to Hunt Whales." Sea Shepherd. November 6. Accessed January 8, 2023. https://seashepherd.org/2019/11/06/for-the-whales-sea-shepherd-on-makahs-tribe-request-to-hunt-whales.

Altherr, Sandra. 2003. "Iceland's Whaling Comeback: Preparations for the Resumption of Whaling." Human Society International, University of California.

[66] The compromise included negotiated catch quotas. But in the end, Australia, New Zealand, and the European states pulled out of the deal. A glimpse into the negotiating process and the central role of the US and that of the former US Commissioner and IWC Chair William (Bill) Hogarth can be gained in WikiLeaks Cables: US Embassy Canberra (2010); US Department of State (2009a); US Embassy Tokyo (2010).

Accessed September 12, 2022. http://www.hsi.org/assets/pdfs/icelands_whaling_comeback_pt1.pdf.

Altherr, Sandra, Kate O'Connell, Sue Fisher, and Sigrid Lüber. 2016. "Frozen in Time: How Modern Norway Clings to Its Whaling Past." Animal Welfare Institute. Accessed September 12, 2022. https://awionline.org/sites/default/files/uploads/documents/AWI-ML-NorwayReport-2016.pdf.

Andresen, Steinar. 2004. "Whaling: Peace at Home, War Abroad." In *International Regimes and Norway's Environmental Policy: Crossfire and Coherence*, ed. Jon B. Skjærseth. Aldershot: Ashgate, pp. 41–63.

Andresen, Steinar. 2019. "Science and Policy in the International Whaling Commission." In *Contesting Global Environmental Knowledge, Norms, and Governance*, ed. M. J. Peterson. Abingdon: Routledge, pp. 110–24.

Animal Welfare Institute. 2013. "Briefing on Whaling Links and Cooperation between Norway and Iceland, Including Whale Meat Exports." *Animal Welfare Institute, Briefing*. April. Accessed January 8, 2023. https://www.awionline.org/sites/default/files/uploads/documents/ML-AWI-Briefing-on-Whaling-Norway-Exports-April2013.pdf.

Bailey, Jennifer L. 2008. "Arrested Development: The Fight to End Commercial Whaling as a Case of Failed Norm Change." *European Journal of International Relations* 14 (2): pp. 289–318. doi: 10.1177/1354066108089244.

Bailey, Jennifer L. 2009. "Norway, the United States, and Commercial Whaling: Political Culture and Social Movement Framing." *Journal of Environment & Development* 18 (1): pp. 79–102. doi: 10.1177/1070496508329358.

Bale, Rachael. 2016. "How Whales Are Deliberately Hunted by 'Accident.'" National Geographic, June 16. Accessed January 8, 2023. https://www.nationalgeographic.com/news/2016/06/south-korea-whaling-bycatch.

Bowett, Julia, and Pete Hay. 2009. "Whaling and Its Controversies: Examining the Attitudes of Japan's Youth." *Marine Policy* 3 (5): pp. 775–83. doi: 10.1016/j.marpol.2009.02.01.

Brydon, Anne. 2006. "The Predicament of Nature: Keiko the Whale and the Cultural Politics of Whaling in Iceland." *Anthropological Quarterly* 79 (2): pp. 225–60. doi: 10.1353/anq.2006.0016.

Caddell, Richard. 2014. "Science Friction: Antarctic Research Whaling and the International Court of Justice." *Journal of Environmental Law* 26 (2): pp. 331–40. doi: 10.1093/jel/equ018.

Catalinac, Amy L.M.Y., and Gerald Chan. 2005. "Japan, the West, and the Whaling Issue: Understanding the Japanese Side." *Japan Forum* 17 (1): pp. 133–63. doi: 10.1080/0955580052000337512.

Clapham, Phillip J. 2015. "Japan's Whaling Following the International Court of Justice Ruling: Brave New World—or Business as Usual?" *Marine Policy* 51 (Suppl. C): pp. 238–41. doi: 10.1016/j.marpol.2014.08.011.

Couzens, Ed. 2013. *Whales and Elephants in International Conservation Law and Politics: A Comparative Study*. Hoboken, NJ: Taylor and Francis.

Darby, Andrew. 2008. *Harpoon: Into the Heart of Whaling*. Cambridge, MA: Da Capo Press.

Deitelhoff, Nicole, and Lisbeth Zimmermann. 2020. "Things We Lost in the Fire: How Different Types of Contestation Affect the Robustness of International Norms." *International Studies Review* 22 (1): pp. 51–76. doi: 10.1093/isr/viy080.

Dorsey, Kurkpatrick. 2013. *Whales & Nations: Environmental Diplomacy on the Seas*. Seattle, WA: University of Washington Press.

Emont, Jon. 2017. "A Whaling Way of Life under Threat." New York Times, August 3. Accessed January 8, 2023. https://www.nytimes.com/2017/08/03/world/asia/whaling-lamalera-indonesia.html.

Epstein, Charlotte. 2008. *The Power of Words in International Relations: Birth of an Anti-Whaling Discourse*. Cambridge, MA: MIT Press.

Erikson, Patricia. 1999. "A-Whaling We Will Go: Encounters of Knowledge and Memory at the Makah Cultural and Research Center." *Cultural Anthropology* 14 (4): pp. 556–83. doi: 10.1525/can.1999.14.4.556.

Faroe Islands. 2019. "Opening Address by Mr Poul Michelsen, Minister of Foreign Affairs and Trade at the 27th Annual Meeting of the North Atlantic Marine Mammal Commission." NAMMCO (North Atlantic Marine Mammal Commission), April 3, 2019. Accessed January 8, 2023. https://lms.cdn.fo/media/12261/nammco-welcome-address-030419.pdf?s=xuyO9_RWVq9Nx8HQ_KzeK7O80ts#:~:text=Let%20me%20begin%20by%20wishing,the%20annual%20meeting%20of%20NAMMCO.

Flowers, Petrice R. 2008. "Shaping State Identity: International Law and Whaling in Japan." *Pacific Focus* 23 (1): pp. 97–120. doi: 10.1111/j.1976-5118.2008.00006.x.

Freeman, Milton M. R., and Stephen Robert Kellert. 1992. *Public Attitudes to Whales: Results of a Six-Country Survey*. Edmonton, AB: The University of Alberta Press.

Friedheim, Robert L. 1996. "Moderation in the Pursuit of Justice: Explaining Japan's Failure in the International Whaling Negotiations." *Ocean Development & International Law* 27 (4): pp. 349–78. doi: 10.1080/00908329609546089.

Friedheim, Robert L. 2001. "Introduction: The IWC as Contested Regime." In Toward a Sustainable Whaling Regime, ed. Robert L. Friedham. Seattle, WA: University of Washington Press, pp. 1–45.

Friedheim, Robert L., ed. 2001. *Toward a Sustainable Whaling Regime*. Seattle, WA: University of Washington Press.

Gillespie, Alexander. 2005. *Whaling Diplomacy: Defining Issues in International Environmental Law*. Cheltenham: Edward Elgar.

Government of Japan. 2015. "Proposed Research Plan for New Scientific Research Program in the Antarctic Ocean (NEWREP-a)." December 11. Accessed January 8, 2023. https://www.mofa.go.jp/ecm/fsh/page4e_000357.html.

Guardian. 2003. "Japan Denounces Whale Conservation Vote." The Guardian, June 17. Accessed January 8, https://www.theguardian.com/environment/2000/jun/29/whaling.uknews.

Hasham, Nicole. 2018. "Japan Slaughtered 122 Pregnant Whales to Prove They Were Fertile." *Sydney Morning Herald*. June 4. Accessed January 9, 2023. https://www.smh.com.au/politics/federal/japan-slaughtered-122-pregnant-whales-to-prove-they-were-fertile-20180604-p4zjcs.html.

Hirata, Keiko. 2005. "Why Japan Supports Whaling." *Journal of International Wildlife Law & Policy* 8 (2–3): pp. 129–49. doi: 10.1080/13880290590096527.

Holm, Fynn. 2019. "After Withdrawal from the IWC: The Future of Japanese Whaling." *Asia-Pacific Journal | Japan Focus* 17 (4): pp. 1–16.

Howe Verhovek, Sam. 1998. "Protesters Shadow Tribe's Pursuit of Whales and Its History." New York Times, October 2.

Hurd, Ian. 2012. "Almost Saving Whales: The Ambiguity of Success at the International Whaling Commission." *Ethics & International Affairs* 26 (1): pp. 103–12. doi: 10.1017/S0892679412000081.

Hurd, Ian. 2013. "Whaling in Europe Is Dependent on the Continued Willingness of Governments to Fund It at a Loss." London School of Economics, Europpblog. February 18. Accessed January 8, 2023. http://blogs.lse.ac.uk/europpblog/2013/02/18/whaling-europe-eu-norway-iceland-greenland-faroe-islands-cites-international-whaling-commission.

ICJ (International Court of Justice). 2012. "Declaration of Intervention of the Government of New Zealand: Whaling in the Antarctic (Australia v. Japan)." ICJ General List, no. 148 (November 20, 2012).

ICJ. 2014. "Whaling in the Antarctic (Australia v. Japan: New Zealand Intervening)." *ICJ Reports*, 2014, p. 226 (March 14).

ICRW (International Convention for the Regulation of Whaling). 1946. "International Convention for the Regulation of Whaling." United Nations Treaty Series, no. 2124, vol. 161 at 72 (December 2).

Iliff, Mike. 2008a. "Modernisation of the International Convention for the Regulation of Whaling." *Marine Policy* 32 (3): pp. 402–7. doi: 10.1016/j.marpol.2007.08.003.

Iliff, Mike. 2008b. "Normalization of the International Whaling Commission." *Marine Policy* 32 (3): pp. 333–38. doi: 10.1016/j.marpol.2007.07.002.

Iliff, Mike. 2010. "The Hogarth Initiative on the Future of the International Whaling Commission." *Marine Policy* 34 (3): pp. 360–66. doi: 10.1016/j.marpol.2009.08.004.

Independent. 1992. "Whaling Ship Attacked." *The Independent*, December 29. Accessed January 8, 2023. https://www.independent.co.uk/news/world/whaling-ship-attacked-1565789.html.

Ishii, Atsushi. 2011. *Kaitai Shinsho 'Hogei Ronsō'*. Tokyo: Shinhyōron.

Ivarsson, Johann Vidar. 1994. *Science, Sanctions and Cetaceans: Iceland and the Whaling Issue*. Reykjavík: Iceland University Press.

IWC (International Whaling Commission). 1982. "Chairman's Report: 34th Annual Meeting, 1982." IWC Doc. Annual Report 1983.

IWC. 1985. "Chairman's Report: 36th Annual Meeting, 1985." IWC Doc. Annual Report 1986.

IWC. 1986a. "Resolution 1986-2: Resolution on Special Permits for Scientific Research." IWC Doc. IWC/38/28.

IWC. 1986b. "Verbatim Record: 38th Annual Meeting, 1986." IWC Doc. Verbatim Record 1986.

IWC. 1987a. "Chairman's Report: 39th Annual Meeting, 1987." IWC Doc. Annual Report 1988.

IWC. 1987b. "Verbatim Record: 39th Annual Meeting, 1987." IWC Doc. Verbatim Record 1987.

IWC. 1988. "Chairman's Report: 39th Annual Meeting, 1988." IWC Doc. Annual Report 1989.

IWC. 1989. "Verbatim Record: 41st Annual Meeting, 1989." IWC Doc. Verbatim Record 1989.

IWC. 1990a. "Chairman's Report: 42nd Annual Meeting, 1990." IWC Doc. Annual Report 1991.

IWC. 1990b. "Verbatim Record: 42nd Annual Meeting, 1990." IWC Doc. Verbatim Record 1990.

IWC. 1991. "Verbatim Record: 43rd Annual Meeting, 1991." IWC Doc. Verbatim Record 1991.

IWC. 1992a. "Chairman's Report: 44th Annual Meeting, 1992." IWC Doc. Annual Report 1993.

IWC. 1992b. "Verbatim Record: 44th Annual Meeting, 1992." IWC Doc. Verbatim Record 1992.

IWC. 1993a. "Chairman's Report: 45th Annual Meeting, 1993." IWC Doc. Annual Report 1994.

IWC. 1993b. "Verbatim Record: 45th Annual Meeting, 1993." IWC Doc. Verbatim Record 1993.

IWC. 1994. "Verbatim Record: 46th Annual Meeting, 1994." IWC Doc. Verbatim Record 1994.

IWC. 1995. "Chairman's Report: 47th Annual Meeting, 1995." IWC Doc. Annual Report 1996.

IWC. 1996a. "Chairman's Report: 48th Annual Meeting, 1996." IWC Doc. Annual Report 1997 (Part 1).

IWC. 1996b. "Verbatim Record: 48th Annual Meeting, 1996." IWC Doc. Verbatim Record 1996.

IWC. 1997a. "Chairman's Report: 49th Annual Meeting, 1997." IWC Doc. Annual Report 1997.

IWC. 1997b. "Verbatim Record: 49th Annual Meeting, 1997." IWC Doc. Verbatim Record 1997.

IWC. 1998. "Verbatim Record: 50th Annual Meeting, 1998." IWC Doc. Verbatim Record 1998.

IWC. 2000. "Verbatim Record: 52nd Annual Meeting, 2000." IWC Doc. Verbatim Record 2000.

IWC. 2004. "Chairman's Report: 56th Annual Meeting, 2004." IWC Doc. Annual Report 2004.

IWC. 2005. "Chairman's Report: 57th Annual Meeting, 2005." IWC Doc. Annual Report 2005.

IWC. 2006a. "Chair's Report: 58th Annual Meeting, 2006." IWC Doc. Annual Report 2006.

IWC. 2006b. "St. Kitts and Nevis Declaration." IWC Doc. Resolution 2006-1 (June 2006).

IWC. 2007a. "Chair's Report: 59th Annual Meeting, 2007." IWC Doc. Annual Report 2007.

IWC. 2007b. "Jarpa Review: Extract from the Full Report of the JARPA Review Workshop 2007." International Whaling Commission. Accessed September 12, 2022. https://iwc.int/jarpa#extract.

IWC. 2008. "Chair's Report: 60th Annual Meeting, 2008." IWC Doc. Annual Report 2008.

IWC. 2010. "Chair's Report: 62nd Annual Meeting, 2010." IWC Doc. Annual Report 2010.

IWC. 2011a. "Chair's Report: 63rd Annual Meeting, 2011." IWC Doc. Annual Report 2011.

IWC. 2011b. "Rules of Procedure and Financial Regulations: As Amended by the Commission at the 63rd Annual Meeting, July 2011." IWC Doc. 2011.

IWC. 2012. "Chair's Report: 64th Annual Meeting, 2012." IWC Doc. Annual Report 2012.

IWC. 2014. "Chair's Report: 65th Annual Meeting, 2014." IWC Doc. Annual Report 2014.

IWC. 2015. "Report of the IWC Expert Workshop on Aboriginal Subsistence Whaling (ASW)." IWC Doc. IWC/66ASW Rep01.

IWC. 2016. "Chair's Report: 66th Annual Meeting, 2016." IWC Doc. Annual Report 2016.

IWC. 2018a. "Chair's Report: 67th Annual Meeting, 2018." IWC Doc. Annual Report 2018.

IWC. 2018b. "Resolution 2018-5: The Florianópolis Declaration on the Role of the International Whaling Commission in the Conservation and Management of Whales in the 21st Century." IWC Doc. 2018-5.

Jonassen, Trine. 2022. "Iceland to End Whaling in 2024 as Demand Dwindles." High North News, February 7. Accessed February 06, 2023. https://www.highnorthnews.com/en/iceland-end-whaling-2024-demand-dwindles.

Kalland, Arne. 2009. *Unveiling the Whale: Discourses on Whales and Whaling.* New York: Berghahn Books.

Knauss, John A. 1997. "The International Whaling Commission: Its Past and Possible Future." *Ocean Development & International Law* 28 (1): pp. 79–88. doi: 10.1080/0090832970954609.

Lieberman, Sarah, Tim Gray, and A. J. R. Groom. 2012. "Moratoria in International Politics: A Comparative Analysis of the Moratoria on Genetically Modified Products and Commercial Whaling." *British Journal of Politics & International Relations* 14 (4): pp. 518–33. doi: 10.1111/j.1467-856X.2011.00479.x.

Maquieira, Cristian. 2019. "Japan's Withdrawal from the International Whaling Commission: A Disaster That Could Have Been Avoided." *Ethics & International Affairs Blog.* January 10, 2019. Accessed January 8, 2023. https://www.ethicsandinternationalaffairs.org/2019/japans-withdrawal-from-the-international-whaling-commission-a-disaster-that-could-have-been-avoided.

McCurry, Justin. 2005. "Japan Loses Key Votes at Whaling Summit." The Guardian, June 21. Accessed January 8, 2023. https://www.theguardian.com/environment/2005/jun/21/whaling.japan.

McCurry, Justin. 2008. "Greenpeace Calls Off Japanese Anti-Whaling Mission." The Guardian, November 4. Accessed January 8, 2023. https://www.theguardian.com/environment/2008/nov/04/whaling-japan.

McCurry, Justin. 2019. "Japan Resumes Commercial Whaling for First Time in 30 Years." The Guardian, July 1. Accessed January 8, 2023. https://www.theguardian.com/world/2019/jul/01/japan-resumes-commercial-whaling-for-first-time-in-30-years.

Meadows, Alan. 2013. "Japanese Whaling: Polls, Perceptions, and Pointers to the Future." *Language and Culture* 10 (1): pp. 101–49. doi: 10.15002/00008540.

Miller, Andrew R., and Nives Dolšak. 2007. "Issue Linkages in International Environmental Policy: The International Whaling Commission and Japanese Development Aid." *Global Environmental Politics* 7 (1): pp. 69–96. doi: 10.1162/glep.2007.7.1.69.

Mitchell, Ronald B. 1998. "Discourse and Sovereignty: Interests, Science, and Morality in the Regulation of Whaling." *Global Governance* 4 (3): pp. 275–93. doi: 10.1163/19426720-00403003.

Miyaoka, Isao. 2004. *Legitimacy in International Society: Japan's Reaction to Global Wildlife Preservation*. New York: Palgrave Macmillan.

Nadelmann, Ethan A. 1990. "Global Prohibition Regimes: The Evolution of Norms in International Society." *International Organization* 44 (4): pp. 479–526. doi: 10.1017/S0020818300035384.

New Zealand Herald. 2012. "Fight for Maori Whaling Traditions." New Zealand Herald, July 5. Accessed January 8, 2023. https://www.nzherald.co.nz/nz/news/article.cfm?c_id=1&objectid=10817502.

Oltermann, Philip. 2014. "Whale Meat Snacks Seized at German Trade Fair." The Guardian, January 24. Accessed January 8, 2023. http://www.theguardian.com/environment/2014/jan/24/whale-meat-snacks-seized-german-trade-fair.

Peez, Anton, and Lisbeth Zimmermann. 2022. "Contestation and Norm Change in Whale and Elephant Conservation: Non-Use or Sustainable Use?" *Cooperation and Conflict* 57 (2): pp. 226–45. doi: 10.1177/00108367211047138.

Peterson, M. J., ed. 2019. *Contesting Global Environmental Knowledge, Norms, and Governance*. Abingdon: Routledge.

Riese, Juliane. 2017. *Hairy Hippies and Bloody Butchers: The Greenpeace Anti-Whaling Campaign in Norway*. New York: Berghahn.

Sakaguchi, Isao. 2013. "The Roles of Activist NGOs in the Development and Transformation of IWC Regime: The Interaction of Norms and Power." *Journal of Environmental Studies and Sciences* 3 (2): pp. 194–208. doi: 10.1007/s13412-013-0114-3.

Scarce, Rik. 2016. *Eco-Warriors: Understanding the Radical Environmental Movement*. London: Routledge.

Scott, Shirley V. 2014. "Australia's Decision to Initiate Whaling in the Antarctic: Winning the Case Versus Resolving the Dispute." *Australian Journal of International Affairs* 68 (1): pp. 1–16. doi: 10.1080/10357718.2013.841121.

Sigvaldsson, Herluf. 1996. "The International Whaling Commission: The Transition from a 'Whaling Club' to a 'Preservation Club'." *Cooperation and Conflict* 31 (3): pp. 311–52. doi: 10.1177/0010836796031003003.

Smith, Roger. 2015. *Japan's International Fisheries Policy: Law, Diplomacy and Policy Governing Resource Security*. Abingdon: Routledge.

Spiegel. 1992. "Ein Stück Schlaraffenland." Spiegel, July 6.

Stoett, Peter J. 1997. *The International Politics of Whaling*. Vancouver: UBC Press.

Strand, Jonathan R., and John P. Tuman. 2012. "Foreign Aid and Voting Behavior in an International Organization: The Case of Japan and the International Whaling Commission." *Foreign Policy Analysis* 8 (4): pp. 409–30. doi: 10.1111/j.1743-8594.2011.00173.x.

Strausz, Michael. 2018. "Japan's Whaling Diplomacy: Science, Morality, and International Norms." In *Routledge Handbook of Japanese Foreign Policy*, ed. Mary M. McCarthy. London: Taylor and Francis, pp. 381–90.

Struck, Doug. 2002. "Japan Rebuffed in Fight to Ease Ban on Whaling." Washington Post, May 23. Accessed January 8, 2023. https://www.washingtonpost.com/archive/politics/2002/05/23/japan-rebuffed-in-fight-to-ease-ban-on-whaling/ca96490a-84d6-44a5-a8af-b3bca458ac49.

Tallberg, Jonas, Thomas Sommerer, Theresa Squatrito, and Christer Jönsson. 2013. *The Opening Up of International Organizations: Transnational Access in Global Governance*. Cambridge: Cambridge University Press.

Tatar, Bradley. 2014. "The Safety of Bycatch: South Korean Responses to the Moratorium on Commercial Whaling." *Journal of Marine and Island Cultures* 3 (2): pp. 89–97. doi: 10.1016/j.imic.2014.08.002.

Teigen, Lars Petter. 2018. "Norway's Green Delusions: The Country May Seem a Haven for Clean Energy, But That's Because It Exports Its Pollution." Foreign Policy, September 19. Accessed January 8, 2023. https://foreignpolicy.com/2018/09/19/norways-green-delusions-oil-gas-drilling.

The White House. 2014. "Message to the Congress: Iceland and the Fisherman's Protective Act." The White House: Office of the Press Secretary, April 1. Accessed February 06, 2023. https://obamawhitehouse.archives.gov/the-press-office/2014/04/01/message-congress-iceland-and-fisherman-s-protective-act.

UNCLOS (United Nations Convention on the Law of the Sea). 1982. "United Nations Convention on the Law of the Sea." United Nations Treaty Series, no. 31363, vol. 1833 at 3 (December 10).

US Department of State. 2009a. "Reply from Secretary Clinton to Foreign Minister McCully." Wikileaks Cables, 09STATE124245 (December 4).

US Department of State. 2009b. "US Participation in Joint Demarche to Iceland on Its Whaling Activities." Wikileaks Cables, 09STATE99783 (September 24).

US Embassy Ankara. 2006. "Turkey Will Not Join International Whaling Commission." Wikileaks Cables 03ANKARA1637 (March 14).

US Embassy Canberra. 2010. "Corrected Copy: Garrett Cool to Whaling Deal, Seeks More on Coral Research." Wikileaks Cables, 10CANBERRA93 (May 2).

US Embassy Helsinki. 2007. "Finns Ask 8 EU Countries to Join IWC." Wikileaks Cables, 07HELSINKI64 (February 1).

US Embassy London. 2007. "HMG Response to International Whaling Commission Demarche." Wikileaks Cables, 07LONDON1666 (May 3).

US Embassy Oslo. 2009. “A Whale of a Cable: Whaling in Norway.” Wikileaks Cables, 09OSLO111 (February 13).

US Embassy Reykjavik. 2007. “Icelandic PM, FM Host U/S Burns for First Blast Bilat ‘Security Dialogue.’” Wikileaks Cables, 07REYKJAVIK192 (July 3).

US Embassy Reykjavik. 2009a. “Icelandic Fisheries Minister Pessimistic on Reversing Predecessor’s Whale Hunt Quotas for 2009.” Wikileaks Cables, 09REYKJAVIK36 (February 18).

US Embassy Reykjavik. 2009b. “Icelandic Minister Confirms Commercial Whaling Decision Stands.” Wikileaks Cables, 09REYKJAVIK37 (February 20).

US Embassy Tel Aviv. 2006. “Israel Looking to Join Whaling Commission by June.” Wikileaks Cables, 06TELAVIV1645 (April 26).

US Embassy Tokyo. 2006. “U.S. Policy Priorities for Abe Administration.” Wikileaks Cables, 06TOKYO5568 (September 26).

US Embassy Tokyo. 2007. “Whaling: Tentative Agreement Not to Kill Humpbacks This Season.” Wikileaks Cables, 07TOKYO5536 (December 12).

US Embassy Tokyo. 2010. “Whaling Commission Chair Discusses Upcoming IWC Working Group with Japan.” Wikileaks Cables, 08TOKYO2193 (August 10).

US Embassy Wellington. 2006. “Pacific Islands Betray New Zealand over Whales.” Wikileaks Cables, 06WELLINGTON600 (August 1).

Victor, David G. 2001. “Whale Sausage: Why the Whaling Regime Does Not Need to Be Fixed.” In Friedheim 2001, pp. 292–310.

Wong, Anny. 2001. *The Roots of Japan’s International Environmental Policies*. London: Routledge.

Zangl, Bernhard. 1999. *Interessen Auf Zwei Ebenen: Internationale Regime in Der Agrarhandels-, Währungs- und Walfangpolitik*. Baden-Baden: Nomos.

Zimmermann, Lisbeth. 2021. “Law and Science in Environmental Governance: The Effects of Legal and Scientific Argumentation in the International Whaling Commission.” In *Talking International Law: Legal Argumentation outside the Courtroom*, eds. Ian Johnstone and Steven R. Ratner. Oxford: Oxford University Press, pp. 263–81.

5

Losing Africa?

Contestation and the decline in the International Criminal Court's regional robustness

5.1 Introduction

The Rome Statute establishing the International Criminal Court (ICC) was adopted in 1998. With it, the international community called for an end to impunity and codified the *duty to prosecute* all serious violations of international humanitarian and human rights law. When the treaty entered into force in 2002, the ICC—the first permanent court mandated to prosecute individuals responsible for the gravest internationally recognized crimes, including sitting heads of state—began operations. Following formulation of the Nuremberg Principles that included definitions of crimes against peace, war crimes, and crimes against humanity in the 1950 report of the International Law Commission (ILC), international criminal law had stagnated for decades (Schabas 2017: 8–9). Finally, in the 1990s, several ad hoc tribunals were established (Sikkink 2011), which led to the Rome Statute, the "culmination of international law-making of the twentieth century" (Weller 2002: 693). The ICC has criminal jurisdiction for international crimes, irrespective of the accused's position, and does not require approval from the United Nations Security Council (UNSC) when states parties refer cases or the ICC prosecutor takes the initiative. However, the relatively new court has already faced many attacks, some of them shaking its foundations.

The United States (US) has always been wary of the ICC's far-reaching powers and the possible implications for its citizens (Ralph 2007; Jorgensen 2021). African states and the African Union (AU) have also criticized the ICC—beginning with the arrest warrant for Sudan's President Omar Al Bashir (García Iommi 2020; Han and Rosenberg 2021). The contestation culminated in 2016 when, in a matter of weeks, Burundi, South Africa, and the Republic of the Gambia, claiming the ICC was unduly focusing on African states, gave notice that they were withdrawing from the Rome Statute. Although South Africa and The Gambia did not actually withdraw, along with

International Norm Disputes. Lisbeth Zimmermann et al., Oxford University Press. © Lisbeth Zimmermann, Nicole Deitelhoff, Max Lesch, Antonio Arcudi, and Anton Peez (2023). DOI: 10.1093/oso/9780198873235.003.0005

growing pressure from the AU, they sent a clear signal to the ICC that support for the court was declining on the African continent. On March 17, 2019, the Philippines withdrew from the ICC after it opened an investigation into extrajudicial killings by the police in the context of the government's "war on drugs."[1]

In light of these ongoing disputes, some scholars caution that "[T]he momentum for international criminal law seems to be gone and its success story—[. . .] culminating in the adoption of the Rome Statute—has come to a close" (Luban 2013: 505). Several studies conclude that AU contestation of the ICC is eroding the international duty to prosecute (e.g. Boehme 2017; Mills and Bloomfield 2018; García Iommi 2020). They emphasize that the ICC cannot deliver on its promises because it has been instrumentalized by many states (Ba 2020) and enjoys only partial compliance (Boehme 2022) and because of its mixed effects on conflict situations (Kersten 2016; Clark 2018). Other scholars argue that despite challenges, the duty to prosecute, international criminal law, and the ICC remain robust (Bower 2019; Simmons and Jo 2019). The various opinions result from different interpretations of norm contestation and its effect on robustness. In this chapter, we contribute to the debate by mapping validity and applicatory contestation patterns worldwide and on the African continent and examine how they influence norm robustness.

We argue that the robustness of duty to prosecute and the ICC have indeed begun to weaken—at least on the African continent, which has long been its focus. We evaluate this trend with respect to decreasing compliance with the court, African states' failure to criticize norm violations, and relatively stable—but low—implementation and concordance in Africa. The main reason for the norm's declining robustness is the rise in validity contestation, which is due to the lack of institutional pathways for African critique (Arcudi 2019; Deitelhoff 2020). While some argue that non-cooperation and contestation can be best explained by interest-based calculations (Ba 2020; Boehme 2022), our findings support the argument that justice dynamics on the African continent (see Clarke 2019) had the strongest effect on contestation and robustness.

We begin by sketching out how the ICC was established and define the core claims of its underlying norm, the duty to prosecute. We then introduce data to assess contestation and norm robustness in two phases: The first was from the Rome Statute's adoption in 1998 to the court's first activities, which were mainly based on self-referrals after the establishment of the ICC in 2002. The

[1] The court still has jurisdiction over crimes allegedly committed in the Philippines between November 1 and March 16, 2019, when it was a member.

second phase begins in 2008, after Omar Al Bashir's arrest warrant was issued, and examines disputes regarding Sudan and Kenya. It ends in 2016, when three African ICC members announced they intended to withdraw from the ICC. Section 5.3 analyzes contestation trends in international discourse and Section 5.4 traces the norm's robustness. We finish by discussing explanatory factors, particularly perceptions of procedural fairness.

5.2 Duty to prosecute: History and data

5.2.1 Norm evolution

The duty to prosecute institutionalized in the ICC is a fairly recent norm with a long history. The Rome Statute of 1998 specified and expanded the notion of criminal accountability beyond the scope that was used when, between 1945 and 1948, the Allied forces prosecuted members of the Axis powers in Nuremberg and Tokyo for the crimes against peace, war crimes, and crimes against humanity. Subsequent calls to universalize the Charter of the International Military Tribunal (IMT)—the legal basis for the Nuremburg trials—and establish a permanent international criminal court quickly subsided in the evolving Cold War (Deitelhoff 2009: 36; Schabas 2017: 9–11). Only after the end of the Cold War did we see "a shift in the legitimacy of the norm of criminal accountability for human rights violations and increase in prosecutions on behalf of that norm" (Sikkink 2011: 5). In 1989, Trinidad and Tobago called upon the United Nations (UN) to establish an international criminal court to prosecute illicit drug trafficking and other transnational crimes, giving new impetus to the UN debate about a permanent court (Trinidad & Tobago 1989).

The UN General Assembly (UNGA) reacted by assigning the International Law Commission (ILC)—a body of experts that had been established in 1947 to help develop international law—with creating the framework for an international criminal court. In 1994, the ILC presented its "Draft Statute for an International Criminal Court" that, in addition to drug trafficking, also included genocide, war crimes, and crimes against humanity. However, the ILC hesitated to infringe on state sovereignty, debating options to opt in or opt out from jurisdiction which would have limited its applicatory reach (Crawford 1994). Meanwhile, the UN ad hoc tribunals for the former Yugoslavia (1993–2017) and Rwanda (1994–2016) had reinforced the norm that perpetrators of international crimes must be held accountable.

Based on the ILC draft statute and experience gained at the tribunals for former Yugoslavia and Rwanda, the Preparatory Committee on the

Establishment of an International Criminal Court began work in 1995. The Like-Minded Group (LMG)—at the beginning mainly small and middle powers supported by the Coalition for the International Criminal Court (CICC)—pushed for an independent court led by a prosecutor authorized to open investigations and in which heads of state and government officials enjoy no immunity (Deitelhoff 2009: 37). In contrast, the "P-5" negotiating block—led by the five permanent UNSC members, France, the United Kingdom (UK), the US, Russia, and China—remained committed to state sovereignty and favored the ILC's conservative draft, which assigned the UNSC a central role, according states more influence on ICC cases (Deitelhoff 2009: 36–37; Goodliffe and Hawkins 2009: 977).

Despite dissent, the draft statute for an international criminal court was completed in April 1998 (Bassiouni 1999: 444–45). That June, the United Nations Diplomatic Conference of Plenipotentiaries on the Establishment of an International Criminal Court (the Rome Conference) opened in Italy and, after five weeks of negotiations, adopted the Rome Statute, with 120 states voting in favor, 21 abstaining, and 7, including the US, China, and India, dissenting (Goldstone and Smith 2008: 110–11). France and the UK were among the most prominent states that changed their position and now supported the Rome Statute (Deitelhoff 2009: 50–51), which met many LMG demands: The ICC has more far-reaching competencies than the ILC draft had envisaged.

The Rome Statute authorizes the ICC to prosecute genocide, war crimes, crimes against humanity, and, since 2018, the crime of aggression. In addition to referrals by states parties (Art. 14), the UNSC can refer situations, including those of non-members, to the ICC (Art. 13(b), whose prosecutor can also initiate investigations (Art. 15, *proprio motu*) in ICC member states (see Schabas 2017: 141–63). Although in principle the UNSC can postpone an ICC case for a renewable period of 12 months, that requires a majority within the UNSC without any permanent member's veto (Art. 16; see Schabas 2017: 163–68). The Rome Statute entered into force in 2002 with the establishment of the ICC, which quickly opened its first cases.

5.2.2 Normative core claims

The Rome Statute codified the duty to prosecute that was institutionalized in the ICC: "[I]t is the duty of every state to exercise its criminal jurisdiction over those responsible for international crimes [and] to put an end to impunity for the perpetrators of these crimes" (Rome Statute

1998: 1). The duty to prosecute refers to the universal obligation to investigate *and* prosecute the most serious atrocities: genocide, war crimes, and crimes against humanity—and, since 2018, aggression. While focused at the national level, under the "complementarity principle," the obligation passes to the international level—the ICC—if national jurisdictions are incapable, or unwilling, to prosecute (Deitelhoff 2009: 37–38). The ICC's duty to prosecute means that individuals, including heads of state, are no longer protected by the principles of state sovereignty and heads of state immunity—which, as part of customary international law, made heads of states immune from prosecution in other states in the past:

> This Statute shall apply equally to all persons without any distinction based on official capacity. [...] Immunities or special procedural rules which may attach to the official capacity of a person, whether under national or international law, shall not bar the Court from exercising its jurisdiction over such a person.
>
> **(Rome Statute 1998: Art. 27)**

States parties to the Rome Statute agree to waive their senior officials' immunity. Even citizens of non-states parties do not enjoy immunity in cases referred to the ICC by the UNSC and if the alleged crimes were committed on a state party's territory (Schabas 2017: 59, 62).

We define challenges to this core claim as *validity* contestation, which, in its most radical form, rejects the norm or the ICC as the competent implementing authority, for example, by invoking neocolonialism or imperialism. Calls to exempt certain groups from the duty to prosecute that generally prioritize other norms such as sovereignty or "peace" also contest the norm's validity by challenging its core claims. When states challenge the appropriateness of norms in specific situations, we speak of *applicatory* contestation, for example, when they doubt the ICC's impartiality, criticize its double standards and politicization, or question the duty to prosecute in specific situations.[2] As we noted in Chapter 1, the distinction between contestation types is often muddy in the empirical analysis, and applicatory contestation can be linked to or disguise more fundamental—validity—challenges to the norm. In ambiguous cases, we decided to code statements as applicatory. Despite this conservative coding approach, we see a strong increase in validity contestation, which buttresses our findings.

[2] For detailed coding schemes, see the Appendix, Table A.4.

5.2.3 Data collection and analysis

We begin with data from 1998, when the Rome Statute was adopted, and end in 2016, when three African ICC members submitted their notifications of withdrawal from the ICC. We also discuss some recent developments regarding the court. We distinguish two phases—before and after the first warrant to arrest a sitting head of state, Omar Al Bashir of Sudan. The first phase, between 1998 and 2007, covers the establishment of the court, US attempts to undermine it, and the first ICC cases (Section 5.3.1). The second phase, between 2008 and 2016, covers the heated debates about Darfur (Sudan) and Kenya (Section 5.3.2).

To analyze contestation trends and the discursive dimension of norm robustness (affirmations and negative reactions), we coded 1,059 statements by states, regional organizations, and groups of states in the Assembly of States Parties (ASP—the ICC's management oversight and legislative body), in UNSC and UNGA meetings, newspapers articles, and communications between states parties and the ICC as well as AU documents.[3] To manage the huge volume of data, we coded all the country statements in the general debate of every other ASP session (341). We conducted a full-text search of the UN Official Document System to identify relevant UNSC meeting records on the duty to prosecute and the ICC (173), as well as the UNGA Plenary (246) and its Sixth Committee on Legal Affairs (172), and coded a random sample of statements in UN meetings. To get a better picture of African discourse on the ICC, we also coded relevant statements in newspaper articles using LexisNexis to search African newspapers (102).[4] Finally, we coded a random sample of communications from states parties to the ICC (as documented by ICC headquarters) that address the situations in Kenya and the Democratic Republic of the Congo (DRC) (12), and all AU documents on the ICC (13).[5]

For the practical dimension of norm robustness, we collected new data on compliance and relied on data sets and secondary literature to assess implementation of the duty to prosecute (see Dukalskis and Johansen 2013).

[3] Per year, the number of statements is distributed as follows (note that we coded the ASP only every second year, which is reflected in the biannual variation): 1998: 31, 1999: 29, 2000: 27, 2001: 30, 2002: 55, 2003: 51, 2004: 31, 2005: 41, 2006: 63, 2007: 39, 2008: 84, 2009: 37, 2010: 81, 2011: 42, 2012: 79, 2013: 58, 2014: 98, 2015: 75, 2016: 111.

[4] The coded material includes articles in: *Sudan Tribune*, Sudan (45); *Daily Nation*, Kenya (19); *Herald*, Zimbabwe (9); *Pretoria News*, South Africa (9); *Cape Argus*, South Africa (5); *The Mercury*, South Africa (4); *Sunday Independent*, South Africa (4); *Cape Times*, South Africa (3); *Mail & Guardian*, regional (3); *Argus Weekend*, South Africa (2); *Al-Bawaba*, regional (1); *Independent on Saturday*, South Africa (1).

[5] Supplementary material and data is available at the Harvard Dataverse: https://doi.org/10.7910/DVN/6VHFZK.

We measured norm compliance through the degree of ICC cooperation by members and non-members (for this approach, see Berlin 2016; Hillebrecht and Straus 2017; Boehme 2022).[6] We measured *implementation* of the duty to prosecute by assessing existing data about how national criminal codes have been incorporating the Rome Statute and its core crimes (Simmons and Jo 2019; Berlin 2020) and how cooperation between the court and member states was being institutionalized—both of which are needed to enforce the norm. We studied *concordance* by qualitatively analyzing affirmations, Rome Statute ratification rates, and data on the salience of the core crimes in UNGA resolutions, and discuss secondary literature regarding public opinion (Simmons and Jo 2019; Zvobgo 2019). Finally, we assess *negative reactions to norm violations* based on the discourse data sets described here. Our findings are complemented by insights from secondary literature.

5.3 Contestation trends

The duty to prosecute has been contested since the Rome Statute was adopted. Figure 5.1 shows that between 1998 and 2016, both applicatory and validity contestation generally rose. Before 2008, contestation mainly came from states that had criticized the ICC during the Rome Statute negotiations, particularly the US, which sought immunity for its own citizens. After the UNSC referred the situation in Darfur to the ICC in 2005, validity contestation was minimal and even dropped slightly. But in 2009, after the ICC prosecutor issued an arrest warrant for Sudanese President Omar Al Bashir, it rose sharply. In 2010, after the ICC opened investigations into Kenya's post-election violence in 2008 and 2009, it peaked again.

The shift toward contestation is more dramatic among the group of African states parties—with 33 states the largest regional group in the ICC—and the AU (see Figure 5.2).[7] In fact, after 2007, their challenges represent the most contestation worldwide, with challenges to the applicability and validity of the duty to prosecute almost rising in parallel. Before the ICC was established, and during its first cases, only a few African states contested application of the duty to prosecute, and none of them challenged its validity until 2004 before the UNSC referred the situation in Darfur to the ICC. The radicalization of

[6] On the deterring effects of the ICC, see Hillebrecht (2016); Jo and Simmons (2016); Miller (2022).

[7] This includes, among others, Côte d'Ivoire, Kenya, Mali Nigeria, South Africa, Tunisia, Tanzania and Uganda. African non-members are, e.g. Rwanda, Sudan, and Ethiopia.

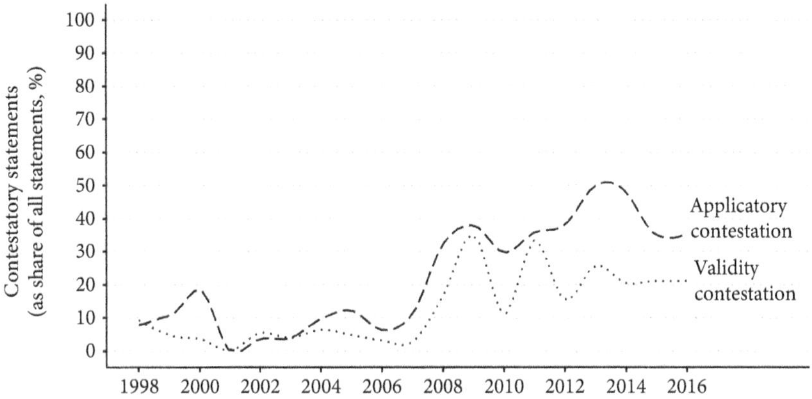

Figure 5.1 Contestation of the duty to prosecute, all states, 1998–2016
Source: Based on 1,059 statements in UN, ICC, and AU documents as well as in African newspaper articles.
Note: Contestation patterns do not significantly shift if we exclude the statements in African newspapers and only focus on discourse in international organizations.

contestation after 2008 was mainly due to African states' growing frustration with the Sudanese and Kenyan cases (see Han and Rosenberg 2021: 741). We now turn our focus to contestation during both phases and show that it mainly became radicalized in African discourse after 2008.

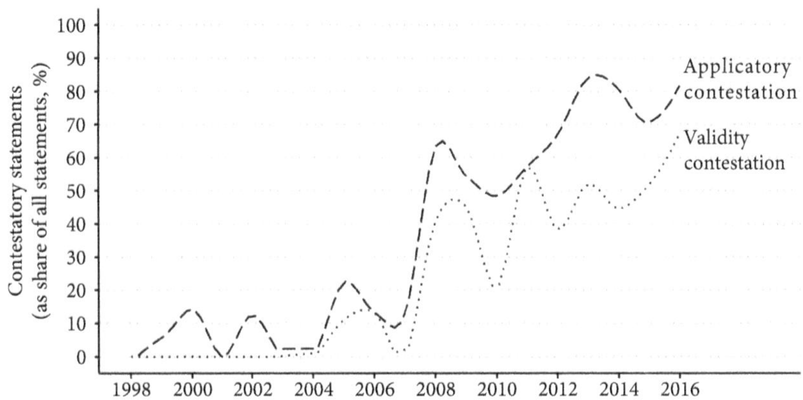

Figure 5.2 Contestation of the duty to prosecute, African states and the AU, 1998–2016
Source: Based on 323 statements in UN, ICC, and AU documents as well as in African newspaper articles. Updated and adapted with permission from Deitelhoff. 2020. "What's in a Name? Contestation and Backlash against International Norms and Institutions." *British Journal of Politics and International Relations* 22 (4): pp. 715–27. doi: 10.1177/1369148120945906.
Note: Contestation patterns do not significantly shift if we exclude the statements in African newspapers and only focus on discourse in international organizations.

5.3.1 From the ICC's establishment to its first cases

After adoption of the Rome Statute, the Preparatory Commission developed the formal and institutional requirements for the court to begin its work after ratification by the sixtieth state (Kirsch and Oosterveld 2001). Until then, the rare contestation mainly came from states that had always been critical of a permanent international criminal court, including the US, who only signed the Rome Statute in 2000 to have a say in the negotiations (Barnidge 2003–04: 739; Birdsall 2010: 456). The US warned that without its support, the ICC would fail (Scheffer 1998, 2000). Yet, the few explicit challenges concerned how the ICC would implement the duty to prosecute and emphasized that national jurisdiction should be prioritized over international.

Questioning the work of the Preparatory Commission and noting that the court would likely be politicized, Israel expressed that it was "deeply concerned at the inclusion, in the list of the gravest war crimes, of formulations tailored to meet the political agenda of certain States" (Israel in UNGA 2000: 4). While Israel addressed the norm's potential application, other countries contested its validity. In UNGA, Pakistan underlined that the:

> Court should complement, and not supplant, the national legal system, failing which it would impinge on the sovereignty of the State. However, some provisions of the Statue, such as the provision concerning the *proprio motu* role of the Prosecutor, tended to dilute that same principle. Similarly, the role assigned to the Security Council in activating the trigger mechanism should be the exclusive realm of States parties, as Security Council decisions were based on political considerations and not on legal principles.
>
> **(Pakistan in UNGA 1998: 8)**

Such statements attack the core claim of the ICC's duty to prosecute by prioritizing domestic legal jurisdiction. That said, in the years immediately following the Rome Statute's adoption, most contestation was applicatory.

In 2002, after 60 states had ratified the Rome Statute, it entered into force—surprising even some of the court's advocates who "had predicted that this goal would not be realized for decades" (Pace 2002: 1). Once established, the US more energetically sought to undermine the court. The newly elected Bush administration declared that it would *not* ratify the Rome Statute, "effectively 'unsigning'" and formally withdrawing from the treaty (Birdsall 2010: 457–58). The US also tried to target the court's operationality by prohibiting any kind of cooperation with the ICC, extraditions to the court and its funding (US Department of State 2003: Sec. 2004). It also entered into bilateral agreements that forbid other countries surrendering US citizens to the ICC (Birdsall 2010: 457; Bosco 2014: 74) and sought to shield its citizens from ICC jurisdiction.

In the court's early years, the greatest challenge to the norm's validity was about exempting US peacekeepers. Shortly after the ICC was established, US diplomats warned that the US would no longer participate in UN peacekeeping missions if its troops were not protected from ICC prosecution (US in *New York Times* 2002) and threatened to veto extensions of peacekeeping missions in the UNSC (Lynch 2002). When that was not assured for the UN peacekeeping mission in East Timor, the US pulled out its troops (Bower 2015: 350). In negotiations over the peacekeeping mission in Bosnia and Herzegovina, the US argued that:

> [W]e are and will remain a special target and cannot have our decision second-guessed by a court whose jurisdiction we do not recognize. With the court coming into being, this problem must be resolved—but in a way that takes into account two hard facts: the United States wants to participate in international peacekeeping, but the United States [. . .] does not and will not accept the jurisdiction of the ICC over the peacekeepers that it contributes.
>
> **(US in UNSC 2002: 2–3)**

Demands for exceptions for special groups—in this case, US peacekeepers—challenge one of the core claims of the duty to prosecute by limiting its reach in cases covered by the Rome Statute. One example of applicatory and validity contestation in legal terms was when the US cited Article 16 of the Rome Statute (Bower 2015: 352) that allows the UNSC to suspend ICC investigations for a year to ensure peace and security (see Section 5.3.2).

Although its challenge was opposed (Bower 2015: 352–53), in 2002, the UNSC agreed to grant immunity for peacekeeping forces from countries' not party to the Court's Statute for 12 months (Thomas 2009: 383). In 2003, the clause was extended for another year (UNSC 2003b). In 2004, the US did not seek a third extension due to growing pressure from allegations of norm violations in its war on terror (Birdsall 2010: 460), which made it difficult for the US to sustain its (legal) contestation (Bower 2015: 356–57). Brazil, for example, criticized that "extending the exemptions of certain categories of individuals from ICC jurisdiction must not be carried out at the expense of the effectiveness of the historic achievement represented by the entry into force of the Rome Statute" (Brazil in UNSC 2003a: 13). Later UNSC resolutions referring the situations in Darfur and Libya to the ICC included exemptions for citizens of non-ICC members—except for the citizens of Sudan and Libya, of course (UNSC 2005b: para. 6, 2011: para. 6).

Although the US was determined to limit the ICC's reach (Birdsall 2010: 462–63), its coercive power could not fully achieve its goals (Bower 2015: 357–58). This episode shows the limits of contestation for even a very powerful state such as the US (see Section 5.5).

That said, US opposition to the ICC could effectively pressure the nascent court because US veto power made it unlikely that the UNSC would refer cases to the ICC, which was seen as the most viable route (Bosco 2014: 78–80). Yet, the ICC soon opened its first investigations of situations referred to the court from an unforeseen direction: Between 2003 and 2005, the governments of Uganda, the DRC, and the Central African Republic (CAR) called on the ICC prosecutor to investigate crimes allegedly committed within their *own* borders during past or current conflicts (see Bower 2017: 139–42; Ba 2020: 15–17). These "self-referrals" reinterpreted the Rome Statute's Article 14 on ICC members referring situations in other states parties (Akhavan 2010: 103). In 2004, the ICC opened investigations into the situations in Uganda and the DRC and, in 2007, investigated the situation in CAR. This innovative approach raised concerns about the referring parties' intentions (Tiemessen 2014; Ba 2020: ch. 3) and the ICC's first Chief Prosecutor Luis Moreno-Ocampo efforts to get early and quick successes for the court (Schabas 2008). The cases themselves were hardly contested.

Sudan, the ICC's fourth case in 2005, was different. The US, China, and Russia abstained (Bower 2017: 159–60), allowing the UNSC to refer the Darfur situation to the ICC for it to investigate war crimes and crimes against humanity allegedly committed by Sudanese forces and allied militias like the notorious Janjaweed (UNSC 2005b). In 2007, the ICC issued its first arrest warrants for Sudanese officials and militia leaders.

Sudan began to challenge both the duty to prosecute and the ICC, mainly at the applicatory level regarding the UNSC's role in referring the situation in Sudan, which did not belong to the ICC (see also Bower 2019: 94). At the ASP, Sudan claimed that:

> [T]he resolution by the Security Council referring the situation in Darfur to the International Criminal Court was, by and large, influenced by political considerations. The resolution came within a series of resolutions aiming at putting pressure on Government of the Sudan. Some powers that were campaigning against the Sudan in the Council were not genuinely interested in bringing about justice.
>
> **(Sudan 2006).**

Contesting the prioritization of peace over justice is at the boundary of application and validity: Instead of questioning the validity of the court or the duty to prosecute, it challenges the legitimacy of the process. We coded such challenges as "applicatory," well aware that they sow the seeds for contestation to radicalize. Foreshadowing many of the debates that would flare up after 2008, Sudan also derided international prosecution as a tool of power politics and hegemony (Sudan in UNSC 2005a: 12)—challenging the validity of the duty to prosecute.

Critique of the Sudanese referral included claims about double standards in only applying the duty to prosecute to a person "if he belongs to a certain category of states" (Sudan in UNSC 2005a: 12). Algeria noted that:

> [T]hose defending the principle of universal justice have in fact ensured that, in this domain, the use of double standards—of which some have accused the Council—and a two-track justice were most unexpectedly demonstrated.
>
> **(Algeria in UNSC 2005a: 5)**

Taking a somewhat different track, some states contested the duty to prosecute by invoking the complementarity principle and prioritizing alternative justice mechanisms. Sudan insisted that atrocities should be tried nationally (Sudan in UNGA 2007: 21) and at the ASP, Namibia emphasized "that justice can also be achieved through reconciliation, not only through punishment and retribution" (Namibia 2006). These statements are also in between applicatory and validity contestation because, as we shall see in section 5.3.2, they can easily be shifted toward more categorical rejections of the ICC and the duty to prosecute.

In sum, before and after the ICC was established, contestation remained rather low—even for African states and the AU. The very few statements challenging the validity of the duty to prosecute—mainly by the US, which does not belong to the ICC—did not diffuse in the broader international discourse. However, contestation is slowly increasing and beginning to shift toward more radical statements—mostly by Sudan—that include allegations of politicization and double standards.

5.3.2 Radicalization of contestation on the African continent

In July 2008, ICC Chief Prosecutor Moreno-Ocampo presented the charges of crimes against humanity and genocide against Sudanese president Omar Al Bashir and requested an arrest warrant, which the ICC Pre-Trial Chamber I issued in March 2009 (ICC 2009). The indictment was a watershed for many African states and the AU with respect to the ICC: The AU Peace and Security Council (PSC) called on the UNSC to suspend the ICC procedure in conformity with Article 16 of the Rome Statute, arguing that it undermined peace-making in Darfur (AU Peace and Security Council 2008). The UNSC first ignored the AU's call that was then merely noted in Resolution 1828 (UNSC 2008). Its refusal to engage outraged the AU and some African states (Mills 2012: 421; Mills and Bloomfield 2018: 110–11). For years, Al Bashir remained at large and little happened in the case. Finally, in April 2022, the ICC began to try former Janjaweed general, Ali Muhammad Ali Abd-Al-Rahman (ICC 2022).

In 2008, tension grew between the ICC and African states and the AU when the ICC chief prosecutor decided to investigate the post-election violence in Kenya (see Chapter 3). After the 2007 presidential elections, violent and ethnicized conflicts erupted over allegations of election fraud by the defeated candidate Raila Odinga against re-elected president Mwai Kibaki. The conflict ended with a power-sharing agreement under which Kibaki remained president and Odinga became prime minister. Yet, in 2010, for the first time, Ocampo-Moreno made use of *proprio mutu*: He opened a case that had not been referred by a state party or the UNSC. Six Kenyan officials—including Uhuru Kenyatta and William Ruto, both members of the new government—were summoned on charges of crimes against humanity (ICC 2011a, b). The two formerly fierce opponents joined ranks and won the 2013 elections, in which the "anti-ICC stance" had been a central theme: Kenyatta became president and Ruto his deputy (Boehme 2022: 118–19). The case set off a lengthy back and forth between Kenya and the ICC, including whether the most powerful of the accused, Kenyatta and Ruto, had to attend the trial in person. Kenya invoked complementarity, arguing that national courts were better suited to address the charges (Bower 2019: 94). Only Kenyatta appeared at the ICC in the Hague for a hearing in October 2014 (Boehme 2022: 107). However, their cases collapsed at the ICC because of a lack of cooperation from Kenya and a lack of evidence due to witnesses repudiating their testimony (Ba 2020: 106–108). Contestation about the Sudanese and Kenyan cases ultimately challenged the norm's core claim about prosecuting sitting heads of state. That said, contestation was almost exclusively driven by African states and did not diffuse into the broader international discourse (see Figures 5.1 and 5.2; see also Bower 2019: 94–95).

Yet, the Sudanese and Kenyan cases served to radicalize contestation of the duty to prosecute, which spread throughout African discourse and increasingly challenged the norm's validity. While a good number of African states have not taken part in the debate (Vilmer 2016: 1326) and some continued to support the ICC (Boehme 2022: 48), it is worth noting that contesting states received little open pushback (see Section 5.4.1). African states challenged the duty to prosecute in four main areas: the immunity of sitting heads of state; a selective (and in their view, illegitimate) focus on Africa; the need to balance making peace with seeking justice; and the principle of complementarity between national, regional, and international judicial mechanisms.

The *immunity of heads of states* has been key to the African challenges and is the clearest example of validity contestation because it is fundamental to the duty to prosecute (see Section 5.2.2). After Al Bashir's arrest warrant had been issued, without singling out the ICC, the AU adopted a declaration criticizing international criminal prosecution and calling for negotiations with the EU "to ensure that those warrants are withdrawn and are not executable in any country" (AU Assembly 2008: para. 7). Other African states joined Sudan's contestation, with the Djibouti Foreign Minister Mahmoud Ali Yousif stating: "The indictment [against Al Bashir] sets a dangerous precedent in dealing with heads of states. It will have dangerous repercussions" (quoted in *Sudan Tribune* 2008). In July 2009, the AU issued a resolution denouncing the violation of Al Bashir's right to immunity, calling on member states to not comply with his arrest warrant (AU Assembly 2009). In 2012, the AU proclaimed:

> [T]he immunities provided for by international law apply not only to proceedings in foreign domestic courts but also to international tribunals: states cannot contract out of their international legal obligations vis-à-vis third states by establishing an international tribunal.
>
> **(AU Assembly 2012: 1)**

For its part, Lesotho rejected the prosecution of heads of state, invoking "the principles deriving from national laws and international customary law by which sitting Heads of State and other senior officials are granted immunities during their tenure of office" (Lesotho 2014). As one of the few non-African states to weigh in on the subject, China supported African claims "on the matter of head-of-state immunity," and called on the ICC to "take into full account the legitimate demands of African states [. . .] instead of causing unnecessary impediment to state leaders in discharging their functions" (China 2014).

Contestation of the ICC's predilection for African cases took various shapes. Arguments directly challenging the application of the duty to prosecute accused the ICC of double standards and politicization. Kenya criticized the "political genesis of the ICC cases" (Kenya in *Daily Nation* 2014a), while Uganda questioned the "politicization and selectivity of the ICC's methods" (Uganda in UNGA 2014b). African states and the AU repeatedly urged the ICC to not turn "a blind eye" to situations involving Western states (e.g. Zimbabwe in Gowans 2011; African Union 2012; Nigeria 2016) and non-African states, such as Colombia and Afghanistan (e.g. Kenya 2011b). The critique of double standards is one of the issues that non-African states supported, with Austria underlining that "other situations would warrant the same decisive action by the Security Council" and calling "for a coherent approach to referrals" because the international community "cannot turn a blind eye to mass killings of innocent civilians, as we are currently witnessing in Syria" (Austria 2011). Although these challenges addressed the way the ICC applies the duty to prosecute, African states used them to more fundamentally contest the ICC. At UNGA in 2014, Sudan reiterated "its clear and firm position on rejecting the so-called International Criminal Court (ICC), as it continues to serve as a forum for politicizing international justice and targeting African leaders" (Sudan in UNGA 2014a: 22). Contestation had begun to challenge the validity of the duty to prosecute and reject the ICC.

More flagrant challenges to the norm's validity are observed in statements based on strong views of African sovereignty that criticize the ICC as an imperialist and neocolonial project. Kenyatta maintained, "We should aim to protect and sustain our independence against all negative forces and uphold the dignity and sovereignty of the African continent and our people" (Kenya in *Daily Nation* 2015). From 2014 onwards, "exit rhetoric" entered official diplomatic debates (Boehme 2022: 143). In 2016 and 2017, this sentiment culminated in the AU calling for African members to withdraw from the ICC (Bower 2019: 99). Kenya, Namibia, and Uganda publicly contemplated withdrawing from the ICC and The Gambia, South Africa, and Burundi officially lodged notices to withdraw (Boehme 2022: 144–55). Although, with the exception of Burundi, they have not (see Section 5.4.2), it shows the general discursive challenge both to the duty to prosecute and the ICC—which a statement from Burundi exemplifies:

> Burundi's accession to the Rome Statute was motivated by the guarantees of respect for the independence and sovereignty of States Parties under the provisions on complementarity, the independence of the statutory bodies of the ICC, in particular, the independence of the Office of the Prosecutor in the administration of international justice. Once the people of Burundi had evidence of violations of these guarantees with so much potential harm to the Republic of Burundi, it took its responsibilities under the Rome Statute and the Constitution of Burundi to denounce the violations and demand the immediate withdrawal of Burundi.
>
> (Burundi 2016)

Echoing the accusation of double standards, it was often argued that international prosecution was being used for "hunting" (Ethiopia in *Sunday Independent* 2013), "harassing," or "targeting" Africans (Kenya in *Daily Nation* 2014b, 2015). Impunity for heads of state was defended on the grounds that "an African [head of state] was not being afforded the same immunity from prosecution that powerful [heads of state] may be afforded" (Han and Rosenberg 2021: 744). Ethiopia argued that the ICC "has transformed [. . .] into a political instrument targeting Africa and Africans" (quoted in *Independent on Saturday* 2013) and Muammar Gaddafi deplored the "attempt by [the West] to re-colonise their former colonies" (quoted in Vilmer 2016: 1321). The Africans' sense of unequal treatment has fueled the broader perception of the court's unfairness (see Section 5.5). It remains to be seen whether the ICC's more recent cases—including the situations in Georgia, Afghanistan, the Philippines, Palestine, Myanmar/ Bangladesh, and, most recently, Ukraine—will help counter the critique.[8]

Contestation also evolved with the conundrum of peace and justice that has shaped criminal justice in general and the ICC's work in particular (for a comprehensive discussion, see Kersten 2016). The Rome Statute acknowledges the tension between peace processes and the pursuit of justice (see Section 5.2.1). We regard challenges addressing this tension that are based on, but do not fundamentally reject, the Rome Statute as applicatory contestation. African states have made several arguments based on the Rome Statute and Article 16 that allows the UNSC to suspend ICC proceedings in the name of ensuring peace and security. In 2008, the AU PSC warned that "[T]he ICC Prosecutor could seriously undermine the ongoing efforts aimed at facilitating the early resolution of the conflict in Darfur and the promotion of long-lasting peace" (AU Peace and Security Council 2008: 2). In support of the national peace process and regional stability, Kenya and the AU called on the UNSC to halt the investigation (Kenya 2013) and discharge Kenyatta and Ruto from having to attend their trials in The Hague (AU Assembly 2013: 1). Although this request resulted in changing the ICC's rules of procedure (ASP 2013), other requests by Kenya and the AU were not taken up by the ICC or its members (Bower 2019: 97).

The reluctance of the ICC and its member states to modify the tenets underlying the duty to prosecute in response to African demands partly explains why applicatory contestation intensified and radicalized into validity challenges (Arcudi 2019). Arguments that call on the ICC to delay its work to protect fragile peace processes mainly address the application of the duty to prosecute but can serve to contest its validity if they generalize that demand. Uganda stated that:

> [J]ustice cannot be sacrificed at the altar of peace, peace too cannot be sacrificed at the altar of justice, or at the very best, a fine balance must be sought.

[8] For all ICC cases, see https://www.icc-cpi.int/Pages/cases.aspx. Accessed February 18, 2022.

> Accordingly, the Continent has on a number of occasions called upon the Court and the United Nations Security Council to strike this balance between the two concepts whenever circumstances so warrant. We regret to note that on most occasions, Africa's voice has gone unheeded.
>
> **(Uganda 2016)**

South Africa similarly held that it was impossible to uphold "an idealistic view striving only to achieve justice and accountability, leaving aside the immediate objectives of attaining peace, security and stability" (South Africa 2016). These statements reject the principle of the duty to prosecute and the ICC by always favoring peace-making over criminal justice, which contradicts the Rome Statute. They also express many African states' frustration over not having their concerns acknowledged by the ICC or the UN. On the African continent, institutional responses to contestation were perceived as unfair and served to radicalize contestation (see Section 5.5).

Finally, the *complementarity principle* of the Rome Statute—whether the duty to prosecute should be applied at the national, regional, or international level—provided an entry point for contestation. This issue has been key to African states, although the UK also invoked the principle to dodge preliminary ICC investigations into the role of British forces in the war on terror by arguing that it was already dealing with those matters (UK 2015). Echoing earlier Sudanese arguments, Kenya wrote to the ICC Appeals Chamber, trying to make a case for national jurisdiction over the alleged crimes:

> A fundamental error was committed by the Pre-Trial Chamber in its finding that no investigation is presently being undertaken by the Government of Kenya into the six Suspects. [. . .] The ICC may retain jurisdiction if "the State is unwilling or unable genuinely to carry out the investigation." The Pre-Trial Chamber did not find that the Government of Kenya was either "unwilling" or "unable" to investigate the six Suspects. The Chamber did not deal with these questions.
>
> **(Kenya 2011b: 3)**

Referring to judicial reforms since the 2007 elections as well as the new Kenyan constitution and arguing that Kenyan courts were able to prosecute the alleged crimes themselves, the Kenyan government argued that the case violated the complementarity principle and was therefore inadmissible in the ICC (Kenya 2011a: 11). Support again came from China's call for the ICC to "strictly comply with the complementarity principle, fully respect the needs and wishes of national courts to handle cases themselves, give positive consideration to the legitimate demands of the regional organizations concerned" (China in UNGA 2013: 23). However, the ICC rejected Kenya's appeal because its judiciary had not taken any concrete steps to prosecute the accused (ICC 2011c). This decision was confirmed by the ICC Appeals Chamber on August 30, 2011 (ICC 2011d). This further fueled perceptions that the African position was not properly recognized by the ICC.

Although technically an issue of *how* the norm is *applied*, contesting the complementarity principle can also tackle its *validity* by aiming to evade international jurisdiction or favoring alternative mechanisms that do not fulfill the universal duty to prosecute codified in the Rome Statute. This was clear in the AU's attempt to establish a regional criminal court. Adopted in 2014, the Malabo Protocol would create a criminal chamber within the African Court of Justice and Human and Peoples' Rights, if ratified (AU Assembly 2014) While such a regional court could complement the ICC under the Rome Statute (Nimigan 2019), it has been coined "an African alternative to the ICC" (Vilmer 2016: 1340). There are concerns about how it could regionally complement the ICC because it protects sitting heads of state from jurisdiction, thus only partially implementing the Rome Statute's basic provisions regarding the core international crimes and universal non-impunity (Vilmer 2016: 1340; Bower 2019: 97). As we have shown, granting immunity to heads of state amounts to validity contestation. The Malabo Protocol has not entered into force because none of the signatories has ratified it (as of 2022).[9] Besides that, the African Court on Human and Peoples' Rights is facing growing resistance within Africa (Daly and Wiebusch 2018).

In sum, contestation of the application and validity of the duty to prosecute has significantly increased among African states but not yet among non-African ones. As the largest regional group among ICC members, African states were crucial for the Rome Statute's adoption and the ICC's rapid establishment (Deitelhoff 2009; Nimigan 2021). The continent has also been the main theater of ICC interventions to date. Unlike Bower (2019: 90), we argue that between 2008 and 2016, contestation on the African continent challenged the validity of the duty to prosecute as a whole. Since 2017, there have been signs for decreasing contestation among African states, after the ICC paused or closed the Kenyan cases (Boehme 2022: 69, 73). It remains to be seen how contestation trends will develop: The states under scrutiny are

[9] The status of the protocol is available at: https://au.int/en/treaties/protocol-amendments-protocol-statute-african-court-justice-and-human-rights. Accessed February 18, 2022.

likely to continue their challenges as they seek to soften the impact of ICC proceedings. This is one reason why African contestation has been greatest (Ba 2020: 139–40), especially when the ICC targeted senior officials (Boehme 2022). As we have shown and discuss in more detail below (Section 5.5), rational consideration was not the sole driver of contestation, which has been shaped by concerns about justice and fair treatment (see also Clarke 2019).

As the ICC has taken up new cases outside Africa, contestation has also begun to flare up elsewhere. To date, the most prominent examples are the withdrawal by the Philippines and the US challenges to the ICC in the Afghanistan situation. Israel, Myanmar, and Venezuela have also challenged ICC activities, mainly questioning the jurisdiction of the court in their cases. In 2006, the ICC began a preliminary investigation into the situation in Afghanistan that could have included the role of US citizens during the US intervention. Then, in 2019, the ICC Pre-Trial Chamber II rejected Chief Prosecutor Fatou Bensouda's request to open an official investigation because it was not in the "interest of justice" (ICC 2019: 32). This decision came as the Trump administration was pressuring the court and had already sanctioned Bensouda and other ICC staff (Zvobgo 2021). Although the investigation was eventually allowed, there has not yet been any comprehensive investigation of the Afghanistan situation. In one of his first acts, the ICC's new prosecutor, Karim Khan, decided *not* to investigate the role of US citizens, instead prioritizing allegations against the Taliban and the Islamic State–Khorasan Province in Afghanistan (Zvobgo 2021). In the Palestinian case, Israel and its allies, like the US and Australia, have challenged ICC jurisdiction, questioning Palestine statehood (*Times of Israel* 2019). With the exception of Georgia (June 2022), none of these cases have resulted in charges against individuals. Further arrest warrants might further fuel contestation dynamics (see Boehme 2022: 43). The broad support for the ICC in the Ukrainian case—partially also coming from the US—might also trigger debates about double standards. The ICC's approach to cases outside of Africa is *key* to reconciling African challengers with the court.

Controversies about the court are also spreading beyond African states due to dissatisfaction regarding implementation of the ICC's mandate and its failure to effectively prosecute. This includes disputes about electing judges who are not independent, the court's difficulty in settling cases (in a total of 27, there have been 4 convictions and 3 acquittals—as of 2022), and its apparent hesitation to take on "hard cases" like Afghanistan (Ba 2020: 157; Hillebrecht 2021: 169).

5.4 Norm robustness trends

Contestation of the duty to prosecute has sharply increased since 2008 but has not reached a global tipping point. In contrast to prognoses that it would remain robust on the African continent (Bower 2019; Simmons and Jo 2019), we find that African states are decreasing their criticism of norm violations and also decreasing compliance with the ICC. Outside of Africa, implementation of, and concordance with, the norm are increasing. Perhaps ICC attempts to bolster global support and react to the specific contestations by the AU and African states (Hillebrecht 2021: 170–71) will subdue the African challenges.

5.4.1 Practice: Decreasing compliance, growing implementation

To study the practical dimension of the duty to prosecute, we examined new data on states parties' cooperation with the ICC and existing data sets on the implementation of atrocity laws and procedural ICC provisions at the domestic level.

The ICC documents cases of non-cooperation. Determining how states respond to requests to help the court fulfill its mandate of universal jurisdiction allows us to assess compliance with the duty to prosecute. Figure 5.3 shows that since 2013 at the latest, states parties' non-cooperation has sharply increased through the refusal to execute arrest warrants, provide evidence

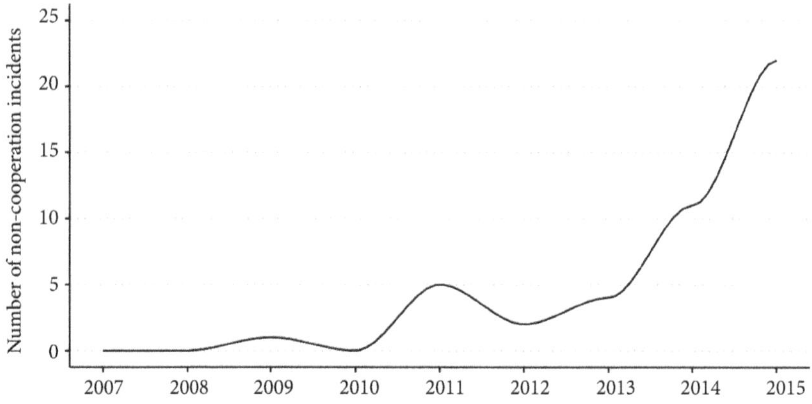

Figure 5.3 Indications of non-cooperation in ICC reports, 2007–15
Source: Based on coding of the ICCs reports of the Bureau on Cooperation, the Bureau on Non-Cooperation, court reports on cooperation, ICC reports to the UN, and reports on the activities of the ICC.

requested, and transfer witnesses. *Compliance* with the duty to prosecute and the court is decreasing. Until 2008, the ICC had operated in a fairly cooperative environment with self-referrals by Uganda, the DRC, and the CAR (see Ba 2020: 92–93; Boehme 2022: 54), although only 12 arrest warrants had been issued. That began to change with Al Bashir's indictment in 2008 and investigations into Kenyan post-election violence starting in 2010 (see also Hillebrecht and Straus 2017: 176).

While the ICC noted that between 2007 and 2009, states were "generally forthcoming" about cooperating, by 2011 their willingness had decreased (Bower 2017: 136–37). It continued to drop until 2016. This is reflected in several requests from the ICC prosecutor for the UNSC to enforce arrest warrants in the situations it had referred to the ICC. Requests were rarely discussed in the UNSC and often went unanswered (Ba 2020: 93). African states were particularly reluctant to cooperate with the court. Of eight situations for which the ICC sought cooperation, Hillebrecht and Straus (2017: 176) find that it only received full cooperation for the CAR and Mali (see also Boehme 2022: 11). In its 2021 report to UNGA, the ICC noted that 12 "requests for arrest and surrender remain outstanding" and called for cooperation by states to apprehend them (UNGA 2021: 3). As noted by the Independent Expert Review of the ICC and the Rome Statute, the lack of cooperation is a continuing concern not only with regard to arrests but also when it comes to the collection of evidence (ASP 2020: paras 751, 756). Cooperating with the ICC also means covering its operating expenses. Continuing constraints on court finances reveal the varying degrees of readiness—including by prominent Western countries like France, Germany, and the UK—to support and facilitate a fully functioning ICC (Hillebrecht 2021: 128–29).

It is important to note that the willingness to cooperate depends on the target of an investigation. African states have been fairly cooperative in cases against rebel leaders or domestic opposition—much less so when it comes to members of government or even heads of state (Boehme 2022: 13). The most glaring example of non-compliance was the arrest warrant for Al Bashir, who traveled more than 75 times to several countries *after* being indicted (Bower 2019: 97; Boehme 2022: 82). Although planned visits by Al Bashir to some countries were cancelled for varying reasons, only Botswana and Malawi officially threatened to arrest him (Boehme 2022: 85–87). The ICC Pre-Trial Chamber II found that, following the AU's call, states parties Malawi and Chad (in rulings in 2011), the DRC (in 2014), and South Africa and Jordan (in 2017), had not complied (Boehme 2022: 102–105). Al Bashir's visit to South Africa in 2015 caused a stand-off between the South African government and its judiciary, with the government even helping Al Bashir to leave the country against an order of the South African Supreme Court (Boehme 2017: 64–67; Bower 2019: 98). The South African position can be seen as the government of a major regional power prioritizing *regional* alliances over its *international* duty to prosecute (Boehme 2017: 68; Ba 2020: 153–54).

As for Sudan, the dynamics recently changed at the ICC: ICC Prosecutor Karim Khan visited Khartoum in August 2021, Sudan's transitional government signed an agreement promising to deliver Al Bashir, who had been ousted from office in 2019 (Chutel 2022). While this suggests a shift toward compliance, as we write, the handover is still pending and the rationale behind the Sudanese decision is suspect because members of its transitional government are also alleged to have been involved in the violence in Darfur. This resembles African–ICC relations in other cases (Ba 2020). Coming to terms with the controversial Sudanese situation that the ICC opened in 2005 is important for its record and relations with African members as well.

Implementation of the duty to prosecute has increased since adoption of the Rome Statute, which obliges states to criminalize core international crimes in their national laws and establish conditions for cooperating with the ICC. Willingness to implement the norm appears to remain—most of all in Europe, the Americas, and Oceania; on the part of some African states; and, least of all, in the Middle East and Asia (Berlin 2020: 87; see also Simmons and Jo 2019: 29–30). By 2019, the Genocide Convention of 1948 and Geneva Conventions of 1949 had resulted in national criminal codes that include crimes against humanity in 90 states, war crimes in 131, and genocide in 133 (Berlin 2020: 85). Criminalizing crimes against humanity quickly increased after adoption of the Rome Statute, the first treaty to codify and oblige states to criminalize such crimes (Berlin 2020: 86). "[J]oining the Court greatly increases the salience of atrocity criminalization" (Berlin 2020: 105)—making it possible for states to act according to the complementarity principle of the duty to prosecute. ICC investigations have also triggered domestic law reforms in some African states (Simmons and Jo 2019: 29; see also Nouwen and Werner 2010; Nouwen 2013). Implementation of the core crimes enshrined in the Rome Statute is increasing.

However, states seem to be less willing to adopt legislation on specific regulations of the Rome Statute to facilitate effective cooperation with the ICC (Bower 2017: 132). These obligations include the facilitation of investigations by the court, to execute arrest warrants, provide evidence, and so forth. The Rome Statute leaves states some discretion to implement these provisions (Bachmann and Nwibo 2018: 497), which could help account for its slow evolution. The Agreement on the Privileges and Immunities of the International

Criminal Court of 2002 facilitates cooperation between the ICC and member states by granting ICC personnel rights like those the UN Charter accords diplomats (Schabas 2017: 384). In ratifying the agreement, countries pledge ICC staff and officials the privileges they need to fulfill their duties. By 2006, a majority of all ICC member states had ratified the agreement; now two-thirds have done so. However, the fact that less than half of African states parties (13 out of 33) have ratified it reflects their slow implementation—similar to other measures (Bower 2017: 150), including the Southern African Development Community's 2001 "Windhoek Plan of Action" (SADC 2001) to boost ratification and implementation of the ICC (Kemp 2014: 75; Bachmann and Nwibo 2018).

In sum, although implementation of the duty to prosecute has grown globally, compliance has been decreasing. Non-compliance rates are highest among African states, where implementation is also lower.

5.4.2 Discourse: Decreasing concordance and negative reactions in Africa

With respect to discourse, we studied concordance with the duty to prosecute by looking at affirmations and ratifications of the norm and public opinion as well as negative reactions to norm violations.

ICC membership grew rapidly between 1999 and 2002, when the court was established. However, the increase in ratifiers has since stagnated. As we write, 123 states are party to the Rome Statute—and one-third of all states are not. Unlike the torture case (see Chapter 2), as contestation about the norm intensified, the pace of ratifications decreased. This might be due to the remaining non-parties being unlikely ratifiers. The ratification trend is reflected in the broader diplomatic discourse: Before 2009, states regularly affirmed the duty to prosecute—and support was also very strong among African states (Figure 5.4; see also Boehme 2022: 68). Until 2013, a growing number of UNGA resolutions mention war crimes and crimes against humanity—a trend that was largely driven by European states (Simmons and Jo 2019: 23), which also shows growing concordance.

But after 2008, African states increasingly contested the ICC and affirmations declined. For the next eight years, only half of all African statements about the ICC affirmed the duty to prosecute. In light of the controversies about the Sudan and Kenya cases, support for the court reached rock bottom in 2015 (see also Boehme 2022: 68–69). This culminated in the AU's threat of mass withdrawals. By leaving the ICC, Burundi (in 2017) and the

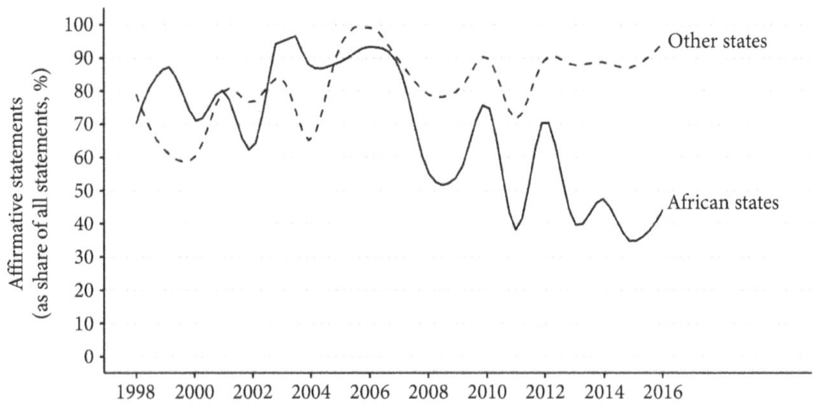

Figure 5.4 Affirmations of the duty to prosecute, 1998–2016
Source: Based on 1,059 statements in UN, ICC, and AU documents as well as in African newspaper articles.

Philippines (in 2019) clearly disavowed the duty to prosecute institutionalized by the ICC. Because states rarely exit international treaties, withdrawals from international criminal and human rights courts "cast doubt on the norm of compulsory jurisdiction" (Hillebrecht 2021: 163). The Gambia and South Africa, the other two African states to lodge official notices of withdrawal, have since retracted their withdrawal notifications—not least due to political and legal developments at home (Ba 2020: 152–54; Boehme 2022: 144–48). In December 2016, several African states announced they would remain in the ICC (Vilmer 2016: 1340; Bower 2019: 99). The threatened mass withdrawal by African states never gained momentum, which could indicate a slight increase in norm concordance. Still, until 2019, support by African states in UNGA never reached the high levels from the pre-2008 era (Boehme 2022: 69). The coming years will show whether concordance can be revived—or not.

Norm concordance in diplomatic discourse is generally reflected in public opinion. Citing a poll covering 67 countries and other country-specific surveys, Simmons and Jo (2019: 24) conclude that "[T]he core norm of anti-impunity and the sense that there is no free pass for atrocities appears to be strong." This attitude, which is also found in the US, could encourage changes in the country's policy toward the ICC (Zvobgo 2019: 1076–77). In 2015, in Kenya, where the president has been under investigation by the ICC, there was also general support for the court, with most of those surveyed opposed to Kenya leaving the ICC (Simmons and Jo 2019: 24); similar results have been reported in polls from Zambia (Bower 2019: 99). African civil society continues to largely support the court (Vilmer 2016: 1337). That said, with little research on public opinion on the whole continent, let alone the world, it is difficult to draw general conclusions.

As fewer states comply with the duty to prosecute (see Section 5.4.1), *negative reactions to violations* have to significantly increase if the norm is to be strengthened. Figure 5.5 contrasts African and non-African actors, showing that African states' negative reactions to norm violations do not offset their growing non-compliance. This is reflected in the ASP's reluctance to adopt critical resolutions on reports about non-cooperation (Mills and Bloomfield 2018: 125). However, since 2013, non-African states have increasingly criticized the growing number of non-cooperation incidents. This could indicate that, at least outside the African group, the non-compliance with the duty to prosecute is criticized more. In Boehme's (2022: 70) analysis, "urging other states to cooperate with the Court and highlighting the importance of cooperation" is one of the most frequent themes of ICC-related statements in UNGA between 2005 and 2019.

African states are the least likely to negatively react to non-cooperation, Burundi's withdrawal, and withdrawal notifications of other states. Our data revealed that Ghana was the only African state to criticize the threats of withdrawals in 2016. Non-African-state criticisms of non-compliance largely concern arrest warrants that are not served and a general lack of cooperation with the ICC.

In sum, the duty to prosecute weathered rare, and sometimes severe, contestations but remained robust until 2007. However, after 2008, African states

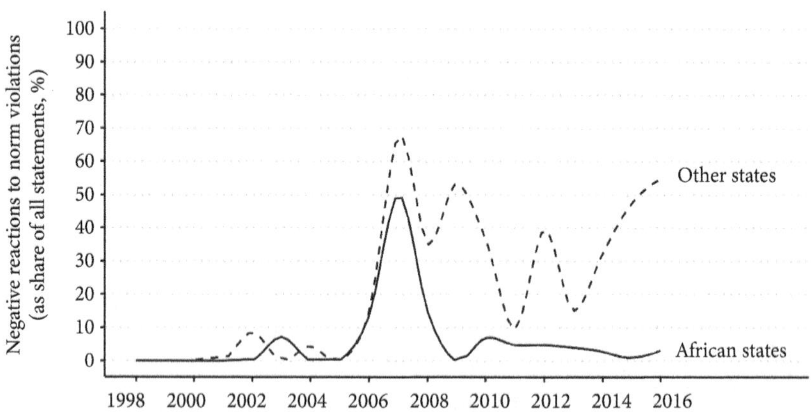

Figure 5.5 Negative reactions to violations of the duty to prosecute, 1998–2016
Source: Based on 1,059 statements in UN, ICC, and AU documents as well as in African newspaper articles.

in particular did not criticize the growing cases of non-compliance. Among African states, implementation of, and concordance with, the duty to prosecute is stable at best. While these trends are, by and large, limited to African states, this can still threaten the norm and the court. By 2016, the duty to prosecute had become less robust on the African continent.

Our findings differ from other studies on the robustness of international criminal law and the anti-impunity norm. We concur with Simmons and Jo (2019) that in terms of concordance with and implementation of the norm, general support for international criminal justice is growing. However, Simmons and Jo do not account for the critical role of non-compliance and its condemnation that have decreased on the African continent. Bower (2019: 100) argues that indications of a negative trend in norm robustness is limited to some African states and did not notably cascade with respect to withdrawals. He concludes that the duty to prosecute remains surprisingly robust because "[T]he coalition of actors seeking to modify the nonimpunity norm is relatively limited in absolute numbers and regionally focused" (Bower 2019: 90). We maintain that the African regional group was, and will remain, critical for the court's success. If the norm weakens there, it is likely to have broader implications. This can already be seen in the first spillover effects: The Philippines withdrew from the ICC in light of the looming investigation (Ba 2020: 155). The experience of African non-cooperation and withdrawals might encourage other states to do the same as they become targeted by the ICC, which would further undermine the duty to prosecute and the ICC.

5.5 Explanatory factors

Contesting African states target both the validity and the application of the duty to prosecute. As expected, the high degree of applicatory contestation and stark increase in validity contestation have weakened the norm—at least in Africa. How did international law and norm clusters, the relative power of norm challengers, and the norm's institutionalization contribute to this development? Why did contestation radicalize among African states and cause the norm to weaken?

The duty to prosecute is a highly legalized international norm (see Section 5.2.1). It is enshrined in the Rome Statute, which very precisely details the crimes falling within its jurisdiction and delegates the ICC to make binding decisions. Of all the cases we studied, the duty to prosecute has the highest degree of legalization—in terms of its obligation, precision, and delegation (see Chapter 1). The norm's formalization did not prevent contestation. Yet, it shapes the content of norm disputes: As Bower argues, the US (Bower 2015) and African states (Bower 2019) use the language of the law in their argumentation. States acknowledge the validity of legal arguments, so legal disputes regarding application actually *reinforce* their commitment to the norm. However, legal argumentation can also be exploited to undermine the duty to prosecute (see Zimmermann 2021).

The duty to prosecute is embedded in a well-established international law norm cluster that includes the laws of war, human rights, criminal accountability, and the broader duty to intervene when atrocities are committed (Fehl 2019: 901; Simmons and Jo 2019: 19). Yet, the norm's embeddedness does not always shield the duty to prosecute from contestation: It also provides avenues for other—sometimes fundamental—challenges. As Han and Rosenberg (2021: 734–37) argue, the duty to prosecute lies in between the principle of the equal accountability of individuals under the Rome Statute and the sovereign equality of states under the UN Charter and customary international law. In this case, contestation of the duty to prosecute uses legal arguments, for instance, when states defend immunity for heads of state. In sum, although the duty to prosecute is embedded in a dense norm cluster (similar to the torture prohibition we examine in Chapter 2), legalization of the cluster did not shield all its core claims from contestation. The US and African states attempted to exploit the complexity of the norm cluster to contest the norm, but the cluster in itself cannot explain the shift in contestation dynamics.

The duty to prosecute codified in the Rome Statute is an international norm that was established without support from the great powers—and indeed, despite them (Deitelhoff 2009; Bower 2017). Despite powerful challenges, the ICC was established in 2002 and soon opened its first cases. Although the US has partly succeeded in protecting its citizens from ICC jurisdiction, the superpower has not been able to garner broad support for its contestations about the norm's validity in order to weaken the norm. In fact, some of its closest allies have not supported US challenges (Thomas 2009; Bower 2015). As we have discussed, open hostility from the US toward the ICC can undermine investigations, so, to a certain extent, unlike the torture case (see Chapter 2), US contestation has been successful.

More serious challenges to the norm and the court have come from prima facie less powerful actors: African states and the AU. However, power relations shape the dynamics of the group of African states: Kenya and South Africa, for instance, are influential regional actors whose contestations affected the entire continent and the politics at the AU. The AU especially was key for orchestrating contestation and providing African states with legitimacy for challenging the ICC (Boehme 2022: 162–63). As long as ICC activities focused solely on situations in Africa, African states and the AU were relatively powerful actors because the ICC has to rely on their cooperation. Although the AU and African states were only able to achieve few changes on a formal level (Arcudi 2019; Bower 2019), Brosig (2021: 131) notes that the AU "achieved most of its tactical goals vis-à-vis the ICC." So far, no African senior official or sitting head of state has successfully been tried by the ICC. The Kenyan cases eventually collapsed and if Al Bashir will ever appear before the ICC, he will do so at the behest of a new government. Yet, African states have not yet been able to create the *global* tipping point needed that would trigger a broader weakening of the duty to prosecute. However, they may be able to garner more support in the future, especially if the ICC cannot respond to their demands—and if cases continue to focus on African states.

The role of law and power cannot fully account for explaining the link between contestation and robustness in this case study. African states have contested the duty to prosecute because of sensing they have been treated unfairly (see also Clarke 2019). During the Rome Statute negotiations, they had advocated for universal jurisdiction, and then most cases involved crimes allegedly committed by Africans (see Nimigan 2021). This perception was largely shaped by the way the institutions first dealt with African contestations. In an ideal scenario, such challenges would be dealt with in the ASP. In addition, they would take place in the UNSC, which can refer cases and also suspend investigations and prosecutions. By referring the Sudanese situation to the ICC, which issued an arrest warrant for Omar Al Bashir, the UNSC spurred African states to contest the duty to prosecute. When the AU requested the UNSC to halt the ICC proceedings to allow them to sponsor a regional solution to the conflict, it merely took note of the request (see Section 5.3.2). African states were not able to achieve a stay of proceedings, nor were they permitted to air their concerns about Al Bashir's arrest warrant in UNSC debates and then their misgivings about the investigation about Kenya (Bower 2019: 96). The council ignored the specific grievances of the African states, which is the ICC's largest regional group.

When the UNSC ignored their request, many African states felt a "sense of betrayal" that pushed them to challenge the norm's validity (Deitelhoff 2020: 722). As Mills put it, "African leaders just wanted some sort of acknowledgement of their concerns and their standing as global leaders" (Mills 2012: 425).

This lack of recognition was underscored by the ICC's alleged selectiveness. As South Africa stated at the ASP meeting in 2016:

> There are perceptions of inequality and unfairness in the practice of the ICC that do not only emanate from the Court's relationship with the Security Council, but also by the perceived focus of the ICC on African states, notwithstanding clear evidence of violations by others.
>
> **(South Africa 2016)**

Before 2008, contestation had sought procedural change. Then it shifted to attack the court itself, promoting non-compliance with court provisions, questioning its rationale, and finally threatening mass withdrawals by African countries (Mills and Bloomfield 2018: 114–16).

As we discuss in Section 5.3.2, African ICC members also sought in vain to discuss their challenges in the seemingly less hierarchical forum of the ASP, where each state has one vote. In light of the power dynamics at the UNSC, the AU suggested granting UNGA the power to defer situations to give peacemaking a chance and also exempt sitting heads of state from ICC jurisdiction. However, despite avoiding the power-politics-prone UNSC, there was no dialogue: African initiatives were met "with little appreciable interest from other ICC members" (Bower 2019: 97; see also Dembinski and Peters 2019: 163). The AU has taken a similar approach regarding the immunity of sitting heads of state. After the ICC reaffirmed that Jordan had been legally obliged to arrest Al Bashir during his visit in March 2017, the AU asked UNGA to seek an advisory opinion from the International Court of Justice (Mudukuti 2020)—so far, without success.

There has been very little room for open dialogue to change African perceptions of unfairness. Contestation by African states radicalized because they were never granted their request for open dialogue—due to their more marginalized positions in international institutions. Since the ICC initiatives to dialogue with the AU in 2010 were not perceived by African states as truly open, they rejected having an ICC–AU liaison office in Addis Ababa (Vilmer 2016: 1339; García Iommi 2020: 118–19). African states' concerns could be alleviated by acknowledging one of their main criticisms and investigating cases outside the continent, which has begun to happen (see also Vilmer 2016: 1338). More modest steps to counter African backlash against the ICC and other international courts have been proposed, starting by increasing transparency about the way they operate (Hillebrecht 2021: 170–71). That is crucial for dialoguing on an equal footing. As we write, it is not yet clear whether attempts to accommodate at least some of the concerns voiced by African states will tone down their contestations.

5.6 Conclusion

After the Rome Statute was adopted in 1998, the duty to prosecute was not very contested—despite US challenges targeting its core. ICC members strongly supported the norm. But that changed in 2008 after an arrest warrant was issued for the Sudanese president Omar Al Bashir. Investigations of the situations in Sudan and Kenya stimulated criticism from African states, who increasingly challenged the core claims of the duty to prosecute and the ICC—especially by seeking to reinstate immunity for sitting heads of state. Their validity contestation weakened the norm. Compliance is decreasing most among the group of African states who had played key roles in the Rome Statute negotiations and the ICC's first cases, which has not been met with stronger critique of norm violations. It is difficult to interpret the degree of concordance and implementation: While global support for the norm is growing, for African states, it is stable at best. The main reason that African states radicalized their contestation and began attacking the norm's validity was frustration about how international institutions responded to their challenges—on top of widespread perceptions of unfairness, particularly ICC "selectivity." Our findings indicate that robustness of the duty to prosecute is weakening in Africa. Without the reconciliation of African states and the ICC, the norm is likely to continue to lose strength. That said, current attempts to respond to the Africans' specific challenges by adapting institutional mechanisms and expanding opportunities for dialogue might soften contestation and bolster the norm.

Reference list

African Union. 2012. "On the Decisions of Pre-Trial Chamber I of the International Criminal Court (ICC) Pursuant to Article 87(7) of the Rome Statute on the Alleged Failure by the Republic of Chad and the Republic of Malawi to Comply with the Cooperation Requests Issued by the Court with Respect to the Arrest and Surrender of President Omar Hassan Al Bashir of the Republic of Sudan." AU press release no. 002/2012 (January 9).

Akhavan, Payam. 2010. "Self-Referrals before the International Criminal Court: Are States the Villains or the Victims of Atrocities?" *Criminal Law Forum* 21 (1): pp. 103–20. doi: 10.1007/s10609-010-9112-2.

Arcudi, Antonio. 2019. "The Absence of Norm Modification and the Intensification of Norm Contestation: Africa and the Responsibility to Prosecute." *Global Responsibility to Protect* 11 (2): pp. 172–97. doi: 10.1163/1875984X-01102004.

ASP (Assembly of States Parties). 2013. "Resolution ICC-ASP/12/Res.7: Amendments to the Rules of Procedure and Evidence." ICC Doc. ICC-ASP/12/20 at 51 (November 27).

ASP. 2020. "Report of the Independent Expert Review of the International Criminal Court and the Rome Statute System." ICC Doc. ICC-ASP/19/16 (September 30).

AU Assembly (African Union Assembly). 2008. "Decision on the Report of the Commission on the Abuse of the Principle of Universal Jurisdiction." AU Doc. Assembly/AU/ Dec.199(XIII) (July 1).

AU Assembly. 2009. "Decision on the Meeting of African States Parties to the Rome Statute of the International Criminal Court (ICC)." AU Doc. Assembly/AU/Dec.245(XIII) Rev.1 (July 3).

AU Assembly. 2012. "Decision on the Progress Report of the Commission on the Implementation of the Assembly Decision on the International Criminal Court (ICC)." AU Doc. Assembly/AU/Dec.397(XVIII) (January 30).

AU Assembly. 2013. "Decision on Africa's Relationship with the International Criminal Court (ICC)." AU Doc. Ext/Assembly/AU/Dec.1 (October 12).

AU Assembly. 2014. "Protocol on Amendments to the Protocol on the Statute of the African Court of Justice and Human Rights." AU Doc. Assembly/AU/Dec.529 (XXIII) (June 27).

AU Peace and Security Council. 2008. "Communique." AU Doc. PSC/MIN/Comm(CXLII) (July 21).

Austria. 2011. "Statement by Konrad G. Bühler, Federal Ministry for European and International Affairs." ASP General Debate, 10th Session (December 14). Accessed January 8, 2023. https://asp.icc-cpi.int/iccdocs/asp_docs/ASP10/Statements/ICC-ASP10-GenDeba-Austriia-ENG.pdf.

Ba, Oumar. 2020. *States of Justice: The Politics of the International Criminal Court*. Cambridge: Cambridge University Press.

Bachmann, Sascha-Dominik D., and Eda L. Nwibo. 2018. "Pull and Push—Implementing the Complementarity Principle of the Rome Statute of the ICC within the AU: Opportunities and Challenges." *Brooklyn Journal of International Law* 43 (2): pp. 457–543.

Barnidge, Robert P. 2003–04. "American Servicemembers' Protection Act and Article 98 Agreements: A Legal Analysis and Case for Constructive Engagement with the International Criminal Court." *Tilburg Foreign Law Review* 11 (4): pp. 738–55.

Bassiouni, Cherif M. 1999. "Negotiating the Treaty of Rome on the Establishment of an International Criminal Court." *Cornell International Law Journal* 32 (3): pp. 443–69.

Berlin, Mark S. 2016. "Why (Not) Arrest? Third-Party State Compliance and Non-compliance with International Criminal Tribunals." *Journal of Human Rights* 15 (4): pp. 509–32. doi: 10.1080/14754835.2015.1103160.

Berlin, Mark S. 2020. *Criminalizing Atrocity: The Global Spread of Criminal Laws against International Crimes*. Oxford: Oxford University Press.

Birdsall, Andrea. 2010. "The 'Monster That We Need to Slay'? Global Governance, the United States, and the International Criminal Court." *Global Governance* 16 (4): pp. 451–69. doi: 10.1163/19426720-01604003.

Boehme, Franziska. 2017. "'We Chose Africa': South Africa and the Regional Politics of Cooperation with the International Criminal Court." *International Journal of Transitional Justice* 11 (1): 50–70. doi: 10.1093/ijtj/ijw024.

Boehme, Franziska. 2022. *State Behavior and the International Criminal Court: Between Cooperation and Resistance*. Abingdon: Routledge.

Bosco, David. 2014. *Rough Justice: The International Criminal Court in a World of Power Politics*. Oxford: Oxford University Press.

Bower, Adam. 2015. "Arguing with Law: Strategic Legal Argumentation, US Diplomacy, and Debates over the International Criminal Court." *Review of International Studies* 41 (2): pp. 337–60. doi: 10.1017/S0260210514000217.

Bower, Adam. 2017. *Norms without the Great Powers: International Law and Changing Social Standards in World Politics*. Oxford: Oxford University Press.

Bower, Adam. 2019. "Contesting the International Criminal Court: Bashir, Kenyatta, and the Status of the Nonimpunity Norm in World Politics." *Journal of Global Security Studies* 4 (1): pp. 88–104. doi: 10.1093/jogss/ogy037.

Brosig, Malte. 2021. *Africa in a Changing Global Order: Marginal But Meaningful?* Cham: Springer.

Burundi. 2016. "Statement by H.E. Vestine Nahimana Ambassador of Burundi." ASP General Debate, 15th Session (November 16–17). Accessed January 8, 2023. https://asp.icc-cpi.int/sites/asp/files/asp_docs/ASP15/GenDeba/ICC-ASP15-GenDeba-Burundi-ENG.pdf.

China. 2014. "Statement by Mr. MA Xinmin, Deputy Director-General of Treaty and Law of the Ministry of Foreign Affairs of China." ASP General Debate, 13th Session (December 8–17). Accessed January 8, 2023. https://asp.icc-cpi.int/iccdocs/asp_docs/ASP13/GenDeba/ICC-ASP13-GenDeba-China-ENG.pdf.

Chutel, Lynsey. 2022. "Will Sudan Send Bashir to the Hague?" Foreign Policy, August 18. Accessed January 8, 2023. https://foreignpolicy.com/2021/08/18/sudan-bashir-icc-hague-justice-darfur-hemeti.

Clark, Philip. 2018. *Distant Justice: The Impact of the International Criminal Court on African Politics*. Cambridge: Cambridge University Press.

Clarke, Kamari Maxine. 2019. *Affective Justice: The International Criminal Court and the Pan-Africanist Pushback*. Durham, NC and London: Duke University Press.

Crawford, James. 1994. "The ILC's Draft Statute for an International Criminal Tribunal." *American Journal of International Law* 88 (1): pp. 140–52. doi: 10.2307/2204031.

Daily Nation. 2014a. "Kenya Writes Protest Letter over Handling of ICC Cases." Daily Nation, October 23.

Daily Nation. 2014b. "Uhuru Says ICC a Threat to Kenya's National Stability." Daily Nation, December 12.

Daily Nation. 2015. "Learn from ICC Treatment of Africa: Uhuru." Daily Nation, June 15.

Daly, Tom Gerald, and Micha Wiebusch. 2018. "The African Court on Human and Peoples' Rights: Mapping Resistance against a Young Court." *International Journal of Law in Context* 14 (2): pp. 294–313. doi: 10.1017/S1744552318000083.

Deitelhoff, Nicole. 2009. "The Discursive Process of Legalization: Charting Islands of Persuasion in the ICC Case." *International Organization* 63 (1): pp. 33–65. doi: 10.1017/S002081830909002X.

Deitelhoff, Nicole. 2020. "What's in a Name? Contestation and Backlash against International Norms and Institutions." *British Journal of Politics and International Relations* 22 (4): pp. 715–27. doi: 10.1177/1369148120945906.

Dembinski, Matthias, and Dirk Peters. 2019. "The Power of Justice: How Procedural Justice Concerns Affect the Legitimacy of International Institutions." *Global Governance* 25 (1): pp. 149–70. doi: 10.1163/19426720-02501010.

Dukalskis, Alexander, and Robert C. Johansen. 2013. "Measuring Acceptance of International Enforcement of Human Rights: The United States, Asia, and the International Criminal Court." *Human Rights Quarterly* 35 (3): pp. 569–97. doi: 10.1353/hrq.2013.0049.

Fehl, Caroline. 2019. "Bombs, Trials, and Rights: Norm Complexity and the Evolution of Liberal Intervention Practices." *Human Rights Quarterly* 41 (4): pp. 893–915. doi: 10.1353/hrq.2019.0066.

García Iommi, Lucrecia. 2020. "Whose Justice? The ICC 'Africa Problem.'" *International Relations* 34 (1): pp. 105–29. doi: 10.1177/0047117819842294.

Goldstone, Richard, and Adam M. Smith. 2008. *International Judicial Institutions: The Architecture of International Justice at Home and Abroad*. London: Routledge.

Goodliffe, Jay, and Darren Hawkins. 2009. "A Funny Thing Happened on the Way to Rome: Explaining International Criminal Court Negotiations." *Journal of Politics* 71 (3): pp. 977–97. doi: 10.1017/S0022381609090835.

Gowans, Stephen. 2011. "U.S. Ambassador Echoes Cecil John Rhodes." The Herald (Harare), September 27.

Han, Yuna, and Sophie T. Rosenberg. 2021. "Claiming Equality: The African Union's Contestation of the Anti-Impunity Norm." *International Studies Review* 23 (3): pp. 726–51. doi: 10.1093/isr/viaa065.

Hillebrecht, Courtney. 2016. "The Deterrent Effects of the International Criminal Court: Evidence from Libya." *International Interactions* 42 (4): pp. 616–43. doi: 10.1080/03050629.2016.1185713.

Hillebrecht, Courtney. 2021. *Saving the International Justice Regime: Beyond Backlash Against International Courts*. Cambridge: Cambridge University Press.

Hillebrecht, Courtney, and Scott Straus. 2017. "Who Pursues the Perpetrators? State Cooperation with the ICC." *Human Rights Quarterly* 39 (1): pp. 162–88. doi: 10.1353/hrq.2017.0006.

ICC (International Criminal Court). 2009. "Pre-Trial Chamber I: Warrant of Arrest for Omar Hassan Ahmad Al Bashir." ICC Doc. ICC-02/05-01/09-1 (March 4).

ICC. 2011a. "Pre-Trial Chamber II: Decision on the Prosecutor's Application for Summonses to Appear for Francis Kirimi Muthaura, Uhuru Muigai Kenyatta and Mohammed Hussein Ali." ICC Doc. ICC-01/09-02/11-1 (March 8).

ICC. 2011b. "Pre-Trial Chamber II: Decision on the Prosecutor's Application for Summons to Appear for William Samoei Ruto, Henry Kiprono Kosgey and Joshua Arap Sang." ICC Doc. ICC-01/09-01/11-1 (March 8).

ICC. 2011c. "Pre-Trial Chamber II: Decision on the Application by the Government of Kenya Challenging the Admissibility of the Case Pursuant to Article 19(2)(B) of the Statute." ICC Doc. ICC-01/09-02/11-96 (May 31).

ICC. 2011d. "Appeals Chamber: Judgment on the Appeal of the Republic of Kenya against the Decision of Pre-Trial Chamber II of 30 May 2011 Entitled 'Decision on the Application by the Government of Kenya Challenging the Admissibility of the Case Pursuant to Article 19(2)(B) of the Statute.'" ICC Doc. ICC-01/09-01/11-307 (August 30).

ICC. 2019. "Pre-Trial Chamber II: Decision Pursuant to Article 15 of the Rome Statute on the Authorisation of an Investigation into the Situation in the Islamic Republic of Afghanistan." ICC Doc. ICC-02/17-33 (April 12).

ICC. 2022. "Abd-Al-Rahman Trial Opens at International Criminal Court." ICC press release ICC-CPI-20220405-PR1650 (April 5).

Independent on Saturday. 2013. "Africans Target of the ICC, Says AU." The Independent on Saturday, October 12.

Jo, Hyeran, and Beth A. Simmons. 2016. "Can the International Criminal Court Deter Atrocity?" *International Organization* 70 (3): pp. 443–75. doi: 10.1017/S0020818316000114.

Jorgensen, Malcolm. 2021. *American Foreign Policy Ideology and the International Rule of Law: Contesting Power through the International Criminal Court*. Cambridge: Cambridge University Press.

Kemp, Gerhard. 2014. "The Implementation of the Rome Statute in Africa." In *Africa and the International Criminal Court*, ed. Gerhard Werle, Lovell Fernandez, and Moritz Vormbaum. New York: Springer, pp. 61–77.

Kenya. 2011a. "Letter Dated 23 March 2011 from the Permanent Representative of Kenya to the United Nations Addressed to the President of the Security Council: Request of Kenya for Deferral under Article 16 of the Rome Statute of the International Criminal Court." UN Doc. S /2011/201 (March 23).

Kenya. 2011b. "Document in Support of the 'Appeal of the Government of Kenya against the Decision on the Application by the Government of Kenya Challenging the Admissibility of the Case Pursuant to Article 19(2)(B) of the Statute.'" ICC Doc. ICC-01/09-01/11-135 (June 20).

Kenya. 2013. "Identical Letters Dated 21 October 2013 from the Permanent Representative of Kenya to the United Nations Addressed to the Secretary-General and the President of the Security-Council." UN Doc. S/2013/624 (October 21).

Kersten, Mark. 2016. *Justice in Conflict: The Effects of the International Criminal Court's Interventions on Ending Wars and Building Peace*. Oxford: Oxford University Press.

Kirsch, Philippe, and Valerie Oosterveld. 2001. "The Preparatory Commission for the International Criminal Court." *Fordham International Law Journal* 25 (3): pp. 563–88.

Lesotho. 2014. "Statement by H.E. Mr. Kelebone A. Maope, Ambassador and Permanent Representative of Lesotho to the United Nations, on Behalf of African State Parties to the Rome Statute." ASP Document (December 8). Accessed January 8, 2023. https://asp.icc-cpi.int/iccdocs/asp_docs/ASP13/GenDeba/ICC-ASP13-GenDeba-Lesotho-AfricanStatesParties-ENG.pdf.

Luban, David. 2013. "After the Honeymoon: Reflections on the Current State of International Criminal Justice." *Journal of International Criminal Justice* 11 (3): pp. 505–15. doi: 10.1093/jicj/mqt023.

Lynch, Colum. 2002. "U. S. Seeks Court Immunity for E. Timor Peacekeepers." Washington Post, May 16.

Miller, Andrew Cesare. 2022. "Without an Army: How ICC Indictments Reduce Atrocities." *Journal of Peace Research* online first: 1–15. doi: 10.1177/00223433221088692.

Mills, Kurt. 2012. "'Bashir Is Dividing Us': Africa and the International Criminal Court." *Human Rights Quarterly* 34 (2): pp. 404–47. doi: 10.1353/hrq.2012.0030.

Mills, Kurt, and Alan Bloomfield. 2018. "African Resistance to the International Criminal Court: Halting the Advance of the Anti-Impunity Norm." *Review of International Studies* 44 (1): pp. 101–27. doi: 10.1017/S0260210517000407.

Mudukuti, Angela. 2020. "Prosecutor v. Omar Hassan Ahmad Al-Bashir: Judgment in the Jordan Referral Re Al-Bashir Appeal." *American Journal of International Law* 114 (1): pp. 103–109. doi: 10.1017/ajil.2019.79.

Namibia. 2006. "Statement by Mr. Issaskar V.K. Ndjoze." ASP General Debate, 15th Session (November 16–24). Accessed January 8, 2023. https://asp.icc-cpi.int/iccdocs/asp_docs/ASP15/GenDeba/ICC-ASP15-GenDeba-Namibia-ENG.pdf.

New York Times. 2002. "U.S. Links Peacekeeping to Immunity from New Court." New York Times, June 19.

Nigeria. 2016. "Statement by the Leader of Nigeria's Delegation Mr. Abubakar Malami, Honourable Attorney General of the Federation and Minister of Justice, Federal Republic of Nigeria." ASP General Debate, 15th Session (November 17). Accessed January 8, 2023. https://asp.icc-cpi.int/iccdocs/asp_docs/ASP15/GenDeba/ICC-ASP15-GenDeba-nigeria-ENG.pdf.

Nimigan, Sarah P. 2019. "The Malabo Protocol, the ICC, and the Idea of 'Regional Complementarity.'" *Journal of International Criminal Justice* 17 (5): pp. 1005–29. doi: 10.1093/jicj/mqz040.

Nimigan, Sarah P. 2021. "Africa and the International Criminal Court: (Re)Constructing the Narrative." *International Criminal Law Review* 21 (2): pp. 203–41. doi: 10.1163/15718123-bja10050.

Nouwen, Sarah M. H. 2013. *Complementarity in the Line of Fire: The Catalysing Effect of the International Criminal Court in Uganda and Sudan*. Cambridge: Cambridge University Press.

Nouwen, Sarah M. H., and W. G. Werner. 2010. "Doing Justice to the Political: The International Criminal Court in Uganda and Sudan." *European Journal of International Law* 21 (4): pp. 941–65. doi: 10.1093/ejil/chq064.

Pace, William. 2002. "A Victory for Peace." *ICC Monitor* 21 (June): pp. 1–2.

Ralph, Jason G. 2007. *Defending the Society of States: Why America Opposes the International Criminal Court and Its Vision of World Society*. Oxford: Oxford University Press.

Rome Statute. 1998. "Rome Statute of the International Criminal Court." United Nations Treaty Series, no. 38544, vol. 2187 at 3 (July 17).

SADC (Southern African Development Community). 2001. "Windoek Plan of Action on ICC Ratification and Implementation in SADC." May 28–30. Accessed April 12, 2018. http://www.pgaction.org/pdf/pre/02_2001_WindhoekPlan.pdf.

Schabas, William A. 2008. "Prosecutorial Discretion v. Judicial Activism at the International Criminal Court." *Journal of International Criminal Justice* 6 (4): pp. 731–61. doi: 10.1093/jicj/mqn045.

Schabas, William A. 2017. *An Introduction to the International Criminal Court*. Cambridge: Cambridge University Press.

Scheffer, David J. 1998. "Remarks before the 6th Committee of the 53rd General Assembly." US Department of State (October 21). Accessed January 8, 2023. http://1997-2001.state.gov/www/policy_remarks/1998/981021_scheffer_icc.html.

Scheffer, David J. 2000. "The U.S. Perspective on the ICC." In *The United States and the International Criminal Court: National Security and International Law*, ed. Sarah B. Sewall. Lanham, MD: Rowman & Littlefield, pp. 115–18.

Sikkink, Kathryn. 2011. *The Justice Cascade: How Human Rights Prosecutions Are Changing World Politics*. New York: Norton.

Simmons, Beth A., and Hyeran Jo. 2019. "Measuring Norms and Normative Contestation: The Case of International Criminal Law." *Journal of Global Security Studies* 4 (1): pp. 18–36. doi: 10.1093/jogss/ogy043.

South Africa. 2016. "Opening Statement by Mr T. M. Masutha, Minister of Justice and Correctional Services, Republic of South Africa." ASP General Debate, 15th Session (November 16–17). Accessed January 8, 2023. https://asp.icc-cpi.int/iccdocs/asp_docs/ASP15/GenDeba/ICC-ASP15-GenDeba-SouthAfrica-ENG.pdf.

Sudan. 2006. "Statement by the Delegation of the Sudan, as Observer." ASP General Debate, 5th Session (November 24). Accessed January 8, 2023. https://asp.icc-cpi.int/iccdocs/asp_docs/library/asp/ICC-ASP5_Statement_sudan.pdf.

Sudan Tribune. 2008. "Myths and Misinformation as NCP Survival Tactics." Sudan Tribune, December 8.

Sunday Independent. 2013. "AU, Kenya and ICC: Beyond Impunity." Sunday Independent, October 13.

Thomas, Daniel C. 2009. "Rejecting the US Challenge to the International Criminal Court: Normative Entrapment and Compromise in EU Policy-Making." *International Politics* 46 (4): pp. 376–94. doi: 10.1057/ip.2009.8.

Tiemessen, Alana. 2014. "The International Criminal Court and the Politics of Prosecutions." *International Journal of Human Rights* 18 (4–5): pp. 444–61. doi: 10.1080/13642987.2014.901310.

Times of Israel. 2019. "Australia Rejects ICC Palestine Probe; Germany Warns against Politicization." Times of Israel, December 25. Accessed January 8, 2023. https://www.timesofisrael.com/australia-rejects-icc-palestine-probe-says-court-has-no-jurisdiction.

Trinidad & Tobago. 1989. "Letter Dated 21 August 1989 from the Permanent Representative of Trinidad and Tobago to the Secretary-General." UN Doc. A/44/195 (August 21).

Uganda. 2016. "Statement by Hon. William Byaruhanga the Attorney General of the Republic of Uganda." ASP General Debate, 15th Session (November 17). Accessed January 8, 2023. https://asp.icc-cpi.int/sites/asp/files/asp_docs/ASP15/GenDeba/ICC-ASP15-GenDeba-Uganda-ENG.pdf.

UK. 2015. "Statement of the United Kingdom of Great Britain and Northern Ireland by Catherine Adams, Legal Director, Foreign and Commonwealth Office." ASP General Debate, 14th Session (November 18). Accessed January 8, 2023. https://asp.icc-cpi.int/iccdocs/asp_docs/ASP14/GenDeb/ASP14-GenDeb-UK-ENG.pdf.

UNGA (United Nations General Assembly). 1998. "UN GAOR: 53rd Session, 11th Sixth Committee Meeting." UN Doc. A/C.6/53/SR.11 (October 22).

UNGA. 2000. "UN General Assembly Official Records (GAOR): 55th Session, 12th Sixth Committee Meeting." UN Doc. A/C.6/55/SR.12 (October 19).

UNGA. 2007. "UN GAOR: 62nd Session, 43rd Plenary Meeting." UN Doc. A/62/PV.43 (November 1).

UNGA. 2013. "UN GAOR: 68th Session, 42nd Plenary Meeting." UN Doc. A/68/PV.42 (October 31).

UNGA. 2014a. "UN GAOR: 68th Session, 107th Plenary Meeting." UN Doc. A/68/PV.107 (September 9).

UNGA. 2014b. "UN GAOR: 69th Session, 36th Plenary Meeting." UN Doc. A/69/PV.36 (October 31).

UNGA. 2021. "Report of the International Criminal Court." UN Doc. A/76/293 (August 24).

UNSC (United Nations Security Council). 2002. "UN Security Council Official Records (SCOR): 57th Session, 4563rd Meeting." UN Doc. S/PV.4563 (June 30).

UNSC. 2003a. "UN SCOR: 58th Session, 4772nd Meeting." UN Doc. S/PV.4772 (June 12).

UNSC. 2003b. "UNSC Resolution 1487." UN Doc. S/RES/1487 (June 12).

UNSC. 2005a. "UN SCOR: 60th Session, 5158th Meeting." UN Doc. S/PV.5158 (March 31).

UNSC. 2005b. "UNSC Resolution 1593." UN Doc. S/RES/1593 (March 31).

UNSC. 2008. "UNSC Resolution 1828." UN Doc. S/RES/1828 (July 31).

UNSC. 2011. "UNSC Resolution 1970." UN Doc. S/RES/1970 (February 26).

US Department of State. 2003. "American Service-Members' Protection Act." US Department of State. July 30. Accessed January 2008, 2023. https://2001-2009.state.gov/t/pm/rls/othr/misc/23425.htm.

Vilmer, Jean-Baptiste Jeangène. 2016. "The African Union and the International Criminal Court: Counteracting the Crisis." *International Affairs* 92 (6): pp. 1319–42. doi: 10.1111/1468-2346.12747.

Weller, Marc. 2002. "Undoing the Global Constitution: UN Security Council Action on the International Criminal Court." *International Affairs* 78 (4): pp. 693–712. doi: 10.1111/1468-2346.00275.

Zimmermann, Lisbeth. 2021. "Law and Science in Environmental Governance: The Effects of Legal and Scientific Argumentation in the International Whaling Commission." In *Talking International Law: Legal Argumentation outside the Courtroom*, ed. Ian Johnstone and Steven R. Ratner. Oxford: Oxford University Press, pp. 263–81.

Zvobgo, Kelebogile. 2019. "Human Rights Versus National Interests: Shifting US Public Attitudes on the International Criminal Court." *International Studies Quarterly* 63 (4): pp. 1065–78. doi: 10.1093/isq/sqz056.

Zvobgo, Kelebogile. 2021. "The ICC's Flawed Afghan Investigation: Why the Court Shouldn't Let America Off the Hook." Foreign Affairs, November 3. Accessed January 8, 2023. https://www.foreignaffairs.com/articles/afghanistan/2021-11-03/iccs-flawed-afghan-investigation.

6

Bad pirates, good privateers?

Surprising robustness of privateering norms

6.1 Introduction

Current research on international norms equates privateering with piracy, which was considered a "common enemy of all nations" from the sixteenth century onward and whose ban was described as an early case of international *jus cogens* (Kempe 2010a: 356).[1] Both practices have been described as "vicious" and in need of broadly similar efforts to criminalize and ban them (Andreas and Nadelmann 2006: 22–26; Sandholtz and Stiles 2009: 35). Widespread transgressions by privateers, as well as the contested boundaries between piracy and privateering, have led International Relations (IR) researchers to describe the distinction as arbitrary and privateering as completely unregulated. Sandholtz and Stiles (2009: 30) argue: "Whether an actor was a pirate or a legitimate privateer was largely a matter of political interest"—and that one would be hard pressed to identify any governing norm between 1500 and 1700.

We argue that this perspective fails to explain why privateering remained robust until the nineteenth century. Based on an elaborate permissive norm covering the legitimate "capture of private property at sea" (Sicking 2018: 457), privateering was regulated by law and adjudication procedures. Different actors strategically used the contested laws, viewing privateering as legitimate—and piracy not.

Scholars often argue that privateering became illegal in the nineteenth century because the practice had become obsolete (e.g. Sandholtz and Stiles 2009: 38). We argue, however, that the privateering norm eroded due to the mid-nineteenth-century shift from contesting its *application* to contesting its *validity*, which was part of the broader shift of norm clusters from mercantilism to capitalism and liberalism, especially in the United Kingdom (UK). Internationally, the privateering ban was a step along the path to finding a

[1] Historians and scholars of historical international relations have a more nuanced viewpoint.

International Norm Disputes. Lisbeth Zimmermann et al., Oxford University Press. © Lisbeth Zimmermann, Nicole Deitelhoff, Max Lesch, Antonio Arcudi, and Anton Peez (2023). DOI: 10.1093/oso/9780198873235.003.0006

solution to permanent applicatory contestation: the perennial strife regarding the rights of neutral states to ship goods during wars. In contrast to the contemporary cases in this volume, where contestation has taken place in densely institutionalized fields at the international level, privateering was replaced as a result of the relative power of a single norm challenger, the UK—although such replacement was a lengthy process.

We begin by discussing how privateering practices changed over time, then show the different levels of regulation and present the data for analyzing contestation and robustness trends (Section 6.2). After that, we give a historical overview of weakening and strengthening trends and explain them through the two types of contestation: application and validity (Section 6.3). We then show that current research on privateering and norm erosion fails to explain the dynamics observed (Section 6.4) and conclude by naming bigger shifts of norm clusters and the relative power of norm challengers as the central factors in privateering's demise (Section 6.5).

6.2 Changing patterns of privateering

6.2.1 Practices of privateering

Although the term "privateer" first emerged in the mid-seventeenth century (Starkey 2011: 130; Rodger 2014: 12),[2] private actors' "capture of private property at sea" (Sicking 2018: 457) had been a widespread practice since the Middle Ages.

Not only did privateering practices and regulations evolve over the centuries but also they were very different around the world. Mediterranean "corsairing" was conducted from the 1500s to the 1800s (Kempe 2010a: 365–67; Rodger 2014: 11; Trivellato et al. 2014; Colás 2016). Off the Northern African coast, Ottoman privateers used "commerce raiding"[3] to acquire not only cargo but also humans for ransom or sale on the Arab slave market. The English long tolerated the West Indies' "buccaneering" that helped them harm Spanish interests in the Americas (Starkey and McCarthy 2014: 134–35). In the seventeenth century, piracy and privateering in the Indian Ocean were "blurred by cycles of inter-imperial war and peace" (Benton 2005: 707).[4]

[2] The German term *Kaperei* and the Dutch term *kaper* are older.

[3] This refers to state navies or privateers attacking merchant ships as a military strategy.

[4] The increased regulation of privateering in Europe and the Americas caused sea robbers to move to the East Indies (Kempe 2010a: 362–64). For the business strategies of privateers over time, see Starkey and McCarthy (2014: 136–42).

Early on in Europe, if one state's subject damaged a second state's subject and the harm went unacknowledged by a court in the damager's country, the damaged subject's sovereign could issue a "letter of marque,"[5] also called a "letter of reprisal," authorizing the capture of property at sea to compensate for the loss. Here, "statehood" does not refer to the fully institutionalized, sovereign, and territorial nation-states that emerged in the nineteenth century but rather the often limited spheres of personalized princely authority (Teschke 2003). Damage was "redeemed" by taking control of ships sailing under the flag of the damaging state ("prizes"), then selling the cargo, and even the vessels, to compensate for the original harm (but not to exceed its total value). Early privateering was not necessarily linked to open warfare: It was a compensation mechanism. Seafaring was understood to involve trading, raiding, and occasional violence:

> Modern historians often present an implicitly dualist contrast between peaceful trader and the aggressive pirate, but in medieval reality the two were often the same person at different times. Robbery under arms was a normal aspect of seaborne trade.
>
> **(Rodger 2014: 6)[6]**

Privateering was significantly expanded in the sixteenth and seventeenth centuries. States issued more letters of marque and reprisal in reaction to foreign privateering (Starkey 1990: 21–22). The growth in activity was primarily driven by conflict over trade monopolies, particularly the Spanish and Portuguese colonies that were "closed" to trade with other European states: Just attempting to trade in off-limit colonies was enough for ships sailing under other flags to be regarded as "pirates." For their part, France, Britain, and the Netherlands refused to honor these restrictions (Kempe 2010b: 43–45) and declared Spanish and Portuguese reprisal acts as piracy. Conflict over trade privileges and monopolies also involved special rights that Britain sought in the slave trade, especially in the second part of the seventeenth century (Kempe 2010b: 137).

Tudor England increasingly used privateering to expand its territory, specifically under Queen Elizabeth (Kempe 2010b: 65; Starkey 2011, 130; Rodger 2014: 9), while European chartered companies used privateering to gain influence in Asia and the Indian Ocean (Kempe 2010b: 91). The dispute between what Hugo Grotius termed the *mare liberum* ("free sea") defended

[5] Linked to "marcher law," "law of the marches, the lawless frontier lands" (Rodger 2014: 6).

[6] A similar conclusion is drawn by Sicking (2018), who studies piracy and privateering activities in medieval Europe and the early modern period.

by France, Britain, and the Netherlands and the *mare clausum* ("closed sea") of Spain and Portugal was not merely over free trading rights but, perhaps more importantly, about the "freedom" to capture private property on all seas (Kempe 2010b: 2).

Increasingly, privateering was not practiced for compensation but as a military strategy: Naval forces were costly for European kings and princes[7] and privateers enhanced their maritime power. Furthermore, targeting enemy trade served to cut enemy supplies and weaken the opponent (Kempe 2010b: 97).[8] Consequently, states began to issue ever more privateering licenses to wage war and demonstrate power.[9] However, it was not just privateers who targeted cargo at sea: Commerce raiding was commonly used by warring state navies until the early twentieth century.[10]

Privateering's apogee is frequently put between the 1650s and the 1750s (Ritchie 1997: 18; Starkey 2011: 138–39). Starkey finds that by the 1730s, "piracy had been largely eradicated from the North Atlantic and privateering had been incorporated into the framework of international relations, a recognition of its potential utility as a tool of war" (Starkey 1990: 19). The practice was widely used in the Seven Years' War, the French Revolutionary Wars, and the wars of independence in North and South America. Then, in 1856, privateering was banned.

6.2.2 Was privateering an international norm?

IR scholars have generally interpreted privateering as a wholly unregulated realm because it was contested over the centuries. In fact, domestic and international customary law did regulate privateering. We conceptualize privateering as a "permissive" norm that, within specific limits, allows, but does not prescribe, certain behaviors, which gradually had European and, in the nineteenth century, even international coverage through the formal codification of "prize law" regulating the wartime capture of an enemy ship and its cargo (Sicking 2018: 432–33).

The "international" law invoked here is, of course, highly Eurocentric; validity and implementation varied greatly between Europe and other parts

[7] Fully fledged state navies only developed in the late seventeenth century.

[8] However, privateers were not especially useful in open battle.

[9] At that stage, "letters of reprisal" were often used by armed trading ships to engage in trade *and*, if the opportunity arose, in prize-taking, too. Privateering licenses were often only for taking prizes (Kempe 2010b: 87; Starkey 2011: 132; see also Starkey 1990: 20–22). French called such licenses *lettres de marque*, the Dutch *kaperbriefven*, the Germans *Kaperbriefe*.

[10] That made the navy a potentially quick way for the lucky few to access rank and fortune, as readers of Jane Austen novels know well.

of the world, including the European colonies (Colás and Mabee 2010a: 88–89). Interpretations of legal practices circulated in other parts of the world and fed back into and shaped European prize law (Benton 2005):

> [T]he laws, treaties, agreements and common regulatory processes of and between nations claiming some jurisdiction over maritime activities formed a broad, fluid spectrum of legitimacy that evolved over time and space.
>
> **(Starkey and McCarthy 2014: 132)**

The basis of the permissive privateering norm was the distinction made between the two ways for private actors to appropriate private property at sea: privateering, which was lawful, and piracy, which was not (Starkey 1990: 19). Originally a means of gaining compensation, privateering was later mostly used in warfare (Kempe 2010b: 45; Starkey 2011: 129). In practice, the division between privateering and piracy was not clear-cut. Below, we focus on privateering as a military strategy used in Europe from the mid-seventeenth century—that was regulated somewhat differently by the various countries.[11]

In general, licenses for privateering were issued by the sovereign, with the legality of prizes and all other legal issues adjudicated in domestic prize and admiralty courts, prize commissions, and other formal bodies. The earliest prize courts were established in the fourteenth and fifteenth centuries (Leira and Carvalho 2010: 60). Sicking (2018: 444–45) shows that, from the late Middle Ages until the seventeenth century, bilateral peace treaties often included joint commissions for dealing with post-war prize issues. The treaties generally featured privateering clauses covering such issues as the reciprocal acknowledgment of wartime prize court decisions, the revocation of outstanding letters of marque and reprisal, and rights to appeal.[12] In the seventeenth and eighteenth centuries, the rules became much more precise. Roelofsen (2012: 154) describes a "semi-internationalized procedure" for settling disputes—although the actual cases were primarily decided by domestic courts.

While the national laws differed as to who was authorized to issue licenses (the parliament, monarch, or other entity) and the specific legal arrangements for privateering and adjudication, there was a widely acknowledged

[11] On French privateering and its *guerre de course*, see Bromley (2010); on Dutch privateering, see Lunsford (2005) and Leira and Carvalho (2010: 63–67); for English privateering, see Starkey (1990); and on nineteenth-century US litigation about privateering, see Arlyck (2012). Mabee (2009: 151) discusses the differences between French state-sponsored privateering and British state-facilitated privateering between 1650 and 1750.

[12] Examples are the 1667 Treaty of Madrid between Great Britain and Spain and the follow-up treaty of 1670 (Kempe 2010b: 140–49). See also the Anglo-Dutch Peace of 1674 (Roelofsen 2012: 158). Sicking (2018: 440–46) gives an overview of medieval treaties that limited reprisals.

set of standards for maritime activities. In the eighteenth and nineteenth centuries, these included rules to "stop, board, search" and "seize" other ships with respect to transferring "ownership" and about how to treat the crew (Anderson and Gifford 1991: 105; Kraska 2009).[13]

All European states had courts or commissions at home—and increasingly, also in their colonies—to decide on the lawfulness of a prize.[14] If privateers raided a ship, they were required to register the prize at a prize court or commission.[15] If the raid was ruled lawful, the privateers could sell or auction the goods and ship. Privateering licenses and domestic laws often spelled out the profit distribution, with shares going to the court, state, shipowner, captain of the ship, and crew. If the court judged a prize unlawful, the owner of the ship had to be fully compensated (for reparation mechanisms, see Musa 2017: 130–38).

However, accountability standards were generally low. Privateers often had to "deposit bonds to guarantee good behavior" (Starkey and McCarthy 2014: 143; see also Musa 2017), although sovereigns were not liable for the non-compliance of privateers using their licenses (Kempe 2010b: 88). Nor were domestic legal systems necessarily good at detecting and punishing non-compliance. Consequently, many seafarers engaged in "legal posturing":

> [T]he sensible seafarer obtained commissions (genuine or fake), carried several flags to disguise a vessel's identity and constructed voyage narratives designed to reduce the scope for accusations of unlawful conduct.
>
> **(Starkey and McCarthy 2014: 141)**

Political and diplomatic considerations further influenced court rulings on prizes (Leira and Carvalho 2010; van Nieuwenhuize 2017). When promised a share in the profits, judges and consuls were motivated to positively decide prizes (see Leira and Carvalho 2010; Sicking 2018: 453). Sicking (2017: 13) describes this as "'flexible interpretation' or 'moulding' of 'victims' and 'neutrality' in individual prize cases depending on the various political and economic interests of the countries at stake."

In the eighteenth century, privateering regulations were further formalized. For example, in the British system, military conflicts had to be accompanied

[13] At the turn of the nineteenth century, Georg Friedrich von Marten published written versions of these rules on privateering in French, English, and German (Kempe 2010a: 367–68). Another central reference was Henry Wheaton's (1815)"Digest of the Law of Maritime Captures and Prizes".

[14] For a comparative overview, see Musa (2017: 130–32).

[15] Under certain conditions, they could also register the prize in a neutral state, as the French did in Norway; see Leira and Carvalho (2010: 64–65). On Spanish-American privateers, see Starkey and McCarthy (2014: 144); for an overview of prize law, see van Nieuwenhuize (2017).

by declarations of war that named the adversaries and specified how prizes were to be adjudicated (Starkey 1990: 22). The High Court of Admiralty based its rulings on standardized regulations. Eighteenth-century legislation, such as the 1759 Privateer's Act that forbid ransoming, tightened the regulations. But the administrative processes continued to be problematic, with limited possibilities for monitoring non-compliance at sea (Starkey 1990: 27).

Anderson and Gifford argue that the prize court decisions rendered in diverse domestic contexts converged because they were based on similar precedents: "While those arrangements differed in some details over time and across countries, there gradually arose a body of international law based on a common set of basic precedents that was employed by prize courts in different countries" (Anderson and Gifford 1991: 106). This perspective of "orderly" privateering is contradicted by Kempe's more skeptical account of how space for privateering was constituted under a fragmentary legal order:

> Based on political interest and the international context, the boundaries between lawful and unlawful commerce raiding were, time and again, adapted and shifted.
> **(Kempe 2010b: 27, our translation).**

6.2.3 Operationalization and data

Privateering allowed private actors to seize private property at sea—first for compensation and later as part of naval warfare. Conduct was codified, and domestic regulations and international customary rules defined lawful prizes and their adjudication.

This analysis of contestation and robustness trends is a desk study on privateering that is largely based on secondary historical sources. No coherent and consolidated quantitative data on privateering exists to supplement our qualitative account. We have attempted to trace contestations of privateering over the centuries. Unlike the slave trade, discussed in Chapter 7, which mostly involved domestic contestation, privateering was always an inter-state affair with parties from European or Western states (privateers, crews, and owners of raided ships, diplomats, judges, etc.).

Here, *applicatory contestation* deals with issues such as whether a certain action should be classified as piracy or privateering and specific cases of compliance or non-compliance. *Validity contestation* questions the very practice of privateering. For example, privateering can be declared wrong for economic or security reasons or because it is inherently immoral. Besides using secondary literature, we also analyzed British debates on privateering between 1780 and 1900 using the online archives of the House of Lords, the House of Commons, and the *Times* newspaper (founded in 1785), which, at that time, was generally considered independent and not shy of innovation, despite being very "establishment."[16]

To assess *norm robustness* with respect to practice, we consulted historical studies about the volume of global privateering. We also studied the amount of non-compliance with domestic regulations and how it evolved over time. Examples of non-compliance included illegal prizes, abuse of the crew, not bringing the case before the responsible prize court or commission, and courts' blatant miscarriage of justice with respect to legal and illegal prizes. Regarding the *discursive robustness* of the privateering norm, we examined historical studies on the international condemnation of privateering practices.

6.3 Contestation and robustness trends

Given the early international consensus against piracy, privateering's longevity is puzzling. We argue that its durability and various shifts in robustness are explained by the dominance of the two contestation types. We divide our analysis into four historical phases. In the *first*, from 1550 to 1650, non-compliance with privateering norms rose while negative reactions to norm violations lessened. This trend reversed in the *second* phase, roughly from 1650 to 1800, when the norm strengthened. We view this as linked to applicatory contestation regarding privateering norms rather than a fundamental challenge to privateering: Debates over the norm's exact application pushed addressees to make it more precise. The norm weakened again in phase *three*, between 1800 and 1856, because of the rise in contestations about privateering's overall validity. After applicatory contestation became permanent because European states (and the United States (US)) were unable to agree on the rights of neutral states, the privateering norm was replaced—in the *fourth* phase, which started in 1856.

6.3.1 Phase 1: 1550–1650

By the early 1600s, conflicts between European states over trade monopolies, territorial influence, sea power, and global colonies had caused privateering to get out of hand: One man's privateer was another man's pirate. Rivalries

[16] See, e.g. Encyclopædia Britannica article, "The Times, British Newspaper." Accessed January 9, 2023. https://www.britannica.com/topic/The-Times; King, Ed. "British Newspaper 1800–1860." Accessed January 9, 2023. https://www.gale.com/intl/essays/ed-king-british-newspapers-1800-1860.

over empire-building—between Spain and Portugal, as well as the Netherlands, France, and Britain—escalated (Section 6.2.1). During this period, "privateering ships outnumbered pirates dramatically" (Carvalho and Leira 2017: 6). The only monitoring concerned individual redress; state impunity enabled a host of activities that violated existing regulations (Kempe 2010b: 46–48). Furthermore, conflicts resulted in ever more unique interpretations of "lawful" commerce raiding.

Although states condemned cases of non-compliance, they did little to sanction them and even urged them on, for example, during Queen Elizabeth I's reign from 1558 to 1603 (see Section 6.2.1). Sometimes states adopted laissez-faire attitudes like those toward buccaneering in the Caribbean in the mid-1600s. In fact, the loosely organized states of the sixteenth and seventeenth centuries were not equipped to enforce order at sea. Uncontrolled privateering led to major confusion about the rules: a sign that the norm was weakening (Kempe 2010b: 138; for the Caribbean, see Colás and Mabee 2010a: 99).

In the ongoing rivalry over empire-building, neutral states—those not involved in the competition between Portugal, Spain, France, Britain, and the Netherlands—challenged uncontrolled private commerce raiding. But privateering was not heavily critiqued: The only demands were for improved monitoring and higher compensation—thus, applicatory issues. For example, Queen Elizabeth I promised Poland and the Hanseatic League that privateering would be better controlled (Kempe 2010b: 68–69).

6.3.2 Phase 2: 1650–1800

Uncertainty about the rules did not cause privateering to decay. Instead, contestation regarding conduct and rules (or the lack thereof) led to incremental norm changes that reduced its scope. This occurred as statehood became more consolidated in Europe, resulting in greater control over privateering and the increased differentiation between state navies and privateers. Sicking (2018: 450) describes the process as the "criminalization of the pirate and the disciplining of the privateer and the admiral." Britain spearheaded this change by tightening its regulations on privateering, establishing a global network of prize courts, more strictly controlling piracy, and beefing up the Royal Navy. Under Elizabeth I, Britain grew to be a major maritime power and preferred to rein in privateering.[17] France did, too

[17] Control was not evenly increased, however, and "legal ambiguities" persisted (Benton 2005: 720). Britain's stronger stance against privateering in the West Indies was certainly also due to its shifting interests: While at first, unhindered privateering was an important tool for gaining territorial influence and a profitable business activity, later, it disturbed trade.

(Ritchie 1997: 12; Mabee 2009, 149; Kempe 2010b: 143–44), while bilateral treaties tightened privateering rules and consolidated the fight against piracy (Kempe 2010b: 141). Paradoxically, the criminalization of piracy stabilized privateering.

Privateering was common during the Nine Years War (1688–97), the War of Spanish Succession (1701–14), the War of Austrian Succession (1740–48), the Anglo-Dutch Wars (1652–54, 1665–67, 1672–74, and 1780–84), and the American War of Independence (1775–83). Ritchie (1997: 18) writes of an "apogee in the late seventeenth and early eighteenth centuries. [. . .] Record numbers of ships obtained licences and [. . .] in turn captured ships on a grand scale." The amount of privateering fluctuated with the number of wars.[18]

During this second phase, privateering per se was not questioned. It was accepted as an efficient strategy of maritime warfare:

> In accord with mercantilist sentiments prevalent in the seventeenth and eighteenth centuries, this utility was deemed to accrue from the destruction wrought upon rival shipping and commerce-injury which was inflicted, moreover, at no expense to the state.
>
> **(Starkey 1990: 13)**

Neither Britain nor France—the main privateering states—considered abandoning it but rather encouraged the practice, while "[mitigating] its worst effects" (Ritchie 1997: 19). States and private traders crafted strategies to counter privateering, including convoying and insurance (Ritchie 1997: 18–19).

Privateering was part of heated debates over the interpretation of rights of neutral states. While Britain and France or Spain were at war, neutral states like the Dutch Republic and Denmark contested the warring states' application of privateering norms and tried to interpret the rules to leave *their* trade untouched. The most common interpretation was that "free ships" (sailing under a neutral flag during a maritime conflict) did not risk capture and could carry goods (even those belonging to subjects of enemy states, except for contraband). Then, in 1756, at the start of the Seven Years' War, Great Britain unilaterally made enemy goods on neutral ships a "good prize"; that is, British privateers were allowed to seize enemy goods on free ships (Ritchie 1997: 20–21)—much to the displeasure of neutral states.

Debates in the British parliament included regular references to privateering (e.g. Grey [1693] 1769). Unsurprisingly, the enemy's wartime privateering

[18] Quantification is difficult: Starkey (1990: Appendix 7) counts 1,785 British privateering vessels between 1793 and 1801 and Starkey and McCarthy (2014: 133–34) around 9,000 British vessels between 1739 and 1815, many of which were dual-purpose ships engaged in trade and/or prize-taking.

activities were cast in a negative light. For example, during the Franco-Dutch War, MP William Garraway complained: "The *French* are not so formidable as they make themselves in their insolent way of privateering" (Grey [1677] 1769; also Grey [1689] 1769). The online archive of *The Times* (from 1785 on) contains no critical discussions of privateering practices at that time, which leads us to conclude that, although privateering in general was not questioned, specific applications were. In 1791, revolutionary France was the first state to propose a ban on privateering. However, it got no support from other European states and eventually also permitted the practice (Ritchie 1997: 22).

6.3.3 Phase 3: 1800–56

Privateering activities climaxed in the early nineteenth century as more letters of marque were issued during the wars of independence in North and South America (Starkey and McCarthy 2014: 135–36). British privateering activities were still in full swing (Starkey 1990: Appendix 8). Kempe describes this phase as one of new regulatory confusion:

> The privateering war had reached such a level of irregularity that none of the participating powers on either side of the Atlantic could safely assess what was defined as legitimate privateering in terms of international standards.
>
> **(Kempe 2010a: 367)**

The third phase also saw abundant applicatory contestation of privateering, including the crucial dispute over the trading rights of neutrals during maritime conflicts (Kraska 2009: para. 11). In 1756, Great Britain had unilaterally decided that neutral commerce was subject to search and that on neutral ships, even non-contraband "enemy" goods were a good prize for British privateers.[19] During the Seven Years' War, the British declared that Dutch trade was subject to seizure because the Dutch were handling most of France's colonial shipping (Anderson and Gifford 1991: 108). At the same time, France declared a neutral national's property on an enemy ship a good prize (Ritchie 1997: 21), thereby limiting trading opportunities for subjects of neutral states.

These developments caused neutral states to more openly contest privateering, particularly in 1780 and 1800, by forming "armed neutralities" to prevent Great Britain from searching their ships and seizing goods (Lemnitzer 2013: 1069). The first armed neutrality aimed to block British attempts to attack Russian vessels trading with the British colonies in North America

[19] Later, US courts also applied this interpretation (Parillo 2007: 18).

during the war for independence. In 1800, the second armed neutrality that Russia initiated against Great Britain was less successful.

During the Crimean War (1853–1856), France and the UK, together with the Ottoman Empire and Sardinia, allied against Russia. In an attempt to prevent neutral states from enforcing a threatened *third* armed neutrality (Lemnitzer 2013: 1072), France and the UK voluntarily accepted the neutral states' broad interpretation of their rights: freedom for enemy goods on neutral vessels and immunity for neutral goods on enemy vessels. In addition, France and the UK jointly declared that they would not issue privateering licenses because the latter feared that US privateers would operate under Russian licenses in the Crimean War (Kempe 2010b: 337). The UK also wanted to further sideline the US, which had started to encourage European states to join a US–Russian treaty that more broadly interpreted neutral rights (for details about this and the UK's counter-campaign, see Lemnitzer 2013: 1075–77).

Privateering itself—and thus, the validity of the permissive norm—was particularly challenged by the UK—but only in the mid-nineteenth century. Lemnitzer (2014: 174) observes that between 1815 and 1853, there was hardly any public debate on privateering in the UK, although some critical voices were raised during the Napoleonic Wars (1803–15) and the Mexican–American War (1846–48). *The Times* published only a few articles on privateering during the Latin American wars of independence (*Times* 1826) that included criticism of abuses (*Times* 1828). Early nineteenth-century parliamentary debates contested the validity of privateering, but not severely (e.g. Lord Musgrave in UK Parliamentary Debates 1801: 206). During the Spanish–American wars of independence between 1808 and 1833, European countries and the US heavily criticized both Spanish and South American privateering as "piratical" (Starkey and McCarthy 2014: 136).

However, general criticism of privateering grew in the years leading up to the Crimean War. For example, in a book chapter published in *The Times*, the author, John Barrow, argues:

> If, indeed, the whole system of privateering could be got rid of, by agreement of the belligerents, it would prove the greatest benefit to mankind in general, as well as to these engaged in it; for it is frequently carried on in a manner little short of legalized and licensed piracy.
>
> (*Times* 1839)

In 1841, in the House of Commons, Whig politician David Barclay demanded that they "put an end for ever [sic] to the barbarous, cruel, and unchristian practice of privateering" (*Times* 1841). In 1846, *The Times* reprinted an article from the French newspaper, *Le Siècle*, describing privateering as a "barbarous practice" (while endorsing commerce raiding):

> Privateering, which has rendered services to France which we are far from forgetting [. . .] engenders passions of lucre, and hatred, from which it is of the highest importance to purge a well-organized society.
>
> (*Times* 1846)

In 1854, as the Crimean War was in full swing, fears about privateers mounted in the UK, which had become the world's greatest naval and trading power. Russian letters of marque (most likely for US privateers) would have disrupted British trade and raised the cost of insurance, putting UK traders at a significant disadvantage. That year, *The Times* and other British newspapers emphatically called for an end to privateering (Lemnitzer 2013: 1073). A short article in *The Times* attacked privateering, which was likened to ground warfare:

> What if the Duke of Wellington on crossing the Pyrenees had brought with him a swarm of Spanish guerillas, and given them written licenses to plunder the peaceful inhabitants of France, and murder all those who resisted their exaction? The very idea is monstrous and incredible.
>
> (*Times* 1854a)

Liberalism is invoked to justify the rejection of privateering:

> A more humane, enlightened, and liberal spirit has searched and reformed the institutions of society. [. . .] It now becomes our duty to consider and to ascertain whether the same period which has served to remove so many prejudices and misconceptions in most of the relations of social life may not also have enabled us to deal in a more liberal and humane spirit with the laws and usages of war itself.
>
> (*Times* 1854b)

That same year, the UK *Daily News* opined that a privateer was "merely a pirate with a pardon in his pocket" (cited in Lemnitzer 2013: 1073), while Prime Minister Lord Aberdeen called privateering "a most intolerable relic of a barbarous age" (cited in Lemnitzer 2013: 1075). In the House of Commons, his position was echoed in an 1854 debate on the rights of neutrals that did not uphold privateering (HC Deb 1854).

The British envisioned a drive to end privateering that resembled their anti-slave-trade campaign (Lemnitzer 2013: 1073; see also Chapter 7). An 1854 letter to the editor of *The Times* shows the relation:

> The "law of nations" is the law of the strong; and yet it is essentially republican in its character, because it is the law of the strong for the protection of, and to secure equal rights to, the weak; but like all other human laws, it is subservient to the public opinion of the world [. . .]. Thirty-five years ago the slave trade—that abominable traffic in human flesh, which is now the horror of the whole civilized world—was in conformity with the "law of nations;" [. . .] In like manner, privateering, under certain restrictions, is in conformity with the "law of nations." But this, too, is a relic of a barbarous age.
>
> **(Werb 1854)**

Privateers were increasingly equated with pirates: Both were enemies of humankind. Privateering was described as a barbaric, inhuman, and brutal kind of warfare. A British trade lobby described it as detrimental to trade and violating the right to private property, which was to be ensured even in wartime (Anderson and Gifford 1991: 113). The general rise of liberalism and capitalism, which replaced mercantilist thinking and more clearly separated economics from politics, as well as the changing strategies for naval warfare, heavily influenced perceptions of privateering (Mabee 2009; Colás and Mabee 2010a).[20]

Privateering practices also changed: To support the UK during the Crimean War, neutral states such as the Union between Sweden and Norway, the Netherlands, Spain, and the Kingdom of the Two Sicilies all closed their harbors to privateers (Lemnitzer 2013: 1074). The British also pressured other neutral states, including Austria, Belgium, Hanover, Portugal, Brazil, Argentina, and Chile, into denying privateers entry.

Some states were more skeptical of a privateering ban. The French, who were allied with the UK against Russia, were torn, with a sizable group within the government inclined to keep its privateering option (Lemnitzer 2013: 1073). Most importantly, the US was against a ban on privateering (Lemnitzer 2013: 1074) because it was key to marine warfare for states without major navies. However, contemporaneous debates in France and the US show

[20] For more on the rise of industrialism and capitalism, changing interpretations of property rights, and the growing anti-privateering lobby in the UK, see O'Malley (1990). Some scholars hold that the criticism was really the British navy's pretext for getting rid of competition as it sought good prizes and potential recruits (Anderson and Gifford 1991: 118).

that privateering was becoming more complex because, to keep up with technology, privateers had switched from sailing ships to steamers, which needed regular port access to load coal (Lemnitzer 2013: 1074).

The unresolved contestation over neutral rights (permanent applicatory contestation) and society's increasing doubts about privateering (validity contestation) brought about a swift decline of the permissive norm during the negotiations to end the Crimean War. In consultation with the UK (Lemnitzer 2013: 1079), the French proposed a thorough codification of the law on naval warfare. While most of the smaller European states were keen to codify their broader interpretation of neutral rights, the UK was mostly concerned about mounting hostilities with the US: A ban on privateering could weaken the US, which had a small navy and relied on privateering.

Signed in 1856, the final agreement on privateering, which also included rules on blockades and contraband, represents a negotiated outcome that sidelined the US. The European states happily accepted the British offer of neutral rights in exchange for a complete ban on privateering. The declaration also included a clause that granted its interpretation of neutral rights only to signatories.

The Paris Declaration Respecting Maritime Law that was signed in April 1856 by the eight states participating in the conference to settle the Crimean War (the UK, France, Russia, Prussia, Austria, Sardinia, and the Ottoman Empire) was the very first multilateral law-making project. By mid-year, most European powers—aside from Spain—had joined. Subsequently opened to all, 40 more states signed in the following years. Non-European countries, including Argentina, Brazil, Chile, and Peru, followed suit (Haule 2008), making this the first codified international legal norm (Lemnitzer 2013: 1068).[21]

The Paris Declaration was not primarily a case of one great power single-handedly eroding a set of permissive norms. Instead, it was a compromise struck between strong maritime powers that had become less reliant on privateering and smaller seafaring nations with divergent interests (Kempe 2010b: 341). It principally accommodated UK interests.

Surprised by the far-reaching law-making project, the US suggested amending the Paris Declaration to ban not just privateering but all commerce raiding, including by state navies. The UK blocked the proposal (Lemnitzer 2013, 2014), and the US did not sign the declaration. Neither did Spain, Mexico, or Venezuela (at least initially), who all maintained that privateering was

[21] On the ratifications, see the International Red Cross, Declaration Respecting Maritime Law. Paris, 16 April 1856. Accessed May 24, 2019. https://ihl-databases.icrc.org/applic/ihl/ihl.nsf/States.xsp?xp_viewStates=XPages_NORMStatesParties&xp_treatySelected=105.

a necessary strategy for small warring states who lacked the means to equip navies. In the following years, their position became increasingly isolated.

6.3.4 Phase 4: After 1856

Interestingly enough, after the Paris Declaration, privateering was not immediately viewed as a repulsive military strategy—not even in the UK. Instead, the replacement process was very slow—in which privateering and its ban competed as states negotiated the scope of the privateering ban. Parliamentary debates in that year reveal that many members of parliament (MPs) were critical of privateering but believed that giving up the British practice of searching neutral ships for enemy goods was too great a sacrifice (HL Deb 1875). Moreover, British debates during the American Civil War (1861–65) show that most MPs believed that the privateering ban was not yet part of the "laws of nations" and was only valid between signatories. They assumed that Confederate privateering was legal and that British citizens could get privateering licenses and participate in the war, although they could not expect the British Crown's protection (HL Deb 1861). Also, after 1856, several applicatory debates arose about how to interpret the Declaration of Paris, for example, with respect to the role of auxiliary cruisers in the German *Seewehr* (private ships under the German navy's command), which signatories seemed not to consider privateering.[22]

Still, the ban on privateering was accompanied by privateering's slow decline in both practice and discourse. Paris Declaration signatories strongly condemned threats of privateering (Lemnitzer 2014: 178), including German Chancellor Otto von Bismarck's menace to use letters of marque against Denmark for not respecting the principle of "effective blockades" in 1864. Chile, another signatory, was denounced for offering letters of marque in the Chincha Islands War (1864–66) between Spain and its former colonies of Chile and Peru, and signatory Bolivia was criticized for offering them against Chile in the War of the Pacific (1879–84). In the end, no letters were taken by privateers during both because privateering did not seem to be lucrative or practical (Lemnitzer 2014: 184–85). In the 1870s and 1880s, Russian threats to use privateering against Britain were condemned by the other signatories of the Paris Declaration (Lemnitzer 2014: 184).

The general decline in privateering is also exemplified by its very limited use in the American Civil War. At its start, realizing that the Confederacy

[22] In later conflicts, "voluntary armies" were not interpreted as privateers (Thomson 1994: 76; Kempe 2010a: 367–68).

was planning to use privateers, the US attempted to join the Paris Declaration (Thomson 1994: 76), only to withdraw the application when European states did not promise their support against Confederate privateers (HL Deb 1861). However, anticipating strong European disapproval, under President Abraham Lincoln, the US refrained from privateering. As for the Confederate side, the closure of "neutral" ports in European colonies in the Caribbean made the practice untenable: Privateering ships were assigned other tasks (Lemnitzer 2014: ch. 6).

Neither side issued privateering licenses during the Spanish–American War, although neither had ratified the Paris Declaration. Analyzing US foreign policy debates, Parillo (2007: 4) argues that privateering remained an option for the US government until the 1880s, when it was finally dropped as a military practice. The US never joined the Paris Declaration; Spain and Mexico joined in 1908 and 1909.

Privateering was replaced as an international norm, yet commerce raiding by state navies persisted. At the second Peace Conference at the Hague (1907), states worked to make international law on commerce raiding more specific and proposed an international prize court—*the very first* international court. However, neither the protocols nor the court were ratified, and the world wars that followed led to major reinterpretations and the erosion of many Paris Declaration rules (Haule 2008; Lemnitzer 2014: 173–96). However, although many principles had been weakened, there was no resurgence in privateering.

Formal support thus grew for a privateering ban to replace the permissive norm. Then, in 1856, the permissive norm was formally replaced by a ban and its robustness eroded over time. Practical instances of privateering declined, accompanied by hefty negative reactions to threatened and actual privateering.

6.4 Factors driving contestation

The explanatory factors for privateering's astonishingly long robustness followed by its swift decay are somewhat different from those for our contemporary cases of norm contestation. The law seems to have played no significant role with respect to privateering. For centuries, the permissive norm was customary international law: The *legal quality* of privateering remained unchanged, although its lack of precision enabled major contestation. In fact, the contestation between 1550 and 1650 focused on practical issues, resulting in tighter rules and further specification that strengthened the norm. The lack of delegation also carries no explanatory weight: Privateering was never formally institutionalized internationally, yet it persisted for centuries.

At first glance, embeddedness in normative clusters also does not seem to apply to privateering—as it is generally linked to the banned practice of piracy. Yet, privateering's embeddedness in broader conceptions of economic activity and statehood does explain its stability and later its decline. At first, the practice was linked to mercantilist notions that intertwined economic activities with political interests. Harming enemy trade was seen as a successful, relatively bloodless, strategy; distinctions between public and private actors and interests were blurred. Privateering was also linked to early forms of state-building, when private actors had great "political-economic usefulness" (Mabee 2009: 140). Then, with the advent of capitalism and liberalism, the right of individuals to own property and the separation of "private" and "public" became more common. As a result, privateering seemed more harmful and also less useful for organizing trade relationships than the general "centralization and bureaucratization of naval power" in state navies (Mabee 2009: 148). Furthermore, privateering was presented as an outdated strategy of warfare that was especially "barbarous" and inhumane.

The relative power of norm challengers significantly helped to get the privateering ban accepted. The mighty UK was forced to compromise with other European states that did not view privateering as a central security concern, yet it managed to get the practice outlawed. Unlike our contemporary cases, in the nineteenth century, there were no dense institutions embedding contestation processes and (somewhat) counterbalancing dominant norm challengers. Even without the offsetting effect of such institutions, the UK had to make deals to get privateering banned—all the while, pioneering multilateral treaty-making as key to creating and championing norms in the international system. In this historical case, the absence of formal international institutions dealing with maritime conflict meant that perceptions of institutional fairness played no role.

Sandholtz and Stiles (2009: 29–30) argue that privateering's demise was due to nineteenth-century technological developments. They write that steamboats, modern gunnery, submarines, and faster communications technology made privateering much more difficult. Yet, these technological developments led to the demise only of privateering, not of commerce raiding by state navies, which had similar circumstances. If commerce raiding by state navies was technologically impractical, why did states continue to defend it as a tool of war? Military strategies, such as the role of blockades and the use of sea versus land power, also changed. However, although privateering became more costly and complicated, states continued to engage in it. Activities only waned after many states closed their ports to privateers.

In her famous work on unauthorized non-state violence in early modern Europe, Thomson (1994) describes the demise of private security actors over the course of the nineteenth century as a consequence of new conceptions of statehood and state-building (see also Ritchie 1997: 23). Thomson argues that we observe not only changing notions of private property but also changing conceptions of the way states should be organized, including their accountability for subjects' extraterritorial acts. Her narrative has been criticized for assuming too clear a distinction between public and private. Thomson also exaggerates the state's interest in monopolizing power during early state-building (Mabee 2009: 142). Although state-building was certainly relevant to privateering, most of the fundamental critics of privateering in the nineteenth century justified its ban using liberal arguments about private property and the inhuman nature of privateering—not the need for monopolization of power.

6.5 Conclusion

For centuries, privateering was a highly contested practice, albeit one that was subject to a set of permissive norms agreed upon by states. This historical case contradicts the dominant IR discourse that equates contestation with norm death (see Chapter 1). It also contradicts the view that privateering and piracy are essentially the same, although we acknowledge that the dividing line long remained dynamic. We hold that both the surprising longevity of privateering and its rapid decline in the nineteenth century are explained by the dominant types of contestation. In the seventeenth century, privateering reached a peak as European states fought over trade monopolies and zones of influence. It did not erode during the ensuing applicatory contestation. Instead, privateering regulations were made more specific, and privateering's scope was reduced. At the turn of the nineteenth century, activity reached another high. But European states could not agree on how to apply neutral rights—and applicatory contestation became permanent.

In the mid-nineteenth century, during negotiations over the rules of naval warfare, the UK pushed for a ban on privateering in exchange for broader neutral rights for smaller European states. The ban on privateering came about when ideas and practices of (mercantilist) economic and social organization—that did not clearly distinguish between private and public—shifted toward liberalism and capitalism. UK society in particular increasingly challenged privateering's validity: Normative clusters changed and privateering was increasingly seen as harmful to private property and immoral. Unlike our contemporary cases, where norm contestation is often channeled in international institutions, the swift codification of the prohibition of privateering was largely determined by the relative power of the primary norm challenger and hegemon. The UK employed strategies from its earlier campaigns against the slave trade to pioneer modern multilateral law-making. With the Paris Declaration, the UK exploited its powerful position to lock in and institutionalize discussion about rules on maritime conflict. Privateering was replaced with a ban—as a result of shifts in normative clusters and the norm challenger's relative power.

Reference list

Anderson, Gary M., and Adam Gifford. 1991. "Privateering and the Private Production of Naval Power." *Cato Journal* 11 (1): pp. 99–122.

Andreas, Peter, and Ethan A. Nadelmann. 2006. *Policing the Globe: Criminalization and Crime Control in International Relations*. Oxford: Oxford University Press.

Arlyck, Kevin. 2012. "Plaintiffs v. Privateers: Litigation and Foreign Affairs in the Federal Courts, 1816–1822." *Law and History Review* 30 (1): pp. 245–78. doi: 10.1017/S0738248011000666.

Benton, Lauren. 2005. "Legal Spaces of Empire: Piracy and the Origins of Ocean Regionalism." *Comparative Studies in Society and History* 47 (4): pp. 700–24. doi: 10.1017/S0010417505000320.

Bromley, John Selwyn. 2010. *Corsairs and Navies, 1660–1760*. London: Hambledon Press.

Carvalho, Benjamin de, and Halvard Leira. 2017. "Empires, Privateering, and the Sea: A Research Program." Paper presented at the ISA Annual Convention in Baltimore, MD, February 22–25.

Colás, Alejandro. 2016. "Barbary Coast in the Expansion of International Society: Piracy, Privateering, and Corsairing as Primary Institutions." *Review of International Studies* 42 (5): pp. 840–57. doi: 10.1017/S0260210516000152.

Colás, Alejandro, and Bryan Mabee. 2010a. "The Flow and Ebb of Private Seaborne Violence in Global Politics: Lessons from the Atlantic World, 1689–1815." In *Mercenaries, Pirates, Bandits, and Empires: Private Violence in Historical Context*, edited by Alejandro Colás and Bryan Mabee, pp. 83–107. Oxford: Oxford University Press.

Encyclopædia Britannica. "The Times, British Newspaper." Accessed January 9, 2023. https://www.britannica.com/topic/The-Times.

Grey, Anchitell. (1677) 1769. “Debates in 1677: May 21st–23rd.” In *Grey's Debates of the House of Commons: Volume 4*, ed. Anchitell Grey. London: T. Becket and P.A. De Hondt, pp. 355–75.

Grey, Anchitell. (1689) 1769. “Debates in 1689: November 10th–19th.” In *Grey's Debates of the House of Commons: Volume 9*, ed. Anchitell Grey. London: T. Becket and P.A. De Hondt, pp. 404–38.

Grey, Anchitell. (1693) 1769. “Debates in 1693: November 7th–29th.” In *Grey's Debates of the House of Commons: Volume 10*, ed. Anchitell Grey. London: T. Becket and P.A. De Hondt, pp. 311–38.

Haule, Romuald R. 2008. “Paris, Declaration of (1856).” In *Max Planck Encyclopedia of Public International Law*, ed. Anne Peters and Rüdiger Wolfrum. Oxford: Oxford University Press. Last updated November 2008. Accessed January 9, 2023. https://opil.ouplaw.com/view/10.1093/law:epil/9780199231690/law-9780199231690-e732.

HC Deb (House of Commons Debates). 1854. “House of Commons Debates: Rights of Neutrals.” HC Deb. vol. 131, cols 955–73 (March 17).

HL Deb (House of Lords Debates). 1861. “House of Lord Debates: The United States—the Civil War—Privateering.” HL Deb. vol. 162, cols 2077–88 (May 16).

HL Deb. 1875. “House of Lords Debates: France—Declaration of Paris, 1856.” HL Deb. vol. 223, cols 822–64 (April 13).

Kempe, Michael. 2010a. “‘Even in the Remotest Corners of the World’: Globalized Piracy and International Law, 1500–1900.” *Journal of Global History* 5 (3): pp. 353–72. doi: 10.1017/S1740022810000185.

Kempe, Michael. 2010b. *Fluch Der Weltmeere: Piraterie, Völkerrecht und Internationale Beziehungen 1500–1900*. Wiesbaden: Campus Verlag.

King, Ed. 2007. “British Newspaper, 1800–1860.” Accessed January 9, 2023. https://www.gale.com/intl/essays/ed-king-british-newspapers-1800-1860.

Kraska, James. 2009. “Prize Law.” In Peters and Wolfrum, eds. Last updated December 2009. Accessed January 9, 2023. https://opil.ouplaw.com/view/10.1093/law:epil/9780199231690/law-9780199231690-e383.

Leira, Halvard, and Benjamin de Carvalho. 2010. “Privateers of the North Sea: At Worlds End—French Privateers in Norwegian Waters.” In Colás and Mabee 2010, pp. 55–82.

Lemnitzer, Jan Martin. 2013. “‘That Moral League of Nations against the United States’: The Origins of the 1856 Declaration of Paris.” *International History Review* 35 (5): pp. 1068–88. doi: 10.1080/07075332.2013.844194.

Lemnitzer, Jan Martin. 2014. *Power, Law and the End of Privateering*. Basingstoke: Palgrave Macmillan.

Lunsford, Virginia West. 2005. *Piracy and Privateering in the Golden Age Netherlands*. New York: Palgrave Macmillan.

Mabee, Bryan. 2009. "Pirates, Privateers and the Political Economy of Private Violence." *Global Change, Peace & Security* 21 (2): pp. 139–52. doi: 10.1080/14781150902871994.

Musa, Shavana. 2017. "Victims of Maritime Conflict, Compensation Claims and the Role of the Admiralty Court in the Early Modern Period." *Comparative Legal History* 5 (1): pp. 125–41. doi: 10.1080/2049677X.2017.1311548.

O'Malley, Pat. 1990. "Peace, Trade and Treaties." *Australian and New Zealand Journal of Sociology* 26 (2): pp. 170–86. doi: 10.1177/144078339002600202.

Parillo, Nicholas. 2007. "The De-Privatization of American Warfare: How the U.S. Government Used, Regulated, and Ultimately Abandoned Privateering in the Nineteenth Century." *Yale Journal of Law & the Humanities* 19 (1): pp. 1–95.

Ritchie, Robert C. 1997. "Government Measures against Piracy and Privateering in the Atlantic Area, 1750–1850." In *Pirates and Privateers: New Perspectives on the War on Trade in the Eighteenth and Nineteenth Centuries*, ed. David J. Starkey. Exeter: University of Exeter Press, pp. 10–28.

Rodger, N. A. M. 2014. "The Law and Language of Private Naval Warfare." *Mariner's Mirror* 100 (1): pp. 5–16. doi: 10.1080/00253359.2014.866371.

Roelofsen, Cornelis G. 2012. "International Arbitration and Courts." In *The Oxford Handbook of the History of International Law*, ed. Bardo Fassbender, Anne Peters, and Simone Peter. Oxford: Oxford University Press, pp. 145–69.

Sandholtz, Wayne, and Kendall W. Stiles. 2009. *International Norms and Cycles of Change*. Oxford: Oxford University Press.

Sicking, Louis. 2017. "Introduction: Maritime Conflict Management, Diplomacy and International Law, 1100–1800." *Comparative Legal History* 5 (1): pp. 2–15. doi: 10.1080/2049677X.2017.1314604.

Sicking, Louis. 2018. "The Pirate and the Admiral: Europeanisation and Globalisation of Maritime Conflict Management." *Journal of the History of International Law* 20 (4): pp. 429–70. doi: 10.1163/15718050-12340098.

Starkey, David J. 1990. *British Privateering Enterprise in the Eighteenth Century*. Exeter: University of Exeter Press.

Starkey, David J. 2011. "Voluntaries and Sea Robbers: A Review of the Academic Literature on Privateering, Corsairing, Buccaneering and Piracy." *Mariner's Mirror* 97 (1): pp. 127–47. doi: 10.1080/00253359.2011.10709036.

Starkey, David J., and Matthew McCarthy. 2014. "A Persistent Phenomenon: Private Prize-Taking in the British Atlantic World, c. 1540–1856." In *Persistent Piracy: Maritime Violence and State-Formation in Global Historical Perspective*, ed. Leos Müller and Stefan Eklöf Amirell. Basingstoke: Palgrave Macmillan, pp. 131–51.

Teschke, Benno. 2003. *The Myth of 1648: Class, Geopolitics, and the Making of Modern International Relations*. London: Verso.

Thomson, Janice E. 1994. *Mercenaries, Pirates, and Sovereigns: State-Building and Extraterritorial Violence in Early Modern Europe*. Princeton, NJ: Princeton University Press.

Times. 1826. "Law of Nations." The Times, October 20.

Times. 1828. "Some Most Extraordinary Facts Have Been Brought to Light, Relative to the System of Privateering." The Times, December 13.

Times. 1839. "Navies of Great Britain, France, &c." The Times, January 19.

Times. 1841. "Parliamentary Notices." The Times, October 9.

Times. 1846. "Letters of Marque." The Times, June 15.

Times. 1854a. "With the Heroism, the Glory, and the Triumphs." The Times, February 28.

Times. 1854b. "The Period of Forty Years Which Has Elapsed Since." The Times, March 10.

Trivellato, Francesca, Leor Halevi, and Cátia Antunes, eds. 2014. *Religion and Trade: Cross-Cultural Exchanges in World History, 1000–1900*. Oxford: Oxford University Press.

UK Parliamentary Debates. 1801. "House of Lords: November 13, 1801." House of Lords Sessional Papers; vol. 16, 183–208.

van Nieuwenhuize, Hielke. 2017. "Prize Law, International Diplomacy and the Treatment of Foreign Prizes in the Seventeenth Century: A Case Study." *Comparative Legal History* 5 (1): pp. 142–61. doi: 10.1080/2049677X.2017.1311550.

Werb, J. Watson. 1854. "Letter to the Editor: Privateering." The Times, March 9.

Wheaton, Henry. 1815. *Digest of the Law of Maritime Captures and Prizes*. New York: R. M'Dermut & D.D. Arden.

7

Atlantic slave trade

Stabilization through contestation

7.1 Introduction

Much is unique about the Atlantic slave trade, including the suffering it caused and how it changed the course of modern history. Over more than three centuries, well over 12 million human beings were brutally torn from their homes and surroundings in one part of the world, transported to and sold in a second region of the world—by and benefiting people in a third. How did Europe's leading seafaring nations normatively justify and establish this immense system of forced relocation? How did the slave trade align with the normative environments of the time? We argue that Atlantic slave trading was a (collection of) permissive norm(s) that allowed states to facilitate the capture, transport, and sale of Africans. It is one of the few major international norms that completely eroded over time and has been replaced—at least partly in response to contestation.[1]

This chapter examines the two most active Atlantic slave traders, the Kingdom of Portugal and the British Empire, and how they justified their activity. Portuguese slavery and slave trading were religiously defended from the outset in the 1500s with precise details about how enslaved Africans were to be transported and "led" to Christianity (Marques 2006: 17, 21). British debates in the early 1700s framed the slave trade as an expression of free trade and property rights (Geggus 2001: 119). This chapter shows that in both cases, applicatory contestation largely prevailed and had stabilizing effects. By debating the "how" and "when" of a norm's application, applicatory contestation clarifies the meaning of certain claims of a norm and helps reinforce the underlying normative beliefs.

The two cases also speak to the ways a norm is strengthened by being embedded in a broader normative environment or cluster (see Ruggie 1982;

[1] The practice still exists in different parts of the world through "modern slavery," human trafficking, forced and bonded labor, and forced marriage. Today, however, slavery is prohibited by international humanitarian law and most domestic law. We examine slave trading's transition from legality to full abolition.

International Norm Disputes. Lisbeth Zimmermann et al., Oxford University Press. © Lisbeth Zimmermann, Nicole Deitelhoff, Max Lesch, Antonio Arcudi, and Anton Peez (2023). DOI: 10.1093/oso/9780198873235.003.0007

Lantis and Wunderlich 2018; Winston 2018). In most of the periods and cases examined here, the slave trade was a fully accepted element of the normative settings of colonialism, Christian doctrine, and the emergent practice of free trade.

In this chapter, we compare domestic contestation of the slave trade in the Kingdom of Portugal and the British Empire because of their substantive significance (Koivu and Hinze 2017) as the leading seafaring and slave-trading powers and hegemons of different periods. The cases extend from the beginning of the trade in the sixteenth century to its end in the early nineteenth century and are presented alongside timelines of each country's estimated annual trade volume (Slave Voyages 2022a) to roughly indicate the norm's robustness and pervasiveness.[2]

In Section 7.2, after discussing the Atlantic slave trade as an international social norm, we discuss its normativity. We define and operationalize applicatory and validity contestation of the slave trade, as well as its robustness, in Section 7.2.2. In Sections 7.3 and 7.4, we examine debates about the slave trade in Great Britain and Portugal, tracing the relative strength and types of norm contestation and robustness at various stages. We discuss the major explanatory factors in Section 7.5 and conclude in Section 7.6.

7.2 Slave trade as an international norm

IR norm researchers typically examine slavery and the slave trade as historical cases of norm "demise" (Shilliam 2014; see also Ray 1989; Sandholtz and Stiles 2009: ch. 7; Panke and Petersohn 2012). They focus on the *end* of the slave trade—the emergence of *anti*-slave-trade norms and abolition—rather than on the origins of the slave trade or how it persisted for centuries. For their part, historians have more comprehensively addressed the issue but, until the mid-1900s, they also focused on abolition (Stein 1979: xvi). In our study, we examine the *persistence* of Atlantic slave trading to gain a better understanding of the link between contestation and norm robustness. We focus on transnational slave trading as a crucial part of the institution of slavery (Finnemore and Sikkink 1998: 891).

IR literature seldom categorizes slavery and slave trading as *norms* but rather as *practices* that became increasingly contested and eventually changed

[2] Annual trade volumes are a very rough proxy for practical robustness because they cannot be directly translated into norm compliance. The slave-trading norm was permissive: It *allowed* a certain practice rather than pro- or prescribing it. *Not* engaging in the norm does not equal *non-compliance*. Despite problems regarding the accuracy of historical data and various confounding factors such as naval warfare, trade volumes can roughly indicate how established or widespread the norm was in its time.

into an anti-slavery norm (Ray 1989; Nadelmann 1990). However, as the following sections highlight, slavery and the slave trade were indeed norms: regular practices that specific groups grounded in shared normative justifications (see Section 7.2.1). These included the right to own captured Africans and the obligation to spread Christianity and the promise of salvation, combined with notions of racial superiority and support for free trade.

Norms do not develop from moral conviction alone. They can also be sparked by practical considerations or routinized habit (Axelrod 1986). Williams's *Capitalism and Slavery* famously argues that the primary impetus for the rise and fall of the slave trade was not humanitarian ideals but rather financial profit. According to Williams, slavery was not abolished because of moral debate but because it was made redundant by capitalist exploitation in the metropolis (Williams 1944; Blackburn 1988: 26). Williams ignited the debate between the relative importance of economic considerations and moral argument, with Crawford (2002: 199) concluding that while "[a]ll sorts of arguments were used," "slavery and forced labor ended because those who made ethical arguments against those practices were able to convince enough people to support abolition" (see, generally Crawford 2002: 159–200).

In contrast to most of our contemporary cases of international norms, the norms surrounding the Atlantic slave trade neither demanded nor prohibited certain practices that were usually tied to particular role identities. Instead, slavery and the slave trade reflected *permissive* norms. The trade appealed to imperial, seafaring, Christian nations (see Pagden 1998). Because Portugal (and Brazil after 1822) and Great Britain ran most of the Atlantic slave trade for hundreds of years (Slave Voyages 2022a), they can be considered crucial case studies of the norm. They were the dominant powers in two decisive slave-trading periods: Portugal was the major sea power in the first half of the sixteenth century, when transatlantic slave trading emerged, and Britain was the major sea power beginning in the eighteenth century, when it ended (Modelski and Thompson 1988: 16, 105–106).

Contestation and justification varied in intensity and type within and between the cases. Annual trade figures indicate that the norm's robustness also varied. In the eighteenth and nineteenth centuries, transatlantic trading was impacted by technological innovations and naval warfare (Rahman 2010). We argue that it also responded to the domestic normative debates that helped stabilize and erode the norm.

7.2.1 Normative core claims and environment of the Atlantic slave trade

To understand how the Atlantic slave trade was sustained, we have to understand the normative environment of the age (Crawford 2002: 160). Enslaved Africans were traded by European nations from the late 1400s to the mid-1800s. We argue that the norms that framed slave trading as a "positive good" (Clay 2016: 269) were deeply embedded in broader normative and socio-economic structures over the centuries and across countries (Ruggie 1982). The slave trade was justified on religious and racial grounds, although the British slave trade primarily gained currency in the early 1700s with trade liberalization and free markets. From the outset, Portuguese slave trading was predominantly religious, justified by the duty to spread Christianity.[3]

Although there is a risk of oversimplifying any description of a normative field over centuries and countries (see Niemann and Schillinger 2017), we can safely say that European slave trading was accompanied by two successive tenets in all participating countries: (1) the duty to spread Christianity and "industrious labor" and (2) the belief that Europeans were morally superior to Africans (Dahomay 2003: 5). As a result, the slave trade was viewed as normatively desirable (see Crawford 2002: 140–43; Clay 2016: 269).

The essence of the Atlantic slave-trading norm within the larger institution of slavery was that all European states had the right to facilitate the capture, transport, and sale of Africans as property (Drescher 2009: 4–5). Following Finnemore and Sikkink's (1998: 891) definition of norms, it was considered a "standard of appropriate behavior" for states with the "given identity" of an empire or a maritime colonial power to engage in enslaving and trading Africans, thus spreading virtue and salvation while also making a profit. A primary impetus was the belief that exposure to Christianity saved souls (Bethell 1970: 5–6; Davis 1975: 375; Thomas 1997: 489; Crawford 2002: 140–43; Clay 2016: 269–70; Young 2016: 401). In 1451, Pope Nicholas V issued a papal bull related to Spanish expeditions along the North African coast that allowed the King of Spain to "reduce [. . .] to perpetual slavery" [. . .] "all enemies of Christ wheresoever placed" (quoted in Davis 1966: 100). Centuries of religious justifications of enslavement followed. Similar views were expressed in all major European slave-trading nations. For example, in 1722, French clergyman Jean-Baptiste Labat argued that the trade *benefited*

[3] There is a debate about whether slavery (and the slave trade) was a ruthless and exploitative practice that, when questioned, was conveniently defended on an ad hoc normative basis (Cohen 2003: 53–59) or whether it sprang from deeply held beliefs of European religious, racial, and moral superiority (see Sandholtz and Stiles 2009: 172; Davis 2012: 17; Young 2016: 402).

enslaved Africans, while in 1764, his countryman, Père Bellon de Saint-Quentin, posited that "slave trading violated neither natural law nor divine law, and actually improved slaves' lot" (Clay 2016: 269). In 1788, the British Reverend Raymund Harris ([1788] 2007: 183–84) similarly made a religious defense of the trade by pointing to the biblical figure Abraham, who owned and traded enslaved peoples. These religious arguments were deployed alongside the notion that enslaved Africans would benefit from their exposure to "industrious labour" on plantations (Swaminathan 2009: 166–67). For these reasons, the trade—"the capture of non-Christians"—was considered an "honorable" endeavor by the Church and other societal authorities (Ray 1989: 408; Sandholtz and Stiles 2009: 172).

A second, parallel, assumption declared that Africans were racially inferior and assailed their "savagery" (Boxer 1975: 263; Rice 1975: 63; Brantlinger 1985: 173–74; Ray 1989: 423; Cohen 2003: 58; Lockley 2016: 338–39). Although slavery had existed for millennia, the "construction of a slave system based so strictly on race was a new development" (Rice 1975: 3). In what Cohen (2003: 14, 19) describes as a racial "impulse to inequality," "Frenchmen saw the blackness of Africans as symbolic of some inner depravity." Starting in the 1600s, the biblical story of Ham was used on both sides of the Atlantic as a "pious justification for the enslavement of Africans" (Azevedo 2003: 117). Because Africans were regarded as lacking civilization, it was widely argued that slavery in fact "spared" or "saved" lives (Davis 1966: 183–84; Cohen 2003: 41–43; Marques 2006: 21, fn. 1). Accordingly, a Christian life in slavery in the Americas was seen as preferable to the "savagery" of the so-called "Dark Continent" (see Brantlinger 1985). With some variations, slavery on all the European powers' plantation complexes was "characterized by racial barriers erected by law and social custom" (Cohen 2003: 58). These two normative elements—(1) the perceived duty to convert Africans to Christianity and (2) the assumption of superiority (Crawford 2002: 142–43)—are reflected in the contradiction of continuing to enslave newly baptized Africans. In France and elsewhere, Africans' supposed inferiority was said to make "religious backsliding" likely; hence, slavery was required to preserve the spark of Christianity within them (Cohen 2003: 45).

In sum, moral debate among political, religious, and merchant elites facilitated and aided the rise of the European slave trade. We argue that their defense of slavery and the slave trade established a moral norm of slave trading from the sixteenth to the nineteenth centuries that both allowed and called for European states to engage in certain behaviors. The norm did not emerge in the earliest days of slavery: It developed as slave trading slowly grew in volume and profit—based on the "strong notions of cultural, religious, and national prejudice [that] had already existed in the sixteenth and seventeenth centuries in the very first contacts" (Cohen 2003: 99).

As we have mentioned, *prescriptive* norms require their addressees to perform certain actions—for example, the responsibility to protect requires states to protect their citizens (see Chapter 3). *Proscriptive* norms demand that their addressees refrain from a specific type of behavior. Examples are manifold in the area of human rights and arms control, such as the prohibitions of torture (see Chapter 2) and chemical weapons (Price 2019). *Permissive* norms such as slave trading and privateering follow a different logic. They merely *allow* or *encourage* their addressees to behave in a certain way and often present rules limiting some facets of the practice: Norm addressees may abstain from the behavior in question without violating the norm. This complicates the examination of norm violation because it is less obvious when the rules for permissive norms are broken than those for proscriptive or prescriptive norms.

7.2.2 Operationalization and data

Applying our framework to the historical slave-trading norm involves specific challenges related to the logic of permissive norms and measuring their robustness, as does the availability of data. The relative lack of formalized international institutions at the time means that contestation primarily occurred domestically—not internationally, as in many of our cases (see also Ray 1989: 421–23).

Contesting the *validity* of a permissive norm resembles contestations for prescriptive or proscriptive norms: when actors directly challenge the norm core in discourse, for example, arguing about the moral wrongness of slavery and the slave trade on religious, ethical, or economic grounds. This includes justifications for rebellions by enslaved Africans, who frequently revolted on land and at sea (Thomas 1997: 422–25). *Applicatory contestation* is made in arguments that address either the application of the norm to a new area (e.g. whether baptized Africans should continue to be enslaved) or contest whether or not a certain behavior is within the bounds of the norm (e.g. the conditions on slave ships). We have consulted secondary sources on both contestation types.

Norm robustness is assessed by mainly focusing on practical dimensions: compliance with the norm and, where appropriate, its implementation. Data limitations require us to leave aside the discursive dimension of robustness, which includes concordance and negative reactions to norm violations (see Chapter 1). During most of the slave trade (especially its beginnings), the permissive norm was not fully codified in international treaties, so there is no way to properly measure concordance or formal affirmation comparatively. We also cannot measure negative reactions to norm violations because permissive norms cannot be as clearly violated as prescriptive and proscriptive norms.

Hence, we rely on measuring practical compliance and behavior in line with the norm and, where possible, we also examine its implementation.[4] For the compliance dimension, we use data from "Slave Voyages," a database on some 34,000 slave-trade crossings between 1500 and 1866, to measure the absolute volume of the trade under the flags of Great Britain and Portugal/Brazil and in relation to the total Atlantic slave trade (see Slave Voyages 2022c). The database "provide[s] an educated guess of how large the slave trade actually was" (Slave Voyages 2022a). While the annual trade volume was volatile and influenced by numerous factors (particularly the domestic and international economic situations and demand, technological improvements, and warfare), it is assumed that growing trade indicates the spread and acceptance of the slave-trading norm in a country. However, because these factors are difficult to disentangle, we only use absolute and relative national slave-trading volumes and their trends to roughly indicate (practical) norm robustness.

7.3 Contestation and robustness trends in Great Britain

The British slave trade may be more studied than that of any other European country. Between 1556 and 1810, the British Empire is estimated to have transported over 3 million captive Africans from their homelands to the Americas, making it the second-largest European slave-trading nation after Portugal/Brazil (Slave Voyages 2022a). Its annual volume peaked in the 1770s and again in the early 1800s. The British slave trade was deeply embedded in the dual systems of imperialism and free trade and markets.

[4] Implementation is indicated by the inclusion of a norm in policy documents such as protocols and standards and the creation of domestic and international institutions tasked with establishing and furthering the norm. The institutionalization of contemporary norms includes the frequency with which norms are referenced in best practices and policy papers as well as the creation of official offices and naming of focal points for a specific issue (e.g. genocide prevention and the responsibility to protect; see Chapter 3). This poses a challenge to measuring the implementation of historical norms: Formalized international interaction and cooperation were not nearly as deep and institutionalized between the sixteenth and eighteenth centuries as today and are far less documented.

The nature and intensity of norm contestation varied greatly in eighteenth- and nineteenth-century Great Britain/United Kingdom (UK), during three periods: (1) the establishment and rise of slave trading alongside free trade debates (until 1715), (2) seven decades of scant public attention (1715–87), and (3) heated mainstream debate in the run-up to abolition (1787–1808). Unlike other European countries, British slave trading and abolition were very public affairs.

7.3.1 Phase 1: The early British slave trade, 1600–1715

By the 1620s, mainly fueled by domestic demand for tobacco, Britain had established its first permanent settlements in the Caribbean and brought enslaved Africans to the West Indian island of Saint Kitts in 1626. Fearing Spain's negative reactions and doubting their financial viability, the Crown did not fully support those colonial expeditions (Blackburn 2010: 222–24). British colonists were supported by Puritan gentry and the British slave trade grew to be linked to British nobility. However, an early colonist of Providence Island,[5] Reverend Samuel Rishworth, opposed the capture and bondage of Africans and even encouraged them to escape. Debate over the first British colony to rely primarily on slave labor led the royally chartered Providence Island Company to declare the legality of enslaving "strangers to Christianity" and so "helped diffuse and normalize the [British] slaveholding habit" (Blackburn 2010: 225–27).

In 1636, the governor of Barbados ruled that all Africans landing on the island were to be considered "chattel" (property) unless otherwise specified. Captive humans were to be handled according to the principles of cattle ownership. The regulation and growth of the British slave trade followed Dutch and Portuguese precedents, which "must have played some role in establishing the acceptability of slavery" (Blackburn 2010: 236), but slavery under the British was harsher than under the Spanish and Portuguese. Blackburn emphasizes the importance of the British institution of private property, which, "sharpened by the rise of capitalist market relationships, was to put the accent on the slave as human chattel and almost entirely to eclipse the notion that the slave was a human being." Following the Bible, influential Puritans framed the plantation master as an "instrument of God's purpose" (Blackburn 2010: 235–37).

[5] Off the east coast of modern-day Nicaragua.

In the North American colony of Massachusetts, which never had an extensive plantation system, the institution of slavery was viewed critically. In the early 1640s, the colony court decreed several times that slavery was only acceptable if the Africans in question were captives of war (Blackburn 2010: 239). This indicates that important aspects of the early slave trade were contested and not uniformly enforced in the Anglophone world. A 1650 embargo and the 1651 Navigation Act ended open trade in the Caribbean and founded the colonial mercantilist system whereby products were barred from being shipped anywhere but Britain using anything but British ships. During early colonialism, the institution of slavery received only limited attention among British decision-makers (Blackburn 2010: 245–47).

In 1660, after the restoration of Charles II, reservations about slave trading were dropped and institutionalized slavery and trading human beings were permitted throughout the British colonies, for example, through the "Act to Regulate the Negroes on the Plantations" of 1667. In 1663 and 1672, monopoly chartered companies were entrusted with the British trade by royal approval. Blackburn (2010: 261) describes "excessive government interest in the colonies" through administration and taxation. The contradictory nature of the religious and racial justifications of early British slave trading is illustrated by the clear legal distinction between Christians and non-Christians, on one hand, and the fact that an enslaved person's baptism did not alter their status on the other (Blackburn 2010: 250–51, 254).

In 1680, the Anglican minister Morgan Godwyn leveled a notable attack against Caribbean slavery by contesting the application of the emerging slave-trade norm. Besides questioning harsh punishment, he criticized West Indian planters' refusal to convert Africans to Christianity. In a 1685/1688 sermon in Westminster Abbey, he argued for baptizing enslaved people. Godwyn questioned the practical conduct of the trade but not its overall validity. Further notable work of the era by English writer Aphra Behn questioned some practices of slavery, though not the institution as a whole, "especially if care was taken to enslave only commoners" (as opposed to African nobility) (Blackburn 2010: 259–60).

Following the Glorious Revolution of 1688, the mercantile Royal African Company lost the monopoly on maritime trade it had held since 1660. In the newfound "highly politicized and institutionally pluralist" climate, the Royal African Company was "branded a deplorable relic of a bygone age, whereas the separate traders [British people who illegally competed in African trade] became emblematic of every British citizen's right to trade" (Pettigrew 2007a: 36). The 1698 "Africa Trade Act" opened the slave trade to any British person willing to pay a 10 percent duty on imports and exports, while the trade in humans was duty free (Pettigrew 2007a: 3, fn. 5, 2007b, 14). This legislation started a "commercial revolution" closely linked to the colonial enterprise (Blackburn 2010: 261). From 1690 to around 1715, an important parliamentary and public movement to liberalize trade with Africa resulted in broad deregulation. Arguments related to the 1689 passage of the Bill of Rights centered on freedom of commerce, property laws, and "contests over who could conduct [the trade with Africa] and on what terms" (Brown 2011: 282; Burnard 2011: 84–85). The "pronounced parliamentary dimension" during those decades and the highly effective lobbying and public petitioning for their cause by separate traders were key to the creation of a free-trade regime for Africa, including slave trading (Pettigrew 2007a: 12, 18, 23). This illustrates Jahn's argument that "[H]istorically liberalism was also intimately associated with slavery and colonialism" and liberalism at home is often associated with oppression abroad (Jahn 2013: 25, 29).

The Bill of Rights guaranteed freedom of speech. By eighteenth- and nineteenth-century European standards, Great Britain—and especially London—allowed very public discourse (Hochschild 2006: 216–18), including early debates over free trade and abolition. Europeans of the time may have had their doubts, but the only recorded organized opposition to slavery and the slave trade arose in religious contexts, mainly Quakers in the North American colonies (Swaminathan 2009: 50). As Blackburn (2010: 263) summarizes, "[t]he Glorious Revolution had been carried through in the name of English liberties, yet in the colonies it confirmed undisguised racial slavery."[6]

Beyond the question of how the trade was to be conducted, one bone of contention was the question of freeing baptized Africans. Most clergy and Crown lawyers dismissed emancipating baptized slaves as a "vulgar opinion" (Swaminathan 2009: 62–63) and asserted that Christianity allowed slavery and slave trading (Davis 1966: 208–10).

Travel writers often described the violence of the slave trade (Drescher 2007: 43). But British society accepted it, viewing slavery as key to their prosperity and economic growth (Swaminathan 2009: 15, 127; Martinez 2014: 16). The Church of England, which in 1710 purchased the 710-acre Codrington Plantation in Barbados through its Society for the Propagation of the Gospel in Foreign Parts, also defended the slave trade (Davis 1966: 219; Hochschild 2006: 61–62, 67–68). The unusually high number of parliamentary proceedings and inquiries in this early phase "offered much

[6] Blackburn (2010: 263–65) discusses John Locke's views on the slave trade.

needed legitimacy to the separate traders' cause" and "such legitimacy proved influential with the public" (Pettigrew 2007b: 24).

7.3.2 Phase 2: Conduct of the trade in relative silence, 1715–87

Following public debate and political contestation that lasted until 1715, there were several decades of relative silence. Between 1715 and 1787—when the British slave trade was busiest in terms of volume—the public "showed only the most passing interest in its conduct, its dimensions, its result, or its character" and it "only rarely became the subject of sustained discussion in parliament" (Brown 2011: 27, 30). British slave trading was largely unquestioned (Finnemore and Sikkink 1998: 895; see Davis 1966: 154, 210; Swaminathan 2009: 30–31).

Once again, only Quakers on both sides of the Atlantic protested against the trade (Klein 1999: 186; Swaminathan 2009: 48). Early examples of organized agitation were the writings and activities of the American abolitionist Anthony Benezet between 1758 and 1769, which were the very first to focus specifically on the slave *trade* as opposed to the entire institution of slavery (Swaminathan 2009: xi, 53–55). However, tales of human sacrifice and cannibalism convinced the general public that enslaving Africans saved lives (Davis 1966: 183–84).

In 1750, the Royal African Company's dissolution resulted in the slave trade being fully deregulated with little parliamentary attention (Brown 2007: 33–37). Around the same time, while scattered individuals expressed aversion to the conditions and conduct of the slave trade, they affirmed its necessity: Plantation owner Samuel Martin recommended treating slaves with "tenderness and generosity" in 1750, and while economist and writer Malachy Postlethwayt stated that economically, "This trade, as it stands, is as good as any we have" (Davis 1966: 148; Morgan 2010: 107), he also pointed toward the nature in which the slave trade was conducted as the main "obstacle to the civilizing process" (Drescher 2009: 75).

Brown (2011: 282) concludes that there "was no more reason to think that the slave trade could be brought to an end in 1750 than there had been in 1550." In 1763, Adam Smith argued that the trade had "hardly any possibility of being abolished, [. . . it] has been universall in the beginnings of society, and the love of dominion and authority over others will probably make it perpetuall" (quoted in Hochschild 2006: 86–87). In other words, the British hardly contested the trade's *validity*: They accepted its core justifications.

In the mid-1700s, enslaved captives frequently revolted at sea, with "at least one insurrection every eight to ten journeys." Most rebellions were countered with extreme violence. Individual revolts were reported from the colonies (Thomas 1997: 422–25) but not interpreted as contesting the slave trade. The Haitian Revolution, which started in 1791, was the most successful slave rebellion (see James 1938; Hazareesingh 2020). The largest slave colony of the day, Haiti, inspired slaves elsewhere to revolt and "enhance[ed] metropolitan opinion" of Africans (Geggus 2001: xv). Assessments of the revolution's overall impact on slave-trading states besides France diverge, but, at the time, each side invoked it as justifying their point of view: Abolitionists saw the Haitian revolt as "a sign of the blacks' humanity," while traders argued that it proved their "barbarity." British abolitionists did not explicitly support the insurrectionists' violence but saw it as an understandable response to oppression (Geggus 1982: 124–27).

In 1772, James Somerset, an enslaved African living in London, was declared free in the *Somerset v. Stewart* judgment, the main rationale being that there was no law that explicitly *permitted* slavery in England (see also Hochschild 2006: 46; Martinez 2014: 20). This sparked a small public information campaign led by Granville Sharp, the first Briton to publish sustained criticism of the slave trade (Swaminathan 2009: 65–69). The judgment also prompted numerous explicit defenses of slavery and antecedent norms, some based on the Old Testament (Swaminathan 2009: 73), others on the racist assertions that had established the norm (Drescher 1992: 368–69).

A trial in 1783 about the killing of 132 Africans aboard the slave ship *Zong* returned the issue to the public's attention. Treated as a matter of insurance, the case demonstrates the persistence of the permissive slave-trading norm. Quaker organizers and Granville Sharp publicly petitioned Parliament, which, expressing the colonial imperative and general view of slave trading at that time, responded, "[A]ll the European maritime powers had to make use of the African trade" (Drescher 2007: 44; see also Swaminathan 2009: 97; Faubert 2018).

Early free-market economists adopted a different angle to question slave trading and its norms. In his 1776 *Wealth of Nations*, Adam Smith argued that because slaves had little incentive to work hard, they were unproductive and artificially inflated the cost of plantation commodities (see Davis 1975: 351–53; Richardson 2007: 131). Smith was surely not an abolitionist, but his line of argument was popular among that growing group (Brown 2010: 94). In the early 1780s, "[A]nti-slavery sentiment had grown fashionable" and "had become associated with politeness, sensibility, patriotism, and a commitment to British liberty" among the educated class (Hilton 2010: 72). However, while

"[N]o major thinker defended slavery, [. . .] few spent real effort attacking it" (Hochschild 2006: 85–86).

7.3.3 Phase 3: Public anti-slave-trade discourse, 1787–1806

By the late 1780s, criticism of the slave trade began to be heard. The institutions of public debate that had facilitated slavery in keeping with the principles of free trade also helped spread abolitionist arguments. Drescher (2007: 43) traces how abolitionists began to mobilize in the second half of the eighteenth century when a "steady stream of articulated distaste" for the trade had accumulated as a result of "casual references" in travel writing. In Great Britain, economic arguments became the only tenable defense of the trade—"precisely those that had easily sustained the system against sporadic hostility for nearly a century." Drescher (2007: 47) concludes that the public abolitionist campaign in Great Britain mainly succeeded because it was a timely moral appeal: "[H]ow could the world's most secure, free, religious, just, prosperous and moral nation allow itself to remain the premier perpetrator of the world's most deadly, brutal, unjust and immoral offences to humanity?" This moved the issue of slavery from the realm of free trade to that of liberal Protestant moral debate (Davis 1966: 401; Azevedo 2003: 102).

In May 1787, the scattered British who had been working for abolition joined forces and founded the Society for Effecting the Abolition of the Slave Trade. Within a year, abolitionist ideas had spread throughout the British Isles: in the numerous London newspapers, coffeehouses, and petitioning and debating societies. Hochschild (2006: 136–38) characterizes February 1788 as the "tipping point month" for the cause (see also Finnemore and Sikkink 1998: 895–96).

The unprecedented flood of petitions on the subject led Parliament to consider the matter, and in July 1788, it passed Dolben's Act, which, for the first time, limited the number of enslaved people shipped in relation to the ship's cargo capacity. This was the first attempt at regulating the British slave trade that accorded any concern for the Africans being transported. Despite supporting it, some abolitionists worried that the bill would establish "the principle that the trade was in itself just but had been abused" (quoted in Hochschild 2006: 140; see also Klein 1999: 149, 162). Here, we see the concern that applicatory contestation could *strengthen* the norm. With respect to slave trading, adaptation was strategically used to contain more radical contestation, just like earlier cases of applicatory contestation. In 1792, the House of Commons voted to gradually end the slave trade, but the House of

Lords voted to prolong it (Davis 1975: 28; Swaminathan 2009: 203; Morgan 2010: 103). Around that time, prominent freedmen in Great Britain such as Olaudah Equiano also spoke out against the slave trade (Gates 2012). Abolitionist campaigns "made a direct appeal to the conscience and to a sense of common humanity beyond caste distinctions" (Blackburn 2010: 140–41).

Abolitionist efforts were countered by the pro-slavery planter lobby, which wielded an "incumbency advantage" in upholding the status quo of slave trading (see Bloomfield and Scott 2017: 13–14). Its principal line of argument was economic, its main strategy behind-the-scenes lobbying: It did not engage in any significant public agitation (Drescher 2007: 50). Drescher (2007: 48–49) finds a "moral versus economic dichotomy" in parliamentary debate between 1788 and 1807: Two-thirds of the time, abolitionists invoked morality, while defenders of the slave trade spent two-thirds of their time on economic arguments.

In 1793, the start of the Anglo-French War slowed the momentum for abolition, with British parliamentarians fearing support would be associated with Jacobinism (Hilton 2010: 69; Morgan 2010: 103, 117). Debate tended to favor regulating the slave trade to ameliorate the conditions (Davis 1975: 30; Hochschild 2006: 85; Swaminathan 2009: 195). In 1799, another bill on shipping conditions was passed, despite the planter lobby arguing that "abolishing a legitimate enterprise without appropriate compensation" would be unjust (Klein 1999: 149; Swaminathan 2009: 204).

These developments pushed British abolitionists to switch tactics, and, around 1805, in the wake of the Anglo-French War that had ended in 1802, they began to advocate ending the slave trade—not only on humanitarian and moral grounds but also for strategic and national security concerns. To decrease trade with the enemy, they suggested barring British citizens from trading slaves in any French colony or ally. Parliament addressed the topic again. Popular opinion remained on the abolitionists' side, and, in 1806, a bill reflecting that passed largely unchallenged (Hochschild 2006: 302–3; Martinez 2014: 22–23; Ford and Parkinson 2021: 830). This made it hard for parliamentarians or slave owners to stem the tide sweeping away the slave trade.

The same year, Parliament appealed to King George III to end the slave trade through international negotiations (Murray 2002: 25). The campaign's internationalization was a turning point in the norm's contestation because the British government was now mandated to convince other states to enact abolition laws and treaties (Marques 2006: 9). The campaign can also be seen as attempting to level the playing field by limiting other states' potential economic benefits. The strategy, which was later pursued by campaigns like those contesting privateering (see Chapter 6), was a way to reconcile normative and economic motives and convince other states to abandon a long-held norm. Softening the economic blow of opposing the norm made it harder for the pro-slavery side to defend its case. Historical accounts reveal that the anti-slavery campaign was very costly. Examining this puzzle of rare "costly international moral action," Kaufmann and Pape (1999: 663–64) find that the greatest influence came from domestic political factors such as coalition strategizing and the wish to be associated with morally righteous causes.

In March 1807, full abolition of the British slave trade was passed and received royal assent: The Act for the Abolition of the Slave Trade entered into force that May (Murray 2002: 26; Martinez 2014: 22–23). With the new ban strictly enforced, the British slave trade eroded rapidly and permanently. Nonetheless, slave labor itself persisted and remained legal, as did similarly cruel "apprenticeship" provisions in the colonies following the Slavery Abolition Act of 1833 (Nwulia 1978; Kaufmann and Pape 1999: 657; Sherwood 2007; Shilliam 2014: 366–68).

In sum, during most of the British slave trade, applicatory contestation predominated, covering issues such as free trade, baptism, and ship conditions—with little public attention (Phases 1 and 2). When the slave trade began, there was hardly any validity contestation, but, in the mid-eighteenth century, moral and economic arguments for outright abolition became louder and widely heard (mid and late Phase 2). National interests and growing tensions with France later increased the momentum for abolition further (Phase 3).

7.3.4 Norm robustness

One measure of norm robustness is practical adherence. Figure 7.1 shows estimated absolute and relative annual British slave-trade volumes between 1600 and 1815 (Slave Voyages 2022a). Note that the period before the British slave trade was abolished likely provides the most accurate data because of a small number of British ships sailing under false Spanish or Portuguese papers to evade the ban after 1807 (Eltis 2018).

The British slave trade had a consistent upward trajectory from its origins in the seventeenth to its end in the early nineteenth century—some 175 years. Dips in annual trade volume are attributable to wars but the trade never came to a complete halt (unlike in France).

The first record of capturing Africans to work as slaves in the Caribbean under the English flag was in 1626. During early colonization, indentured

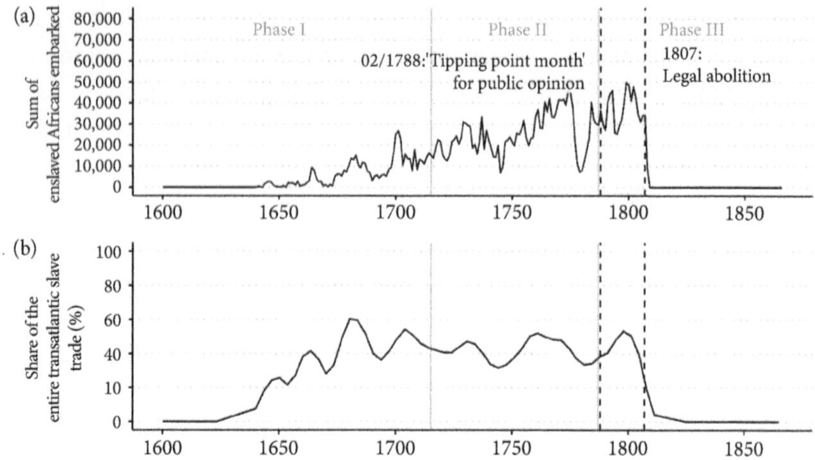

Figure 7.1 Estimated absolute and relative volume of the Atlantic slave trade under the British flag, 1600–1815
Source: Based on the Slave Voyages (2022a) data set.

servants from Ireland and Scotland were the primary source of labor in the Caribbean. But sugarcane cultivation was more labor-intensive than tobacco and required more labor generally. By 1653, enslaved Africans had become the main source of such labor on Barbados and outnumbered indentured servants 20,000 to 8,000 (Blackburn 2010: 225, 231, 235–36).

The English Civil War (1642–51) brought the emerging slave trade to a halt, although the colonies continued to thrive (Blackburn 2010: 243–44). After the end of the monopoly of the Royal African Company, the slave trade reached a new peak, with about 27,000 enslaved Africans forced to embark on the "Middle Passage" in 1701. The triangular slave trade brought manufactured goods to Africa, where they were traded for Africans, who were forced to march from their homelands to coastal ports in their "First Passage." During the subsequent Middle Passage (and second side of the triangle), they were shipped to the Americas, where their "Final Passage" brought them to where they would be forced to work. Shipment to Britain of raw materials purchased with the proceeds from selling the enslaved people and cultivated by them constituted the third side of the trade triangle (O'Malley 2014). The British state benefited significantly from fees and duties related to the Atlantic slave trade (Davis 1966: 134).

Following the intense public "free trade" debate between 1690 and 1715, the slave trade expanded through continual deregulation. In 1715, its "capacity dramatically increased" (Pettigrew 2007b: 12) and in 1729, a new record of more than 30,000 enslaved Africans were traded. In Britain, between 1715 and 1787, planters and merchants gained more influence and the slave trade significantly expanded until it was completely deregulated and "free" (Davis 1966: 154). Throughout the War of the Austrian Succession (1740–48), Britain clashed with Spain and France in the West Indies. The Caribbean trade collapsed, and British slave imports dropped by around 80 percent between 1737 and 1745. Nonetheless, the trade quickly recovered, reaching new heights in 1760 and 1761.

The American Revolutionary War (1775–83) substantially reduced the volume of British slave trading, although it once again proved to be resilient: Decreased trade volume does not indicate any shift in British opinion. On the contrary, the trade's swift rebound indicates the norm's sustained robustness and the British economy's dependence on slave trading. The abolition movement led to validity contestation in the late 1780s and fluctuations in annual trade volume. Nonetheless, enslavement and forced relocation persisted until abolition in 1807.

In sum, the evolution of British slave trading and abolition was embedded in other contemporary debates, particularly those concerning free trade and markets (see also Jahn 2013) and, later, fundamental rights and Protestant morality. In the early 1700s, major public calls for free trade led to deregulating the slave trade and opening it from a trade monopoly to private individuals. Applicatory contestation consistently ended in favor of free trade, gradually increasing the slave trade's practical permissive scope and volume, stabilizing the norm. Free trade arguments were part of a broader push for an "ideology of natural right that was synonymous with individual economic self-interest" that offered slave traders both an earning opportunity and a moral defense for trading slaves (Pettigrew 2007a: 9–10). This shows how the norm's deep embeddedness in the socio-economic system and normative beliefs of the time made it less susceptible to criticism on moral grounds.

As the abolitionist movement gained a significant following in the late 1780s, British campaigners used both applicatory and validity contestation to discredit the slave trade, including the Enlightenment notion that all men are created equal (Ray 1989: 423). However, the discourse only began to shift after abolitionists switched tactics and combined economic and moral reasons for abolishing slave trading. In times of international conflict, particularly with France, economic arguments based on national security concerns and anti-French attitudes convinced the public and Parliament. By 1806, strong abolitionist sentiment had been spreading throughout Britain for almost two decades and openly supporting the slave trade was untenable.

7.4 Contestation and robustness trends in Portugal

We now turn to a very different case: slave trading in the Portuguese Empire, by far the single largest slave-trading state. Between 1500 and 1822 (when Brazil became independent), some 4.4 million Africans were forced to embark on the trans-Atlantic voyage under the Portuguese flag (Slave Voyages 2022a, b, c). As the leading sea power of the 1400s and early 1500s, Portugal was the first country to begin trading slaves across the Atlantic. Between 1500 and 1750, it regularly accounted for more than half of the Atlantic slave trade. The Portuguese trade was deeply embedded in explicit religious arguments and the supposed rights and obligations of Christians. This section describes contestation of the Portuguese slave trade and presents its robustness trends.

Unlike Britain, but along with the Spanish colonies, Portugal "supplemented medieval and classical laws, and traditional religious justifications with new slaveholding doctrines" (Blackburn 2010: 309). Another difference between British and Portuguese slave trading was the actors involved. In Portugal, no open debate was allowed outside of state-sanctioned fora. In the sixteenth and seventeenth centuries, the slave trade was primarily justified by theologians. For hundreds of years, there was hardly any public contestation of slavery in Portugal: Discussion about the slave trade was limited to international negotiations and within the government.

7.4.1 Phase 1: Early trade, 1500–1700

From 1444, when the first Portuguese sailed to sub-Saharan Africa to enslave Africans, religious rhetoric justified capturing the continent's inhabitants. Far earlier and more explicitly than in Britain, introducing "heathens" to the Christian faith in this way was viewed as an act of benevolence in Portugal (Russell-Wood 1978; Magalhães 1997; Marques 2006: 17, 21). The first state to engage in the Atlantic slave trade, Portugal entered into relations with African kingdoms and empires and purchased domestically enslaved Africans (Thornton 2010: 40). This initial Portuguese slave trading defined "a system of concepts and images regarding slavery" that long persisted (Marques 2006: 14–15), with baptism and transport to lands ruled by Christians seen as delivering Africans from "the devil's slavery" (Azevedo 2003: 106–107).

Along with framing enslavement in religion, for centuries Portugal was the only European state to regulate enslaved Africans' treatment during the

Middle Passage. Though "scarcely [. . .] the height of generosity," from the very beginning the Portuguese Crown regulated food supplies, sleeping arrangements, and shipping capacities (Thomas 1997: 125, 291, 411; see also Boxer 1975, 265). While the regulations were only half-heartedly implemented, for hundreds of years, Portugal was the only state to institute regulation of any kind (Thomas 1997: 455; Klein 1999: 148).

In the mid-1500s, individual Portuguese clerics spoke out against the new and growing Atlantic trade, one calling it a custom "never previously used or heard of among human beings," another charging that enslavers used "fraud or violence" on African shores (Boxer 1975: 264; see also Davis 1966: 187; Azevedo 2003: 111). That said, those contesting the conduct of the trade also praised its "virtues" and did not advocate abolition (Bethell 1970: 5). Religion continued to shape Portuguese discourse throughout the sixteenth and seventeenth centuries. For example, in 1633, the prominent cleric and philosopher António Vieira argued that enslaved Africans' safe arrival in Brazil was proof of God's blessing and that Christianity had liberated their souls (Marques 2006: 17–18). Early debates of this type alleviated possible moral doubts and solidified the shared understanding that slave trading and ownership were generous and virtuous acts.

7.4.2 Phase 2: The peak of the trade, 1700–1807

The discovery of gold beyond Rio de Janeiro in the late 1600s considerably increased the demand for slavery and forced labor in Brazil (Russell-Wood 1998: 76; Birmingham 1999: 82). This coincided with Lisbon's attempt to increase its overall influence on Atlantic slave trading (Disney 2009: 80). By 1730, the Brazilian economy had become singularly dependent upon slave labor, as had local church and state institutions (Bethell 1970: 3; Boxer 1975: 191). In the early 1700s, the Portuguese Empire had more enslaved people than all other Christian kingdoms combined (Thomas 1997: 456). Under the Marquis de Pombal, the de facto head of the Portuguese government from 1750 to 1777, two monopolies were founded to develop two northeastern Brazilian regions (Maranhão and Pernambuco) that were granted exclusive rights to import enslaved Africans (Boxer 1975: 192–93; Birmingham 1999: 86–87; Klein 1999: 80–81).

In the early eighteenth century, the Vatican criticized Lisbon for the slave trade, though this may well have been fueled by animosity linked to the War of the Spanish Succession (1701–14), and antisemitic sentiments aimed at seeing whether "some of the slave traders were secret Jews." The Portuguese court did not respond (Thomas 1997: 456). The developing slave trade was monitored diplomatically, and the Portuguese ambassador in London occasionally reported on the growing abolitionist movement in Great Britain. But Lisbon changed neither its policy nor its strategy (Marques 2006: 12; Drescher 2009: 201).

Scholars remain divided over the writings of Manuel Ribeiro da Rocha, an eighteenth-century Portuguese cleric and lawyer active in Brazil (Azevedo 2003). Some interpret his 1758 *Etíope Resgatado empenhado, sustentado, corrigido, instruído, e libertado* [*The Ethiopian Ransomed, Indentured, Sustained, Corrected, Educated, and Liberated*] as the first Portuguese abolitionist text, although others see it as little more than another general plea to improve conditions (Thomas 1997: 461; Marques 2006: 19–20). A key tenet of Rocha's work was that "the traditional ideal of Christianizing the master–slave relationship [i.e. ameliorating it] was combined with a new ideal of preparing the slave for freedom" (Azevedo 2003: 121). Rocha expanded upon the Portuguese fiction of redeeming Africans by baptizing and enslaving them. He considered their enslavement illegitimate, even "piratical," although he conceived of slavery as a decades-long "contract of redemption" between the enslaved and the enslaver (Azevedo 2003: 105–107). Though his work has received attention in recent historical accounts, it almost certainly was barely noticed in the 1760s. At that time, free speech, let alone freedom of the press, were far more limited in Portugal and Brazil than they were in Great Britain. The Portuguese Crown heavily censored the few periodicals available, while abolitionist news from Great Britain went unremarked (Marques 2006: 10–11, 26). As the abolitionist cause gathered steam in London, the "Luso-Brazilian public [remained] almost totally immune to the abolitionist discourse circulating through the Atlantic from the late 1780s" (Drescher 2009: 201; see also Marques 2006: 10–11).

In the late eighteenth century, there were few new arguments about improving enslaved peoples' conditions. Slavery was considered economically necessary for the Portuguese Empire and a righteous endeavor. Popular opinion held that the system needed reform, not abolition (Bethell 1970: 6; Marques 2006: 20–25). Marques (2006: 20–26) notes that centuries of religious justification eventually morphed into more explicit and secular assumptions of "African barbarity."

Enslaved peoples' rebellions against their masters were as common in Portuguese-ruled parts of the Americas as they were elsewhere (Thomas 1997: 610). But rarely—if ever—reported, they had very little influence on public and private opinion regarding the slave trade in Portugal. The Haitian Revolution's influence on the slave trade's eventual abolition in Brazil "seems meager at best" (Drescher 2001: 11). Unlike Britain (see, e.g. Olaudah Equiano and James Somerset above), there were almost no Africans in Portugal at the time (Drescher 2009: 204).

7.4.3 Phase 3: The slave trade comes to a halt, 1807–22

When British officials contacted the Portuguese foreign minister about abolishing the slave trade in 1807 (the year of British abolition), he responded that any form of abolition would be "utterly impracticable" to Portuguese interests (Bethell 1970: 6; Thomas 1997: 571). In other correspondence, the minister seemed unconcerned and ill informed, arguing that Portuguese regulations on the Middle Passage were in line with the abolitionists' humanitarian concerns and that these regulations sufficed (Marques 2006: 13).

In 1807, the Brazilian Bishop Azerado Coutinho published the last explicit Portuguese-language defense of the slave trade (Drescher 2009: 201–202). But with the British abolishing the slave trade and internationalizing the campaign for abolition, Portuguese elites had to acknowledge that slave trading was nearing its end. Suspecting that the UK would start to pressure Portugal, the government and the learned class changed their overt opposition to strategic "foot-dragging." In 1808, the UK established the British Royal Navy's West Africa Squadron to patrol the West African coast and enforce the proscription of slave trading (Thomas 1997: 573).

Meanwhile, Portugal and the UK began to negotiate mainly commercial issues, including most-favored-nation status (Thomas 1997: 571). British councilors consistently raised the question of abolition, but Portuguese diplomats did not react. A draft treaty stated that Portugal would pursue "a gradual abolition in all its domains." As far as the Portuguese were concerned, these were stipulations which "do not require any sacrifice of us: our trade in slaves, despite what is stated at the beginning of the article, will not only remain as it is at present, but will actually be increased." Still, the diplomats produced a memorandum of understanding about how their interpretation was not to be at all limited by their "expression of [. . .] humane sentiments" (Marques 2006: 14). Despite verbal concessions to London, the Portuguese government at the time and Dom João VI himself fully supported maintaining, and even expanding, the slave trade (Bethell 1970: 8–9; Marques 2006: 14; Mason 2009: 813, 816–17; Martinez 2014: 31). Yet, in the wake of deliberations, another round of laws was passed to ostensibly improve conditions on slave ships (Thomas 1997: 607). Throughout those years, there was little church or civil society discourse on the issue.

In 1813, Lisbon's "first priority was to ensure the continued supply of slaves to Brazil" (Marques 2006: 37). Nevertheless, the Portuguese ambassador to the UK had started to advocate measures similar to the Dolben's Act and proposed investigating Portuguese enslavement practices. At home, however, his suggestions were taken to be the ramblings of an Anglophile who had "gone native" in London (Marques 2006: 37–40).

At the Congress of Vienna of 1814–15, the Atlantic slave trade was again brought into international negotiations. Portugal made a concerted effort to coordinate positions with Spain, the only other state actively trying to extend the slave trade (Murray 2002: 56; Mason 2009: 817). But strapped for funds and assuming that enforcement would be lax, Portugal eventually agreed to abandon its slave trading *north* of the equator in exchange for GBP 600,000 (Thomas 1997: 585). With the primary Portuguese slave-trading ports in modern-day Angola and the Brazilian city of Salvador (both well below the equator), that was a negligible concession.

In 1817, Portugal and the UK concluded another treaty that granted states parties reciprocal rights to search and seize ships transporting slaves beyond the boundaries in the treaty. The UK also pressured Portugal, along with Spain and the Netherlands, into setting up a Mixed Commission Court to try possible violations (Kaufmann and Pape 1999; see Martinez 2014). Still recalcitrant, Portugal nonetheless joined the innovative regime, which featured an equal number of judges of each nationality (Bethell 1970: 19). Assuming that applicatory contestation would delay any serious enforcement of abolition, the Portuguese government hoped the new court "would reduce British demands for a firm commitment to final abolition" and effectively preserve "the legality of the Portuguese slave trade" (Mason 2009: 813). But the UK also tasked its ever-growing West Africa Squadron with enforcing the treaty, thereby strengthening the cause of international abolition and sending a strong signal to its Mixed Commission Court partners (Thomas 1997: 581, 651).

In the following years, officials in Lisbon continued to stall strategically and never sincerely considered abolishing its slave trade (Mason 2009: 820). An adamant defender of the slave trade, regardless of the criticism leveled at Portugal, Dom João VI remained unswayed by international developments (Bethell 1970: 22). After Brazil became independent in 1822, the absolute annual volume of Lusophone slave trading increased significantly: Much of the trade to Brazil was conducted by Portuguese nationals, and no abolition movement arose in Portugal. After losing Brazil, the Portuguese Crown expanded its plantations in Angola and on the islands of Cape Verde and São Tomé and Príncipe. Portugal's "tolerationism" implied resigned acceptance that the slave trade would gradually end (Marques 2006: 35–65; Drescher 2009: 203–204).

Portugal had formally ended slave trading in 1835 but only abolished slavery in its empire in 1875. The UK's "aggressive" pressure was instrumental in formally and practically ending the Portuguese trade. Although the slave trade was officially abolished in (independent) Brazil in 1831, thanks to many complicit authorities, it continued illegally for decades (Thomas 1997: 628–29, 633–34; Slave Voyages 2022a). Through an August 1839 act, British ship captains were granted extensive rights to seize Portuguese slave ships, liberate enslaved people, and turn Portuguese traders over to Portuguese authorities. The crackdown was possible due to significant expansions of the West Africa Squadron and especially support from the French Navy (Thomas 1997: 655–59, 729, 788). In the 1840s, the British Navy stepped up its active search-and-capture policy, thereby hastening the end of the Brazilian slave trade, which was formally ended by a second abolition law in 1850 (Thomas 1997: 651–54, 727–46). External coercion was needed to stop Portuguese and Brazilian slave trading.

7.4.4 Norm robustness

Portugal and Brazil are estimated to have shipped a total of 5.8 million enslaved Africans to the Americas between 1500 and 1856. Between 1700 and 1800, yearly trade ranged between 20,000 and 25,000 captives, with the amount suddenly tripling around 1810. Trade then fluctuated during wartime. In 1822, Brazil declared its independence, which Portugal formally recognized in 1825. Our analysis ends with Brazil becoming independent (see also Slave Voyages 2022b). Figure 7.2 shows the estimated annual volume of Portuguese and Brazilian slave trading from 1500 to 1866 in relative and absolute terms.

Compared with Great Britain, from the seventeenth to the early nineteenth century, the Portuguese slave trade—mainly between present-day Angola and Brazil—remained consistently robust. Well into the seventeenth century, Portugal conducted over half the total annual Atlantic slave trade. Despite the British abolishing slavery in 1807, which slowly made the topic creep into elite political debates in Portugal, slave trading continued unabated.

In sum, the Portuguese and British cases exhibit several major differences. Early on, the British slave trade was deregulated and opened up to private traders: The government hardly intervened. In contrast, when the Portuguese Crown began to establish colonies, it implemented rules for

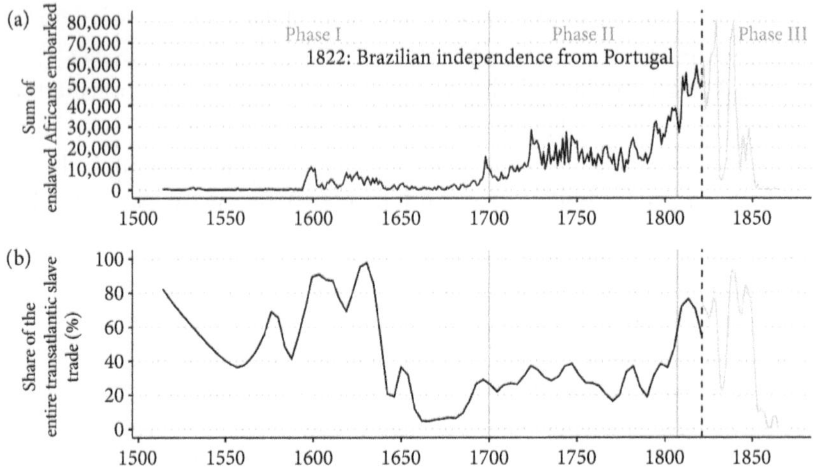

Figure 7.2 Estimated absolute and relative volume of the Atlantic slave trade under the Portuguese and Brazilian flags, 1500–1866
Source: Based on the Slave Voyages (2022a) data set.

conditions on slave ships. The British justified their deregulation through free-trade arguments; Portuguese leaders stressed the moral and religious benefits of converting enslaved Africans to Christianity. Ostensibly, they were aware that the slaves suffered during the Middle Passage and embedded debate about the slave trade in contemporary Catholic teachings: Enslaving Africans was viewed as a generous part of Portugal's civilizing mission. Unlike the British, as the Portuguese slave trade grew, so did regulations and justifications. But the venues for contestation were very different: Britain had a comparatively strong culture of public debate and argument; Portugal did not.

We argue that the combination of consistent applicatory contestation regarding conditions onboard slave ships and Christianization, along with the deep embeddedness of slave trading in Christian belief systems, critically contributed to the acceptance and continuously high volume of the Portuguese slave trade.

7.5 Factors driving contestation

What can we draw from these two cases of persistent Atlantic slave trading with respect to the role of law and norm clusters and the power of norm challengers and international institutions? The cases demonstrate that factors such as the *norm's legal quality* did not affect its continued robustness.

Throughout most of the examined time frame, the slave trade was barely regulated internationally. Furthermore, although the degree of *precision* of national regulations differed markedly, the outcomes were similar: The norm remained robust and contestation moderate both in an environment with little regulation (Great Britain) and in one with increasingly precise regulation (Portugal).

The slave trade's long-term stability can be tied to its *embeddedness* in contemporary norm clusters. In both Portugal and Great Britain, the slave-trading norm was strengthened because the trade and its profits were integral to domestic society, the economy, and culture. In Britain, the norm was embedded in a normative field of free-market ideology and liberalism that promoted private property and trade. It was thus shielded from the potential negative effects of early contestation on moral or religious grounds—which led to a deregulated practice with abhorrent conditions. Only contestation over the morality of the slave trade in liberal Protestant belief that "directly challeng[ed] the traditional Christian view of slavery" (Davis 1966: 401), combined with security concerns and anti-French sentiments in an environment of relatively free speech, proved to be particularly potent in public and parliamentary debates following the 1793–1802 Anglo-French War and the ongoing Napoleonic wars.

In Portugal, the norm was deeply linked to religious beliefs and norms from its fifteenth-century beginnings. Curiously, its firmly religious embeddedness resulted in the earliest slave trade regulations in Europe, which supposedly aimed to mollify the hardships of enslaved Africans and convert them to Christianity. Framing enslavement as an act of charity helped stabilize the norm when it was being heavily attacked in Britain and France. In stark contrast to British political institutions, there was no open, public debate in Portugal on politics in general or the slave trade in particular, which prolonged the trade as a branch of commerce. Only when Britain, the most *powerful norm challenger* of the time, attempted to level the economic playing field and internationalize abolition did Portugal begin to slowly change its practices and ultimately stop the trade (see section 7.4.3). As institutionalization beyond the state was still minimal at the time, perceptions of unfairness in international institutions did not play a major role in this case.

7.6 Conclusion

The most important conclusion to draw from contestation of the slave-trading norm is that in both the British and Portuguese cases, the overall link between validity and applicatory contestation and the practice dimension of norm robustness is rather weak. This might simply result from the lack of data, which makes it difficult to measure contestation and robustness. But it might also come from the norm's permissive nature (see Chapter 6 on privateering). Since permissive norms only *allow* for a certain type of behavior, and neither require nor prohibit it, contestants may have more difficulty in convincingly framing the issue.

Nevertheless, these cases present intriguing findings on (1) the linkage between applicatory contestation and norm robustness, which our contemporary cases often lack, and (2) the role of larger norm clusters and the norm challengers being relatively powerful. In both Britain and Portugal, validity contestation largely remained at the margins of debate: The norm was seldom fundamentally challenged. While validity contestation grew stronger and more severe in late-eighteenth-century Great Britain, in tandem with the rise of free speech and public debate (Hochschild 2006: 216–18), in Portugal there was never any validity contestation.

In both cases, phases of applicatory contestation strengthened the norm, as in the case of privateering (see Chapter 6). The slave-trade norms in both Britain and Portugal were firmly embedded in broader norm clusters. In the British case, initial contestation in the late 1600s and early 1700s resulted in free-trade regulation that legitimized and institutionalized the norm instead of undermining it. Similarly, early in the Portuguese slave trade, applicatory contestation based on interpretations of Christian charity created a number of (nominal) regulations regarding slave ships—this type of justification made it more difficult to attack the norm: Portuguese slave trading was only ended after the UK undertook international negotiations and enforced a ban.

Reference list

Axelrod, Robert. 1986. "An Evolutionary Approach to Norms." *American Political Science Review* 80 (4): pp. 1095–111. doi: 10.2307/1960858.

Azevedo, Celia M. 2003. "Rocha's 'The Ethiopian Redeemed' and the Circulation of Anti-Slavery Ideas." *Slavery & Abolition* 24 (1): pp. 101–26. doi: 10.1080/714005255.

Bethell, Leslie. 1970. *The Abolition of the Brazilian Slave Trade: Britain, Brazil and the Slave Trade Question, 1807–1869*. Cambridge: Cambridge University Press.

Birmingham, David. 1999. *Portugal and Africa*. Basingstoke: Palgrave Macmillan.

Blackburn, Robin. 1988. *The Overthrow of Colonial Slavery, 1776–1848*. London: Verso.

Blackburn, Robin. 2010. *The Making of New World Slavery: From the Baroque to the Modern, 1492–1800*. New York: Verso.

Bloomfield, Alan, and Shirley V. Scott. 2017. "Norm Antipreneurs in World Politics." In *Norm Antipreneurs and the Politics of Resistance to Global Normative Change*, ed. Alan Bloomfield and Shirley V. Scott. London: Routledge, pp. 1–19.

Boxer, Charles Ralph. 1975. *The Portuguese Seaborne Empire, 1415–1825*. New York: A.A. Knopf.

Brantlinger, Patrick. 1985. "Victorians and Africans: The Genealogy of the Myth of the Dark Continent." *Critical Inquiry* 12 (1): pp. 166–203. doi: 10.1086/448326.

Brown, Christopher L. 2007. "The British Government and the Slave Trade: Early Parliamentary Enquiries, 1713–83." *Parliamentary History* 26 (S1): pp. 27–41. doi: 10.1111/j.1750-0206.2007.tb00678.x.

Brown, Christopher L. 2010. "Empire without America: British Plans for Africa in the Era of the American Revolution." In Abolitionism and Imperialism in Britain, Africa, and the Atlantic, ed. Derek R. Peterson. Athens, OH: Ohio University Press, pp. 84–100.

Brown, Christopher L. 2011. "Abolition of the Atlantic Slave Trade." In *The Routledge History of Slavery*, eds Gad J. Heuman and Trevor G. Burnard. Abingdon: Routledge, pp. 281–97.

Burnard, Trevor G. 2011. "The Atlantic Slave Trade." In *The Routledge History of Slavery*, eds Gad J. Heuman and Trevor G. Burnard. Abingdon, pp. 80–97.

Clay, Lauren R. 2016. "'Cruel Necessity': Capitalism, the Discourse of Sympathy, and the Problem of the Slave Trade in the Age of Human Rights." *Slavery & Abolition* 37 (2): pp. 256–83. doi: 10.1080/0144039X.2015.1120103.

Cohen, William B. 2003. *The French Encounter with Africans: White Response to Blacks, 1530-1880*. Bloomington, IN: Indiana University Press.

Crawford, Neta. 2002. *Argument and Change in World Politics: Ethics, Decolonization, and Humanitarian Intervention*. Cambridge: Cambridge University Press.

Dahomay, Jacky. 2003. "Slavery and Law: Legitimations of an Insurrection." In *The Abolitions of Slavery: From Léger Félicité Sonthonax to Victor Schoelcher, 1793, 1794, 1848*, ed. Marcel Dorigny. New York: Berghahn Books, pp. 3–16.

Davis, David Brion. 1966. *The Problem of Slavery in Western Culture*. Ithaca, NY: Cornell University Press.

Davis, David Brion. 1975. *The Problem of Slavery in the Age of Revolution, 1770–1823*. Oxford: Oxford University Press.

Davis, David Brion. 2012. "Slavery, Emancipation, and Progress." In *British Abolitionism and the Question of Moral Progress in History*, ed. Donald A. Yerxa. Columbia, CA: University of South Carolina Press, pp. 13–26.

Disney, A. R. 2009. *A History of Portugal and the Portuguese Empire: From Beginnings to 1807*. Cambridge: Cambridge University Press.

Drescher, Seymour. 1992. "The Ending of the Slave Trade and the Evolution of European Scientific Racism." In *The Atlantic Slave Trade: Effects on Economies, Societies and Peoples in Africa, the Americas, and Europe*, ed. Joseph E. Inikori and Stanley L. Engerman. Durham, NC: Duke University Press, pp. 361–96.

Drescher, Seymour. 2001. "The Limits of Example." In *The Impact of the Haitian Revolution in the Atlantic World*, ed. David Geggus. Columbia, CA: University of South Carolina Press, pp. 10–14.

Drescher, Seymour. 2007. "Public Opinion and Parliament in the Abolition of the British Slave Trade." *Parliamentary History* 26 (S1): pp. 42–65. doi: 10.1111/j.1750-0206.2007.tb00679.x.

Drescher, Seymour. 2009. *Abolition: A History of Slavery and Antislavery*. Cambridge: Cambridge University Press.

Eltis, David. 2018. "Methodology: Methodology, National Carriers." Slave Voyages: The Trans-Atlantic Slave Trade Database." Accessed October 5, 2022. https://www.slavevoyages.org/voyage/about#methodology/national-carriers/17/en.

Faubert, Michelle. 2018. *Granville Sharp's Uncovered Letter and the Zong Massacre*. Cham: Palgrave.

Finnemore, Martha J., and Kathryn Sikkink. 1998. "International Norm Dynamics and Political Change." *International Organization* 52 (4): pp. 887–917. doi: 10.1162/002081898550789.

Ford, Lisa, and Naomi Parkinson. 2021. "Legislating Liberty: Liberated Africans and the Abolition Act, 1806–1824." *Slavery & Abolition* 42 (4): pp. 827–46. doi: 10.1080/0144039X.2021.1972641.

Gates, Henry Louis, ed. 2012. *The Classic Slave Narratives*. 2nd edn. New York: Signet Classics.

Geggus, David. 1982. "British Opinion and the Emergence of Haiti, 1791–1805." In *Slavery and British Society, 1776–1846*, ed. James Walvin. London: Red Globe Press London, pp. 123–49.

Geggus, David. 2001. "The French Slave Trade: An Overview." *The William and Mary Quarterly* 58 (1): pp. 119–38. doi: 10.2307/2674421.

Harris, Raymund. (1788) 2007. "Scriptural Researches on the Licitness of the Slave-Trade, Shewing Its Conformity with the Principles of Natural & Revealed Religion, Delineated in the Sacred Writings of the Word of God." In *The Slave Trade Debate: Contemporary Writings For and Against*, ed. Bodleian Library. Oxford: Bodleian Library University of Oxford, pp. 174–247.

Hazareesingh, Sudhir. 2020. *Black Spartacus: The Epic Life of Toussaint Louverture*. London: Penguin Books.

Hilton, Boyd. 2010. "1807 and All That: Why Britain Outlawed Her Slave Trade." In *Abolitionism and Imperialism in Britain, Africa, and the Atlantic*, ed. Derek R. Peterson. Athens, OH: Ohio University Press, pp. 63–83.

Hochschild, Adam. 2006. *Bury the Chains: Prophets and Rebels in the Fight to Free an Empire's Slaves*. Boston, MA: Mariner Books.

Jahn, Beate. 2013. *Liberal Internationalism: Theory, History, Practice*. Basingstoke: Palgrave.

James, C. L. R. 1938. *The Black Jacobins: Toussaint L'ouverture and the San Domingo Revolution*. London: Penguin.

Kaufmann, Chaim D., and Robert A. Pape. 1999. "Explaining Costly International Moral Action: Britain's Sixty-Year Campaign against the Atlantic Slave Trade." *International Organization* 53 (4): pp. 631–68. doi: 10.1162/002081899551020.

Klein, Herbert S. 1999. *The Atlantic Slave Trade*. Cambridge: Cambridge University Press.

Koivu, Kendra L., and Annika Marlen Hinze. 2017. "Cases of Convenience? The Divergence of Theory from Practice in Case Selection in Qualitative and Mixed-Methods Research." *PS: Political Science & Politics* 50 (4): pp. 1023–27. doi: 10.1017/S1049096517001214.

Lantis, Jeffrey S., and Carmen Wunderlich. 2018. "Resiliency Dynamics of Norm Clusters: Norm Contestation and International Cooperation." *Review of International Studies* 44 (3): pp. 570–93. doi: 10.1017/S0260210517000626.

Lockley, Timothy. 2016. "Race and Slavery." In *The Oxford Handbook of Slavery in the Americas*, ed. Robert L. Paquette and Mark M. Smith. Oxford: Oxford University Press, pp. 336–56.

Magalhães, Joaquim Romero. 1997. "Africans, Indians, and Slavery in Portugal." *Portuguese Studies* 13:143–51. doi: 10.2307/41105067.

Marques, João Pedro. 2006. *The Sounds of Silence: Nineteenth-Century Portugal and the Abolition of the Slave Trade*. New York: Berghahn.

Martinez, Jenny S. 2014. *The Slave Trade and the Origins of International Human Rights Law*. Oxford: Oxford University Press.

Mason, Matthew. 2009. "Keeping up Appearances: The International Politics of Slave Trade Abolition in the Nineteenth-Century Atlantic World." *William and Mary Quarterly* 66 (4): pp. 809–32.

Modelski, George, and William R. Thompson. 1988. *Seapower in Global Politics, 1494–1993*. London: Macmillan.

Morgan, Philip D. 2010. "Ending the Slave Trade: A Caribbean and Atlantic Context." In *Abolitionism and Imperialism in Britain, Africa, and the Atlantic*, ed. Derek R. Peterson. Athens, OH: Ohio University Press, pp. 101–28.

Murray, David R. 2002. *Odious Commerce: Britain, Spain and the Abolition of the Cuban Slave Trade*. Cambridge: Cambridge University Press.

Nadelmann, Ethan A. 1990. "Global Prohibition Regimes: The Evolution of Norms in International Society." *International Organization* 44 (4): pp. 479–526. doi: 10.1017/S0020818300035384.

Niemann, Holger, and Henrik Schillinger. 2017. "Contestation 'All the Way Down'? The Grammar of Contestation in Norm Research." *Review of International Studies* 43 (1): pp. 29–49. doi: 10.1017/S0260210516000188.

Nwulia, Moses D.E. 1978. "The 'Apprenticeship' System in Mauritius: Its Character and Its Impact on Race Relations in the Immediate Post-Emancipation Period, 1839–1879." *African Studies Review* 21 (1): pp. 89–101. doi: 10.1017/S0002020600019090.

O'Malley, Gregory E. 2014. *Final Passages: The Intercolonial Slave Trade of British America, 1619–1807*. Chapel Hill, NC: University of North Carolina Press.

Pagden, Anthony. 1998. *Lords of All the World: Ideologies of Empire in Spain, Britain and France, 1492–1830*. New Haven, CT: Yale University Press.

Panke, Diana, and Ulrich Petersohn. 2012. "Why International Norms Disappear Sometimes." *European Journal of International Relations* 18 (4): pp. 719–42. doi: 10.1177/1354066111407690.

Pettigrew, William A. 2007a. "Free to Enslave: Politics and the Escalation of Britain's Transatlantic Slave Trade, 1688–1714." *William and Mary Quarterly* 64 (1): pp. 3–38.

Pettigrew, William A. 2007b. "Parliament and the Escalation of the Slave Trade, 1690–1714." *Parliamentary History* 26 (S1): pp. 12–26. doi: 10.1111/j.1750-0206.2007.tb00677.x.

Price, Richard. 2019. "Syria and the Chemical Weapons Taboo." *Journal of Global Security Studies* 4 (1): pp. 37–52. doi: 10.1093/jogss/ogy040.

Rahman, Ahmed S. 2010. "Fighting the Forces of Gravity: Seapower and Maritime Trade Between the 18th and 20th Centuries." *Explorations in Economic History* 47 (1): pp. 28–48. doi: 10.1016/j.eeh.2009.05.007.

Ray, James Lee. 1989. "The Abolition of Slavery and the End of International War." *International Organization* 43 (3): pp. 405–39. doi: 10.1017/S0020818300032987.

Rice, C. Duncan. 1975. *The Rise and Fall of Black Slavery*. London: MacMillan Press.

Richardson, David. 2007. "The Ending of the British Slave Trade in 1807: The Economic Context." *Parliamentary History* 26 (S1): pp. 127–40. doi: 10.1111/j.1750-0206.2007.tb00684.x.

Ruggie, John Gerard. 1982. "International Regimes, Transactions, and Change: Embedded Liberalism in the Postwar Economic Order." *International Organization* 36 (2): pp. 379–415. doi: 10.1017/S0020818300018993.

Russell-Wood, Anthony J. R. 1978. "Iberian Expansion and the Issue of Black Slavery: Changing Portuguese Attitudes, 1440–1770." *American Historical Review* 83 (1): pp. 16–42. doi: 10.1086/ahr/83.1.16.

Russell-Wood, Anthony J. R. 1998. *The Portuguese Empire, 1415–1808: A World on the Move*. Baltimore, MD: John Hopkins University Press.

Sandholtz, Wayne, and Kendall W. Stiles. 2009. *International Norms and Cycles of Change*. Oxford: Oxford University Press.

Sherwood, Marika. 2007. *After Abolition: Britain and the Slave Trade Since 1807*. London: I.B. Tauris & Co. Ltd.

Shilliam, Robbie. 2014. "'Open the Gates Mek We Repatriate': Caribbean Slavery, Constructivism, and Hermeneutic Tensions." *International Theory* 6 (2): pp. 349–72. doi: 10.1017/S1752971914000165.

Slave Voyages. 2022a. "Estimates Database, 1501–1866." Slave Voyages: The Trans-Atlantic Slave Trade Database." Accessed October 5, 2022. http://www.slavevoyages.org/estimates/UMyFr5g7.

Slave Voyages. 2022b. "Glossary: Brazil." Slave Voyages: The Trans-Atlantic Slave Trade Database." Accessed October 5, 2022. http://www.slavevoyages.org/help/page_glossary#glossary-letter-B.

Slave Voyages. 2022c. "Glossary: Flag/National Flag." Slave Voyages: The Trans-Atlantic Slave Trade Database." Accessed October 5, 2022. http://www.slavevoyages.org/help/page_glossary#glossary-letter-F.

Stein, Robert Louis. 1979. *The French Slave Trade in the Eighteenth Century: On Old Regime Business*. Madison. WI: University of Wisconsin Press.

Swaminathan, Srividhya. 2009. *Debating the Slave Trade: Rhetoric of British National Identity, 1759–1815*. London: Routledge.

Thomas, Hugh. 1997. *The Slave Trade: The Story of the Atlantic Slave Trade, 1440–1870*. New York: Simon & Schuster.

Thornton, John K. 2010. "African Political Ethics and the Slave Trade." In Peterson 2010, pp. 38–62.

Williams, Eric. 1944. *Capitalism and Slavery*. Chapel Hill, NC: University of North Carolina Press.

Winston, Carla. 2018. "Norm Structure, Diffusion, and Evolution: A Conceptual Approach." *European Journal of International Relations* 24 (3): pp. 638–61. doi: 10.1177/1354066117720794.

Young, Jeffrey Robert. 2016. "Proslavery Ideology." In *The Oxford Handbook of Slavery in the Americas*, ed. Robert L. Paquette and Mark M. Smith. Oxford: Oxford University Press, pp. 399–423.

8
International norm disputes
Comparative insights for theory and practice

8.1 Introduction

Contestation abounds in world politics: International norms, institutions, and the international order itself are increasingly under challenge in virtually every policy area—from human rights and global health, through trade and climate change, to arms control and international peace and security law. Scholars of International Relations (IR) have begun to study the effects of norm contestation, backlash against institutions and courts, and the broader crisis of the liberal international order (LIO) (see Lake et al. 2021). Our book contributes to the debate with a comparative analysis of how contestation has affected international norm robustness in six cases. IR norm researchers have long discussed that contestation is key to the emergence, diffusion, change, and potential erosion of international norms. Our goal was to answer whether contestation affects the robustness of international norms—and if so, how. We have used six case studies (the torture prohibition, the responsibility to protect, the commercial whaling moratorium, the duty to prosecute, privateering, and the slave trade) to show that norms begin to weaken, and even erode, when contestation impugns their core claims or when applicatory contestation becomes permanent. We have shown that one main reason for contestation to radicalize and diffuse, and thereby weaken norms, is the character of the institutional setting—its fairness and hierarchies—in which norm disputes take place. In the historical cases, the relative power of norm challengers mattered most, while in all cases, embeddedness in broader norm clusters affected norm contestation and robustness—albeit in different ways.

This final chapter presents our comparative findings on contestation trends (Section 8.2), robustness trends (Section 8.3), and the factors that explain how contestation and robustness are linked (Section 8.4). We then turn to major issues in international norm disputes not explicitly addressed in the case studies and discuss their implications (Section 8.5). Section 8.6 concludes by delineating how our research agenda on contestation and norm robustness informs the debate over the LIO's crisis.

International Norm Disputes. Lisbeth Zimmermann et al., Oxford University Press. © Lisbeth Zimmermann, Nicole Deitelhoff, Max Lesch, Antonio Arcudi, and Anton Peez (2023). DOI: 10.1093/oso/9780198873235.003.0008

8.2 Contestation trends

In this book, we map contestation trends in six cases to trace the causes, dynamics, and consequences of challenges to international norms. Distinguishing between applicatory and validity contestation proved key to unpacking and systematizing the often heated and complex disputes about international norms (Deitelhoff and Zimmermann 2020). This distinction has helped us systematically identify which aspects of an international norm actors challenge (how the norm is applied or also the validity of its core claims), trace gradual changes in contestation patterns, and show critical junctures.

Since the adoption of the UN Convention against Torture (CAT) in 1984, only a few states have challenged the application, let alone the validity, of the international torture prohibition in the UN General Assembly (UNGA). Mainly, states have disputed specific charges of torture. One reason is because contesting a core human rights norm—the absolute and non-derogable prohibition of torture—in UNGA would sully a state's reputation. But central challengers, such as Chile and the United Kingdom (UK) in the 1970s, Israel in the 1990s, and the United States (US) in the early 2000s, maintained that existential threats justified their violent interrogation techniques. At least for a time, those four states contested the validity of the torture prohibition by seeking to exploit loopholes in the norm with respect to the special circumstances of terrorist or existential threats. Most of their norm challenges, however, addressed the definition of torture: whether specific interrogation techniques such as waterboarding constitute torture. As disturbing and worrying as this contestation was, we found that all four states eventually walked back from their occasionally radical challenges to the norm. Since these kinds of challenges have also not spread to other states, we did not expect the norm to be weakened internationally.

The responsibility to protect (R2P) is a non-legal norm whose emergence was contested and that has remained contested since it was adopted in the World Summit Outcome Document (WSOD) by UNGA in 2005. Our main finding is that R2P challenges have rarely attacked its core claim regarding the national and international responsibility to protect populations from atrocities. Instead, contestation has remained applicatory: States contest the *conditions* that trigger R2P, *who* is supposed to apply it (domestic, regional, or international actors), and *how* (through prevention or intervention). Disputes about R2P heated up when the UN Security Council (UNSC) authorized the Libya intervention in 2011 that caused the end of Muammar Gaddafi's rule. During that, and since then, Russia,

China, and countries from the Global South have taken very critical positions, generally questioning the norm's third pillar of military intervention. Because contestation has predominantly been applicatory, we expected that R2P will not be weakened—although the norm may be incrementally changing.

The 1986 moratorium that prohibits all types of commercial whaling can be described as a soft law regulation. It is not a formal part of the International Convention for the Regulation of Whaling, the founding document of the International Whaling Commission (IWC), but is part of the IWC Schedule, which regulates specific whaling activities. In this case, we observe that, at first, contestation was mostly applicatory: concerning the interpretation of specific exemptions from the moratorium, such as aboriginal subsistence and scientific whaling. Because of the lack of any agreed interpretations of central issues such as scientific whaling, certain types of applicatory contestation became permanent. Moreover, more and more states began to contest the norm's validity by invoking sustainability as justification for limited whaling. This culminated in a stand-off between pro-whalers and anti-whalers in the 2000s, which subsided somewhat in the 2010s after the failure to renegotiate the moratorium. The diffusion of contestation led us to expect that the whaling moratorium would become less robust.

In 1998, the Rome Statute enshrined the duty to prosecute grave international crimes, establishing the International Criminal Court (ICC) in 2002. At the beginning, only a few states contested the norm and the ICC. A notable exception was the non-member US, which repeatedly sought to limit the court's jurisdiction over its citizens. Among ICC members, contestation remained low throughout the early 2000s as the court opened its first cases of self-referrals by African states. Challenges to the norm mounted in 2005, when the UNSC referred the situation in Darfur, Sudan to the ICC, and flared up again in 2010, when, on his own initiative, the prosecutor began to investigate post-election violence in Kenya. These cases targeted sitting heads of state and members of government: Omar Al Bashir in Sudan and Uhuru Kenyatta and William Ruto in Kenya. Since the arrest warrant for Al Bashir was issued in 2008, contestation has increased, mainly by African states and the African Union (AU). Validity contestation almost matched applicatory contestation, which mainly attacks the non-immunity of sitting heads of state in the Rome Statute and accuses the ICC of being an instrument of Western domination. Like the commercial whaling moratorium, based on this finding, we expected that radicalized contestation will weaken the duty to prosecute.

Our first historical case study examined contestation patterns around the permissive norm that allowed states to commission private ships to seize foreign vessels at sea. Privateering existed in different forms and under different names from the Middle Ages to the nineteenth century, during which it changed from largely being a mechanism of inter-state compensation into a central strategy of naval warfare. Applicatory contestation always existed, albeit to different extents at different periods: States mainly challenged how privateering was organized, regulated, and adjudicated in "prize law." Challengers did not question the basic notion of privateering but rather criticized some privateers for not complying with regulations. In the nineteenth century, most discussion focused on the kinds of trade that could be classified as "neutral" and thereby exempt from wartime privateering. Only in the mid-1800s validity contestation appeared, particularly in the UK, which more generally questioned privateering in moral and liberal arguments regarding private property and free trade. Between European states, applicatory contestation about the definition of neutral trade had become permanent and validity contestation increased—a general shift that could lead to norm weakening.

We observe a similar pattern with respect to Atlantic slave trade, another permissive norm. The European slave trading remained in place from the late fifteenth to the nineteenth centuries. Comparing domestic discourse around the trading of enslaved people in Portugal and the UK reveals interesting similarities. In both states, for centuries, contestation was applicatory. In Portugal, the widespread applicatory contestation was part of a religious discourse aimed at converting enslaved Africans to Christianity. In the UK, where applicatory contestation was limited, slave trade discourse mainly concerned free trade and property ownership. Applicatory contestation remained dominant in Portugal until the 1800s, while, in the UK at the turn of the nineteenth century, there was a radical change to strong validity contestation couched in moral and national security arguments—a strong sign of the norm's swift replacement.

In these six case studies, we have found that the two types of contestation mostly evolve in parallel. At first, we expected norm challengers to shift from applicatory to validity contestation when norm disputes escalated. We observed, however, that as contestation radicalizes, actors begin to attack international norms at *both* levels. More research is needed to better understand why states target a norm's application, validity—*or both*. In addition, under which conditions is contestation driven by rational or normative considerations (see March and Olsen 1998: 949–51)? Often challengers are aware that applicatory contestation can stabilize norms. With respect to the slave trade, radical challengers in the UK often had misgivings about supporting applicatory contestation and adaptive changes, fearing that to do so would leave the slave-trading norm intact and perhaps even legitimize it (see Chapter 7). As for the torture prohibition, the US tried to couch challenges in terms of applicatory contestation to avoid being seen as *radical* (see Chapter 2). The context and discursive settings seem to at least partly influence the choice of specific contestation strategies (see Anderl et al. 2021; Jongen and Scholte 2022).

8.3 Robustness trends

Only quite recently have researchers begun the challenging undertaking of systematically and comparatively measuring the robustness of international norms (Bower 2017; Deitelhoff and Zimmermann 2019; Ben-Josef Hirsch and Dixon 2021; Girard 2021; Blair et al. 2022; Percy and Sandholtz 2022; Scherzinger 2023). We propose a four-dimensional approach to trace trends in norm discourse and practice. In each case study, we combined indicators to generate a comprehensive view of norm robustness. We assessed compliance rates and implementation levels (practice) as well as norm concordance and negative reactions to norm violations (discourse). This allowed us to cover the regulative and evaluative dimensions of international norms (Finnemore and Sikkink 1998: 891) as well as their validity and facticity (Deitelhoff and Zimmermann 2019: 3).

In the torture prohibition case, norm robustness was more or less stable—in line with its mostly applicatory patterns of contestation. Discovering the facts of a clandestine practice like torture is difficult, but existing data sets based on human rights reporting show that globally, compliance with the prohibition of torture remains constant and might even be slightly improving. Ongoing instances of torture are consistently criticized and condemned in international discourse, which is a strong sign that the norm is robust. It is buttressed by increasing implementation, including codification in domestic law and the establishment of National Human Rights Institutions (NHRIs) mandated to improve compliance and implementation. In international discourse, most states affirm the torture prohibition in statements at the United Nations (UN) and, after US contestations and violations were made public, began to affirm that the norm is non-derogable. This finding does not ignore the fact that torture is widespread in some states, such as Syria (Austin 2016), and sometimes involves multistate collaboration, as during the US-led extraordinary rendition program (Austin 2017). However, such cases of rampant norm violation have not proliferated and the torture prohibition generally guides the behavior and discourse of all states. In contrast to fears that the torture prohibition was being eroded (e.g. McKeown 2009; Brunnée and Toope 2010; Kutz 2014), our results show that, the notorious war on terror notwithstanding, the norm has remained robust.

Applicatory contestation has similarly shaped debates about the responsibility to protect, which has also remained robust. Although it is more challenging to determine the robustness of a norm like R2P because of its mainly positive duties—unlike a prohibitive norm such as the torture ban or the commercial whaling moratorium—we observe R2P shaping both international practice and discourse. Since its adoption in 2005, the UNSC has increasingly addressed conflict situations that could threaten civilian populations by referring to R2P, a clear change from evaluating very few situations with respect to "protection." This does not mean that all mass atrocities have been met with military interventions, nor that they should be. However, we see the UN and other actors undertaking military interventions, including robust peacekeeping, in the name of humanitarian protection. The norm is also being implemented using National Focal Points and is increasingly institutionalized in the UN System. The international responsibility to protect vulnerable populations is reaffirmed in most statements regarding the norm. Affirmation recovered surprisingly quickly after the heavily disputed intervention in Libya in 2011. Moreover, states criticize atrocities and the international community's inaction. While scholars and commentators alike expect the demise of R2P, we find the norm robust in both practice and discourse—at least during the first decade after its adoption. That said, R2P's effectiveness will always depend on the political will—shaped by global power dynamics. The question remains as to how widely the norm is currently being reinterpreted to only cover *prevention*, which changes its core claims and saps its robustness. The unopposed non-application of R2P's military dimension could indicate that it is weakening (see our discussion of "silence" in Section 8.5).

The commercial whaling moratorium was weakened by unresolvable applicatory contestation and rising validity contestation. Commercial whaling had nearly completely stopped after the moratorium took effect. It increased again when Norway restarted in the 1990s and Iceland in the 2000s. After withdrawing from the IWC in 2019, Japan also began to hunt whales commercially again (as opposed to "scientifically," as it had for years). In recent years, the Japanese whale meat market has shrunk and commercial whaling activity has decreased slightly in Iceland and Norway. At the same time, negative reactions also decreased—with fewer and fewer IWC resolutions condemning commercial whaling in general and scientific whaling in particular—while domestic opinion polls, in this case an indicator for concordance, revealed that opinions on commercial whaling continued to be highly polarized.

The duty to prosecute, too, has been weakened through validity contestation by African states, the ICC's largest regional group, which has been the object of most ICC investigations. This supports our argument that shifts to validity contestation impact norm robustness. Like R2P, it is difficult to assess global compliance with the positive obligation to prosecute perpetrators of international crimes. However, we note that cooperation with the ICC has decreased since 2008, when African states increased contestation. The group's failure to criticize non-cooperation undermines the norm, a regional trend that is reflected by many African states only slowly implementing the Rome Statute and the dearth of laws criminalizing atrocities. We also observe the decreasing willingness of African states to affirm the duty to prosecute. It remains to be seen whether the norm's weakening is contained or further escalates and whether the ICC exercises self-restraint in controversial cases such as Afghanistan—potentially reshaping the core claims of the duty to prosecute.

In the historical case of privateering, applicatory contestation led to tighter regulation and similarly stabilized the practice—as reflected in its prevalence—and increased its legitimacy. Not until the mid-nineteenth century did validity contestation and permanent applicatory contestation of "neutral" trade push the British to support total prohibition, which became enshrined in a multilateral treaty, the Paris Declaration Respecting Maritime Law of 1856. Although that did not immediately end privateering, criticism of ongoing or potential privateering gradually increased. By the late nineteenth century, it had been stopped and the norm has been replaced.

The permissive norm regarding slave trading was stabilized by ongoing applicatory contestation. In Portugal, contestation along religious grounds influenced slave trade regulations but reinforced the normative conviction that trading humans could be justified, which was reflected in centuries of vigorous activity. This belief remained firmly in place until the mid-nineteenth century, when British pressure pushed Portugal to stop. Most British applicatory contestation about the practice focused on issues like free trade, which served to widen the norm's permissiveness and gradually stabilize it, thereby increasing the numbers of people enslaved and traded. However, when validity contestation gained ground at the end of the nineteenth century, the legal space to trade human beings was restricted and turned into total prohibition, which was quickly implemented in the UK and accompanied by international campaigns.

However, there are caveats to making a clear, global assessment of norm robustness trends. First of all, we note the phenomenon of *partial* robustness, especially in our contemporary case studies: The duty to prosecute has been weakened among African states but remains strong among many other ICC members; the commercial whaling moratorium is weak among whaling states and their allies but relatively strong in the large anti-whaling camp; R2P's Pillars 1 and 2—on states' responsibility to protect their populations and the international community's responsibility to assist them—are strong, but Pillar 3 on military interventions is weak; and the prohibition of torture was weakened among a small group of states during the war on terror, yet remains globally robust.

A norm applies to a specific situation and a particular group of actors: Its weakening for some could cause it to weaken across the board—especially when that happens among a key group of norm addressees such as African states at the ICC. Only the two historical cases showed complete decay and replacement, which was swift for slave trading but dragged on another 50 years for privateering. The latter case supports our general finding that only a long-term perspective can detect trends in norm robustness (Price 1997; Sandholtz 2007). Slave trading's and privateering's complete decay could also be linked to the UK's position as the unchallenged naval power after defeating combined French and Spanish forces in the Battle of Trafalgar in 1805 (Kennedy 1997). In the more multipolar, institutionalized setting of the late twentieth and early twenty-first centuries, norms are more likely to show more complex robustness patterns as a result of challenges. While it thus remains difficult to make generalizations about norm robustness—our contextualized approach is particularly apt to assess such complexity.

This makes it unsurprising that in all our case studies—and many others beyond the scope of this book—weakening processes have not created a normative void: Norms have instead been replaced by other norms or alternative normative arrangements (Sandholtz 2019: 145; Percy and Sandholtz 2022: 942–43; Pratt 2022: 8–9). Norms evolve gradually, adapting to changing social and technical circumstances. With respect to the ICC, we might be witnessing the universal duty to prosecute slowly being replaced by a version of individual criminal accountability that has a much more limited regional reach (e.g. does not include Africa) and applicatory scope (e.g. heads of states have immunity). Even for R2P, there are signs that prevention and assistance are gradually replacing military intervention.

Finally, assessing norm robustness comes with methodological challenges in *measuring* norms. There is a long tradition of measuring compliance with international norms—especially in human rights research (Hathaway 2002; Hafner-Burton and Tsutsui 2005; Simmons 2009; Cingranelli and Richards 2010; Conrad et al. 2013; Fariss 2014, 2018). Despite limitations (see Chapter 2), the various approaches help assess the practical dimension of norm robustness. Novel text-mining approaches for analyzing human rights reports are opening pathways to expand existing data sets and to collect compliance data for further international norms (Cordell et al. 2022). In addition, there is a growing body of quantitative work assessing national implementation of international norms and advancing our knowledge about norm adoption and diffusion. These approaches map the adoption, changes, and effects of anti-torture laws (Berlin 2021), the criminalization of atrocities (Berlin 2020), and equality norms on sexual orientation (Girard 2021) across countries.

For the discourse-based dimensions of norm robustness, it has been much harder to find valid indicators for studying norm robustness globally and in various countries. Innovative and often quantitative work has recently expanded the means to assess the concordance and implementation of international norms. Scherzinger (2023) used a sentiment analysis to show that R2P is positively connoted in most UNSC debates. This useful addition to our findings on affirmative R2P discourse goes beyond qualitative content analysis. But it does not provide an in-depth analysis of the substantive nuances in UN diplomatic discourse, such as positive mention of the specific elements and pillars of R2P. Recent survey-based public opinion studies on the use of certain types of weapons have also expanded the methodological tool kit and our knowledge about how international norms are grounded in shared understandings at national and societal levels (Nylen and Carpenter 2019; Carpenter and Montgomery 2020; Carpenter et al. 2021; Blair et al. 2022). Yet, there is still a dire need for global surveys of public opinion to grasp norms' international scope and national and regional variations. More thorough sentiment analyses and public opinion research could complement the study of concordance with international norms.

Overall, these approaches seek to make claims about norm robustness—albeit to different degrees—although they usually focus on just one dimension of robustness and thereby create an incomplete picture. Moreover, with few exceptions (e.g. Panke and Petersohn 2012, 2016; Ben-Josef Hirsch and Dixon 2021), research on norm robustness is based on single-case studies (but see Sandholtz and Stiles 2009 with a related focus on norm change). Future research should explore more comparative and multimethod approaches for measuring norm robustness (Peez 2022: 16–18, 22).

8.4 Explanatory factors

Our six cases support the expectation that validity contestation is more detrimental to a norm's robustness than applicatory challenges. In addition, if the latter becomes permanent, norm challengers are more likely to shift contestation towards validity contestation. Our comparative findings suggest that neither legalization nor legal discourse fully explains these developments. In our contemporary cases, the most decisive factor influencing the dynamics of norm disputes was the institutional setting: When it is perceived as fair and non-hierarchical, contestation is less likely to radicalize from applicatory to validity and less likely to diffuse in the broader global discourse. In the historical cases, the relative power of norm challengers was decisive.

In this book, we look at three aspects of the role of law: how much "hard" (binding) legal instruments matter, how much legal discourse matters, and how embeddedness in a broader norm cluster explains contestation types and robustness trends. All our case studies show that hard law does not prevent contestation, nor do precision and institutionalized adjudication clearly contain challenges at the level of applicatory contestation. Although the duty to prosecute is a hard law with regard to precision and delegation, it encountered widespread validity contestation. In contrast, R2P—a very imprecise, non-legal norm whose imprecision lent itself to reinterpretation—remained fairly robust. The commercial whaling moratorium is a soft law norm instituted by the IWC: While applicatory contestation was fueled by the moratorium's imprecision and lack of delegation, they did not obviously increase validity contestation. As for the torture prohibition, it is a peremptory norm of customary international law that is codified in international treaties. But it remains open to validity contestation, sometimes disguised in legal language. Even a very precise definition of torture did not prevent states from contesting specific elements of the definition. However, precision and delegation helped restrain contestation to the level of application and reject validity contestation.

There was no relevant hard law at the international level regulating the two historical norms on privateering and slave trading, which remained robust for centuries. These cases show how domestic legal systems channel applicatory contestation, something we have also observed in more recent cases, for instance, national responses to torture in the US and the legal–political fallout from South Africa's failure to extradite Omar Al Bashir.

It is also difficult to argue that anchoring a norm in international law creates a specific kind of legal discourse that tames and restricts the type of argument about its application. We did observe that the language of contestation changed with further legalization (see also Zimmermann 2021). In the torture case, disputes in the 1970s were over using "brutality" to define torture; in the 1990s and early 2000s, it was about "severity," the term used in the UN Convention against Torture. However, the change did not block contestation and has even provided cover for fundamental challenges (Schmidt and Sikkink 2019: 106). Contestation of the duty to prosecute differs when it is carried out in international institutions or is voiced for the general public. In the Assembly of States Parties, African states contested and attempted to modify specific ICC rules, whereas elsewhere, they criticize neocolonialism and imperialism outright.

Embeddedness in norm clusters had varying effects on the dynamics of contestation and robustness. Its stabilizing effect is probably clearest in the torture prohibition that is central to the international human rights architecture. In the historical case studies, embeddedness in broader, albeit competing, norm clusters helped stabilize the permissive norms of privateering and slave trading: the former closely linked to mercantilism, the latter to free trade and the Christian mission. Whereas the decline of privateering was accompanied by the whole norm cluster weakening, the demise of slave trading was brought about by linking the norm to *alternative* norm clusters. With respect to the whaling moratorium, R2P, and the duty to prosecute, embeddedness in complex norm clusters provides pathways for contestation because arguments can be linked to competing sets of norms. But this does not explain shift in contestation types and patterns. Since a norm always functions in a broad normative environment and in more than one norm cluster, it is difficult to pinpoint how embeddedness affects contestation and norm robustness. To understand how norm clusters work in international norm dynamics, we still need to know how and why such embeddedness gradually changes and how it can be reframed by challengers.

Across the case studies, contestation came from states very differently positioned in the international system in terms of relative power. Like others before us (Sandholtz and Stiles 2009: 332–34), we conclude that in our contemporary case studies, powerful states did not more successfully challenge international norms even by mobilizing their soft and hard power capacities. With respect to the torture prohibition, although the US actively collaborated with other states to torture terror suspects, US challenges did not widely diffuse. Only in this specific group, and for a limited period, do we observe instances of states emulating US arguments and practices. In the R2P case, Russia and China were powerful veto players, but they were unable to fundamentally shift contestation dynamics about R2P—although it remains to be seen whether they will continue to prevent the norm's application. As for challenges to the duty to protect and the commercial whaling moratorium, the main initiators were considerably less powerful (e.g. Kenya and other African states for the ICC) or at least less powerful than the norm supporters (e.g. Norway or Japan for whaling). Interestingly, in both cases, outspoken challengers gathered support based on the asymmetry, presenting themselves as abused small states bullied by the West and especially the US—a resonant discourse that broadened their support (see also Peez and Zimmermann 2022: 235–37). Although in both cases the norm challengers are less powerful, the norms' robustness hinges on their cooperation. If all whaling states, states investigated by the ICC, and their allies exited the IWC and the ICC, it would be much harder to put into effect and sustain the norms. Their relative power was reinforced by perceptions of institutional unfairness and hierarchies.

This contrasts with our findings on privateering and slave trade. In both cases, the relatively powerful UK was able to promote international prohibitions—even without other states widely contesting the norms' validity. Slave trading swiftly decayed due to enforcement by the UK, which relied on its hard power (see also Sandholtz and Stiles 2009: 333). International negotiations, multilateral treaties, and shaming were still necessary to fundamentally change the privateering norm. We argue that this resulted from the UK's naval power in the nineteenth century as well as the more institutionalized international order with more actor groups in the second half of the twentieth- and in the twenty-first centuries. In such settings, norm negotiations are often more formalized, with more complex maneuvering by many actors—which curbs unilateral shaming and sanctioning strategies such as those the UK had used earlier.

Finally, we showed that procedures were significant in the contemporary cases. In the two cases of weakening (the duty to prosecute and the whaling moratorium), international negotiations of the norm and the process of channeling contestation were perceived as unfair and not offering equal recognition: Anti-whaling actors engaged in several lengthy adaptation negotiations only to vote against them while passing resolutions criticizing whaling. Simultaneously, boycott campaigns and direct action by US and European non-governmental organizations (NGOs) deepened pro-whaling states' perceptions of being unfairly targeted for their "traditions," although in other policy fields they were "good" members of international society. Whaling was hardly a profitable business in any of the whaling states like Japan, Norway, and Iceland, and anything but an immediate objective of many African and Caribbean states, and there were plenty of loopholes for limited whaling activities, yet the discourse of unfair treatment united the pro-whalers and hardened their positions.

In the case of the duty to prosecute, African states considered the UNSC's role in the ICC's institutional set-up as unresponsive and hierarchical. African states also maintained that the Assembly of States Parties did not take their views seriously. Some governments had good reason to fear prosecution; others did not but nonetheless severely criticized the duty to prosecute as institutionalized in the ICC. This is evident in South African criticism of the ICC's focus on Africa, which other states portrayed as a selective prosecution of Africans shaped by neocolonial and imperialist world views. African states' attempts to present their critique at the UNSC and in the Assembly of States Parties—especially regarding immunity for heads of state and postponing investigations to allow peace-making efforts to succeed—did not receive the hoped-for recognition. On the African continent, the sense of being unfairly treated in an international system deeply shaped by asymmetric power relations and the selective application of the duty to prosecute radicalized contestation and weakened the norm.

Validity contestation did not diffuse with respect to the torture prohibition and R2P. This was partly due to the embeddedness in norm clusters, especially in the torture case we discuss in Chapter 2. The institutional settings where the two norms were disputed were more conducive of dialogue and not perceived as especially unfair or hierarchical. For R2P, this is seen in the Informal Interactive Dialogue which helped create shared understandings of the norm. However, open dialogue also opened pathways for norm change. For the torture prohibition, the "constructive dialogue" about the torture prohibition at UN treaty bodies and negotiations at UNGA provided fora in which each state was on an equal footing. The European human rights bodies provided legal procedures for the UK to defend its position. Contestation was thereby prevented from becoming permanent and radicalizing into validity challenges, while other states did not join in because charges of "unfair treatment" were implausible.

To summarize, calling for harder sanctions or harder law in reaction to norm challenges could backfire in many cases. But to keep certain international norms robust, more reflection is necessary about institutional mechanisms and processes to manage norm contestation in international institutions.

8.5 Broader debates about international norms

For this book, we set out to study international norms using theoretical and methodological assumptions to enable a comparative project. In this section, we discuss alternatives and limitations to our approach: norm change and complexity, practice, silence, and critique regarding international norm disputes.

The case studies in this book examine individual norms, taking their core claims at the point of adoption as the starting point to analyze the effects of contestation. This does not neglect the fact that norms are always open to *change* (Sandholtz and Stiles 2009; Krook and True 2012; Wiener 2014; Niemann and Schillinger 2017) and are embedded in broader social and normative environments (Lantis and Wunderlich 2018: 571, 2022: 5; Fehl and Rosert 2020: 1–2; Gholiagha et al. 2020: 294). Our case studies also demonstrate that contestation shapes norm content—and potentially, core claims as well—in recurring processes of change; that is, the definition of torture has been broadened, which affects the measurement of compliance, while R2P may have changed its original aims, making it difficult to assess with our indicators for discourse and practice. As for the ICC, one potential future course could fundamentally reinterpret the norm's core claims. Such changes can result from both applicatory and validity contestation. Future research should analyze how processes of norm change and robustness trends are interlinked.

Our comparison of the robustness of individual norms does not exclude their embeddedness in complex *norm clusters*: Brief case histories in each chapter show that norms are embedded in broader normative environments. Indeed, norm complexity is one of the main bases for both applicatory and validity contestation, as clearly shown with respect to R2P and the duty to prosecute.

This book studies contestation as a discursive phenomenon and distinguishes it from norm robustness. Such contestation can be linked to performative acts such as tearing up a copy of the UN Charter in UNGA. In our cases, Omar Al Bashir openly visiting ICC member states who refused to deliver him to the court also had such performative qualities. With this conceptualization, we differ from authors that would conceptualize contestation also as *behaviors*, arguing that "actions can be louder than words" (Stimmer and Wisken 2019: 520). They focus on the non-implementation of international norms—an aspect that we would analyze as part of the practice dimension of norm robustness—and on more expressive disobedient actions that challenge international norms (Stimmer and Wisken 2019: 521–22).

Our approach also differs from practice theorists which take practices as their starting point and study their performative effects on international norms (Bode and Huelss 2018; Pratt 2022). Pratt (2022), for instance, demonstrates how changes in practices led to far-reaching normative transformations of targeted killings, torture, and private military contracting during the US war on terrorism. Yet, while practice theories analytically prioritize practices over norms (Gadinger 2022: 119), they often evaluate their normativity using similar concepts: fields, normative configurations, orders of worth, and repertoires shared by communities of practice (see the discussions in Lesch 2017, 2021; Lesch and Loh 2022).

Targeted killings and autonomous weapon systems are a case in point. Technological changes have certainly contributed to creating a new normality of carrying out assassinations around the globe—albeit only to a limited degree in a few states (Jose 2017). The emergence of autonomous weapon systems might further undermine existing norms on the use of force and humanitarian law (Bode and Huelss 2018). Yet, at what point does this normality also transform normativity, that is, a sense of appropriateness shared beyond the few states that actually practice targeted killings?

In our understanding, these practices have also resulted in disputes regarding their application and sometimes even validity. To systematically analyze how these disputes impact robustness, we employed a traditional definition of norms and consider these and similar practices as non-compliance. International norms only lose robustness or shift toward new standards of appropriateness if non-compliance is no longer criticized. We show, for example, that torture (Chapter 2) has remained limited to a small group of states that have been unable to change or erode international norms (for a similar finding on targeted killings, see Keating 2022).

A broad assertion, to which we also subscribe holds that actions—including norm violations—come with some kind of justification. For some, this can trigger "rhetorical entrapment" that eventually leads to compliant behavior (Risse 2000: 23; Schimmelfennig 2001: 65). Others argue that it dissolves international norms in endless rounds of argumentation, making the distinction between compliance and non-compliance meaningless (Koskenniemi 2005; Hurd 2017). In the 1984 *Nicaragua v. United States*, the International Court of Justice (ICJ) held that states affirm international norms by justifying their violations through referring to international law (ICJ 1986: para. 186; for a critical discussion, see Marxsen 2018: 21–22). Thus, outright "disregard" or "neglect" of norms might give more cause for concern than open contestation (Wiener 2014: 49; Dixon 2017: 85–86). *Neglect and silence* take three forms: States deliberately avoid invoking and applying certain norms, do not attempt to justify their actions by referring to international norms, and, if they are legal norms, do not couch their arguments in legal language. They thereby prevent communicative engagement and the opportunity to maintain shared understanding about contested norms (see Lewis et al. 2019 for a similar debate in international law). That can destabilize them more than open challenges. None of our cases exhibited complete silence, but in R2P we observed that as state and non-state actors at the UN began to shy away from referring to the norm and applying it (Chapter 3). This shows that interpreting contestation and robustness trends requires in-depth knowledge of policy processes based, for example, on interviews with experts who clarify whether there is strategic neglect and silence.

One could also criticize a project like ours for *reifying extant—mostly Western—norms* and reproducing international rule (see Adler-Nissen 2014; Zarakol 2014). This also raises the normative question of whether applicatory contestation is the preferable form of contestation because—unlike validity contestation—it is less likely to disrupt international norms. As our historical case studies like the one on the slave trade show, even validity contestation can be an important source for progress in international politics (see Wolff and Zimmermann 2016). In addition, our findings can be linked to a critique of the asymmetrical structures of the liberal international order and its institutional hierarchies, which we see as key, for example, for the radicalization of the contestation of the duty to prosecute and the ICC's weakening.

This book has taken a mostly empirical approach to studying how contestation affects norm robustness without prioritizing stability over weakness or applicatory over validity challenges. With norms constantly evolving, we do not judge the normative quality of change *or* contestation. We assume that contestation drives norm development and is indispensable for political orders to reproduce and adapt to changing social and technological circumstances. Our task is to assess *when*, in terms of change and robustness, *which* effects are more or less likely. We can conceive of norms being undermined by actors as diverse as a decolonial movement that seeks to disentangle global governance processes, extremist religious groups, and far-right networks seeking to curtail individual rights and freedoms. In our understanding, the normative judgments attached to any norm weakening are then determined by the substance, direction, and process of challenges and norm-weakening processes.

Our findings offer fertile ground for a variety of pathways to make such normative judgments regarding particular international norm disputes. An *internal* critique of the duty to prosecute would evaluate both contestation and robustness based on the norm's core claims enshrined in the Rome Statute, an *external* critique would adopt a postcolonial or universalist perspective to question the same norm, and an *immanent* critique would take the arguments and normative reference points of the disputants that we have mapped as a starting point to criticize the implementation of the duty to prosecute by the ICC (on the distinction between internal, external, and immanent critique in IR, see Anderl and Wallmeier 2018; see also Schindler and Wille 2019).

8.6 Crisis of the liberal international order

The "crisis of the liberal international order" has become the new buzzword in IR scholarship and the broader discourse. The more optimistic prognoses of the 1990s have given way to growing concerns. In this final section, we sketch the main lines of the debate, identify gaps in the literature, and discuss what can be learned from norm contestation scholarship. We argue that scholars of the LIO and its crisis have a lot to learn from the rich debates about norm contestation. At the same time, norm researchers should pay more attention to challenges that do more than contest individual norms and study how norm contestation simultaneously triggers and reinforces order-defiant contestation.

Early LIO debates discussed whether a coherent international order even exists, its foundation, and the relation between liberal and multilateral orders. Cooley and Nexon (2020: 23) describe the LIO as an "assemblage of many different orders at different scales" (similarly Ikenberry 2018). Based on nineteenth-century antecedents, the current LIO emerged under US leadership after the end of the Second World War (Ikenberry 2011; Zürn 2018), then broadened and deepened after the Cold War (Patrick 2016; Börzel and Zürn 2021). Most scholars seem to share an understanding of the LIO based on a broad notion of liberal internationalism, which can be summarized as an "ideational disposition to embrace liberal core values and to promote their global implementation through cooperative institutions" (Kreuder-Sonnen and Rittberger 2020: 5). The order is usually presented as the success story that brought peace, security, and prosperity; embedded great powers; and nurtured interstate trust and cooperation (Ikenberry 2018: 11). This is not to say that the LIO has been without discontents. It has been shaped by the profound power asymmetries in its treaties and organizations (Cox 1992) that are reflected in its core ideas and principles (Acharya 2017; Duncombe and Dunne 2018). Its promises of peace, individual equality, and development have been described as always partial—at best (Barkawi and Laffey 1999; Viola 2020; Bello 2021; Búzás 2021). Nonetheless, scholars agree that the numerous current crises are subjecting the LIO to a critical stress test.

On one hand, scholars argue that the changing international system has added outside pressure to the LIO. They write about the unraveling US hegemony (Mearsheimer 2019). Particularly under the Trump presidency, the US withdrew and heavily criticized core LIO institutions (Cooley and Nexon 2020: 168–70), while the emerging economies of Brazil, Russia, India, China, and South Africa (BRICS) have their own views about the design of multilateral institutions (Kahler 2013; Stephen 2014; Zangl et al. 2016; Ikenberry 2018; Bettiza and Lewis 2020; Schmitt 2020). Scholars also note that the democratization wave of the 1990s has been succeeded by a backlash from autocrats (Carothers 2006; Ambrosio 2016) who care less for cooperation or international law (Ginsburg 2020). According to Bettiza (2020), Drezner (2020), and McNamara and Newman (2020), the COVID-19 pandemic has accelerated the crisis of the LIO.

Other scholars emphasize that some processes and outcomes of the LIO itself are undermining the order. An economic version of that argument posits that advancing globalization and the neoliberal economic system that the multilateral order helped develop have put immense pressure on societies (e.g. Colgan and Keohane 2017; Flaherty and Rogowski 2021). Although adverse reactions are often attributed to the "losers" of globalization, they also come from global elites (Slobodian 2021). A second interpretation is that liberal internationalism has fueled populist movements around the world that are calling for more radical changes of existing institutions and the return to strong nation-states (Hooghe and Marks 2018; Hooghe et al. 2019; Norris and Inglehart 2019; Stengel et al. 2019). The ensuing struggles for recognition merged challenges from populist movements and authoritarian regimes into a major cause of the LIO crisis (Adler-Nissen and Zarakol 2021). In a third version, it is the authority and rule of international institutions themselves which are to blame for the backlash: Börzel and Zürn (2021) claim that inbuilt legitimation problems are shaping current challenges. Kreuder-Sonnen and Rittberger (2020) maintain that high political authority and technocratic legitimation by international institutions produce contestation that cannot be reconciled by existing institutional channels and fora. Daase and Deitelhoff (2021: 186) see the problem in a "triumphant propagation and asymmetric enforcement of [liberal] principles" [our translation].

How will the LIO be affected? Some expect resilience (Deudney and Ikenberry 2018; Ikenberry 2018); others adaptation (Acharya 2017; Eilstrup-Sangiovanni and Hofmann 2020); a third group expects a "shallower" and "thinner" version (Ginsburg 2020: 258); still others decay and fundamental change (Wright 2017; Duncombe and Dunne 2018; Mearsheimer 2019). However, few theorists consider the empirical effects of current challenges to the LIO. Like earlier debates about norm dynamics (Chapter 1), recent research often assumes that contestation per se—or certain types of it—can be equated with crisis (Kreuder-Sonnen and Rittberger 2020: 3). Yet, the link between challenges and their outcome is not automatic and far from obvious (Madsen et al. 2018: 201). Like earlier debates about international norms, the current debate is confused about when the order changed or eroded: Some see events like Brexit as embodying the world order's fundamental change (Magnuson 2017), while others are skeptical (Benner 2020). Some see the World Trade Organization as upholding economic liberalism (Felbermayr 2019), others see alternative arrangements emerging (Bello 2000; Nakatomi 2013). Distinguishing incremental adaptation from more fundamental change is a ticklish undertaking: Drawing the line at different points returns very different assessments about the current situation—echoing problems in norms research.

What can our approach to studying the link between contestation and norm robustness reveal about the nature and outcomes of the LIO crisis? To begin with, future research should identify the key norms that are currently jeopardized to reveal how contestation is affecting the LIO. This book offers insights into central norms like the international torture prohibition, individual criminal accountability, and the prohibition of slavery. The framework developed in this book also offers promising pathways for studying other aspects of the LIO such as its fundamental principles, institutions, and policies. We need to identify the LIO's core normative claims to assess how it is being contested and whether it is weakening, remaining robust, or strengthening. Although there is no commonly accepted definition of the LIO, scholars point to three pillars: (1) multilateral cooperation or the concept that states should tackle global problems in shared institutions; (2) free trade or economic liberalism; and (3) political liberalism, which generally refers to individual rights (see the discussions in Nye 2017; Ikenberry 2018; Eilstrup-Sangiovanni and Hofmann 2020). *Applicatory contestation* challenges specific aspects of how these pillars are implemented in policies, norms, and institutions. It can call for more integration to solve the crisis—or warn about the need to reduce the authority of international governance (Hooghe et al. 2019). *Validity contestation* represents a fundamental rejection of one pillar of the LIO (e.g. multilateral cooperation) along with its constitutive norms and institutions. In addition, we might be facing an even broader challenge: a form of *order-defiant contestation* that questions the current order in itself (see also Lesch and Marxsen 2013). In line with our core argument, we expect that applicatory contestation likely strengthens the LIO, and validity and order-defiant contestations weaken it.

Our understanding of robustness applied to the LIO would mean that its three pillars were *no longer broadly accepted as legitimate, no longer practiced*, and were perhaps *replaced*—with the international community *no longer condemning such attitudes and behavior*. The current order is not weakened by individual states withdrawing from specific international institutions or creating alternatives. However, widespread withdrawals combined with unilateral or bilateral actions or a shift to completely different forms of authority (medieval, colonial, and others), together with no condemnation of such attitudes, would signal that the LIO is weakening (see also Eilstrup-Sangiovanni and Hofmann 2020: 1080).

There have long been challenges to the application and interpretation of the LIO's foundation. Addressing global problems looked different in the 1950s than it did in the 2010s, and interstate cooperation has had to include more actors to increase its legitimacy (Tallberg et al. 2013; Dingwerth et al. 2019). Economic liberalism, which had its heyday in the 1980s and 1990s, has been viewed more cautiously since the financial crisis of 2008–09 (Nölke 2018). In recent decades, the focus on individual rights—enshrined in the Universal Declaration of Human Rights and subsequent human rights treaties—has been expanded to include significantly more positive and group rights (on indigenous rights, see Chen 2017). Other liberal norms are even contested in the West (see Lesch 2021). So far, these challenges have not weakened or fundamentally changed the LIO: Some have even strengthened it.

This book's case studies shed light on the varying degrees to which states are willing to address global challenges through the institutions of the LIO: human rights protection at the UN, whaling in the IWC, and the prosecution of core crimes before the ICC. We have demonstrated how the US contested a core individual human right in the prohibition of torture (see Chapter 2). At that time, some observers held that fundamental human rights were in peril and feared that the "rules of the game are changing" (Dunne 2007). In hindsight, the challenges did not weaken those norms because they were met with strong pushback. While growing validity contestation did sap the duty to prosecute, the handful of threatened withdrawals—with Burundi and the Philippines actually exiting the ICC—have not seriously undermined, much less replaced, the ordering principles of individual criminal accountability (Chapter 5). While current crises may confront us with more severe challenges in the form of validity or even order-defiant contestations, we also see a "rally 'round the flag'" effect, with several states protesting the challenges and calling for the norms' defense. As long as deviations from the LIO's key pillars meet with such criticism, its boundaries might shift but the order will likely remain intact.

This illustration invites scholars of international norms and the LIO to further integrate these closely related, though still often separate, research agendas and study the interplay of contestation on different levels (policies, norms, institutions, and orders) and their effects. It begs the question of how those seeking to defend the LIO should react to the current crisis. One central concern has been that if US hegemony ends, smaller states and non-state actors will have more exit options and alternative patrons that make enforcement more difficult (Cooley and Nexon 2020) because it will cost more to uphold the order (Daase and Deitelhoff 2021: 185). Our case studies suggest that stronger legalization and sanctions against deviant actors will not necessarily do the trick. Norms are less likely to weaken in non-hierarchical, fair settings that facilitate dialogue and lead to mutual recognition (see Section 8.4). Maintaining room for honest disputes seems to be particularly important in the current "struggles for recognition" (Adler-Nissen and Zarakol 2021). The current crisis, especially expressed in order-defiant contestations, might decide the limits of conciliation: Fundamental rejection is hard to accommodate and would probably gut some of the LIO's essential characteristics. Keeping pathways for contestation open is critical for coping with the current crisis and defending the LIO from its many challenges. At the same time, such pathways need minimal agreement about its underlying principles, which might be missing for order-defiant contestation.

This book has provided an important contribution to better theorize how contestation dynamics unfold and affect the further development of international norms. This framework can also inform research on international institutions and global orders. Tracing contestation types and robustness dynamics has the potential to identifity tipping-points in the current crisis of the liberal international order.

Reference list

Acharya, Amitav. 2017. "After Liberal Hegemony: The Advent of a Multiplex World Order." *Ethics & International Affairs* 31 (3): pp. 271–85. doi: 10.1017/S089267941700020X.

Adler-Nissen, Rebecca. 2014. "Stigma Management in International Relations: Transgressive Identities, Norms, and Order in International Society." *International Organization* 68 (1): pp. 143–76. doi: 10.1017/S0020818313000337.

Adler-Nissen, Rebecca, and Ayşe Zarakol. 2021. "Struggles for Recognition: The Liberal International Order and the Merger of Its Discontents." *International Organization* 75 (2): pp. 611–34. doi: 10.1017/S0020818320000454.

Ambrosio, Thomas. 2016. *Authoritarian Backlash: Russian Resistance to Democratization in the Former Soviet Union*. London: Routledge.

Anderl, Felix, Priska Daphi, and Nicole Deitelhoff. 2021. "Keeping Your Enemies Close? The Variety of Social Movements' Reactions to International Organizations' Opening Up." *International Studies Review* 23 (4): pp. 1273–99. doi: 10.1093/isr/viaa103.

Anderl, Felix, and Philip Wallmeier. 2018. "Modi der Kritik des internationalen Regierens: Ein Plädoyer für immanente Kritik." *Zeitschrift für Internationale Beziehungen* 25 (1): pp. 65–89. doi: 10.5771/0946-7165-2018-1-65.

Austin, Jonathan Luke. 2016. "Torture and the Material-Semiotic Networks of Violence across Borders." *International Political Sociology* 10 (1): pp. 3–21. doi: 10.1093/ips/olv001.

Austin, Jonathan Luke. 2017. "We Have Never Been Civilized: Torture and the Materiality of World Political Binaries." *European Journal of International Relations* 23 (1): pp. 49–73. doi: 10.1177/1354066115616466.

Barkawi, Tarak, and Mark Laffey. 1999. "The Imperial Peace." *European Journal of International Relations* 5 (4): pp. 403–34. doi: 10.1177/1354066199005004001.

Bello, Walden. 2000. "UNCTAD: Time to Lead, Time to Challenge the WTO." Transnational Institute. May 1. Accessed January 9, 2023. https://www.tni.org/en/article/unctad-time-to-lead-time-to-challenge-the-wto.

Bello, Walden. 2021. "The Rise and Fall of Multilateralism." *Dissent* 68 (2): pp. 56–64. doi: 10.1353/dss.2021.0036.

Ben-Josef Hirsch, Michal, and Jennifer M. Dixon. 2021. "Conceptualizing and Assessing Norm Strength in International Relations." *European Journal of International Relations* 27 (2): pp. 521–47. doi: 10.1177/1354066120949628.

Benner, Thorsten. 2020. "Kindred Spirits: How a Post-Brexit Britain and the EU Can Work Together to Strengthen Multilateralism." The Foreign Policy Centre. December 16. Accessed January 9, 2023. https://fpc.org.uk/kindred-spirits-how-a-post-brexit-britain-and-the-eu-can-work-together-to-strengthen-multilateralism/.

Berlin, Mark S. 2020. *Criminalizing Atrocity: The Global Spread of Criminal Laws against International Crimes*. Oxford: Oxford University Press.

Berlin, Mark S. 2021. "Does Criminalizing Torture Deter Police Torture?" *American Journal of Political Science*, pp. 1–24. doi: 10.1111/ajps.12684.

Bettiza, Gregorio. 2020. "Pandemipolitics and the (Potential) Unmaking of the Liberal World Order." Accessed September 23, 2022. http://www.gregoriobettiza.com/publication_3276.html.

Bettiza, Gregorio, and David Lewis. 2020. "Authoritarian Powers and Norm Contestation in the Liberal International Order: Theorizing the Power Politics of

Ideas and Identity." *Journal of Global Security Studies* 5 (4): pp. 559–77. doi: 10.1093/jogss/ogz075.

Blair, Christopher W., Jonathan A. Chu, and Joshua A. Schwartz. 2022. "The Two Faces of Opposition to Chemical Weapons: Sincere Versus Insincere Norm-Holders." *Journal of Conflict Resolution* 66 (4–5): pp. 677–703. doi: 10.1177/00220027211057057.

Bode, Ingvild, and Hendrik Huelss. 2018. "Autonomous Weapons Systems and Changing Norms in International Relations." *Review of International Studies* 44 (3): pp. 393–413. doi: 10.1017/S0260210517000614.

Börzel, Tanja, and Michael Zürn. 2021. "Contestation of the Liberal International Order: From Liberal Multilateralism to Postnational Liberalism." *International Organization* 75 (2): pp. 282–305. doi: 10.1017/S0020818320000570.

Bower, Adam. 2017. *Norms without the Great Powers: International Law and Changing Social Standards in World Politics*. Oxford: Oxford University Press.

Brunnée, Jutta, and Stephen J. Toope. 2010. *Legitimacy and Legality in International Law: An Interactional Account*. Cambridge: Cambridge University Press.

Búzás, Zoltán I. 2021. "Racism and Antiracism in the Liberal International Order." *International Organization* 75 (2): pp. 440–63. doi: 10.1017/S0020818320000521.

Carothers, Thomas. 2006. "The Backlash against Democracy Promotion." *Foreign Affairs* 85 (2): pp. 55–68.

Carpenter, Charli, and Alexander H. Montgomery. 2020. "The Stopping Power of Norms: Saturation Bombing, Civilian Immunity, and U.S. Attitudes toward the Laws of War." *International Security* 45 (2): pp. 140–69. doi: 10.1162/isec_a_00392.

Carpenter, Charli, Alexander H. Montgomery, and Alexandria Nylen. 2021. "Breaking Bad? How Survey Experiments Prime Americans for War Crimes." *Perspectives on Politics* 19 (3): pp. 912–24. doi: 10.1017/S1537592720002376.

Chen, Cher Weixia. 2017. "Indigenous Rights in International Law." In *Oxford Research Encyclopedia of International Studies*. Oxford: Oxford University Press. Last updated November 2017. Accessed January 9, 2023. https://doi.org/10.1093/acrefore/9780190846626.013.77.

Cingranelli, David L., and David L. Richards. 2010. "The Cingranelli and Richards (CIRI) Human Rights Data Project." *Human Rights Quarterly* 32 (2): pp. 401–24. doi: 10.1353/hrq.0.0141.

Colgan, Jeff D., and Robert O. Keohane. 2017. "The Liberal Order Is Rigged: Fix It Now or Watch It Wither." *Foreign Affairs* 96 (3): pp. 36–44.

Conrad, Courtenay R., Jillienne Haglund, and Will H. Moore. 2013. "Disaggregating Torture Allegations: Introducing the Ill-Treatment and Torture (ITT) Country–Year Data." *International Studies Perspectives* 14 (2): pp. 199–220. doi: 10.1111/j.1528-3585.2012.00471.x.

Cooley, Alexander, and Daniel H. Nexon. 2020. *Exit from Hegemony: The Unraveling of the American Global Order*. Oxford: Oxford University Press.

Cordell, Rebecca, K. Chad Clay, Christopher J. Fariss, Reed M. Wood, and Thorin M. Wright. 2022. "Disaggregating Repression: Identifying Physical Integrity Rights Allegations in Human Rights Reports." *International Studies Quarterly* 66 (2). doi: 10.1093/isq/sqac016.

Cox, Robert W. 1992. "Multilateralism and World Order." *Review of International Studies* 18 (2): pp. 161–80. doi: 10.1017/S0260210500118883.

Daase, Christopher, and Nicole Deitelhoff. 2021. "Wenn die Geltung schwindet: Die Krise Der liberalen Weltordnung und die Herrschaftsproblematik internationaler Politik." In *Normative Ordnungen*, ed. Rainer Forst and Klaus Günther. Berlin: Suhrkamp, pp. 162–97.

Deitelhoff, Nicole, and Lisbeth Zimmermann. 2019. "Norms under Challenge: Unpacking the Dynamics of Norm Robustness." *Journal of Global Security Studies* 4 (1): pp. 2–17. doi: 10.1093/jogss/ogy041.

Deitelhoff, Nicole, and Lisbeth Zimmermann. 2020. "Things We Lost in the Fire: How Different Types of Contestation Affect the Robustness of International Norms." *International Studies Review* 22 (1): pp. 51–76. doi: 10.1093/isr/viy080.

Deudney, Daniel, and G. John Ikenberry. 2018. "Liberal World: The Resilient Order." *Foreign Affairs* 97 (4): pp. 16–24.

Dingwerth, Klaus, Antonia Witt, Ina Lehmann, Ellen Reichel, and Tobias Weise. 2019. *International Organizations under Pressure: Legitimating Global Governance in Challenging Times*. Oxford: Oxford University Press.

Dixon, Jennifer M. 2017. "Rhetorical Adaptation and Resistance to International Norms." *Perspectives on Politics* 15 (1): pp. 83–99. doi: 10.1017/S1537 59271600414X.

Drezner, Daniel W. 2020. "The Song Remains the Same: International Relations After COVID-19." *International Organization* 74 (S1): E18–E35. doi: 10.1017/S0020818320000351.

Duncombe, Constance, and Tim Dunne. 2018. "After Liberal World Order." *International Affairs* 94 (1): pp. 25–42. doi: 10.1093/ia/iix234.

Dunne, Tim. 2007. "'The Rules of the Game Are Changing': Fundamental Human Rights in Crisis after 9/11." *International Politics* 44 (2–3): pp. 269–86. doi: 10.1057/palgrave.ip.8800188.

Eilstrup-Sangiovanni, Mette, and Stephanie C. Hofmann. 2020. "Of the Contemporary Global Order, Crisis, and Change." *Journal of European Public Policy* 27 (7): pp. 1077–89. doi: 10.1080/13501763.2019.1678665.

Fariss, Christopher J. 2014. "Respect for Human Rights Has Improved over Time: Modeling the Changing Standard of Accountability." *American Political Science Review* 108 (2): pp. 297–318. doi: 10.1017/S0003055414000070.

Fariss, Christopher J. 2018. "The Changing Standard of Accountability and the Positive Relationship Between Human Rights Treaty Ratification and Compliance." *British Journal of Political Science* 48 (1): pp. 239–71. doi: 10.1017/S000712341500054X.

Fehl, Caroline, and Elvira Rosert. 2020. "It's Complicated: A Conceptual Framework for Studying Relations and Interactions Between International Norms." PRIF Working Papers no. 49. Peace Research Institute Frankfurt.

Felbermayr, Gabriel. 2019. "25 Years of the WTO: Causes of Decay and Reform Proposals for the Future." Kiel Focus. December. Accessed January 9, 2023. https://www.ifw-kiel.de/publications/kiel-focus/2019/25-years-of-the-wto-causes-of-decay-and-reform-proposals-for-the-future-13610.

Finnemore, Martha J., and Kathryn Sikkink. 1998. "International Norm Dynamics and Political Change." *International Organization* 52 (4): pp. 887–917. doi: 10.1162/002081898550789.

Flaherty, Thomas M., and Ronald Rogowski. 2021. "Rising Inequality as a Threat to the Liberal International Order." *International Organization* 75 (2): pp. 495–523. doi: 10.1017/S0020818321000163.

Gadinger, Frank. 2022. "The Normativity of International Practices." In *Conceptualizing International Practices: Directions for the Practice Turn in International Relations*, ed. Alena Drieschova, Christian Bueger, and Ted Hopf. Cambridge: Cambridge University Press, pp. 100–21.

Gholiagha, Sassan, Anna Holzscheiter, and Andrea Liese. 2020. "Activating Norm Collisions: Interface Conflicts in International Drug Control." *Global Constitutionalism* 9 (2): pp. 290–317. doi: 10.1017/S2045381719000388.

Ginsburg, Tom. 2020. "Authoritarian International Law?" *American Journal of International Law* 114 (2): pp. 221–60. doi: 10.1017/ajil.2020.3.

Girard, Tyler. 2021. "Reconciling the Theoretical and Empirical Study of International Norms: A New Approach to Measurement." *American Political Science Review* 115 (1): pp. 331–38. doi: 10.1017/S0003055420000854.

Hafner-Burton, Emilie M., and Kiyoteru Tsutsui. 2005. "Human Rights in a Globalizing World: The Paradox of Empty Promises." *American Journal of Sociology* 110 (5): pp. 1373–411. doi: 10.1086/428442.

Hathaway, Oona A. 2002. "Do Human Rights Treaties Make a Difference?" *Yale Law Journal* 111 (8): pp. 1934–2042.

Hooghe, Liesbet, and Gary Marks. 2018. "Cleavage Theory Meets Europe's Crises: Lipset, Rokkan, and the Transnational Cleavage." *Journal of European Public Policy* 25 (1): pp. 109–35. doi: 10.1080/13501763.2017.1310279.

Hooghe, Liesbet, Tobias Lenz, and Gary Marks. 2019. "Contested World Order: The Delegitimation of International Governance." *Review of International Organizations* 14 (4): pp. 731–43. doi: 10.1007/s11558-018-9334-3.

Hurd, Ian. 2017. *How to Do Things with International Law*. Princeton, NJ: Princeton University Press.

ICJ (International Court of Justice). 1986. “Military and Paramilitary Activities in and against Nicaragua (Nicaragua V. United States of America).” Merits, ICJ Reports 1986, p. 14 (June 26).

Ikenberry, G. John. 2011. *Liberal Leviathan: The Origins, Crisis, and Transformation of the American World Order*. Princeton, NJ: Princeton University Press.

Ikenberry, G. John. 2018. “The End of Liberal International Order?” *International Affairs* 94 (1): pp. 7–23. doi: 10.1093/ia/iix241.

Jongen, Hortense, and Jan Aart Scholte. 2022. “Inequality and Legitimacy in Global Governance: An Empirical Study.” *European Journal of International Relations* 28 (3): 667–95. doi: 10.1177/13540661221098218.

Jose, Betcy. 2017. “Not Completely the New Normal: How Human Rights Watch Tried to Suppress the Targeted Killing Norm.” *Contemporary Security Policy* 38 (2): pp. 237–59. doi: 10.1080/13523260.2017.1334856.

Kahler, Miles. 2013. “Rising Powers and Global Governance: Negotiating Change in a Resilient Status Quo.” *International Affairs* 89 (3): pp. 711–29. doi: 10.1111/1468-2346.12041.

Keating, Vincent Charles. 2022. “Membership Has Its Privileges: Targeted Killing Norms and the Firewall of International Society.” *International Studies Quarterly* 66 (3): pp. 1–12. doi: 10.1093/isq/sqac040.

Kennedy, Greg. 1997. “Maritime Strength and the British Economy, 1840–1850.” *Northern Mariner* 7 (2): pp. 51–69.

Koskenniemi, Martti. 2005. *From Apology to Utopia: The Structure of International Legal Argument*. Reissue with a New Epilogue. Cambridge: Cambridge University Press.

Kreuder-Sonnen, Christian, and Berthold Rittberger. 2020. “The LIOn’s Share: How the Liberal International Order Contributes to Its Own Legitimacy Crisis.” Harvard CES Open Forum Series 2019–20. Center for European Studies, Harvard.

Krook, Mona Lena, and Jacqui True. 2012. “Rethinking the Life Cycles of International Norms: The United Nations and the Global Promotion of Gender Equality.” *European Journal of International Relations* 18 (1): pp. 103–27. doi: 10.1177/1354066110380963.

Kutz, Christopher. 2014. “How Norms Die: Torture and Assassination in American Security Policy.” *Ethics & International Affairs* 28 (4): pp. 425–49. doi: 10.1017/S0892679414000598.

Lake, David A., Lisa L. Martin, and Thomas Risse. 2021. “Challenges to the Liberal Order: Reflections on International Organization.” *International Organization*, pp. 1–33. doi: 10.1017/S0020818320000636.

Lantis, Jeffrey S., and Carmen Wunderlich. 2018. "Resiliency Dynamics of Norm Clusters: Norm Contestation and International Cooperation." *Review of International Studies* 44 (3): pp. 570–93. doi: 10.1017/S0260210517000626.

Lantis, Jeffrey S., and Carmen Wunderlich. 2022. "Reevaluating Constructivist Norm Theory: A Three-Dimensional Norms Research Program." *International Studies Review* 24 (1): pp. 1–27. doi: 10.1093/isr/viab059.

Lesch, Max. 2017. "Praxistheorien und Normenforschung in den internationalen Beziehungen: Zum Beitrag der pragmatischen Soziologie." *Zeitschrift diskurs* 2: pp. 31–54.

Lesch, Max. 2021. "Multiplicity, Hybridity and Normativity: Disputes about the UN Convention against Corruption in Germany." *International Relations* 35 (4): pp. 613–33. doi: 10.1177/0047117820965662.

Lesch, Max, and Christian Marxsen. 2023. "Norm Contestation in the Law Against War: Towards an Interdisciplinary Analytical Framework." *Heidelberg Journal of International Law* 83 (1). Forthcoming.

Lesch, Max, and Dylan Loh. 2022. "Field overlaps, normativity, and the contestation of practices in China's Belt and Road Initiative." *Global Studies Quarterly* 2 (4): 1–12. doi: 10.1093/isagsq/ksac068.

Lewis, Dustin A., Naz K. Modirzadeh, and Gabriela Blum. 2019. "Quantum of Silence: Inaction and Jus Ad Bellum." Harvard Law School Program on International Law and Armed Conflict. July. Accessed January 9, 2023. https://papers.ssrn.com/sol3/papers.cfm?abstract_id=3420959.

Madsen, Mikael Rask, Pola Cebulak, and Micha Wiebusch. 2018. "Backlash against International Courts: Explaining the Forms and Patterns of Resistance to International Courts." *International Journal of Law in Context* 14 (02): pp. 197–220. doi: 10.1017/S1744552318000034.

Magnuson, William. 2017. "Is Brexit the Beginning of the End for International Cooperation?" The Conversation, March 30. Accessed January 9, 2023. https://theconversation.com/is-brexit-the-beginning-of-the-end-for-international-cooperation-70865.

March, James G., and Johan P. Olsen. 1998. "The Institutional Dynamics of International Political Orders." *International Organization* 52 (4): pp. 943–69. doi: 10.1162/002081898550699.

Marxsen, Christian. 2018. "Violation and Confirmation of the Law: The Intricate Effects of the Invocation of the Law in Armed Conflict." *Journal on the Use of Force and International Law* 5 (1): pp. 8–39. doi: 10.1080/20531702.2017.1365488.

McKeown, Ryder. 2009. "Norm Regress: US Revisionism and the Slow Death of the Torture Norm." *International Relations* 23 (1): pp. 5–25. doi: 10.1177/0047117808100607.

McNamara, Kathleen R., and Abraham L. Newman. 2020. "The Big Reveal: COVID-19 and Globalization's Great Transformations." *International Organization* 74 (S1): E59–E77. doi: 10.1017/S0020818320000387.

Mearsheimer, John J. 2019. "Bound to Fail: The Rise and Fall of the Liberal International Order." *International Security* 43 (4): pp. 7–50. doi: 10.1162/isec_a_00342.

Nakatomi, Michitaka. 2013. "Plurilateral Agreements: A Viable Alternative to the World Trade Organization?" ADBI Working Paper Series no. 439. Asian Development Bank Institute.

Niemann, Holger, and Henrik Schillinger. 2017. "Contestation 'All the Way Down'? The Grammar of Contestation in Norm Research." *Review of International Studies* 43 (1): pp. 29–49. doi: 10.1017/S0260210516000188.

Nölke, Andreas. 2018. "Vom liberalen zum organisierten Kapitalismus." *Zeitschrift für Internationale Beziehungen* 25 (2): pp. 181–98. doi: 10.5771/0946-7165-2018-2-181.

Norris, Pippa, and Ronald Inglehart. 2019. *Cultural Backlash: Trump, Brexit, and Authoritarian Populism*. Cambridge: Cambridge University Press.

Nye, Joseph. 2017. "Will the Liberal Order Survive? The History of an Idea." *Foreign Affairs* 96 (1): pp. 10–16.

Nylen, Alexandria, and Charli Carpenter. 2019. "Questions of Life and Death: (De)Constructing Human Rights Norms through US Public Opinion Surveys." *European Journal of International Security* 4 (2): pp. 142–62. doi: 10.1017/eis.2019.3.

Panke, Diana, and Ulrich Petersohn. 2012. "Why International Norms Disappear Sometimes." *European Journal of International Relations* 18 (4): pp. 719–42. doi: 10.1177/1354066111407690.

Panke, Diana, and Ulrich Petersohn. 2016. "Norm Challenges and Norm Death: The Inexplicable?" *Cooperation and Conflict* 51 (1): pp. 3–19. doi: 10.1177/0010836715597948.

Patrick, Stewart. 2016. "World Order: What, Exactly, Are the Rules?" *Washington Quarterly* 39 (1): pp. 7–27. doi: 10.1080/0163660X.2016.1170477.

Peez, Anton. 2022. "Contributions and Blind Spots of Constructivist Norms Research in International Relations, 1980–2018: A Systematic Evidence and Gap Analysis." *International Studies Review* 24 (1): pp. 1–33. doi: 10.1093/isr/viab055.

Peez, Anton, and Lisbeth Zimmermann. 2022. "Contestation and Norm Change in Whale and Elephant Conservation: Non-Use or Sustainable Use?" *Cooperation and Conflict* 57 (2): pp. 226–45. doi: 10.1177/00108367211047138.

Percy, Sarah V., and Wayne Sandholtz. 2022. "Why Norms Rarely Die." *European Journal of International Relations* 28 (4): 934–54. doi: 10.1177/13540661221126018.

Pratt, Simon Frankel. 2022. *Normative Transformation and the War on Terrorism: The Evolution of Targeted Killing, Torture, and Private Military Contracting*. Cambridge: Cambridge University Press.

Price, Richard. 1997. *The Chemical Weapons Taboo*. Ithaca, NY: Cornell University Press.

Risse, Thomas. 2000. "'Let's Argue!' Communicative Action in World Politics." *International Organization* 54 (1): pp. 1–39. doi: 10.1162/002081800551109.

Sandholtz, Wayne. 2007. *Prohibiting Plunder: How Norms Change*. Oxford: Oxford University Press.

Sandholtz, Wayne. 2019. "Norm Contestation, Robustness, and Replacement." *Journal of Global Security Studies* 4 (1): pp. 139–46. doi: 10.1093/jogss/ogy042.

Sandholtz, Wayne, and Kendall W. Stiles. 2009. *International Norms and Cycles of Change*. Oxford: Oxford University Press.

Scherzinger, Johannes. 2023. "Unbowed, Unbent, Unbroken? Examining the Validity of the Responsibility to Protect." *Cooperation and Conflict* 58 (1): pp. 81–101. doi: 10.1177/00108367221093155.

Schimmelfennig, Frank. 2001. "The Community Trap: Liberal Norms, Rhetorical Action, and the Eastern Enlargement of the European Union." *International Organization* 55 (1): pp. 47–80. doi: 10.1162/002081801551414.

Schindler, Sebastian, and Tobias Wille. 2019. "How Can We Criticise International Practices?" *International Studies Quarterly* 63 (4): pp. 1014–24. doi: 10.1093/isq/sqz057.

Schmidt, Averell, and Kathryn Sikkink. 2019. "Breaking the Ban? The Heterogeneous Impact of US Contestation of the Torture Norm." *Journal of Global Security Studies* 4 (1): pp. 105–22. doi: 10.1093/jogss/ogy036.

Schmitt, Olivier. 2020. "How to Challenge an International Order: Russian Diplomatic Practices in Multilateral Security Organisations." *European Journal of International Relations* 26 (3): pp. 922–46. doi: 10.1177/1354066119886024.

Simmons, Beth A. 2009. *Mobilizing for Human Rights: International Law in Domestic Politics*. Cambridge: Cambridge University Press.

Slobodian, Quinn. 2021. "The Backlash against Neoliberal Globalization from Above: Elite Origins of the Crisis of the New Constitutionalism." *Theory, Culture & Society* 38 (6): pp. 51–69. doi: 10.1177/0263276421999440.

Stengel, Frank A., David B. MacDonald, and Dirk Nabers, eds. 2019. *Populism and World Politics: Exploring Inter- and Transnational Dimensions*. Cham: Springer.

Stephen, Matthew D. 2014. "Rising Powers, Global Capitalism and Liberal Global Governance: A Historical Materialist Account of the BRICs Challenge." *European Journal of International Relations* 20 (4): pp. 912–38. doi: 10.1177/1354066114523655.

Stimmer, Anette, and Lea Wisken. 2019. "The Dynamics of Dissent: When Actions Are Louder Than Words." *International Affairs* 95 (3): pp. 515–33. doi: 10.1093/ia/iiz019.

Tallberg, Jonas, Thomas Sommerer, Theresa Squatrito, and Christer Jönsson. 2013. *The Opening Up of International Organizations: Transnational Access in Global Governance*. Cambridge: Cambridge University Press.

Viola, Lora Anne. 2020. *The Closure of the International System: How Institutions Create Political Equalities and Hierarchies.* Cambridge: Cambridge University Press.

Wiener, Antje. 2014. *A Theory of Contestation*. Heidelberg: Springer.

Wolff, Jonas, and Lisbeth Zimmermann. 2016. "Between Banyans and Battle Scenes: Liberal Norms, Contestation, and the Limits of Critique." *Review of International Studies* 42 (3): pp. 513–34. doi: 10.1017/S0260210515000534.

Wright, Thomas. 2017. *All Measures Short of War: The Contest for the Twenty-First Century and the Future of American Power*. New Haven, CT: Yale University Press.

Zangl, Bernhard, Frederick Heußner, Andreas Kruck, and Xenia Lanzendörfer. 2016. "Imperfect Adaptation: How the WTO and the IMF Adjust to Shifting Power Distributions among Their Members." *Review of International Organizations* 11 (2): pp. 171–96. doi: 10.1007/s11558-016-9246-z.

Zarakol, Ayşe. 2014. "What Made the Modern World Hang Together: Socialisation or Stigmatisation?" *International Theory* 6 (2): pp. 311–32. doi: 10.1017/S1752971914000141.

Zimmermann, Lisbeth. 2021. "Law and Science in Environmental Governance: The Effects of Legal and Scientific Argumentation in the International Whaling Commission." In *Talking International Law: Legal Argumentation outside the Courtroom*, eds. Ian Johnstone and Steven R. Ratner. Oxford: Oxford University Press, pp. 263–81.

Zürn, Michael. 2018. *A Theory of Global Governance: Authority, Legitimacy, and Contestation*. Oxford: Oxford University Press.

APPENDIX

Coding schemes for applicatory and validity contestation

Table A.1 Coding scheme for the international torture prohibition

Categories	Dimensions	Themes	Description
Validity contestation	Categorical exceptions	Territories Groups of persons Special circumstances	Statements that demand exceptions from the non-derogable prohibition of torture
	Norm conflicts	Sovereignty Safety of the state/population	Statements that prioritize another norm over the prohibition of torture
	Rejection	Abolishing prohibition Permissive norm of torture	Statements that outright reject the torture prohibition and/or human rights
Applicatory contestation	Fairness	Impartiality Hypocrisy	Statements that criticize the one-sided treatment or double standards with regard to certain states
	Norm application	Definition of torture Trivialization Denial	Statements that questions whether the practices in question actually took place or amount to torture and/or ill-treatment
	Institutional implementation	Competence Procedures	Statements that challenge the activities of international institutions in specific cases.

Source: Authors.

Table A.2 Coding scheme for the responsibility to protect

Categories	Dimensions	Themes	Description
Validity contestation	Categorical exceptions	Use of force Coercive measures	Statements that generally reject the military or coercive dimension of the responsibility to protect
	Norm conflicts	Sovereignty Violation of international law	Statements that prioritize another norm over the responsibility to protect
	Rejection	Colonialism Imperialism Abuse as a tool of power	Statements that outright reject the responsibility to protect

Applicatory contestation	Fairness	Impartiality	Statements that criticize the one-sided treatment of certain states
		Hypocrisy Selectivity	Statements that criticize double standards in the use of the norm with regards to certain states
	Norm application	Politicization Situation Security Council Mandates	Statements that question whether the responsibility to protect is appropriately applied to the specific situation and by competent actors
	Applied measures	Use of force Sanction Coercion Regime change Unilateralism	Statements that challenge the measures applied under the responsibility to protect in specific cases

Source: Authors.

Table A.3 Coding scheme for the commercial whaling moratorium

Categories	Dimensions	Themes	Description
Validity contestation	Norm conflicts	Sovereignty/self-determination Food security Cultural identity Sustainability	Statements that prioritize another norm over the whaling moratorium
	Rejection	Colonialism Negative consequences	Statements that reject the commercial whaling moratorium because of profound asymmetries in the global system, inherent flaws, and unintended consequences
Applicatory contestation	Fairness	Impartiality	Statements that criticize the one-sided treatment of certain states
		Hypocrisy	Statements that criticize double standards in the use of the norm with regards to certain states
	Exemptions	Scientific whaling Aboriginal subsistence whaling Small-type whaling	Statements that question existing rules for exemption or call for the creation of new exemptions with regard to aboriginal subsistence whaling, scientific whaling, and small-type whaling

Source: Authors.

Table A.4 Coding scheme for the duty to prosecute

Categories	Dimensions	Themes	Description
Validity contestation	Categorical exceptions	Certain groups Heads of state	Statements that demand exceptions from the duty to persecute
	Norm conflicts	Sovereignty Peace National jurisdiction	Statements that prioritize another norm over the duty to prosecute
	Rejection	Colonialism Imperialism	Statements that outright reject the duty to prosecute and/or the ICC
Applicatory contestation	Fairness	Impartiality	Statements that criticize the unfair treatment of certain states
		Hypocrisy	Statements that criticize double standards in the use of the norm with regards to certain states
	Performance of the ICC	Selectivity Politicization Complementarity Procedures	Statement that question the ICC's activities in its application and implementation of the duty to prosecute

Source: Authors.

Index